DEBT-FOR-DEVELOPMENT EXCHANGES

Debt-for-development exchanges are an important financing tool for development. They make debt relief more politically and practically attractive to donor countries, and serve the development of recipient countries through the cancellation of external debt and the funding of important development projects. This book commences by chronicling the emergence of debt-for-development exchanges from their forebears, debt–equity exchanges, and analyses why debt for development suffers from very few of the problems that plagued debt–equity. The book also analyses the different types of debt-for-development exchanges and the different ways they have been used by donor nations. The book then explores a range of critical perspectives on exchanges and concludes by considering a wide range of innovative uses for the funds generated by exchanges.

Ross P. Buckley is a Professor of Law at University of New South Wales, a Fellow of the Asian Institute of International Financial Law of the University of Hong Kong and a Fellow of Australia21, a national research organisation. He is the founding series editor of the *Global Trade Law Series*; series co-editor of the *International Banking and Finance Law Series*; and founding editor of the 'Overseas Law' column in the *Australian Law Journal*. He has written or edited eleven books and authored more than 90 book chapters and articles.

Debt-for-Development Exchanges

HISTORY AND NEW APPLICATIONS

Written and edited by

ROSS P. BUCKLEY

Faculty of Law, University of New South Wales

CAMBRIDGE
UNIVERSITY PRESS

CAMBRIDGE UNIVERSITY PRESS
Cambridge, New York, Melbourne, Madrid, Cape Town,
Singapore, São Paulo, Delhi, Tokyo, Mexico City

Cambridge University Press
32 Avenue of the Americas, New York, NY 10013-2473, USA

www.cambridge.org
Information on this title: www.cambridge.org/9781107009424

First published 2011

Printed in the United States of America

A catalog record for this publication is available from the British Library.

Library of Congress Cataloging in Publication data
  Debt-for-development exchanges : history and new
  applications / [edited by] Ross P. Buckley.
     p.   cm.
  Includes index.
  ISBN 978-1-107-00942-4 (hardback)
  1. Economic development projects – Finance – Law and legislation.
  I. Buckley, Ross P.   II. Title.
  K3820.D43   2011
  338.91–dc22   2010052877

ISBN 978-1-107-00942-4 Hardback

To family and friends. When all is said and done, all we have that matters are family and friends, and along the way all that is best is family and friends. Yet somehow it can be easy to forget to be filled with gratitude for that which gives our lives its greatest richness and meaning.

Contents

Acknowledgments

My greatest debt is to the Australian Research Council for the Discovery Grant without the funding from which this book would not have been possible: a debt I don't wish to exchange, in any way. In addition I would like to thank all of the participants at the workshop at the University of New South Wales, Sydney, Australia, in March 2010, especially those who travelled long distances to join us, such as Jürgen Kaiser from Germany and M. D. Shamsuddoha from Bangladesh. I would also, of course, like to express my gratitude to all who have contributed to this book, brief profiles of whom appear in the list of contributors.

Thank you also to the publishers of the following journals for permission to reproduce here edited and adapted portions of the following articles:

- "US Debt-for-Development Legislation: A Missed Opportunity to Enhance United States National Security?" *Banking and Finance Law Review* 26: 233–257 (with S. Freeland)
- "Debt-for-Development Exchanges: Using External Debt to Mitigate Environmental Damage in Developing Countries", *West Northwest Journal of Environmental Law* 16 (Winter 2010): 77–101 (with S. Freeland)
- "Debt-for-Development Exchanges: A Potentially Innovative Response to the Global Financial Crisis", *University of New South Wales Law Journal* 32 (2009): 620–645
- "Debt-for-Development Exchanges: The Origins of a Financial Technique", *Law and Development Review* 2, No. 1 (2009), 24–49

And the final thank you, and it is a big one, is to the indefatigable Lara K. Hall, who did much of the research for my early chapters and then managed the editing and compilation of the entire volume. Her contribution was invaluable. Hers is a name to watch out for in the coming years.

Ross P. Buckley
Sydney, October 2010

Contributors

Principal Contributor and Editor

Ross P. Buckley is Professor of International Finance Law at the University of New South Wales in Sydney; founding series editor of the *Global Trade Law Series* of Kluwer Law International of The Hague; and series co-editor of Kluwer's *International Banking and Finance Law Series*. He is a Fellow of the Asian Institute for International Finance Law at the University of Hong Kong. His work focusses on ways to improve the regulation and resilience of the global financial system. He has consulted to government departments in Australia, Indonesia, Vietnam and the United States and to banks and finance houses in Australia and England. Before becoming an academic, he worked as a banking lawyer in Australia, in Hong Kong and on Wall Street.

Other Contributors

Joffre Balce is the Convenor for Macquarie University's Global Leaders Forum on Developing Countries' Debt and serves as an advisor for Jubilee Australia and the Association for Good Government. He formerly consulted to former President Corazon Aquino in the areas of co-operative and countryside development and then Vice President Gloria Macapagal-Arroyo for antipoverty socioeconomic development. He headed the Foundation for a Sustainable Society, Inc. (a nongovernmental organisation entrusted with the management of a Swiss–Philippine debt-for-development exchange counterpart fund), the Planning and Research Center of the Philippine Deposit Insurance Corporation and the equities research section of Pryce Securities.

Luke Fletcher has been working with Jubilee Australia in various capacities since 2005, including as National Coordinator from 2005 to 2007. He recently

commenced a PhD in politics and international studies at the University of
Cambridge as a Gates Scholar.

Steven Freeland is Professor of International Law, University of Western
Sydney, and Visiting Professor of International Law, University of Copenhagen.

Philip Ireland works with a range of nongovernmental organisations on
development issues and climate change, engaging with research, policy and
advocacy in the Australian and international contexts.

Jürgen Kaiser, originally a development education worker of the Protestant
Church in Germany, cofounded Erlaßjahr2000 (the Germany Jubilee2000
campaign) in 1997. He has been working on third world debt ever since, temporarily as Financial Flows and Debt Relief Advisor at the United Nations
Development Programme (New York).

John Langmore is a Professorial Fellow, School of Social and Political
Sciences, University of Melbourne, and formerly an Australian Member of
Parliament and Representative of the International Labour Organization to
the United Nations in New York.

Emmanuel T. Laryea is a Senior Lecturer in the Law Faculty of Monash
University, Australia. He taught at the University of Ghana, Bond University
and Lancaster University, England, before joining Monash in 2001.

Gillian Moon is a Senior Lecturer in the School of Law, University of New
South Wales, and Director of the Trade, Human Rights and Development
Project in the Australian Human Rights Centre, University of New South
Wales. She specialises in the intersections between human rights law, international economic law and development policy, her particular interest being
the impact of international trade law and foreign investment rules on human
rights, inequality and development.

Alicia C. Qian is the holder of the Australian Nuclear Science Technology
Organisation (ANSTO) Industry Partner Award for Biological, Earth and
Environmental Sciences and works for ANSTO's Institute of Environmental
Research. She also studies law and science at the University of New South
Wales.

Tony Rinaudo joined World Vision Australia in 1999 and oversaw projects in a
number of African countries. Today he is the Natural Resource Management
Advisor at World Vision Australia and in this capacity gives input into agricultural, forestry and environmental projects in a wide range of countries

where World Vision operates. Rinaudo has 17 years' field experience in West Africa, where he promoted rapid reforestation methods and diversified food production systems.

Julia Roy is a Sessional Lecturer of Ethics in the School of Law and an Associate Lecturer of Business Law in the Australian School of Business at the University of New South Wales. She is a director of Jubilee Australia, and has a professional background in refugee and genocide prevention advocacy and policy. She has represented Australian civil society at the United Nations and nongovernmental forums in New York, Europe, the Asia-Pacific and Australia.

M. D. Shamsuddoha is the Chief Executive of a research-based nongovernmental organisation, Participatory Research and Development Initiatives (PRDI) in Bangladesh. He is involved with different regional and global networks campaigning for climate and trade justice. Shamsuddoha also represents the government of Bangladesh in the negotiations on climate change at the United Nations Framework on Climate Change.

Tanvir A. Uddin is the International Programs Manager at Muslim Aid Australia. He is also a Scientia Scholar Arts/Law student majoring in development studies and economics at the University of New South Wales.

Bill Walker is World Vision Australia's Governance and Citizenship Policy Advisor. A major focus of this role is on developing a social accountability approach, Citizen Voice and Action. Prior to this, he was active in campaigning for debt cancellation from the inception of Jubilee 2000 in 1995 and provided policy advice on various issues of sovereign debt.

Adele Webb is the National Coordinator of Jubilee Australia, having worked with the organisation since 2006. Adele has spent time living and working in South Africa, Malawi and the Philippines, and has studied at the University of New South Wales and the University of South Africa in a range of disciplines, including law, history, economics, development and anthropology.

Introduction

A Productive Partnership between Civil Society and the Academy

Ross P. Buckley

There is a considerable history behind this volume. I first researched and wrote about debt exchanges some 12 years ago.[1] Five years later Bill Walker, who then chaired Jubilee Australia's Policy Working Group, approached me with the idea of drafting a submission to the Australian government on why it should consider undertaking such exchanges. Steven Freeland and I wrote this submission to Treasury in 2003. In 2005 Bill Walker and I together wrote Jubilee Australia's official submission to AusAid for its white paper consultation. Later in that year I spoke at an AusAid event in Sydney.

In late 2006 I spoke at a Make Poverty History conference in Melbourne on debt-for-development exchanges, and that campaign's media liaison staff worked to ensure that an opinion piece I'd written on the idea appeared in the *Australian Financial Review* on the day of the conference.[2] As a result of reading the opinion piece, Bob Sercombe, opposition spokesman on overseas development assistance, came along to listen and asked questions in private afterwards. At about the same time, World Vision Australia (where Bill Walker has his day job) sponsored a research assistant to work on more formal scholarly research on the topic, and the outcome of that work appeared in 2007.[3]

In April 2007 Adele Webb and Luke Fletcher of Jubilee Australia organised an event titled "Is Australia a Responsible Lender?" as part of the 'fringe festival' for the national conference of the Australian Labor Party (ALP, which was then in opposition) at which the ALP Shadow Parliamentary Secretary for Overseas Development Assistance, Bob McMullan, and I spoke.

---

[1] Ross Buckley, "Debt Exchanges Revisited: Lessons from Latin America for Eastern Europe", *Northwestern Journal of International Law and Business* 18 (1998): 655–684.
[2] Ross Buckley, "Transparency Helps Narrow the Gap", *Australian Financial Review*, November 16, 2006, 63.
[3] Ross Buckley and A. Small, "Leveraging Australia's Debt Relief to the Philippines Using Debt-for- Investment Projects", *Macquarie Law Journal* 7 (2007): 107–124.

Debt-for-development exchanges were discussed at this event. Shortly there-after, these years of advocacy efforts culminated in the Labor Party adopting a debt-for-health exchange with Indonesia as part of its policy platform. This became government policy with Labor's electoral victory in November 2007.

In this way was policy shaped. Adele and Luke's advocacy efforts at Jubilee Australia led the way, ably supported by Bill Walker at World Vision Australia and by the Make Poverty History campaign, a coalition involving the above nongovernmental organisations plus TEAR, Oxfam and many others.

The Debt2Health exchange was implemented in mid-2010. Under the exchange, Australia has cancelled A$75 million of its loans to Indonesia in return for Indonesia paying one-half of that sum to the Global Fund to be used in the fight against tuberculosis in Indonesia. May this be but the first of many productive debt-for-development exchanges between the two countries. Adele Webb and Luke Fletcher tell the complete story of how the Debt2Health exchange that Australia and Indonesia entered into in 2010 came about.

In 2007 I applied for, and was lucky enough to receive, a major three-year Australian Research Council grant to explore debt-for-development exchanges and their potential to contribute to the security of our region. This volume is one significant outcome of the research undertaken under that grant.

I tell this story in part to show the genesis of this volume and its long historical roots. But more significantly I tell the story to show the potential of partnerships between civil society organisations and university academics. It is almost inconceivable that my research would ever have influenced federal government policy without the input of two civil society organisations, Jubilee Australia and World Vision Australia. Likewise, however, the representations to government of those organisations may have been less credible without the support of my research. Civil society, around the world, may find in universities a well of resources that are highly valuable in their advocacy activities and yet have been tapped but lightly. This is particularly so if civil society under-stands that academic talent can be used in diverse ways: to generate research to underpin arguments and, depending upon the academics' personality and inclinations, to advocate for those arguments. If academics are invited to work on issues in ways that will generate publications, they are far more likely to be able to say yes than if they are asked merely to write reports or submissions that will never be formally published. People often go into university teaching wanting to make a difference in the world. A partnership with civil society can enable academics to bring about that difference.

Anyway, enough of this history; let's move on to the history of debt exchanges. These are the subject of the nine chapters in the first two parts of this book. These chapters commence by chronicling the emergence of debt-for-development exchanges from their forebears, debt–equity exchanges, and analyse why debt for development suffers from very few of the problems that plagued debt–equity. The different types of debt-for-development exchange by development project are then considered. So, for instance, one chapter considers debt-for-nature exchanges and another debt-for-education exchanges, and so on. Part II of the book proceeds to analyse the practices and trends in exchanges by donor countries, seeking to demonstrate the lessons learned in how each donor country has used, or in the case of France abused, this technique.

Part III introduces critical and analytical perspectives on exchanges. The chapters in Parts IV and V were presented initially at a workshop funded by the Australian Research Council and held at the University of New South Wales in March 2010. This one-day workshop allowed these authors and other interested participants to come together to learn of each other's work and thoughts and to explore new uses for this well-established financial technique.

In the initial chapter in Part III, Julia Roy makes the case that debt audits to determine the legitimacy of the debt are prerequisites of credible exchanges. Jürgen Kaiser then grapples with the sad reality that, in the absence of other mechanisms that enable the cancellation of illegitimate or odious debt, a nation may be better served by exchanging debt, notwithstanding the fact that in an ideal world it would be set aside as illegitimate or odious, because we don't live in that world and the nation will otherwise simply have to keep servicing the debt.

Gillian Moon then explores the human rights dimensions of exchanges, and M. D. Shamsuddoha considers Bangladesh's experience with debt and development and the contributions exchanges could make to that country.

In the final chapter in Part III, Joffre Balce explores some of the interesting applications of the debt-exchange technique in the Philippines, as well as some potentially innovative applications. Joffre's chapter ends on a provocative note, for he questions whether, while productive in a micro sense, exchanges are destructive in a macro sense, as they perpetuate the dependency of the financial systems of developing countries upon external finance. Joffre's question is significant, for it challenges directly a fundamental working assumption of the entire international financial system, namely that poor nations have inadequate domestic financial resources and are best served by borrowing from abroad. Certainly in East Asia, from where Joffre hails, this appears to be a deeply questionable assumption, and Joffre explores the idea of using exchanges to make the most of domestic financial resources within, and being remitted to, the Philippines.

The fourth and final part of the book is in many ways the most important, as it considers new and innovative uses for the funds generated by exchanges.

It begins with a chapter about one of the most exciting development projects I have encountered, projects to teach African farmers how to restore tree cover to their farms by caring for the stumps of indigenous trees, which in the past have been treated as impediments to farming. Most antidesertification efforts in Africa have focussed upon the planting of exotic varieties of trees. Tony Rinaudo in his excellent work with World Vision in a number of sub-Saharan countries has proved that the best trees with which to combat soil and wind erosion and to turn back the encroachment of the world's largest desert are the trees that are already there, in the ground, as stumps. These projects are perfectly adapted to funding by debt-for-development exchanges. Their costs are modest. The benefits are very substantial, and the projects in time become self-sustaining as farmers teach other farmers how to improve yields and generate other sources of income by nurturing stumps into coppiced trees.

The next brief chapter in Part IV considers the massive returns available from restoring mangrove forests, both as breeding grounds for fish and sea-food catches, and as tsunami protection zones.

This is followed by John Langmore's analysis of how debt exchanges could be used to fund social protection programs (basic welfare support). John's chapter contains important and previously unpublished calculations by Professor Anthony Clunies-Ross of the amount it would actually cost the world to lift all who live in extreme poverty around the world out of it – an amount that is almost certainly beyond the capacity of debt exchanges to fund but is nonetheless surprisingly affordable for rich countries. And, of course, the fact that debt exchanges cannot fund the world's entire social protection needs doesn't mean exchanges cannot begin to do so for some specific countries that currently lack such programs. As I write this introduction, I have been sick for a month with whooping cough, a very nasty affliction in middle age. The incredible exhaustion this disease has caused me has brought home the hard truth of what it must be like for poor people in poor countries without social protection. It has been extremely sobering for me to realise that, as I have struggled to make lunches and help my children get off to school (before collapsing on the bed in exhaustion), people in the world as sick or sicker than I have had to work all day in physically demanding roles because for them to fail to work is to fail to eat. Social protection schemes are part of the answer to this inhumanity.

The two succeeding chapters, the first by Philip Ireland, the second by Alicia C. Qian and Tanvir A. Uddin, explore ways that debt exchanges could fund the general climate change adaptation efforts our world is going to need in abundance, and one specific climate change adaptation measure: climate change schools to teach Bangladeshi farmers how to respond to a changing climate.

The next chapter considers briefly the idea of debt-for-peace exchanges and explores the contribution that funding from a debt exchange could make in supporting community-based peace initiatives in Mindanao in the Philippines, the potential of US legislative schemes to fund debt-for-nuclear-nonproliferation exchanges and, finally, the security threats posed by environmental degradation and climate change.

The penultimate chapter in the volume is by Emmanuel T. Laryea and explores how information and communication technology systems funded by debt-for-development exchanges could be used to promote good governance and in turn development in developing countries.

The final chapter is written, most fittingly, by the man who first had the idea of Australia entering into debt-for-development exchanges, Bill Walker. Bill explores the potential of these exchanges to promote citizen action and voice in developing countries. Bill's contribution answers in part the question Joffre Balce raises at the end of Part III. The most sustainable long-term development path of all is one that empowers developing countries to develop and rely upon their own human and financial capital. Debt exchanges could play a role in this regard, but to realise this role will require a fundamental shift in thinking: a new paradigm. But I am getting ahead of myself, to material best considered in the book's conclusion.

PART I

Types of Exchanges and Their Development
over Time

1

The Early Years: The Evolution of a Technique

Ross P. Buckley

I. INTRODUCTION

The beginning was the early 1980s. And in the beginning were bad loans, and from the loins of these bad loans sprang debt–equity exchanges, which quickly begat debt-for-nature exchanges, and then debt-for-education exchanges, and most recently, debt-for-health exchanges. And today, when all the begatting has been done, the progeny are known mostly as debt-for-development exchanges, or sometimes as debt-for-investment projects (by those who wish to suggest for the technique a more commercial focus).[1]

The first debt-for-development exchange was undertaken in 1987. Two decades later, in 2007, it was estimated that these financial techniques had resulted in the cancellation of US$5.7 billion of debt and the application of US$3.6 billion to development projects.[2] Early debt-for-development exchanges typically involved an environmental or other nongovernmental organisation (NGO), which purchased the debt for a discount in the secondary market and tendered it to the debtor government in return for a promise to apply an agreed-upon amount of local currency to mutually agreed-upon environmental or other projects in the debtor nation. The most common type of debt-for-development exchange today takes place directly between a creditor and debtor nation without NGO involvement. Under a typical exchange, the creditor nation will offer to cancel a specified part of a loan or loans if the debtor nation applies a portion of the amount cancelled (or perhaps the repayments

---

[1] R. P. Buckley and A. Small, "Leveraging Australia's Debt Relief to the Philippines Using Debt-for-Investment Projects", *Macquarie Law Journal* 7 (2007): 107.

[2] Working Group on Debt Swaps for Education, "Draft Report for the Director-General of UNESCO" (August 2007), 5, accessed August 2, 2010, http://www.unesco.org/education/ EFAWGSDE/WGDSE_2nd_draftreportforDG_EN.pdf.

it would have made on the loan over the next 5 to 10 years) towards mutually determined development projects in the debtor nation.

Debt-for-development exchanges matter. In 2005 the United Nations urged developed nations to seek a 'durable solution to the debt problems of develop- ing countries', and further noted that 'such mechanisms may include debt for sustainable development swaps',[3] and in 2007 the European Network on Debt and Development noted that 'debt-swaps have a real and growing presence on the political agendas of donor countries'.[4]

So it is worth understanding where these techniques came from and how they evolved. Indeed, it is the evolution of the idea that explains the tech- nique's quaint title, for as my wife pointed out:

> Where is the exchange when a rich country offers to cancel some of its loans to a poor country, if the poor country spends money on a development project? Surely that's like our saying to our daughter, 'You don't have to repay the advance we gave you last week, provided you spend half of it at the shops next week'.

The history explains all this: not the shopping proclivities of women, I am not sufficiently erudite to explain that, but the title and evolution of a significant financial technique.

But first we must begin, and in the beginning bad loans were needed, loans that traded at a discount to their face value. For without a discount there is no reason to undertake a debt-for-equity exchange, and debt-for-development exchanges, while still worthwhile without a source of discounted debt, cer- tainly lose some of their attraction.

Sadly, bad loans are rarely in short supply, and oceans of bad loans became available in late 1982. In mid-August 1982, Mexico announced the suspension of principal payments on its foreign debt and the debt crisis began.[5] Shortly afterwards, Brazil, Argentina and other Latin American nations announced that they required substantial additional funding to avoid defaulting on their debts.[6] Commercial banks stopped virtually all lending to the region and,

[3]   United Nations General Assembly, "Draft Resolution Referred to the High-level Plenary Meeting of the General Assembly by the General Assembly at Its Fifty-ninth Session: 2005 World Summit Outcome", September 15, 2005.
[4]   Marta Ruiz, "Debt Swaps for Development: Creative Solution or Smoke Screen?" (European Network on Debt and Development, October 2007), 4, accessed August 2, 2010, http://www. eurodad.org/uploadedFiles/Whats_New/Reports/Debt_swaps_ENG(2).pdf.
[5]   Darrel Delamaide, *Debt Shock* (London: Weidenfeld & Nicholson,1984), 6.
[6]   Allegra C. Biggs, "Nibbling Away at the Debt Crisis: Debt-for-Nature Swaps", *Annual Review of Banking Law* 10 (1991): 436; E. Webb, "Debt for Nature Swaps: The Past, the Present and Some Possibilities for the Future", *Environmental and Planning Law Journal* 11 (1994): 222.

within 15 months, 27 countries had rescheduled their debt or were in the process of doing so.[7] More were to follow.

The traditional sources of foreign capital for Latin America before 1970 were bonds, direct investment, official loans and supplier's credits.[8] Thus each wave of defaults was not a crisis for the international financial system, as the losses fell on a broad range of individual investors and suppliers, not on a relatively small number of banks.[9] For instance, the development of the United States in the nineteenth century was financed mainly by the issuance of bonds, principally to European nonbank investors,[10] and the defaults, of which there were plenty,[11] therefore did not threaten the financial system.

In the early 1970s, aided by the development of syndicated loans, the major commercial banks began to lend to Latin America. The lenders were now banks, not investors in bonds or projects or exports to the region.[12] For the first time in history the major thrust of development finance was commercial bank lending.[13] The pace of lending accelerated throughout the decade. The total external debt of the 17 highly indebted countries[14] in 1975 was US$76.6 billion.[15] This doubled by 1979, and doubled again by 1982, to a total of US$276.5 billion.[16]

[7] Philip A. Wellons, *Passing the Buck: Banks, Government and Third World Debt* (Boston: Harvard Business School Press, 1987), 255.

[8] Richard A. Debs, David L. Roberts and Eli M. Remolona, *Finance for Developing Countries: Alternative Sources of Finance – Debt Swaps* (New York: Group of Thirty, 1987), 10; Marilyn E. Skiles, "Latin American International Loan Defaults in the 1930s: Lessons for the 1980s?" Federal Reserve Bank of New York, Research Paper No. 8812, April 1988, 41–42. Stallings notes that suppliers' credits became significant only after World War II; see Barbara Stallings, *Banker to the Third World: U.S. Portfolio Investment in Latin America, 1900–1986* (Berkeley: University of California Press, 1987), 109–110.

[9] Frank Griffith Dawson, *The First Latin American Debt Crisis: The City of London and the 1822–1825 Loan Bubble* (New Haven, CT: Yale University Press, 1990), 237; Delamaide, *Debt Shock*, 49.

[10] Delamaide, *Debt Shock*, 49; Cleona Lewis, *America's Stake in International Investments* (Washington, DC: Brookings Institution, 1983), 17–24, 30, 35, 36–39, 45–48.

[11] Delamaide, *Debt Shock*, 49, and Lewis, *America's Stake*, 25–26, 35, 45–46.

[12] Barry Eichengreen and Richard Portes, "After the Deluge: Default, Negotiation, and Readjustment during the Interwar Years", in Barry Eichengreen and Peter Lindert (eds.), *The International Debt Crisis in Historical Perspective* (Cambridge, MA: MIT Press, 1989), 40–41.

[13] Debs, Roberts and Remolona, *Finance for Developing Countries*, 10; Delamaide, *Debt Shock*, 49.

[14] Argentina, Bolivia, Brazil, Chile, Colombia, Costa Rica, Cote d'Ivoire, Ecuador, Jamaica, Mexico, Morocco, Nigeria, Peru, Philippines, Uruguay, Venezuela and Yugoslavia.

[15] World Bank, *Developing Country Debt: Implementing a Consensus* (Washington, DC: World Bank, 1987), 26.

[16] Jeffrey D. Sachs, "Introduction", in Jeffrey D. Sachs (ed.), *Developing Country Debt and the World Economy* (Chicago: Chicago University Press, 1989), 9. For instance, the net liabilities of Argentina, Brazil and Mexico to developed country international banks increased from US$56.6 billion in December 1979 to US$104.5 billion in December 1981; and almost as many net loans were made to the major debtors in 1981 and 1982 as in the entire period from 1973 to 1979.

Certainly, when Mexico's inability to service its debt triggered the debt crisis, there was an abundance of bad loans to be used in debt exchanges. However, to facilitate the process there needed to be a market upon which entities interested in initiating debt-for-development exchanges could acquire the debt.

II. THE SECONDARY MARKET IN DISCOUNTED DEBT

A form of secondary market for the discounted debt of less developed countries and their corporations had 'existed on a relatively small scale since well before the onset of the crisis in 1982'.[17] But the secondary market really began to grow after 1982.[18] I have written at length elsewhere about the development of this market.[19]

The market began as a swap market in which a US bank with one or two loans to Poland in its portfolio might exchange them with a German bank for some Latin American loans that the German bank no longer wanted. Each bank was refocussing its portfolio on regions of the world it knew best, or at least to which it had sizeable exposures. After some months, some brave and wise bankers began to actually sell loans and absorb the losses. In the words of Lee Buchheit:

> Fortunate indeed are those bankers who in 1983 sold off their Argentine exposure at a 15 or 20% discount although, at the time, this was accompanied by a good deal of hand-wringing, tooth-gnashing and piteous wailing about the cruelty of international lending.[20]

This secondary market provided the source of funds that were soon to be used in debt–equity exchanges and debt-for-nature exchanges.

III. DEBT–EQUITY EXCHANGES

Debt–equity agreements involve the sale of external debt by an investor to the debtor government in return for a discounted amount of local currency,

---

[17] United Nations Centre on Transnational Corporations, *Debt Equity Conversions: A Guide for Decision-Makers* (New York: United Nations, 1990).

[18] Ibid.

[19] R. P. Buckley, *Emerging Markets Debt: An Analysis of the Secondary Market* (Kluwer: London, 1999), 1–330; and R. P. Buckley, "A Force for Globalisation: Emerging Markets Debt Trading from 1994 to 1999", *Fordham International Law Journal* 30 (2007): 185–259.

[20] Lee C. Buchheit, "Return of the Living Debt", *International Financial Law Review* (May 1990): 28.

which must then be invested in shares in, or otherwise injected as capital into, a local company.[21] Their attraction for investors and debtor nations is that the secondary market discount is 'recaptured' and divided between them. In effect a debt–equity exchange results in some debt relief for the debtor nation and a preferential exchange rate for the foreign investor.[22] In exchange for this preference there are usually limitations. Often eligible investment is limited to certain industries and has to meet certain requirements, and there are usually limitations on the repatriation of capital and the remittance of dividends. Furthermore, many countries nominate only a portion of their outstanding indebtedness as eligible for conversion into equity.

In a typical scheme the central bank of the debtor nation announces that the debt can be exchanged at a certain rate for equity in local businesses or used for capital investments in the debtor nation. The rate of exchange of debt for equity may be set by the central bank (e.g., the central bank may stipulate that it will retain 12 cents on the dollar so that, for every dollar tendered, the investor receives local currency to the value of 88 cents). Alternatively, the rate may be set by an auction so that investors bid for the right to convert debt into equity, and those willing to accept the largest discounts receive the right to convert their debt.[23] For instance, in 1986 Nissan acquired some US$60 million of Mexican government debt on the secondary market at a price of US$40 million. It then resold the debt to the Mexican central bank for US$54 million in pesos for investment into its Mexican subsidiary. As a result some US$60 million in Mexican government debt was cancelled and Nissan was able to inject some US$54 million of equity into its Mexican operation for a cost of US$40 million.[24] In other words, as a result of this debt–equity exchange Nissan received a preferential exchange rate some 35% better than the market rate.

In summary, debt–equity schemes can increase investment and permit debtor nations to recapture part of the secondary market discount in the

[21] Paris Club, "Debt Swap Reporting: Rules and Principles" (2006), accessed August 2, 2010, www.clubdeparis.org/en/public_debt.html.
[22] Debs, Robertson and Remolona, *Finance for Developing Countries*, 23. For an analysis of the preferential exchange rate involved in debt–equity swaps, see George Anayiotos and Jamie De Pinies, "The Secondary Market and the International Debt Problem", *World Development* 18 (1990): 1657.
[23] For two contemporaneous accounts of debt–equity schemes, see Martin W. Schubert, "Trading Debt for Equity", *Banker* 137 (February 1987); and Martin W. Schubert, "Third World Debt as a Trading and Investment Tool", *Countertrade and Barter* (April–May 1987): 38.
[24] Eric N. Berg, "U.S. Banks Swap Latin Debt", *New York Times*, September 11, 1986; Steven Freeland, "Turning to a Trusted Friend: Using Debt Exchanges for Environmental and Development Purposes", *Australian International Law Journal* (2001): 105.

value of their loans at the cost of conferring a preferential exchange rate upon foreign investors.

Chile was the first country to implement a formal debt–equity exchange program in 1985, which in time proved to be perhaps the most successful debt–equity scheme of all. Within the first three years, Chile reduced its external debt by some US$3.8 billion, or 19%.[25] Chile's ability to operate the debt-exchange program consistently over a prolonged period encouraged foreign investment in addition to that which otherwise would have been made. Strict limitations on the repatriation of principal and the remission of dividends abroad restricted the drain on Chile's foreign exchange reserves, and perhaps most important, Chile's economy had a remarkable capacity to absorb credit without leading to inflation. These factors allowed the program to be opened to local investors, which promoted its acceptance by the Chilean people.[26] Despite its apparent success, it had been suggested that the rapid decline in foreign direct investment (FDI) that occurred upon the scheme's termination resulted from market saturation and the inferior quality of remaining investment opportunities.[27]

Mexico's debt–equity scheme commenced in April 1986 and had retired US$3 billion of Mexico's US$107 billion foreign debt when it was suspended in November 1987.[28] It was suspended because it was highly inflationary. Rather than issuing bonds, as Chile had done, Mexico printed pesos, which led to inflation. The exchange rate afforded to inbound investments by the scheme was highly preferential, and the scheme, in the main, supported only investments that would have been made anyway (as will virtually always be the case in schemes of short duration due to the long lead times of international investment decisions).[29]

The popularity of debt–equity schemes was enhanced in this period by the liberalisation of US banking regulations. US banks had been limited to holding 20% of the equity in any nonfinancial company. Regulation K was amended by the Federal Reserve Board in August 1987 to permit 100% ownership of nonfinancial companies in the 33 most heavily indebted less developed countries, provided that the companies were state owned and the acquisitions

[25]   R. P. Buckley, "Debt Exchanges Revisited: Lessons from Latin America for Eastern Europe", *Northwestern Journal of International Law and Business* 18, No. 3 (1998): 666.
[26]   Ibid.
[27]   Ibid.
[28]   Melanie Tammen, *Energizing Third World Economies: The Role of Debt–Equity Swaps* (Washington, DC: Heritage Foundation, 1989), 7.
[29]   Ibid.

were from the government[30] – a change enacted specifically to promote debt–equity privatisations.[31]

IV. CONCLUSION

Debt–equity exchanges have had vociferous critics. In the words of Rudiger Dornbusch:

> Washington has been obscene in advocating debt–equity swaps and in insisting that they be part of the debt strategy. The U.S. Treasury has made this dogma, and the IMF and the World Bank, against their staff's professional advice and judgment, have simply caved in.[32]

The principal objections of the critics have been the extent to which debt–equity schemes proved to be inflationary and, because these inflationary consequences meant most schemes couldn't be maintained for more than about 18 consecutive months, the failure of the schemes to encourage additional investment. The short tenors of most schemes meant that a preferential exchange rate was, in effect, granted to inbound investment that was going to come into the country anyway. The potential for such an exchange rate to encourage genuinely additional investment was lost due to the relatively long lead times for foreign investment and the relatively short periods nations could afford to operate these schemes before inflationary pressures became so extreme the schemes had to be shut down.

---

[30] 12 CFR section 211.5(f). See also Eduardo C. G. de Faria, J. Andrew Scott and Nigel J. C. Buchanan, *PW/Euromoney Debt–Equity Swap Guide* (London: Euromoney Publications PL, 1988), Ch. 2, "U.S. Legal Considerations"; Lee C Buchheit, "The Capitalization of Sovereign Debt: An Introduction", *University of Illinois Law Review* 2 (1988): 410; and Lee C. Buchheit, "Banking Regulation: Federal Reserve Liberalises Foreign Investment Rules for US Banks", *Journal of International Banking Law* 3 (1987): 111–113.

[31] With their potential for reducing both the debt burden on a country and the perceived inefficiencies of state-owned enterprises. See also David Spencer, "Regulation K Allows 100 Percent Ownership", *International Financial Law Review* 6, No. 10 (October 1987): 13–14, citing the Federal Reserve Board's commentary on the amendment. For an example of a conversion that took advantage of this liberalised regulatory environment, see OCC Unpublished Interpretative Letter of February 27, 1989, from the Comptroller of the Currency to the President, Miami National Bank, NA (Ref 12 USC 29a, 12 USC 24(7)). The Comptroller approved a transaction in which the named bank proposed to exchange its Argentine debt for Honduran debt and then swap the Honduran debt for local currency with which to acquire 100% of the common stock in a Honduran steel foundry.

[32] Rudiger Dornbusch, "Panel Discussion on Latin American Adjustment: The Record and Next Step", in John Williamson (ed.), *Latin American Adjustment: How Much Has Happened?* (Washington, DC: Institute for International Economics, 1990), 324.

Exchanging debt for equity is not new. In the 1880s Peru crafted a resolution of its indebtedness in one, novel, massive debt–equity exchange: British bonds were exchanged for stock in Peruvian Corp., the owner of the state railways, lands and mining concessions.[33] Exchanging debt for equity is also often used by banks to resolve domestic corporate defaults. However, it was in exchanging external debt for equity in national companies in the aftermath of the debt crises in Latin America in the 1980s that gave commentators the idea of exchanging external debt for nature conservancy. Debt-for-equity exchanges had shown how the discount on the debt in the secondary market multiplied the buying power of the funds available for the task. A truly innovative idea was thereby born.

[33] Carlos Marichal, *A Century of Debt Crises in Latin America* (Princeton, NJ: Princeton University Press, 1989); Werner Baer and Kent Hargis, "Forms of External Capital and Economic Development in Latin America: 1820–1997", *World Development* 25 (November 1997): 1805–1820.

2

Debt-for-Nature Exchanges

Ross P. Buckley and Steven Freeland

I. INTRODUCTION

The idea of debt-for-nature exchanges was first proposed in 1984, following the groundwork laid by debt–equity schemes. In the words of one market participant, 'The ideas for debt-for-nature didn't really get off the ground until debt–equity programs had been launched.... Really these programs can be viewed as son-of-debt-equity'.[1]

In October 1984 Dr Thomas Lovejoy, then Executive Vice President of the World Wildlife Fund (WWF), wrote an opinion piece for the *New York Times* that is generally credited with having provided the first public formulation of the debt-for-nature idea.[2]

Lovejoy proposed that a developing country's external debt be reduced in return for its taking steps to address issues of environmental concern and that governments provide tax relief to commercial creditor banks for participating in these transactions.[3] Lovejoy emphasised the correlation between developing country indebtedness and environmental degradation[4] and encouraged environmental nongovernmental organisations (NGOs) to investigate using the developing country secondary debt market to finance conservation projects.

---

[1] Randall Curtis, Director of Costa Rica's debt-for-nature program for the Nature Conservancy, quoted in "The Debt-for-Nature Option", 2 *Swaps – The Newsletter of New Financial Institutions* 11 (November 1988): 1.

[2] Thomas Lovejoy, "Aid Debtor Nations' Ecology", *New York Times*, October 4, 1984; J. Eugene Gibson and Randall K. Curtis, "A Debt for Nature Blueprint", *Columbia Journal of Transnational Law* 28 (1990): 333 n. 9.

[3] Julian C. Juergensmeyer and James C. Nicholas, "Debt for Nature Swaps: A Modest but Meaningful Response to Two International Crises", *Florida Journal of international Law* 5 (1990): 198; Timothy B. Hamlin, "Debt-for-Nature Swaps: A New Strategy for Protecting Environmental Interests in Developing Nations", *Ecology Law Quarterly* 16 (1989): 1067.

[4] Nancy Knupfer, "Debt-for-Nature Swaps: Innovation or Intrusion?" *New York International Law Review* 4 (1991): 87.

He noted that discounted developing country debt could potentially leverage 'conservation dollars to preserve some of the world's most biologically valuable natural areas while helping countries reduce their external debt'.[5]

This type of debt-exchange transaction is based on the simple notion of a reduction in external debt in return for domestic conservation activities.[6] In the 1980s most developing country foreign debt was denominated in US dollars (or other hard currencies). Many developing nations employed short-term, often indiscriminate strategies to produce exports to generate foreign exchange for debt repayment. One of the most destructive activities undertaken in this regard was the clearing of rainforests.[7] Tropical rainforests are found primarily in developing countries, with 25% of such forests in Latin America alone.[8] In the late 1980s approximately 140,000 acres of tropical rainforest were being cleared in Latin America every day,[9] prompting predictions that by 2000 'tropical forests will have been largely destroyed'.[10] As well as forests being cleared to convert land to pasture or agriculture, significant amounts of timber were harvested for export,[11] much of it illegally.[12]

The use of debt-for-nature exchanges has evolved since the early exchanges and are now used to address a broad range of environmental challenges. Two broad forms of debt-for-nature exchanges have developed. In the first form, a nation's debts are purchased by an environmental NGO and offered to the debtor for cancellation in exchange principally for its undertaking to protect ongoingly a designated parcel of its land. In the second form, the debt

[5] WWF, "World Wildlife Fund and Ecuador Sign Large Debt-for-Nature Swap" (press release, December 14, 1987), 2, quoted in Derek Asiedu-Akrofi, "Debt-for-Nature Swaps: Extending the Frontiers of Innovative Financing in Support of the Global Environment", *International Lawyer* 25 (1991): 564.

[6] Konrad von Moltke, "Debt-for-Nature: The Second Generation", *Hastings International and Comparative Law Review* 14 (1991): 975; Asiedu-Akrofi, "Debt-for-Nature Swaps", 581.

[7] Michael S. Sher, "Can Lawyers Save the Rainforest? Enforcing the Second Generation of Debt-for-Nature Swaps", *Harvard Environmental Law Review* 17 (1993): 157.

[8] Andrew Wolman, "Review of Conservation Payment Initiatives in Latin America: Conservation Concessions Conservation Incentive Agreements and Permit Retirement Schemes", *William and Mary Environmental Law and Policy Review* 28 (2004): 860.

[9] Nina M. Dillon, "The Feasibility of Debt-for-Nature Swaps", *North Carolina Journal of International Law and Commercial Regulation* 16 (1991): 127.

[10] "Ecologists Make Friends with Economists", *Economist*, October 15, 1988, 25.

[11] Robert J. Buschbacher, "Ecological Analysis of Natural Forest Management in the Humid Tropic", in *Race to Save the Tropics: Ecology and Economics for a Sustainable Future*, ed. Robert Doogland (Washington, DC: Island Press, 1990), 59.

[12] Despite the United Nations' international efforts and some domestic measures, illegal logging continues to increase in countries such as Cambodia, Laos, Nigeria, Papua New Guinea, Philippines, Solomon Islands and Thailand. See Jenifer Lynn Peters, "Land and Resource Management: The Illegal Trafficking of Timber in Cambodia", *Colorado Journal of International Environmental Law and Policy* 11 (2000): 104.

is exchanged, usually at a discount, for local currency that is then used by local conservation groups or government agencies for various environmental projects in the debtor country.

The so-called first-generation exchanges involve the purchase on the secondary market of commercial bank debt by NGOs. 'Second-generation' mechanisms are bilateral agreements between donor and recipient governments and use official debt (loans by one nation to another). Second-generation transactions have used large amounts of debt for a broad range of environmental and developmental purposes, impetus for which was provided by the enactment of a range of legislative provisions in the United States (considered in Chapter 4). The most recent debt-for-nature exchanges have evolved even further, as we shall see, to address a broader array of environmental issues and to place the debtor nation at the centre of each exchange.

II. FIRST-GENERATION DEBT EXCHANGES

Early debt-for-nature exchanges involved the co-operation and agreement of environmental NGOs, the developing country government and its central bank. The very first of these first-generation debt exchanges was undertaken in 1987 in Bolivia.

A. *Bolivia (1987): 'Debt for Conservation'*

In 1987 Conservation International (CI), a Washington-based environmental NGO, bought US$650,000 of Bolivia's debt in the international secondary debt market for about US$100,000. Funding came from a grant given by a private charitable foundation.[13] Under the debt-exchange agreement,[14] this debt was exchanged for shares in a newly established company set up to preserve approximately 3.7 million acres of forests and grasslands surrounding the Beni Biosphere Reserve in north-eastern Bolivia,[15] an area noted for its biological richness.[16] CI agreed to provide ongoing assistance to Bolivia as 'official advisor' to plan and design the protected areas.[17] For its part, Bolivia undertook

---

[13]   The Frank Weeden Foundation based in San Francisco.

[14]   Agreement between the government of Bolivia and Conservation International, July 13, 1987.

[15]   Asiedu-Akrofi, "Debt-for-Nature Swaps", 565.

[16]   The reserve supports 6,000–8,000 species of vascular plants, including at least 500 bird species and 13 endangered animal species. See Gibson and Curtis, "A Debt for Nature Blueprint", 354.

[17]   Conservation International, "Bolivia Sets Precedent with First Ever 'Debt-for-Nature'" (press release, July 16, 1987), 1, reprinted in Priya Alagiri, "Give Us Sovereignty or Give Us

to provide legal protection for the 334,200-acre reserve[18] and to establish a local currency fund equivalent to US$250,000 to manage and administer these protected areas. Bolivia was to contribute US$100,000 of this sum, with the remainder to come from the United States Agency for International Development (USAID).[19] Bolivia and a local NGO shared the management of the land, and title to it remained with Bolivia.[20]

This first debt-for-nature transaction highlighted a range of potential problems with the debt-exchange mechanism. The primary problems that emerged concerned national sovereignty, the position of indigenous peoples and the enforceability of the agreement.

When the proposed transaction with Bolivia was announced, various Latin American newspapers reported (incorrectly) that a foreign organisation had purchased Bolivian 'lands considered the national patrimony'.[21] Several Latin American countries criticised the idea of debt exchanges,[22] and even though the local organisation involved was able to explain the true position, this lingering mistrust associated with the transaction highlighted some of the potential sensitivities associated with debt exchanges.

The local indigenous people were not adequately consulted during the design phase of the project. The Chimane Indians lived in the forest without formal land tenure,[23] but with the advent of the debt exchange, they sought to obtain title to the land. However, the terms of this debt exchange made this

Debt: Debtor Countries' Perspective on Debt-for-Nature Swaps", *American University Law Review* 41 (1992): 495 n. 58.

[18] Marilyn Post, "The Debt-for-Nature Swap: A Long-Term Investment for the Economic Stability of Less Developed Countries", *International Lawyer* 24 (1990): 1082; Robert M. Sadler, "Debt-for-Nature Swaps: Assessing the Future", *Journal of Contemporary Health Law and Policy* 6 (1990): 326.

[19] J. Eugene Gibson and William J. Schrenk, "The Enterprise for the Americas Initiative: A Second Generation of Debt-for-Nature Exchanges – With an Overview of Other Recent Exchange Initiatives", *George Washington Journal of International Law and Economics* 25 (1991): 17; Gibson and Curtis, "A Debt for Nature Blueprint", 356 n.118.

[20] Post, "The Debt-for-Nature Swap", 1082.

[21] Gibson and Curtis, "A Debt for Nature Blueprint", 356.

[22] Brazil was initially one of the most vehement critics of the debt-for-nature mechanism. See Antonio N. Picirillo, "The Metamorphosis: Expected Changes in the Brazilian Debt-for-Nature Swap Process and Policy Implications", *Fordham Environmental Law Review* 17 (1994): 563–564. In 1989 Brazil's president, Jose Sarney, ruled out debt-for-nature swaps, citing national sovereignty, and declared that '[w]e accept international aid but we don't accept conditions'. See James Brooke, "Brazil Announces Plan to Protect the Amazon", *New York Times*, April 7, 1989.

[23] Eve Burton, "Debt for Development: A New Opportunity for Non-Profits, Commercial Banks, and Developing States", *Harvard International Law Review* 31 (1990): 242 n. 63.

impossible.[24] Already threatened with the destruction of their natural habitat through indiscriminate and illegal logging, they were now presented with an 'American-type' national park model,[25] in which their ability to engage in traditional foraging for food and fuel was further restricted. In effect, the debt-exchange agreement divested the Chimane of their land rights,[26] as many of their traditional activities conflicted with the conservation goals that underpinned the transaction.[27] The lack of timely local input represented a major failing of this transaction.

To complicate matters, Bolivia failed to contribute its equivalent of US$100,000 to the local currency account until almost two years after the agreement was signed.[28] As a result, the USAID funding that was contingent upon Bolivia's contribution was not forthcoming and the project was significantly underfunded.[29] Furthermore, Bolivia initially failed to enact national legislation designed to legally protect the Reserve. This issue was made even more complex by the fact that the Beni region was one of Bolivia's principal areas for illegal cocaine processing. Bolivia did not fully comply with its responsibilities, and the debt-for-nature agreement did not contain mechanisms to require it do so.[30]

Despite the problems associated with the Bolivian transaction, several positive outcomes ensued from this pioneering arrangement. It confirmed that exchanging developing country debt, even when the amounts involved were relatively small, to advance conservation, environmental and perhaps developmental goals was feasible, as long as due account was taken of relevant local conditions and the need for enforceability. Clearly, this local-conditions caveat is crucial, since each debt exchange must accommodate the recipient region's specific circumstances.

[24] Amanda Lewis, "The Evolving Process of Swapping Debt for Nature", *Colorado Journal of International Environmental Law and Policy* 10 (1999): 436.

[25] Knupfer, "Debt-for-Nature Swaps", 89.

[26] E. Webb, "Debt for Nature Swaps: The Past, the Present and some Possibilities for the Future", *Environment and Planning Law Journal* 11 (1994): 227.

[27] Lewis, "The Evolving Process", 437.

[28] Gibson and Curtis, "A Debt for Nature Blueprint", 357.

[29] Ibid.

[30] For a more detailed discussion of the nonenforceable character of many of the early debt-exchange transactions, see Tamara J. Hrynik, "Debt-for-Nature Swaps: Effective but Not Enforceable", *Case Western Journal of International Law* 22 (1990): 141. The issue of enforceability is of greater significance when developed country 'public funds', such as US taxpayers' money, are involved. See Rosanne Model, "Debt-for-Nature Swaps: Environmental Investments Using Taxpayer Funds without Adequate Remedies for Expropriation", *University of Miami Law Review* 45 (1991): 1203.

In addition, the exchange led to a positive spin-off: after Bolivia implemented the debt-for-nature exchange, the International Tropical Timber Organisation (ITTO)[31] provided it with a US$1.26 million grant for continued forestry conservation.[32]

B. *Other First-Generation Debt-for-Nature Exchanges*

Early debt-for-nature transactions in Ecuador and Costa Rica were structured to address some of the concerns that arose in the Bolivian exchange. In 1987 a second debt-for-nature exchange was undertaken, with the World Wide Fund (WWF), the Nature Conservancy (TNC) and the Missouri Botanical Gardens purchasing US$10 million of Ecuador's external debt at a massive discount for only US$1.5 million.[33] The funds were then assigned to a private Ecuadorian conservation group, Fundacion Natura.[34] Upon conversion, the debt was exchanged at full face value into local currency bonds in Fundacion Natura's favour.[35] The principal amount funded the foundation's establishment[36] together with an endowment fund to support its general activities.[37] Fundacion Natura uses the interest generated by the bonds to undertake a diverse range of environmental projects to protect Ecuadorian national parks and reserves.[38] Its work continues to this day.[39]

In contrast to the Bolivian transaction, in Ecuador the agreed-upon conservation activities were undertaken by the local NGO without government

[31] The ITTO is an international organisation that 'encourages the development of forestry alternatives that can be replicated in other countries'. See Conservation International Foundation, *The Debt-for-Nature Exchange: A Tool for International Conservation* (Washington, DC: Conservation International, 1991), 14 n. 4.

[32] Gibson and Schrenk, "The Enterprise for the Americas Initiative", 9. However, this forest management plan was difficult to implement, due to conflicts of interest between various groups and the lack of interest in reforestation demonstrated by the timber companies (9 n. 32).

[33] Catherine A. O'Neill and Cass R Sunstein, "Economics and the Environment: Trading Debt and Technology for Nature", *Colorado Journal of International Environmental Law and Policy* 17 (1992): 108.

[34] Lewis, "The Evolving Process", 437.

[35] The local currency of Ecuador at the time was the sucre. However, in 1999 Ecuador changed its local currency to US dollars as part of an extensive restructuring of its financial system. "As U.S. Military Settles In, Some in Ecuador Have Doubts", *New York Times*, December 31, 2000. See also "Divided about the Dollar", *Economist*, January 6, 2001, 36.

[36] Lewis, "The Evolving Process", 437.

[37] Gibson and Curtis, "A Debt for Nature Blueprint", 361.

[38] Allegra C. Biggs, "Nibbling Away at the Debt Crisis: Debt-for-Nature Swaps", *Annual Review of Banking and Finance Law* 10 (1991): 456.

[39] See http://www.fnatura.org.

participation. From an environmental funding viewpoint, the transaction was a success. Like many developing countries, Ecuador had found it difficult to devote significant financial resources to the environment.[40] Even though the US$10 million of debt represented only a fraction of Ecuador's total external debt, the resulting environmental funding was very significant in the circumstances. Interest payments in the first year alone doubled Ecuador's entire budget for national parks.[41]

Through the use of an endowment fund, the perception within Ecuador of a loss of sovereignty was far less than it had been in Bolivia. The range of projects was selected with local input rather than the entire transaction being for the preservation of one area of a country designated important by a foreign conservation group.

In 1987 the Costa Rican 'Debt-for-Conservation' Agreement followed a structure similar to that utilised in the Ecuadorian exchange.[42] Within three years, in excess of US$70 million of Costa Rica's external debt was exchanged into local currency bonds (equivalent to US$36 million) through the implementation of four debt exchanges.[43]

Under debt-exchange agreements in 1987 and 1998,[44] US$5.4 million of Costa Rica's debt was purchased in the international secondary market for US$918,000, funded by the WWF and donations to the Costa Rican National Parks Foundation from a variety of other NGOs.[45] The debt was converted at 75% of face value into medium-term local currency bonds,[46] with an average annual interest rate of 25%.[47] Interest income was used to establish a fund for conservation projects, including the Guanacaste National Park project, with title to land purchased reverting to the government only after the park was fully completed and endowed.[48]

---

[40] Ronny J. Halperin, "Revenue Ruling 87–124: Treasuries' Flawed Interpretation of Debt for Nature Swaps", *University of Miami Law Review* 43 (1989): 721.

[41] Gibson and Curtis, "A Debt for Nature Blueprint", 360.

[42] Lewis, "The Evolving Process", 437.

[43] Two of these transactions were second-generation debt-exchange transactions.

[44] Costa Rican Debt-for-Nature Agreement, dated October 27, 1987, between the Costa Rican Central Bank, the Ministry of Natural Resources, Energy and Mines, the Costa Rican Cooperative Bank RL and Fundacion de Parques Nacionales (the Costa Rican National Parks Foundation, a Costa Rican NGO). See Gibson and Curtis, "A Debt for Nature Blueprint", 336 n. 172.

[45] These included the Nature Conservancy, Asociacion Ecologica La Pacifica, P. W. Charitable Fund, MacArthur Foundation, J. S. Noyes Foundation, Swedish Society for the Conservation of Nature, W. Alton Jones Foundation and Organisation for Tropical Studies and Conservation International. See ibid., 369 n. 187.

[46] These bonds were structured to mature after five years and nine months.

[47] Gibson and Curtis, "A Debt for Nature Blueprint", 367.

[48] Alagiri, "Give Us Sovereignty", 496.

III. SECOND-GENERATION DEBT-FOR-NATURE EXCHANGES

The success of some first-generation transactions, coupled with the growing international awareness of the relationship between the environment and development, opened the way for a new form of debt exchange involving official debt (i.e., debt between nations) rather than commercial bank debt.[49] These transactions were on a bilateral government-to-government basis, with the developed country donor governments playing a central role. This form of debt exchange reflected a convergence of interests between the respective governments.[50]

The advent of government-to-government agreements was an important development in the evolution of the debt-exchange mechanism, because it allowed for the exchange of much larger amounts of debt. This was facilitated in part by the introduction of a debt-exchange clause by the Paris Club in 1991, through which bilateral debt was deemed eligible to be exchanged and debt-exchange programs for the conversion of official development assistance were approved.[51]

The expansion of debt exchanges to include official debt pushed the concerns of enforceability, political viability and transparency to the fore. Governments needed to consider the potential for political fallout from a failure to satisfactorily implement an agreement.[52] These government-to-government transactions became known as 'second-generation'[53] debt exchanges.

A. *Costa Rica (1989): 'Debt for Conservation' and 'Debt for Industry'*

Costa Rica, with 12% of its land designated as national parks or protected biological reserves, represented a prime candidate for debt-for-nature exchanges and benefitted from early exchanges.[54] In the late 1980s Costa Rica participated in six debt-for-nature agreements, which retired 6.5% of its national debt.[55] In January 1989 the Netherlands and Costa Rica agreed that the former

49 Lewis, "The Evolving Process", 439.
50 von Moltke, "Debt-for-Nature", 983.
51 Melissa Moye, *Overview of Debt Conversions* (London: Debt Relief International, 2001), 10.
52 Sadler, "Debt-for-Nature Swaps", 335.
53 For example, see von Moltke, "Debt-for-Nature", and Sher, "Can Lawyers Save the Rainforest?"
54 Brijesh Thapa, "The Relationship between Debt-for-Nature Swaps and Protected Area Tourism: A Plausible Strategy for Developing Countries", *USDA Forest Service Proceedings* 15 (2000): 269.
55 Sean Michael Neal, "Bringing Developing Nations on Board the Climate Change Protocol: Using Debt-for-Nature Swaps to Implement the Clean Development Mechanism", *Georgetown International Environmental Law Review* 11 (1998): 172 (1998).

would purchase US$33 million of Costa Rican debt in the secondary debt market, to be converted into local currency four-year bonds, equivalent in value to US$9.9 million.[56] Interest was to be calculated at an annual rate of 15%, and these bonds were held in a trust fund, administered by both governments, in order to fund projects in reforestation and forest management.[57]

This was the first government-to-government debt-for-nature exchange and was innovative for the inclusion within the agreement of enforcement measures. These measures enabled each government to retain control over the projects financed, both through the requirement that both countries sign every project agreed to and by virtue of their ongoing ability to inspect projects and, if appropriate, to suspend finance for noncomplying projects.[58] The agreement, however, did not go so far as to include a dispute resolution mechanism.[59]

Another oversight of the agreement was the failure to provide any role for NGOs in the selection of projects or with respect to governance.[60] While the value of the debt exchanged was not large, through the creation of a trust fund, interest continued to accrue, which provided an ongoing source of conservation finance. The interest generated was in itself greater than the total annual Costa Rican Park Service budget.[61]

In the same year, Sweden purchased about US$28 million of Costa Rica's external debt for US$3.5 million and donated it to Costa Rica's National Parks Foundation. Upon conversion, four-year bonds were created paying annual interest at a rate of 15%, which went into an endowment for research, environmental education, park management and land acquisition.[62] The primary focus was to fund sustainable management of tropical forests in the Guanacaste province.[63]

B. *Poland (1991): 'Debt for Democracy'*

The early 1990s saw the debt-exchange mechanism developed further to apply to much larger amounts of a developing country's external debt. In March

[56] Agreement on Financial Cooperation in Order to Support Forest Development, January 1989, in Sher, "Can Lawyers Save the Rainforest?" 170.
[57] Karel von Kester, "The Use of Aid Money for Debt Reduction from the Inside", *Journal of International Development* 6 (1994): 243.
[58] Lewis, "The Evolving Process", 442.
[59] Sher, "Can Lawyers Save the Rainforest?" 171.
[60] Ibid., 172.
[61] Thapa, "Debt-for-Nature Swaps and Protected Area Tourism", 269.
[62] The Guanacaste National Park Project Foundation. See Gibson and Curtis, "A Debt for Nature Blueprint", 370.
[63] Neal, "Bringing Developing Nations on Board", 172.

1991 seven major industrialised countries agreed to forgive half of Poland's US$33 billion debt.[64] In addition some Paris Club countries agreed to channel interest payments and principal on some of the remaining debt into a Polish Ecofund to finance projects aimed at halting environmental damage. The Paris Club rescheduling had authorised members to sell their debt for exchanges involving local currency funding. In total, US$473 million in local currency was invested in the Ecofund, with the United States the largest single donor, contributing US$367 million to EcoFund projects.[65]

These actions were intended to show support for the democratic and economic reforms instituted in Poland following the introduction of a post-Communist government.[66] Poland was suffering from severe economic stagnation, which, coupled with its unsustainable debt burden, had pushed it to the brink of insolvency.[67] Furthermore, Poland was highly polluted.[68] To reduce the 'transboundary' effects of its pollution on neighbouring countries, the Paris Club Agreement was made conditional upon the implementation of environmental clean-up programs and antipollution measures in Poland.

The EcoFund provided grants to approved conservation projects. Approved projects were in the areas of transboundary air pollution, climate change, biological diversity and a clean-up of the Baltic Sea.[69] Between 1992 and 2007, the EcoFund financed 1,500 programs. The financing agreements typically provided for annual payments until 2010.[70]

The successful near completion of this program demonstrates the adaptability of the exchange mechanism and its ability to be applied to significant amounts of debt in order to facilitate social and economic development.

[64] The Paris Club consists of the major creditors of a country seeking a rescheduling of its debt. It is named after its usual meeting place and was first 'formed' in 1956. It has no fixed membership, officers or permanent administrative staff. See Ross P. Buckley, "Rescheduling as the Groundwork of Secondary Markets in Sovereign Debt", *Denver Journal of International Law and Policy* 26 (1998): 300 n. 9; and Lewis, "The Evolving Process", 443.

[65] Pervaze A. Sheikh, "Debt-for-Nature Initiatives and the Tropical Forest Conservation Act", CRS Report for Congress RL31286 (October 11, 2006), CRS-5.

[66] Gibson and Schrenk, "The Enterprise for the Americas Initiative", 66.

[67] D. H. Cole, "Cleaning up Krakow: Poland's Ecological Crisis and the Political Economy of the International Environmental Assistance", *Colorado Journal of International Environmental Law and Policy* 2 (1991): 217.

[68] At the time Poland had the fourth-largest external debt in the world. See ibid.

[69] Organisation for Economic Co-operation and Development (OECD), "Lessons Learnt from Experience with Debt-for-Environment Swaps in Economies in Transition", (2007), 5, accessed August 2, 2010, http://www.oecd.org/dataoecd/49/28/39352290.pdf.

[70] Environmental Technologies Action Plan, "Polish EcoFund Offers Template for Eco-innovation Funding", accessed August 2, 2010, http://ec.europa.eu/environment/etap/inaction/functions/New_Services/225_en.html.

The Polish debt-for-democracy exchange is the largest debt-for-nature exchange to date.[71]

The developed world's response to Poland's problems also highlights the extent to which geopolitical concerns consistently attract far higher levels and amounts of debt cancellation than do developmental or environmental concerns. In Poland's case, US$16.5 billion of debt was cancelled to promote Poland's transition to democracy, whereas only slightly less than half a billion dollars was exchanged to address Poland's massive environmental challenges. The same dynamic played out after the Iraq war.

Iraq, with the world's second-largest recorded oil reserves (10.8%), behind those of Saudi Arabia (25.2%),[72] and pre-conflict income levels at least three times higher than those generally accepted as defining poverty, is not a strong candidate for debt relief. The challenge has been to restore a functional economy to Iraq and rebuild its infrastructure so that it can again enjoy the benefits nature has bestowed upon it. To this end, Iraq is a very strong candidate for aid. However, the immediate cash flow benefits of debt cancellation are limited to the interest payments saved. Nonetheless, though far poorer countries usually have only 35% to 50% of their debts cancelled,[73] the Paris Club creditors agreed in 2004 to cancel 80% of Iraq's loans to them (after refusing to meet US demands for total cancellation of its debts). Much like Europe in the aftermath of World War II, Iraq needs to be rebuilt, and once it has been rebuilt its long-term economic capacity should not be in doubt. Debt relief, which is essentially long term in impact, was thus peculiar to Iraq's situation. Nonetheless, the United States later proceeded unilaterally to cancel all of its loans to Iraq.[74]

C. Bulgaria

Nonetheless, to return to our chronology, following on from the example of Poland, Bulgaria was the second Eastern European country to participate in

---

[71] OECD, "Lessons Learnt", 26.
[72] Centre for Strategic and International Studies, *The Changing Geopolitics of Energy – Part IV: Regional Developments in the Gulf, and Energy Issues Affecting Iran, Iraq, and Libya* (1998), 6, http://www.geni.org/globalenergy/library/technical-articles/links/CSIS/the-changing-geopolitics-of-energy/energyiv81298.pdf.
[73] International Monetary Fund and International Development Association, "Heavily Indebted Poor Countries (HIPC) Initiative – Statistical Update" (2004), accessed August 2, 2010, http://www.imf.org/external/np/hipc/2004/033104.htm.
[74] Ross P. Buckley, "Iraqi Sovereign Debt and Its Curious Global Implications", in *Beyond the Iraq War: The Promises, Perils and Pitfalls of External Interventionism*, eds. Michael Heazle and Iyanatul Islam (London: Edward Elgar, 2006), 141–155.

a debt-for-nature exchange. In 1995 Switzerland and Bulgaria signed a debt-for-nature exchange of SF 20 million, with the stipulation that the equivalent amount in local currency be invested in environmental protection and clean-up in Bulgaria.[75] The exchange amounted to 23% of Bulgaria's external debt owed to Switzerland, and the National Trust EcoFund (NTEF) was established to administer the funds.[76] The World Bank provided a grant to cover the costs of establishing the NTEF before disbursements to projects were made from the revenue from the debt exchange.[77] The NTEF has four priority areas: clean-up of past pollution, reduction of air pollution, protection of clean water and biodiversity.[78] The Fund's objective is 'the management of means provided under debt-for-environment and debt-for-nature swap agreements' and other environmental financing.[79]

The NTEF plays only a co-financing role in environmental projects.[80] By 2006 it had financed 72 projects.[81] These included hazardous waste and substances disposal, the funding of waste treatment plants and the management and development of infrastructure in protected areas.[82] While the NTEF was established with the revenue generated by the debt exchange, it has since expanded its financing base. In a 2003 assessment, its strength was attributed to its role in securing co-financing from other international sources, using the publicity created by the debt-for-nature exchange as a platform to seek further contributions.[83] The political independence and stable revenue provided by the debt exchange were found to be important factors in the NTEF's success.[84] The total cost of completed programs is slightly more than US$64 million, with US$11 million coming from the Fund and the rest of the money provided by international financial, government and independent institutions.[85] More recently the NTEF has established a new financial branch of a Protected Areas Fund that disperses money for landscape, natural habitats and biodiversity preservation.[86]

[75] Thapa, "Debt-for-Nature Swaps and Protected Area Tourism", 54, 271–272.
[76] OECD, *Debt-for-Environment Swap in Georgia: Pre-feasibility Study and Institutional Options* (Paris: OECD, 2006), 44, accessed August 2, 2010, http://www.oecd.org/dataoecd/8/56/35178696.pdf.
[77] OECD, "Lessons Learnt", 43.
[78] National Trust EcoFund, "Home", accessed August 2, 2010, http://www.ecofund-bg.org/.
[79] Patrick Francis, Michael Betts and Joanna Fiedler, "Review and Assessment of the Bulgarian National Trust Eco Fund" (September 2003), 6, accessed August 2, 2010, http://www.aequiconsult.com/images/NTEF_Review_2003_final_report.pdf.
[80] Ibid, 8.
[81] National Trust EcoFund, "Projects", accessed August 2, 2010, http://www.ecofund-bg.org.
[82] Ibid.
[83] Francis, Betts and Fiedler, "Review and Assessment", 8.
[84] Ibid., 9.
[85] National Trust EcoFund, "Home", accessed August 2, 2010, http://www.ecofund-bg.org/.
[86] OECD, "Lessons Learnt", 48.

The Polish and Bulgarian debt-for-nature exchanges provide good examples of a structure to allow for the transparent administration of a debt-for-nature exchange using an environmental fund. The Organisation for Economic Co-operation and Development (OECD) notes that the Bulgarian EcoFund has proved to be a model of good governance 'known for its rigorous project selection procedures and transparent decision-making'.[87]

Moreover, creating an environment fund establishes a long-term financing mechanism.[88] The strength of such funds lies in their organised and enduring structure and their independence from government.[89] The creation of environmental funds has repeatedly provided stability and direction to conservation policies in developing countries.[90]

The Peruvian Trust Fund for National Parks and Protected Areas (PROFONANPE) is a similar environmental fund, which finances biodiversity, conservation and sustainable development programs.[91] It was established by a contribution of US$5.2 million from the Global Environmental Facility as an endowment fund. Since then it has been funded principally through debt-for-nature exchanges and now has a capital of US$95.9 million.[92] Debt-for-nature exchanges have thus far been undertaken by PROFONANPE with Germany, Canada, Finland and the United States.[93]

IV. MORE RECENT DEBT-FOR-NATURE EXCHANGES

The range of extensive multilateral debt-relief initiatives since 2000 has led to the continued utility of debt-for-nature exchanges being challenged. One commentator has asked, 'Has the multilateral HIPC ended the era of bilateral debt-for-nature swaps?'[94] However, support for, and the use of, debt-for-nature exchanges, particularly as a tool for conservation finance in the many highly indebted nations that have failed to qualify for the Highly Indebted

---

[87] Ibid.

[88] David M. Leon, "Expanding the Scope of the Tropical Conservation Act: Exchanging Foreign Debt for Sustainable Development", *University of Miami International and Comparative Law Review* 11 (2003): 147.

[89] Marianne Guerin-McManus, "Conservation Trust Funds", *UCLA Journal of Environmental Law and Policy* 20 (2001–2002): 2.

[90] Francis, Betts and Fiedler, "Review and Assessment", 6.

[91] Alberto Paniagua, "Bilateral Debt-for-Nature Swaps: The PROFONANPE Experience – Peru", Paper for the Fifth World Parks Congress: *Sustainable Finance Stream*, September 2003, 4.

[92] PROFONANPE'S portfolio, accessed August 2, 2010, www.profonanpe.org.pe.

[93] Paniagua, "Bilateral Debt-for-Nature Swaps", 3.

[94] Eugenio Gonzales, "Roles and Challenges for Foundations in Debt-for-Development Swaps" (Synergos Institute), 13 (copy on file with second author).

Poor Countries (HIPC) Initiative or the Multilateral Debt Relief Initiative (MDRI), have continued to grow. Indeed, several international organisations and NGOs have continued to argue for greater use of debt-for-nature exchanges in a wide range of countries across Africa, Asia, Latin America and elsewhere.[95] The United States has consistently used debt-for-nature exchanges as a means of financing forest conservation around the word. The three US legislative initiatives that have enabled the exchange of debt for conservation purposes are examined in detail in Chapter 4.

The United Nations Economic Commission (UNEC) in 2001 considered the debt-exchange mechanism as 'underutilised' for conservation purposes and advocated the potential of debt exchanges to help limit deforestation, preserve other resources such as water and biodiversity and promote clean energy.[96] The OECD has endorsed the use of debt-for-nature exchanges as a conservation financing mechanism, stating:

> A debt-for-environment swap is among the very few mechanisms that can provide sustainable support for local economic development and at the same time mobilise domestic spending to protect purely public and common goods (such as biodiversity) or pure externalities (such as transboundary or global pollution) in low-income countries.[97]

The successes of the debt-for-nature programs in Poland, Bulgaria and elsewhere have encouraged the OECD to seek to implement such mechanisms in other nations.

The OECD has argued for the use of debt-for-nature exchanges in Eastern Europe, the Caucasus and Central Asia, given that, of all the nations in these regions, only the Kyrgyz Republic is eligible for debt relief under multilateral initiatives.[98] The OECD has emphasised the importance of 'a thorough

---

95 Arturo López Ornat and Sira Jiménez-Caballero, "Sustainable Financing Sources for Protected Areas in the Mediterranean", Paper presented at IUCN Conference on Finance Sources for Protected Areas in the Mediterranean, Seville (January 29–31, 2006), 54; Alain Lambert, "Sustainable Financing for Environmental Projects in Africa: Some Ideas for Consideration", Prepared for the 11th Regular Session of the African Ministerial Conference on the Environment, Brazzaville, Congo, May, 22–26, 2006; Agus Purnomo, "Debt Swap for Nature Opportunities in Indonesia", Prepared for KEHATI (Indonesian Biodiversity Foundation) (2004), 5, accessed August 2, 2010, http://www.fundses.org.ar/deuxedu/biblioteca/5_estudios_mecanismos_de_conversion_de_deuda/debt_swap_nature_opportunities_indonesia_synergos2004.pdf; United Nations Economic Commission of Latin American and the Caribbean, "Debt for Nature: A Swap Whose Time Has Gone?" LC/MEX/L.497 (November 6, 2001).
96 United Nations Economic Commission of Latin American and the Caribbean, "Debt for Nature", 18.
97 OECD, "Lessons Learnt".
98 Ibid, 13. In 2002 the CIS 7 initiative was launched as a collaborative effort to facilitate economic growth and poverty reduction for the Kyrgyz Republic, Moldova, Armenia, Azerbaijan, Tajikistan, Uzbekistan and Georgia, but this initiative has not resulted in debt

and rigorous analysis of the debt portfolio' before engaging in debt-for-nature exchanges.[99] In international rescheduling agreements, both the Kyrgyz Republic and Georgia have included debt-exchange provisions in the rescheduling of their Paris Club debt, and both governments have established inter-ministerial working groups on debt-for-environment exchanges.[100]

The OECD argues that the best results are achieved through Paris Club negotiations and has conducted feasibility studies of the Kyrgyz Republic and Georgia in order to examine the possibility and potential of such debt exchanges.[101] Despite the high hopes of the Kyrgyz government, the feasibility study revealed limited potential. Most of its foreign debt is multilateral,[102] and of the small proportion of bilateral debt, the only creditors to have engaged in exchanges are Germany and France (the other main creditors were Russia and Turkey, which have not undertaken any debt exchanges or thus far demonstrated a willingness to do so). Priority projects that have been identified include biogas production from animal waste and the prevention of irreversible loss of biodiversity. Germany was identified as the most likely creditor with which to pursue a debt-for-nature exchange, and the Kyrgyz government is currently attempting to secure such an agreement.[103]

Georgia has sought to utilise the debt-exchange mechanism since 2000, when it asked the World Bank for assistance in negotiating debt-for-environment schemes with creditor governments. It sought similar assistance from the OECD in 2001.[104]

Following the feasibility study of debt-for-environment exchanges for Georgia, the OECD recommended that 'Georgia pursue a comprehensive debt-for-environment swap scheme to take advantage of the synergies that exist between environment and development objectives'.[105] In its assessment, the OECD noted a number of promising project sectors, including reducing emissions of greenhouse gases, reducing pollution of international waters, protecting biological diversity and facilitating access for the poor to safe water and sanitation services.[106]

forgiveness. For more information, see the IMF and World Bank, "A New Initiative for the CIS 7" (February 2002).
[99] OECD, "Lessons Learnt", 54.
[100] OECD, "Facilitating Policy Dialogue on Opportunities and Risks of Debt-for-Environment Swaps", accessed August 2, 2010, http://www.oecd.org/document/7/0,3343,en_2649_34335_35165319_1_1_1_1,00.html.
[101] OECD, "Lessons Learnt", 26.
[102] Until the establishment of the MDRI, there was a reluctance to forgo any multilateral debt; see ibid., 14.
[103] Ibid., 30.
[104] Ibid., 16.
[105] Ibid., 26.
[106] Ibid., 10.

The report did, however, note that '[p]reparation for the transaction and financial transfer of a debt-for-environment swap scheme is not going to be short, easy and cheap'.[107] This has proved to be correct, as Georgia has yet to finalise an agreement for a debt-for-nature exchange with any creditor nation.[108]

In terms of potential negative impacts of debt-for-nature transactions, the OECD has highlighted the threats of inflationary impact, credit-rating down-grades and inefficient public administration,[109] but at the same time has noted that the potential benefits of such exchanges are far greater.[110] The United Nations Environmental Program (UNEP) is also of the view that debt-for-nature transactions are potentially highly useful.

Alain Lambert has argued that there is a dire need to expand innovative funding mechanisms for environmental projects, as '[t]he traditional 'project approach' does not work anymore'.[111] The innovative funding mechanisms he suggests could more broadly tackle environmental concerns in Africa and include environmental trust funds, payment schemes for environmental services, debt-for-nature exchanges and carbon-offset programs. He considered that 'Debt-for-Sustainable Development swaps will never be the single or definitive solution to the problem but its much more extensive use could certainly be part of a more global solution'.[112]

Lambert provided three reasons for the failure of traditional project funding for environmental conservation:

1. the failure to provide long-term financing, with conservation activities largely ceasing at the conclusion of a project;
2. too great a dependence on donor funding; and
3. the continuing tendency to view the environment and development as separate issues.[113]

The use of debt-for-nature exchanges in the past decade highlights their ability to address the short-falls in other conservation mechanisms and foster long-term financing and an integrated approach to the environment. Examples of this are set out in the following subsections.

---

[107] Ibid., 58.
[108] Ibid., 9.
[109] Ibid., 18.
[110] Ibid., 17–18.
[111] Lambert, "Sustainable Financing", 3.
[112] Ibid., 20.
[113] Ibid., 3.

A. *The Madagascar Foundation*

Recent debt-for-nature exchanges undertaken by Madagascar demonstrate the success of trust funds as a means to secure long-term financing for environmental projects. In 2000 Madagascar was declared eligible for debt relief under the HIPC Initiative. In the preparation of its Poverty Reduction Strategy Paper, the environment was 'considered to be a crosscutting theme in poverty reduction strategy'.[114] In the same year, the Malagasy government established the Sustainable Financing Commission to design a sustainable financing strategy for Madagascar's Third Environmental Program.[115] Environmental priorities included environmental impact evaluations for all projects, sustainable management of coastal and marine ecosystems and sustainable financing for protected areas.[116]

In 2003 Germany undertook a debt-for-nature exchange with Madagascar in relation to debt that was excluded from HIPC treatment.[117] Germany agreed to cancel €23.3 million of debt in exchange for the Malagasy government's paying €13.8 million into a counterpart fund to be disbursed to finance environmental projects over 20 years.[118] The agreement was contingent on the establishment of a Madagascar Foundation for Protected Areas and Biodiversity, with a management structure acceptable to the German government.[119] The Madagascar Foundation was established in 2005. The debt-for-nature exchange reflected the priorities established in Madagascar's Third Environmental Program.[120]

The Madagascar Foundation has continued to be funded through debt-for-nature exchanges. Most recently, in 2008, France announced a debt-for-nature transaction with Madagascar, which will contribute US$20 million in funding. This is the largest debt-for-nature exchange in Madagascar's history and has brought the Foundation's total endowment to more than US$50 million.[121]

---

[114] Melissa Moye and Jean-Paul Paddack, "Madagascar's Experience with Swapping Debt for the Environment", Background paper for the fifth World Parks Conference, Durban, South Africa (WWF, 2003), 8.

[115] Ibid., 7.

[116] Ibid., 8.

[117] Germany has long been a leader in debt-for-nature exchanges; see e.g., Ross P. Buckley, "Debt-for-Development Exchanges: A Potentially Innovative Response to the Global Financial Crisis", *University of New South Wales Law Journal* 32 (2009): 620.

[118] Moye and Paddack, "Madagascar's Experience", 9.

[119] Ibid.

[120] Ibid., 11.

[121] WWF, "Debt-for-Nature Swaps", accessed August 2, 2010, http://www.worldwildlife.org/what/howwedoit/conservationfinance/debtfornatureswaps.html.

B. *Millennium Development Goals, the Paris Declaration and Debt-for-Nature Exchanges*

The OECD argues that debt-for-nature exchanges should be used to facilitate the achievement of water and environmental Millennium Development Goals (MDGs).[122] The seventh MDG seeks to promote 'environmental stability' and takes a broad view of environmental imperatives, including the integration of principles of sustainable development into country policies and programs, the reduction of biodiversity loss, the promotion of sustainable access to safe drinking water and basic sanitation by 2015 and the achievement of significant improvements in the lives of slum dwellers.[123]

These targets have been directly incorporated into more recent debt-for-nature agreements. For example, recent Italian exchanges use the MDGs to provide a framework for debt-for-nature exchanges. These exchanges, which are analysed in Part II, have environmental protection as a central goal, and the environmental protection goals pursued were framed with reference to the MDGs.

Two project clusters of the Italy–Egyptian Debt Swap Agreements (IEDS) of 2001, examined in more detail in Chapter 5, were in line with the seventh MDG. These were to increase access to safe drinking water and to 'integrate principles of sustainable development' into national projects. Under these targets, dams were constructed and pilot programs undertaken to facilitate treatment of agricultural drainage using low-cost technology. Research was also undertaken into the establishment of desalination plants.[124] In order to foster principles of sustainable development, projects undertaken ranged from environmentally sustainable tourism to measures to decrease industrial pollution. These included the relocation of tanneries to outside Cairo in order to contribute to cleaner industrial production and the training of neighbourhood leaders in environmental awareness. Solid waste management and marine biodiversity projects were also funded.[125]

In 2006 Italy signed a debt-for-development exchange with Kenya for €44 million, which focussed primarily on environmental projects. Water and irrigation were priority sectors in light of the National Water Services Strategy, 2007–2015, which aims to upgrade water systems in rural areas.[126] The

---

[122] OECD, "Lessons Learnt", 34.

[123] See www.un.org/millenniumgoals/, accessed February 17, 2010.

[124] Samir Radwan, Sherif Kamel and Nevine El Oraby, "Partners for Development: The Experience of the Italian–Egyptian Debt Swap Program (2001–08)" (2008), 39, accessed August 2, 2010, http://www.utlcairo.org/stampa/Final%20study%20IEDS.pdf.

[125] Ibid., 36.

[126] Kenya–Italy Debt-for-Development Program (KIDDP), "Sectors of Intervention", accessed August 2, 2010, http://www.kiddp.org/.

upgrading of the Korogocho slum, another purpose of the exchange, was also aligned with the MDGs and the National Slum Upgrading Programme.

The debt-for-development exchanges undertaken by Italy demonstrate how debt exchanges can be used effectively and sustainably to address environmental challenges. They also establish how environmental concerns can be viewed as part of broader development concerns, and not as merely ancillary to poverty alleviation.

The second development in these debt-for-nature exchanges is the way Italy has sought to implement the agreements under the dictates of the Paris Declaration on Aid Effectiveness. In 2005 the Paris Declaration established five key principles for overseas development assistance: ownership, alignment, harmonisation, results and mutual accountability.[127] The insistence on conditions by creditor nations – known as 'conditionality' – is no longer viewed as appropriate in an international aid program. Despite the absence of conditions, the principles of the Paris Declaration have provided a coherent framework by which debt-for-nature transactions can promote, rather than undermine, good governance in debtor nations.

In a final report on the IEDS in 2008, the criteria against which the implementation of programs was assessed were their alignment with the MDGs and the principles of the Paris Declaration.[128] The report concluded that debt exchanges could conform to the two frameworks.[129] In line with the Paris Declaration, projects in the IEDS were selected by the Egyptian government mainly in accordance with national priorities. The majority of projects were implemented by Egyptian government entities, and both nations were concurrently responsible for monitoring the implementation of the agreement.[130]

C. *Indonesia, Debt-for-Nature Exchanges and the Clean Development Mechanism*

Although initially resistant to the idea of debt exchanges, since 2000 the government of Indonesia has expressed interest in participating in exchanges with other nations. In a 1998 feasibility assessment, USAID concluded that 'debt-for-nature swaps are likely to be feasible in Indonesia and should be actively pursued as a debt relief and conservation funding mechanism'.[131]

---

[127] OECD, "The Paris Declaration and AAA", accessed August 2, 2010, http://www.oecd.org/document/18/0,3343,en_2649_3236398_35401554_1_1_1_1,00.html.
[128] Radwan, Kamel and El Oraby, "Partners for Development", 19.
[129] Ibid., 24.
[130] Ibid., 29–30.
[131] "Assessment of the Feasibility: Debt-for-Nature Swaps in Indonesia", Prepared for the US Agency for International Development (December 14, 1998), vi.

Indonesia was seen as a prime candidate for debt-for-nature exchanges, due to the ready availability of restructured debt and because the rate of deforestation in Indonesia has been alarmingly high.[132] The East Asian crisis had a substantial impact on conservation funding in Indonesia, with the budget for national parks management slashed by 30% in 1998–1999 in nominal terms (a 60% reduction in real terms).[133]

Recognising that the environment was ripe for debt-for-nature exchanges, WWF, CI, TNC and KEHATI (the Indonesian Biodiversity Foundation) created a Joint Steering Committee to explore and co-ordinate the possibilities for debt-for-nature exchanges and promote them to government.[134] KEHATI organised a seminar on debt-for-nature exchanges in October 2004, where papers presented by the Indonesian Central Bank and the National Planning Agency asserted that about US$800 million worth of the country's debt might be eligible for exchange.[135]

Following debt-for-education exchanges with Germany in 2002, Germany and Indonesia entered into an innovative debt-for-nature exchange in September 2006 under which €6.25 million was invested to increase environmental quality through targeted funding for small and micro businesses.[136] In June 2009, Indonesia and the United States finalised a US$19.6 million debt-for-nature agreement to finance forest conservation programs in Sumatra. Including interest and with $2 million contributed by environmental NGOs, $30 million will be paid into a trust fund over eight years. Discussions are now under way about a second debt-for-nature exchange with the United States,[137] and Indonesia is currently in the final stages of negotiating a €20 million debt-for-nature exchange with Germany.[138]

While enthusiasm for debt-for-nature exchanges has not been uniform within Indonesia,[139] there has been continuing advocacy for a more widespread use of the mechanism and greater dialogue with creditor nations.

---

[132] Between 2000 and 2005, Indonesia had the fastest rate of deforestation worldwide: Tony Hotland, "RI–Germany Eye Cooperation Around Renewable Energy Sources", *Jakarta Post*, February 28, 2008.

[133] "Assessment of the Feasibility", 1.

[134] Purnomo, "Debt Swap for Nature Opportunities in Indonesia", 5.

[135] Gonzales, "Roles and Challenges", 13.

[136] Republic of Indonesia, "Debt-for-Nature Swap Program on Environmental Investment for Micro and Small Business" (press release, October 3, 2006).

[137] "Government Secures Debt Swap with Italy", *Jakarta Post*, January 10, 2009.

[138] "RI, US Begin Discussion on Second Debt-for-Nature Deal", *Jakarta Post*, January 16, 2010.

[139] Indonesian environmental NGO WHALI (Indonesia Forum for the Environment and Friends of the Earth Indonesia) has expressed reservations about the use of debt-for-nature exchanges, due to a perceived exclusion of indigenous populations from the projects; Interview with Feri Irawan (October 4, 2007), accessed August 2, 2010, http://home.snafu.de/watchin/redamazon12.11.07.htm.

Most recently, the Borneo Orangutan Survival Foundation (BOS) has sought to implement a debt-for-nature exchange in conjunction with the Clean Development Mechanism (CDM).

In 1997 the Indonesian government saved a 364,000-hectare area in Central Kalimantan from becoming an oil palm plantation. The area is home to an estimated 3,000 wild orangutans. The Indonesian government had authorised the BOS to negotiate with the World Bank for the debt-for-nature exchange to raise funds for ongoing protection of this area.[140] The founder of the BOS, Willie Smits, had envisioned that 'we could offer this area to become a new permanent reserve, but under the condition that a part of Indonesia's debt be forgiven', with the area then managed not by the Indonesian government but by the BOS.[141]

The innovative nature of his project, however, was that Smits conceived of the original conservation project being established under a bilateral debt-for-nature agreement and the continued financing being funded through the CDM, whereby the preservation of peat swamps could create a sustainable income through a voluntary carbon-offset program.[142]

There were some initial difficulties with such a project. For example, Indonesia had, prior to 2004, not ratified the Kyoto Protocol to the United Nations Framework Convention on Climate Change[143] and therefore was not eligible to market carbon credits. To overcome this obstacle, Smits reached an agreement with Shell Canada, which has a voluntary carbon credit scheme.[144] Upon ratification of the Kyoto Protocol, the possibilities of this scheme widened, with expressions of interest from the Netherlands and Germany to participate in carbon trading for the purpose.[145] This would be the first such debt exchange to take place within the framework of the CDM. Whilst negotiations for this initiative appeared promising, no concrete agreements have yet been signed.[146]

---

[140] Orangutan Conservancy, "Mawas-BOSF: A New Habitat Protection Project", accessed August 2, 2010, http://www.orangutan.net/projects/mawas.

[141] ABC Radio National, "The Science Show: 10 July 2004 – Orangutan – Person of the Forest", accessed August 2, 2010, http://www.abc.net.au/rn/science/ss/stories/s1127766.htm.

[142] Ibid. The possibility of utilising the CDM for peat swamps in the Central Kalimantan has also been recognised by the Institute for Environmental Security; see, e.g., Jenna Heyde Hecker, "Promoting Environmental Security and Poverty Alleviation in the Peat Swamps of Central Kalimantan, Indonesia" (October 2005), accessed August 2, 2010, http://www.envirosecurity.org/espa/PDF/IES_ESA_CS_Kalimantan_Case_Study.pdf.

[143] Kyoto Protocol to the United Nations Framework Conventions on Climate Change, accessed August 2, 2010, http://unfccc.int/essential_background/kyoto_protocol/items/1678.php.

[144] ABC Radio National, "The Science Show".

[145] Annie Lawson, "A Race Against Time", *The Age*, November 7, 2004.

[146] BOS, "Do the Orangutans of Mawas Hold a Key to Helping Prevent the Effects of Global Warming in the Asia/Pacific Area?", accessed August 2, 2010, http://www.orangutans.com.au/Orangutans-Survival-Information/Mawas-Reserve.aspx.

Progress has been slow with debt-for-nature exchanges in Indonesia, despite a strong commitment by environmental NGOs to be involved in innovative approaches. Smits has noted the difficulty of engaging creditor support for debt exchanges, due to systemic corruption within Indonesia.[147] The International NGO Forum on Indonesian Development has cited disappointment with Indonesia's most recent collaborative initiative on international aid, the Jakarta Commitment, which has failed to articulate an obligation to eradicate corruption. The Jakarta Commitment is an intergovernmental initiative for the management of foreign aid involving 22 donor countries and multilateral institutions.[148] The commitment has, however, failed to seek diplomatic debt reduction and debt relief. A greater acceptance of debt restructuring and an increased commitment to wiping out corruption may be required before debt-for-nature exchanges can begin to fulfil their potential within Indonesia.

V. CONCLUSION

Originally conceived and implemented for relatively modest purposes, the debt-for-nature exchange mechanism has disproved the doubts of those who suggested it was a financing technique with relatively limited capacities that had passed its use-by date. Despite some hiccups along the way, it seems that, much like standby letters of credit, the debt-exchange mechanism has a flexibility and simplicity that allows it to be adapted for an increasing variety of purposes. Indeed, as has been discussed, where there is sufficient political will and interest, the mechanism can involve very significant amounts of money and be used for historically groundbreaking purposes.

Yet despite its advantages, the exchange mechanism is still underutilised, particularly when compared with the extent of more traditional funding of developing countries through development aid and when compared with the extent of straight debt cancellation. This may be due to a number of factors: a misunderstanding of the purposes of the technique, an overblown fear that the technique cannot accommodate the needs of indigenous peoples, traditional notions of sovereignty, a failure in the past to implement appropriate enforcement and governance structures and a shortage, particularly in developing countries, of the time, energy and expertise needed to negotiate and properly implement debt exchanges.

The need for increased environmental financing is, however, more crucial than ever. As discussed with reference to Indonesia, climate change is an area in

---

[147] ABC Radio National, "The Science Show".
[148] INFID, "The 'Jakarta Commitment': A Reincarnation of CGI and a Commitment to Dependency" (press release, February 2, 2009).

need of innovative financing mechanisms, and some are explored in Chapters 18 and 19. There are estimated global financing gaps of US$120 billion to $200 billion for climate change adaptation and mitigation.[149] Indonesia is the world's third-largest emitter of greenhouse gases, with 80% of emissions due to deforestation.[150] In late May 2010 Indonesian President Susilo Bambang Yudhoyno announced a two-year moratorium on logging under a Deforestation and Forest Degradation (REDD) agreement with Norway.[151] The agreement is worth US$1 billion over seven to eight years. The money will initially be spent on completing a REDD strategy for Indonesia. The funds are tied to verified emissions reductions by Indonesia, from deforestation, forest degradation or peatland destruction.[152] This initiative has, however, missed an opportunity to reduce Indonesia's foreign debt whilst pursuing climate change reduction. An agreement between the United States and Indonesia targeting environmental funding has, conversely, included a debt exchange, as discussed in Chapter 4. There has, indeed, been growing recognition of the potential for using debt-for-nature exchanges to target climate change specifically.

The underutilisation of the debt-exchange mechanism for environmental purposes was noted by Development Finance International in a report to the Joint Ministerial Forum on Debt Sustainability held at the World Bank in 2009.[153] It was noted that, in the past five years, only six Paris Club members have exchanged debts but that Paris Club nations 'acknowledge that, provided debt relief can be well spent by debtor governments, it is a good means of providing reliable, predictable long term aid'.[154] A study was undertaken to assess the feasibility of debt exchanges to combat climate change in 58 countries that might be vulnerable to both climate change and unsustainable debt levels.[155] Climate change is not a priority for developing countries struggling to meet the needs of their people. Urgent actions identified by the less developed countries in the National Action Plans for Adaptation (NAPAs) are forecast to cost US$2 billion a year.[156] In this context, and given the acceleration of rising sea levels in low-level coastal countries, desertification and deforestation,

---

[149] Development Finance International, "Debt Relief to Combat Climate Change", Paper presented to the Joint Ministerial Forum on Debt Sustainability, April 2009, 2.

[150] Tom Allard, "Norway to Pay to Indonesian Logging Moratorium", *Sydney Morning Herald*, May 28, 2010.

[151] Ibid.

[152] Royal Norwegian Embassy in Jakarta, "Norway–Indonesia REDD+ Partnership: Frequently Asked Questions", May 31, 2010, accessed August 2, 2010, http://www.norway.or.id/Norway_in_Indonesia/Environment/-FAQ-Norway-Indonesia-REDD-Partnership-/.

[153] Development Finance International, "Debt Relief to Combat Climate Change".

[154] Ibid., 2.

[155] Ibid., 4.

[156] Ibid., 13.

alternative financing mechanisms are being explored. The study concluded that debt relief 'is technically feasible and is a high-quality way to provide additional aid to developing countries; that a large amount of debt is potentially eligible; that funding is needed to combat climate change and maintain debt sustainability; and that ways exist to convince creditors and debtors to participate'.[157]

A particularly shocking comparison suggesting that debt-for-nature exchanges have been grossly underutilised is that between the typical size of debt-for-nature exchanges considered herein and the size of debt cancellations afforded by the United States to promote its national security interests, narrowly defined, and its geopolitical interests. When the success of Poland's transition to democracy was seen as important for Eastern Europe in the early 1990s, the United States cancelled $2.5 billion of its debt.[158] When Jordan's moderating influence in the Middle East was seen to matter, the United States cancelled $700 million of its debt.[159] When Egypt's support of US policy in the Middle East was particularly valued, the United States cancelled $7 billion of its debt.[160] And when the United States was seeking to rebuild Iraq after the second Gulf war, the United States cancelled $3.5 billion of its debt, for a nation with the world's second-largest oil reserves and thus the long-term capacity to repay the debt readily.[161]

However, more recent developments are encouraging, and the embryonic steps that have been taken to incorporate the debt-exchange process into the CDM regime under the Kyoto Protocol may represent a further opportunity to promote environmental and developmental progress through the use of a time-tested financing technique. Chapters 18 and 19 explore the potential of debt exchanges to address climate change adaption. Certainly these exchanges are a tool that should be used far more often, and on much larger scales, than has been the case to date, as the world seeks to address the ever more complex environmental and developmental challenges of the 21st century.

---

[157] Ibid., 16.
[158] Sheikh, "Debt-for-Nature Initiatives", CRS-5.
[159] James Fuller, "Debt for Nonproliferation: The Next Step in Threat Reduction", *Arms Control Today* (January–February 2002), accessed August 2, 2010, http://www.armscontrol.org/print/975.
[160] Ibid.
[161] Ross P. Buckley, "Iraqi Sovereign Debt and Its Curious Global Implications", in *Beyond the Iraq War: The Promises, Perils and Pitfalls of External Interventionism*, eds. Michael Heazle and Jyanatul Islam (London: Edward Elgar, 2006), 141–155.

3

Other Debt-for-Development Exchanges

Ross P. Buckley

Debt-for-nature exchanges demonstrated that debt exchanges can operate without the inherent weaknesses of debt-for-equity exchanges: they don't tend to be inflationary and can be run consistently for long periods. As a consequence debt-exchange mechanisms began to be applied to a wide range of developmental goals. Two prominent examples, debt-for-education and debt-for-health initiatives, are discussed in the following sections.

I. DEBT FOR EDUCATION

Some three years after the early debt-for-nature exchanges in 1987, it was realised that the promotion of education could replace nature conservancy as the purpose of the exchange. Debt-for-education exchanges are another application of the basic principle that the acquisition of debt and its tender to the debtor nation for discharge can, by virtue of the debt's secondary market discount, magnify the purchasing power of hard currency for local currency.[1] Indeed, in the first debt-for-education exchange, Harvard University multiplied the purchasing power of its funding almost three times.[2]

In 1990 Harvard University and Ecuador entered into a debt-for-education agreement. Pursuant to the agreement, Harvard acquired US$5 million of Ecuadorian debt in the secondary market and exchanged these loans with

---

[1] The discount in the secondary market is of the essence of all of these debt exchanges, as noted with respect to debt-for-nature swaps by Facundo Gómes Minujín in "Debt-for-Nature Swaps: A Financial Mechanism to Reduce Debt and Preserve the Environment", *Environment and Policy Law* 21 (1991): 147–148.

[2] Jennifer F. Zaiser, "Swapping Debt for Education: Harvard and Ecuador Provide a Model for Relief", *Boston College Third World Law Journal* 12 (1992): 157.

the Central Bank of Ecuador for 50% of their face value in local currency bonds.[3] As Harvard acquired the loans at a price of 15.5% of face value, their total investment was US$775,000.[4] The bonds were transferred to a local Ecuadorian educational foundation, formed for the purpose. This founda- tion sold the bonds in Ecuador and used the proceeds to purchase US dollars in the local market. The proceeds amounted to some US$2 million, or almost three times Harvard's initial contribution. These funds, now owned by the local foundation, were invested in the United States. The investments were designed to realise about US$150,000 per annum, of which about 85% was used to fund scholarships for Ecuadorian students to attend Harvard and the balance was to fund local research and study in Ecuador by Harvard faculty and students.[5]

Since 1998 there have been 18 debt-for-education exchanges initiated in 14 debtor nations.[6] For example, Germany has undertaken three debt-for-education exchanges with Indonesia and one with Pakistan, and Spain has undertaken debt-for-education exchanges with Ecuador (US$50 million), Nicaragua (US$38.9 million), Honduras (US$138.3 million), El Salvador (US$10 million), Bolivia (US$72 million) and Peru (US$11 million and €6 million). France has entered into exchanges to benefit education with Cameroon, Mauritania, Tanzania, Nicaragua and Uruguay. In most of these exchanges, the proceeds have been directed to funding local schools in the debtor nation. The Harvard model has proved to be highly unusual and not generally copied in later exchanges, although in one French exchange a centre for scientific research and education was funded in the debtor nation.[7]

Debt-for-education exchanges have been pursued more recently to meet commitments under the Millennium Development Goals (MDGs) for universal primary education. In 2007 there were 72 million children world- wide who were still not enrolled in primary education, and in 2006 aid for

---

[3] The Ecuadorian government drove a hard bargain here, recapturing 50% of the loans' value. The reason for insisting on such favourable terms was probably to minimise the inflationary impact of the local currency bonds that had to be issued to 'repurchase' the debt.

[4] Zaiser, "Swapping Debt", 180–181.

[5] Ibid., 182–183.

[6] UNESCO General Conference, "Item 5.17 on the Agenda: Debt Swaps for Education", 35th Session, October 12, 2009, accessed August 2, 2010, http://unesdoc.unesco.org/images/ 0018/001849/184906e.pdf.

[7] UNESCO Working Group on the Debt Swaps for Education, "Draft Report for the Director-General of UNESCO" (August 21, 2007), accessed August 2, 2010, www.unesco. org/education/EFAWGSDE/WGDSE_2nd_draftreportforDG_en.pdf. See also UNESCO, "Education for All, Final Report of the First Meeting of the UNESCO Working Group on Debt Swaps for Education" (2006), accessed August 2, 2010, http://unesdoc.unesco.org/ images/0015/001537/153714e.pdf.

basic education represented only 2.6% of overall official development assistance (ODA).[8] In 2003 the Ibero-American Conference on Education called on heads of state to look at converting debt into funds for education, and in 2005 the Ibero-American Pact for Education had, as a goal, the promotion of techniques for debt-for-education exchanges.[9]

In 2003 the Ministers of Education of Argentina, Brazil and Venezuela and the President of Peru encouraged UNESCO to take a leading role in promoting debt-for-education exchanges. The result was the adoption of the resolution at the 33rd session of the General Conference of UNESCO in 2005 creating a working group for debt swaps for education.[10] The working group has since met twice to exchange lessons learned from past debt-for-education exchanges and to formulate guidelines for best practices. UNICEF had been a pioneer in investing in education through debt exchanges: exchanges it sponsored retired almost US$200 million of debt between 1989 and 1995 for education and other development-focussed programs. UNICEF has not participated in debt exchanges since 1995, and bilateral debt exchanges have emerged as a greater source of education funding.[11] Although the UNESCO working group, unlike UNICEF, has no funding base through which to pursue debt-for-education exchanges directly, its formation has been encouraged as a means to assess implementation, foster facilitation between nations and develop best-practice models.[12]

The context of the global financial crisis (GFC) has led to a renewed interest in alternative financing mechanisms, as public education spending in the developing world is falling behind targets. The UNESCO 2009 General Conference recommended that the Director-General establish an Advisory Panel of Experts on Debt Swaps and Innovative Approaches to Education Financing. UNESCO plans to hold a conference on this topic in the first half of 2010 and to present debt exchanges as one of the several alternative financing initiatives to address the financial crisis. Whilst acknowledging that debt-for-education exchanges cannot solve the debt problem, they nonetheless may provide much needed funding to educational initiatives. UNESCO's General

---

[8]   United Nations, "Millennium Development Goals Report" (2009), 15; UNESCO Working Group on Debt Swaps for Education, "Draft Report", 2.
[9]   "What Are Debt-for-Education Swaps?" Working paper for the UNESCO Working Group on Debt Swaps for Education (2007), 13 (copy on file with author).
[10] UNESCO Working Group on Debt Swaps for Education, "Draft Report", 3.
[11] Melissa Moye, *Overview of Debt Conversion* (London: Debt Financing International, 2001), 13–14.
[12] Marta Ruiz, "Debt Swaps for Development: Creative Solution or Smoke Screen?" (European Network on Debt and Development, October 2007), 25, accessed August 2, 2010, http://www.eurodad.org/uploadedFiles/Whats_New/Reports/Debt_swaps_ENG(2).pdf.

Counsel further indicated the possibility of a role for an expert advisory panel in disseminating information on debt exchanges and acting as a knowledge exchange on best debt-exchange practices.

II. DEBT FOR HEALTH

The adoption of the MDGs in 2000 created a greater awareness of the need to foster development in impoverished nations and of the importance of population health for this process.[13] Indeed, health epidemics threaten progress on all other development goals.[14] The Declaration of Commitment on AIDS/HIV was adopted in June 2001 by all UN member states. It holds that 'the HIV/AIDs challenge cannot be met without new, additional and sustained resources'. Important for our purposes, the Declaration supported 'debt swaps for projects aimed at the prevention, care and treatment of HIV/AIDs'.[15] Debt-exchange programs that generate funding to address HIV/AIDS and other serious epidemics have been vigorously promoted by the UN, in part for the potential to create publicity for 'the need to join forces in the fight against the HIV/AIDS epidemic' and in the hope that this publicity will lead to further private donations,[16] and in part as simply another way to generate funds to tackle the HIV epidemic.

The Global Fund to Fight AIDS, Tuberculosis and Malaria is another UN initiative. It is a public–private partnership that seeks to finance public health initiatives in developing countries.[17] The Global Fund currently finances two-thirds of all international investments in fighting malaria and tuberculosis, and provides more than 20% of worldwide funding for AIDS prevention.[18] In 2007 it launched its Debt2Heath initiative, a debt-exchange program to fight HIV/AIDS, tuberculosis and malaria. The Global Fund proposed itself as a third party in debt-exchange negotiations that seek to persuade creditor

---

[13] For more, see United Nation, "UN Millennium Development Goals", accessed August 2, 2010, www.un.org/millenniumgoals.

[14] Sydney Rosen, Jonathon Simon, Donald Thea and Paul Zeitz, *Exchanging Debt-for-Health in Africa: Lessons from Ten Years of Debt-for-Development Swaps* (November 1999), 5, http://www.cid.harvard.edu/hiid/732.pdf.

[15] UNAIDS, *Debt-for-AIDS: UNAIDS Policy Brief* (Geneva: UNAIDS, 2004), 7.

[16] Ibid., 19.

[17] The Global Fund has a Memorandum of Understanding with UNAIDS, which has been renewed annually since 2003. "Memorandum of Understanding UNAIDS and the Global Fund", accessed August 2, 2010, www.hivpolicy.org/Library/HPP000216.pdf.

[18] The Global Fund to Fight Aids, Tuberculosis and Malaria, "Debt2Health: Innovative Financing of the Global Fund", 6, accessed August 2, 2010, www.theglobalfund.org/documents/publications/other/D2H/Debt2Health.pdf.

nations to forgo payment of sovereign debts if the debtor nation pays a portion of the amount owed in local currency to the Global Fund. Debt2Health is the first debt-for-development exchange that has been organised through 'triangular arrangements' involving a multilateral organisation. The Global Fund has adopted debt-exchange techniques to diversify its resource base and free up domestic resources. The Global Fund's commitment is that all funds generated by debt exchanges will go towards financing grants, and none will be consumed in administrative costs.[19]

A two-year pilot phase was announced in 2007, with Indonesia, Kenya, Pakistan and Peru eligible to participate.[20] Germany was the first donor participant in the program and committed to cancelling €50 million of its debt from Indonesia if Indonesia invested €25 million in the Global Fund over a five-year period from 2008. Germany further agreed to make available a total of €200 million for debt-for-health exchanges under the initiative by 2010. The first instalment was paid by Indonesia in June 2008.[21] The payments to the Global Fund are equal to and in lieu of the periodic interest payments that would otherwise have been due to Germany, which avoids any adverse impact on the Indonesian budget.[22]

Under the Debt2Health initiative, Germany and Pakistan in November 2008 signed an agreement by which Germany agreed to cancel €40 million in debt under an agreement by which Pakistan would invest €20 million with the Global Fund. Annual payments of €5 million will be made by Pakistan, commencing in 2009.[23]

In 2007 the Labor opposition in Australia made a policy commitment to, if elected, enter into a A$75 million debt exchange with Indonesia through the Debt2Health initiative, stating that it 'is time for Australia to join other progressive aid donors'.[24] The commitment to the debt exchange was sustained by the government once it assumed office, with Australia in mid-2009 affirming its commitment to cancel Indonesian debt in return for investment in the Global Fund.[25] The Executive Director of the Global Fund, Dr Michel

[19] Ibid., 7–12.
[20] The Global Fund to Fight Aids, Tuberculosis and Malaria, "Q&A Debt2Health", accessed August 2, 2010, www.theglobalfund.org/documents/innovativefinancing/FAQ_d2h_en.pdf.
[21] Aditya Suharmoko, "RI pursuing Debt-Swap Mechanism", *Jakarta Post*, June 24, 2008.
[22] The Global Fund, "Debt2Health", 12.
[23] The Global Fund to Fight Aids, Tuberculosis and Malaria, "German Financial Co-operation with Pakistan" (November 30, 2008), accessed August 2, 2010, http://www.theglobalfund.org/documents/innovativefinancing/DE-PK.pdf.
[24] Bob McMullan, "Labor Will Swap Indonesia's Debt for Health", June 6, 2007 (press release, June 6, 2007).
[25] Australian Government, "Australia Converts Commercial Debt to Indonesia into Health Programs" (press release, May 28, 2009).

Kazatchkine, in launching the program noted that 'a significant number of countries which do not qualify for debt relief through existing multilateral initiatives still spend as much as one-fifth of their export earnings on servicing debt while at the same time struggling with a high disease burden'.[26] The debt exchange provides for the rupiah equivalent of A\$37.5 million to be invested by Indonesia in the Global Fund in return for A\$75 million of debt being cancelled by Australia.[27] The exchange agreement was finally signed in Jakarta on July 15, 2010.[28] The funds deposited with the Global Fund as a result will be used to finance the procurement of tuberculosis medication. Indonesia has one of the highest rates of tuberculosis in the world, with more than 90,000 people dying from the disease every year. The disbursement of the funds will be monitored by an independent body consisting of members of government, academia and the private sector.[29]

The real benefits of trilateral exchanges lie in enforceability and transparency. A commitment by Indonesia to pay €25 million to the Global Fund to Fight AIDS, Tuberculosis and Malaria within Indonesia is far more enforceable and transparent than a similar commitment by Indonesia to invest these resources to achieve these ends. In the former case, nothing less than a funds transfer to the Global Fund will discharge the obligation. In the latter, it is up to the Indonesia Ministry of Health to seek to ensure that the Ministry of Finance pays the money, which politically may be difficult, as finance ministries tend to be powerful institutions, and it is open to the Ministry of Health to identify measures as being undertaken in pursuance of this commitment, which would have been funded anyway.

III. CONCLUSION

The scale of debt-for-development exchanges has far eclipsed that of the debt-for-nature exchanges out of which they grew. It was estimated that, from 1987 to 1994, between US\$750 million and US\$1 billion face value of foreign debt was cancelled in debt-for-development exchanges,[30] with UNICEF alone

[26] Ibid.
[27] Jubilee Australia states that this contribution 'could fund village and district level support for at least 106,128 HIV tests, the provision of AIDs treatments for over 3,000 people and the purchase of 23,000 TB treatments'. See Jubilee Australia, "Debt-for-Development Swap with Indonesia", Jubilee Australia Policy Paper, April 2007, 15.
[28] The Global Fund, "Supplementary Information on the Occasion of the Signing of the Debt2Health Agreement Between Indonesia, Australia and the Global Fund in Jakarta" (press release, July 15, 2010).
[29] "RI Gets Debt Relief to Aid TB Plan", *Jakarta Post*, July 17, 2010.
[30] J. Kaiser and A. Lambert, *Debt Swaps for Sustainable Development: A Practical Guide for NGOs* (IUCN Gland, Switzerland and Cambridge, UK, 1996), 14. Much of the debt

converting nearly US$193 million of debt for development.[31] In the same period, a total of about US$177 million of foreign debt was converted in debt-for-nature exchanges.[32] Since the mid-1990s the volume of debt exchanges has continued to grow. By 2003 the value of debt-for-nature exchanges was estimated to have reached more than US$1 billion.[33] In 2007 Fundación SES, Latindadd and the Organization of Iberoamerican States estimated that US$5.7 billion had been cancelled in debt-for-development exchanges, with some US$3.6 billion having, as a result, been invested to enhance development.[34]

Debt-for-development exchanges have, however, made only a tiny dent in the overall indebtedness of developing nations; sadly the debt burdens are too large for that. Yet to measure their effect on debt levels is to miss the important roles they have played. Some desperately poor nations, such as Bolivia, have been able to reduce their overall debt burden substantially and preserve some of their ravaged environment through debt-for-nature exchanges using donated funds. Costa Rica received funding for conservation efforts where none would otherwise have been available. Villages in Peru, the Sudan and elsewhere have drinking water and villages in Indonesia, Pakistan, Nicaragua, and many other countries have schools because of debt-for-development exchanges. Most recently, these techniques have begun to serve as a source of additional funds with which to fight the scourges of HIV/AIDs, malaria and tuberculosis.

Debt-for-development exchanges have made a significant contribution to date to development programs. The debt burden on developing countries has severely curtailed spending on health, education and other social programs, and the need to raise exports to service the debt has often damaged the environment in those countries. Debt-for-development exchanges have been important because they have gone some small way towards redressing these damaging social and environmental impacts of external debt.

converted in debt-for-development swaps was official bilateral debt (i.e., loans made by developed nations to less developed countries) and was donated for the purpose by the developed nations. For instance, in 1994 Canada forgave 75% of the C$22.7 million of Peru's official bilateral debt and converted the balance for development purposes. Similar arrangements were entered into between Finland and Peru (1995), Germany and Peru (1994), Switzerland and Bulgaria (1995) and the United States and the Philippines (1995). See ibid., 8.

[31] Ibid., 16.
[32] Ibid., 12–13.
[33] Romy Greiner and Allyson Lankeste, "Debt-for-Conservation Swaps: A Possible Financial Incentive for On-Farm Biodiversity Conservation", Paper presented at the 50th annual conference of the Australian Agricultural and Resource Economics Society, Sydney February 7–10, 2006, accessed August 2, 2010, http://www.riverconsulting.com.au/reports/Greiner_Lankester_AARES-2006.pdf.
[34] UNESCO Working Group on Debt Swaps for Education, "Draft Report", 7, 5.

PART II

Exchanges by Donor Countries

4

United States Debt Exchanges

Ross P. Buckley and Steven Freeland

The development of debt-for-nature exchanges and broader forms of debt exchanges has been encouraged partly by various US congressional initiatives, which have highlighted the relationship between debt and the environmental and developmental problems of developing countries. The motivation for these enactments has, perhaps not unexpectedly, arisen largely from self-interest. The United States has significant bilateral trade, investment and strategic relationships with a number of countries struggling under severe debt burdens, particularly in Latin America – the region that ever since the Monroe Doctrine the United States has considered its backyard and over which it claims an entitlement to exercise a special oversight.[1] Efforts to address their development needs, and the sustainability of their economies, were designed to promote strategic interests in the region. Stronger Latin American economies expand the potential market for US goods, services and investment capital.[2] Consequently, the United States has encouraged its lenders to participate in debt-exchange transactions in the region by way of the legislative initiatives. Debt-for-nature exchanges have since the 1980s been conducted by the United States by way of three legislative initiatives.

I. 1989 GLOBAL ENVIRONMENTAL PROTECTION ASSISTANCE ACT (US)

In April 1988 the United States Agency for International Development (USAID) issued debt-for-development guidelines that proposed funding of

[1] Steven M. Cohen, "Give Me Equity or Give Me Debt: Avoiding a Latin Debt Revolution", *University of Pennsylvania Journal of International Business Law* 10 (1988): 92.
[2] Antonia N. Piccirillo, "The Metamorphosis: Expected Changes in the Brazilian Debt-for-Nature Swap Process and Policy Implications", *Fordham International Law Journal* 17 (1994): 557.

nongovernmental organisation (NGO) intermediaries for approved debt exchanges. The NGOs would then be responsible for negotiating with quali- fying developing countries and for managing the use of the resources acquired through the exchange. The proposal was structured to avoid any suggestion of overt debt forgiveness,[3] which the United States at the time would have found quite unacceptable.[4] The US Congress reacted favourably to these guide- lines and enacted the 1989 Global Environmental Protection Assistance Act (GEPA),[5] which established funding and support for USAID debt-exchange activities.[6]

GEPA was the first US law relating to debt-exchange transactions.[7] Under the heading 'Debt-for-Nature Exchanges', Chapter 7 authorises USAID to grant funds to environmental NGOs for the purchase of secondary mar- ket debt of 'eligible' countries, to be used in debt-exchange transactions.[8] To participate in an authorised transaction, the debtor country must have 'the capacity, commitment and record of environmental concern to oversee the long-term viability of … the project'.[9] To minimise sovereignty concerns, the legislation prohibits the US government from taking title to, or an interest in, land within a recipient country as a condition of the transaction.[10]

In 1989 the World Wide Fund for Nature (WWF) acquired US$3 million of external Malagasy debt with USAID funds, which were then converted at face value into local currency and used to train and fund 400 park rangers.[11] It was also the first debt-exchange transaction that USAID funded.[12] Further debt exchanges have occurred since in Madagascar[13] – which had, by 1998, reduced

---

[3] Scott Wilson, "The United States Agency for International Development as Catalyst for Debt for Nature Swaps", UCLA *Pacific Basin Law Journal* 10 (1991): 275.

[4] However, as part of the HIPC Initiative and in response to the demands of groups such as Jubilee 2000, the United States agreed in late 2000 to fund US$435 million to fulfil its obli- gations under its debt relief obligations for that year. See Joseph Kahn, "Rich Nations Will Forgive Debts of 22 of the Poorest", *New York Times*, December 23, 2000.

[5] 22 U.S.C. §2281–2286 (1989). For a detailed description of the provisions of GEPA, see Wilson, "The United States Agency for International Development as Catalyst", 260.

[6] Wilson, "The United States Agency for International Development as Catalyst", 275.

[7] Amanda Lewis, "The Evolving Process of Swapping Debt for Nature", *Colorado Journal of International Environmental Law and Policy* 10 (1999): 444.

[8] Marilyn Post, "The Debt-for-Nature Swap: A Long-Term Investment for the Economic Stability of Less Developed Countries", *International Lawyer* 24 (1990): 1093.

[9] M. S. Sher, "Can Lawyers Save the Rainforest? Enforcing the Second Generation of Debt- for-Nature Swaps", *Harvard Environmental Law Review* 17 (1993): 172.

[10] Post, "The Debt-for-Nature Swap", 1094.

[11] Lewis, "The Evolving Process", 444.

[12] USAID had agreed to fund part of the financing required under the 1987 Bolivian debt- for-nature exchange but had withdrawn its support following Bolivia's failure to meet its commitments on time.

[13] The second USAID-funded transaction in Madagascar, which was completed in 1990, was the first debt exchange to provide for the cancellation of trade credits. See J. E. Gibson and

its US$100 million commercial debt by half through the implementation of debt exchanges – as well as in the Philippines and Guatemala. By 1998 USAID had provided US$95 million to environmental NGOs for the acquisition of US$146 million of external developing country debt, which was subsequently used in debt-exchange transactions.[14]

Despite these achievements, there are inevitable problems associated with the disbursement of aid money to localised projects by large bodies such as USAID. Bureaucratic overheads often absorb a significant proportion of the funds allocated towards a debt-exchange program.[15] Moreover, decisions to fund (or not to fund) a particular project may be based on internal procedures not necessarily relevant to the proposal.[16] However, previous USAID-sponsored transactions have been significant and have emphasised the role of indigenous people in protected areas.[17] The incorporation into the debt-exchange mechanism of procedures for the education and training of local indigenous people is one way of promoting long-term, sustainable development.[18]

II. 1990 ENTERPRISE FOR THE AMERICAS INITIATIVE ACT (US)

In June 1990, after meeting with South American leaders at the Andean Summit,[19] President Bush proposed a comprehensive plan to stimulate economic growth and reduce trade barriers in the West.[20] This revolved around three 'pillars' (increased capital investment in Latin American and Caribbean countries, a proposed free trade zone and debt reduction)[21], which were intended to show Latin American democracies that they would not be ignored in favour of Eastern Europe.[22]

W. J. Schrenk, "The Enterprise for the Americas Initiative: A Second Generation of Debt-for-Nature Exchanges – With an Overview of Other Recent Exchange Initiatives", *George Washington Journal of International Law and Economics* 25 (1991): 14.

[14] Lewis, "The Evolving Process", 444.

[15] Gibson and Schrenk, "The Enterprise for the Americas Initiative", 48.

[16] USAID has been described as a 'bloated bureaucracy'. During the eight-year term of the Clinton administration, its size was cut from 10,000 to 7,300. President George W. Bush also criticised the bureaucratic nature of USAID, and there have from time to time been calls for its abolishment and replacement with a smaller quasi-government foundation, the International Development Foundation. See, e.g., Eric Schmitt, "Helms Urges Foreign Aid Be Handled by Charities", *New York Times*, January 12, 2001.

[17] Lewis (1999), "The Evolving Process", 445.

[18] P. Alagiri, "Give Us Sovereignty or Give Us Debt: Debtor Countries' Perspective on Debt-for-Nature Swaps", *American University Law Review* 41 (1992): 507.

[19] Gibson and Schrenk, "The Enterprise for the Americas Initiative", 16.

[20] Sher, "Can Lawyers Save the Rainforest?" 174.

[21] Ibid.

[22] Douglas Logsdon, "Debt-for-Nature Evolves: The Enterprise for the Americas Initiative", *Colorado Journal of International Environmental Law and Policy* 3 (1992): 642.

Although it was designed primarily to stimulate growth and free trade,[23] the debt-reduction aspects of this initiative were significant. Debt exchanges were formalised as an important component of US policy for the region,[24] indicating an increased governmental acceptance of the mechanism as an appropriate financing technique. The final form of the 1990 Enterprise for the Americas Initiative Act (US) (EAI)[25] authorised the exchange of bilateral sovereign debt for environmental protection programs, the first time official debt could be utilised in this way.[26] Under the EAI, the United States agreed to reduce debt owed by eligible countries and allow interest to be paid in local currency and at concessionary rates into a local environment fund.[27]

The original proposal envisaged the exchange of approximately US$5 billion of Latin American debt, with another US$12 billion to be completely forgiven. After intense lobbying, Congress agreed to a debt reduction of only US$1.7 billion. A subsequent legislative amendment allowed the relevant debtor countries to purchase up to 40% of debt owed to the US Agriculture Department at market value.[28]

To qualify under the EAI, a country must meet certain eligibility criteria,[29] including 'significant progress' in establishing an open investment regime, which itself may require compliance with various World Bank or International Monetary Fund (IMF) macroeconomic conditions.[30] Implementation is by way of an Environmental Framework Agreement (EFA), the first of which was signed between the United States and Chile on June 27, 1991, the anniversary of the announcement of the initiative. This agreement provided for the forgiveness of US$15.7 million of PL 480 debt, which came from 'food for peace loans', which were low-interest loans given to developing countries to purchase US agricultural products,[31] in return for Chile's allocating the interest payable on the remaining US$23.6 million of debt to fund local environmental projects. By 1993 the United States had also signed EFAs with Argentina, Bolivia, Colombia, El Salvador, Jamaica, Peru and Uruguay, resulting in US$875

---

[23]   The trade and investment components of EAI were pursued through other measures; ibid., 650–651.

[24]   Piccirillo, "The Metamorphosis", 557.

[25]   7 U.S.C. § 1738 (1990).

[26]   Lewis, "The Evolving Process", 445.

[27]   Konrad von Moltke, "Debt-for-Nature: The Second Generation", *Hastings International and Comparative Law Review* 14 (1991): 984–985.

[28]   Ibid.

[29]   For a more detailed description of the mechanics of the EAI, see Logsdon, "Debt-for-Nature Evolves", 635.

[30]   Gibson and Schrenk, "The Enterprise for the Americas Initiative", 16.

[31]   Pervaze A. Sheikh, "CRS Report for Congress: Debt-for-Nature Initiatives and the Tropical Forest Conservation Act", CRS Report RL 32186 (October 11, 2006) CRS-7, accessed August 2, 2010, http://www.au.af.mil/au/awc/awcgate/crs/rl31286.pdf.

million of debt being converted into the local currency equivalent of US$154 million of environmental protection funding.[32]

The EAI illustrated how broad international economic, development and financial policy issues were connected to issues of environmental concern[33] and that these could be incorporated into a debt exchange.[34] Indeed, it highlighted the need to respond to increasing concerns for global environmental and development issues. The program allowed for the funding of a wide range of activities, from conservation to education and from agriculture to sustainable development projects.[35] Overall, under the EAI US$154 million was allocated to environmental funds in seven Latin American and Caribbean countries between 1992 and 1998.[36]

Owing to changes in US budget rules requiring prior appropriation of costs incurred by Treasury through debt reduction, no EFA has been signed since 1993.[37] However, further legislative amendments in 1998 facilitated a Peruvian debt buy-back, by which Peru repurchased 50% of its US$350 million debt to the United States at its then net present value (US$57 million). In return, Peru agreed to place the local currency equivalent of US$22 million into a local environment fund.[38]

III. TROPICAL FOREST CONSERVATION ACT (US)

The 1998 Tropical Forest Conservation Act (US) (TFCA) became law on July 29, 1998. It addresses formally the relationship between levels of external indebtedness and the continuing eradication of tropical rainforests. Geographically, its scope extends further than the EAI, as it is not limited to Latin America and the Caribbean; on the other hand, its focus is limited specifically to the preservation of tropical rainforests. The TFCA relieves developing countries of certain costs associated with foreign debt in exchange for a commitment to allocate resources to the preservation of rainforests.[39] The TFCA provides

[32] Lewis, "The Evolving Process", 446.
[33] The EAI is intended to 'promote debt reduction, investment reforms, and community-based conservation and sustainable use of the environment'. See EAI Section 1738a, cited in Logsdon, "Debt-for-Nature Evolves", 643.
[34] von Moltke, "Debt-for-Nature", 985.
[35] Logsdon, "Debt-for-Nature Evolves", 647.
[36] Jennifer A. Loughrey, "The Tropical Forest Conservation Act of 1998: Can the United States Really Protect the World's Resources? The Need for a Binding International Treaty Convention on Forests", *Emory International Law Review* 14 (2000): 329.
[37] Lewis, "The Evolving Process", 451.
[38] Ibid., 452.
[39] Sean Michael Neal, "Bringing Developing Nations on Board the Climate Change Protocol: Using Debt-for-Nature Swaps to Implement the Clear Development Mechanism", *Georgetown International Environmental Law Review* 11 (1998): 164.

for 'grant' funds, whereby grants are made to tropical forest funds overseen by NGOs and community groups, which implement the conservation projects.[40] This funding initiative seeks to ensure that funds reach the designated programs rather than be dealt with at the discretion of the debtor government.

By providing for three types of debt exchange – debt reductions, debt buybacks and debt exchanges – the TFCA demonstrates the adaptability of the mechanism to particular circumstances or specific debtor nations. Before 1991, no appropriations were required for debt cancellations and the United States cancelled between US$11 billion and US$12 billion in debt between 1988 and 1991. This all changed with the introduction of the Federal Credit Reform Act of 1990,[41] pursuant to which debt exchanges and reductions can be undertaken only up to the amount appropriated for debt reductions in the annual budget approved by Congress.[42] Under the TFCA, debt reduction is intended for the poorest nations. After the debt has been reduced by a certain amount, the interest on the remaining debt is paid into a fund for conservation efforts.[43]

Under the TFCA, the United States can establish partnerships with NGOs under which the NGOs provide additional funding for debt reductions.[44] When a debt reduction is agreed upon, with the involvement of an NGO, three agreements are signed: an agreement for the debt restructuring between the United States and the beneficiary country, an agreement to transfer the funds to the NGO between the United States and the NGO, and the Forest Conservation Agreement between the NGO and the beneficiary country. Therefore, the US government is not a signatory to the Forest Conservation Agreement; however, it is invariably represented on the oversight body for the funded conservation efforts.[45]

As of 2007, NGOs, primarily the Nature Conservancy (TNC), Conservation International (CI) and the WWF, had contributed more than US$9.6 million to TFCA deals.[46] This involvement by NGOs is viewed by the US government

[40] David M. Leon, "Expanding the Scope of the Tropical Conservation Act: Exchanging Foreign Debt for Sustainable Development", *University of Miami International and Comparative Law Review* 11 (2003): 146.

[41] Sheikh, "CRS Report for Congress", CRS-13.

[42] Amanda Lewis, "Land and Resource Management: The Tropical Forest Conservation Act", *Colorado Journal of International Environmental Law and Policy Year Book* (1998): 95.

[43] Ibid., 94.

[44] U.S Department of the Treasury, "Treasury International Programs, Justification for Appropriations: FY2009 Budget Requests", (2008) 26, accessed August 2, 2010, http://www.treas.gov/press/releases/reports/completefy2009cpd.pdf.

[45] Sheikh, "CRS Report for Congress", CRS-15.

[46] Eric Green, "U.S. Program Helps Save Tropical Forests, Cut Foreign Debt", *America.gov*, May 17, 2008.

as a strength of the Act, in that it is seen as facilitating pubic–private partnerships and dialogues about conservation.[47]

The TFCA specifies five eligible conservation projects: (1) the establishment, maintenance and restoration of parks, protected reserves and natural areas and plant and animal life within them; (2) training programs to increase the capacity of personnel to manage the parks; (3) development and support for communities in or near the tropical forests; (4) development of sustainable ecological systems and land management systems; and (5) research to identify the medicinal uses of tropical forest plants and their products.[48]

The TFCA was conceived as a tool in the fight against global warming. In its legislative findings on the TFCA, the US Congress made specific reference to the role that tropical rainforests play in reducing greenhouse gases in the atmosphere.[49] The preservation of tropical rainforests has a significant impact on the environment, and tropical deforestation amounts to a fifth of all greenhouse gas emissions.[50] The TFCA was signed by the Clinton administration, but was reauthorised under President Bush and was partly intended to diffuse international and domestic criticism of President Bush's environment policies following the rejection of the Kyoto Protocol to the United Nations Framework Convention on Climate Change in March 2001.[51] The United States has long opposed binding international treaties on forest preservation and has used bilateral debt-exchange agreements in their place.[52]

A. Measures to Address Indigenous and National Sovereignty Concerns

The two main criticisms often voiced against debt-for-nature transactions are concerns about indigenous rights and the national sovereignty of the debtor

---

47 The American Presidency Project, "Fact Sheet: Tropical Forest Conservation Act", accessed August 2, 2010, http://www.presidency.ucsb.edu/ws/index.php?pid=78814.

48 Sheikh, "CRS Report for Congress", CRS-10.

49 The US Congress noted that '[t]ropical forests provide a wide range of benefits to humankind by ... playing a critical role as carbon sinks in reducing greenhouse gases in the atmosphere, thus moderating global climate change.' Quoted in Neal, "Bringing Developing Nations on Board", 163 n. 5.

50 Linda Yun, "Costa Rica's Debt-for-Nature Swap", October 1, 2007, accessed August 2, 2010, http://www.conservation.org/FMG/Articles/Pages/costa_rica_debt-for-nature_swap.aspx.

51 *International Legal Materials* 37 (1988), 22. For the background to the rejection by the Bush administration of the Kyoto Protocol to the United Nations Framework Convention on Climate Change, see Steven Freeland, "The Kyoto Protocol: An Agreement Without a Future?" *University of New South Wales Law Journal* 24 (2001): 532.

52 Loughrey, "The Tropical Forest Conservation Act of 1998", 315–316.

nations.[53] Concerns about indigenous sovereignty have plagued debt-for-nature exchanges from their conception. In the 1987 debt exchange between CI and Bolivia, the agreement thwarted the claim by the Moxo Indians inhabiting Bolivia's Chiamese Forest, as the claim of sovereignty was pushed aside for the agreed-upon 'conservation' initiatives.[54] The TFCA provides specifically for the protection of the rights of indigenous peoples and, like the EAI, encourages projects that include the involvement of local communities in planning and execution.[55] It goes further than the EAI by facilitating funding for the 'development and support of the livelihoods of individuals living in or near a tropical forest in a manner consistent with protecting such tropical forests'.[56]

The TFCA seeks to quiet concerns about national sovereignty by requiring the formation of an administrative body in each instance to oversee the distribution of the funds. Although the body must include US government officials as well as those from the beneficiary country, the majority of the body is made up of representatives from local organisations in the beneficiary country concerned with environment and community development,[57] so as to dispel the notion of dominance of US objectives and loss of local control over land. Furthermore, the debtor country can veto any grant over US$100,000 even if the administrative body has approved it.[58]

The TFCA was the result of a prolonged campaign for a legislated debt-for-nature program of its type. It was first introduced unsuccessfully as the Debt-for-Nature Bill, sponsored by Senators Richard Lugar and (now Vice President) Joseph Biden in 1989.[59] Long in the making, the final text was weaker than what was originally envisioned. While the TFCA does contain provisions seeking to address concerns of sovereignty and of indigenous populations, the final version passed by the Senate watered down considerably the original provisions. The need for consultation with indigenous leaders before forming the administrative body was deleted, as was the provision that funding support not only individuals living in rainforests but also 'the cultures of such individuals'.[60]

---

[53] In 1989 Brazil's President, Jose Sarney, ruled out debt-for-nature swaps, citing national sovereignty, and declared, 'We accept international aid but we don't accept conditions'. See James Brooke, "Brazil Announces Plan to Protect the Amazon", *New York Times*, April 7, 1989,

[54] Leon, "Expanding the Scope", 140.

[55] Under the EAI, the swap with Chile trained Indians in conservation techniques and the Jamaican swap enhanced the capacity of community organisation to manage resources in the protected areas. See Lewis, "The Evolving Process", 462.

[56] 22 U.S.C. § 2431g(d)(6); quoted in Lewis, "The Evolving Process", 465.

[57] Leon, "Expanding the Scope", 150.

[58] Lewis, "Land and Resource Management", 98.

[59] Richard Lugar and Joseph R. Biden, Jr., "Swapping Debt for Nature", *Christian Science Monitor*, August 5, 1998.

[60] Lewis, "Land and Resource Management", 99.

The provisions that remained have not been entirely successful in over-coming concerns of sovereignty. In September 2001 the United States signed a TFCA agreement with Thailand. The additionally required agreement, however, was never signed. The Thai government subsequently annulled the TFCA agreement on January 30, 2003, following local media speculation that the United States would take control of the tropical forests within Thailand. The US$5.6 million appropriated for the Tropical Forest Fund was subsequently recovered.[61]

B. Eligibility Requirements and Enforcement Measures in the TFCA

The TFCA establishes numerous criteria that debtor nations must meet in order to be eligible to enter into a Tropical Forest Agreement. First, the debtor nation must have a tropical forest of global or regional significance, and be classified as a low- or middle-income country.[62] The nation must have a democratically elected government, must co-operate with international drug control measures and must not support international terrorism or violate human rights.[63]

Furthermore, the Act stipulates criteria that address the economic environ-ment of the developing nation. The beneficiary country must have a loan from certain entities in the World Bank Group or a macroeconomic agreement with the IMF or equivalent. It must also have instituted investment reform, as evidenced by a bilateral investment treaty with the United States, or by an investment sector loan, or by demonstrated progress towards implanting an open investment regime.[64]

The TFCA provides that any agreement must contain 'reasonable provisions for the enforcement of the terms of the agreement'.[65] To ensure enforcement, all agreements and the operation of administrative bodies within the debtor nations are monitored in the United States by the pre-existing Enterprise for Americas Initiative Board.[66] Eight of the 15 members of this board represent US federal agencies. The board monitors the 'program operations and fiscal audits' of all agreements. Reports on the implementation of TFCA agree-ments are made annually to Congress.

---

[61] Sheikh, "CRS Report for Congress", CRS-9.
[62] A low-income country is classified as one with a per capita income of less than US$752 per annum, and a middle-income country has a per capita income of more than US$752 but less than US$8,956. See Loughrey, "The Tropical Forest Conservation Act of 1998", 332.
[63] Lewis, "The Evolving Process", 447.
[64] Sheikh, "CRS Report for Congress", CRS-7.
[65] Lewis, "Land and Resource Management", 99.
[66] John Charles Kunich, "Losing Nemo: The Mass Extinction Now Threatening the World's Ocean Hotspots", *Columbia Journal of Environmental Law* 30 (2005): 118.

Furthermore, the US government can veto any grant larger than US$100,000.[67] Further monitoring of the agreement is provided for by the 'evaluation sheet', which establishes criteria for the programs to meet and is completed each year by the member of the US government on the administrative board.[68] Earlier examples of enforcement measures in a debt-for-nature exchange were included in the first-ever government-to-government debt exchange between the Netherlands and Costa Rica. Both countries had to approve each project and each country had the power to suspend projects.[69] Amanda Lewis notes, however, that the EAI and TFCA 'take enforceability to the next level', as a failure to perform obligations by the debtor country renders the agreement null and void.[70]

C. Tropical Forest Agreements under the TFCA

In 2000 the first agreement under the TFCA was signed with Bangladesh. A debt reduction of US$10 million was entered into to generate US$8.5 million in local currency for a forest fund. The fund was dedicated to conserve mangrove forests and protect Bengal tigers. In 2001 a second debt-reduction agreement was signed with El Salvador as part of a package of initiatives designed to address climate change and 'promote cooperation in the Western Hemisphere and beyond' on environmental matters. The US$14 million 'debt-for-forest' agreement provided that every dollar of debt relief would be exchanged for two dollars of local currency funding for forest conservation.[71]

The first debt-exchange agreement under the TFCA was signed with Belize in August 2001. The United States forgave US$14 million of bilateral debt in exchange for Belize issuing US$7.2 million of local currency to Belizean NGOs entrusted to establish a fund to manage 23,000 acres of forest. In this exchange, CI provided US$800,000 to the US government for the purposes of the exchange, representing the first time that an NGO participated in a TFCA initiative.[72]

The Philippines and the United States signed a debt-for-nature agreement in September 2002, pursuant to which US$5.5 million of the Philippines' debt was cancelled. In return, the Philippine government agreed to fund

[67] Lewis, "Land and Resource Management", 99.
[68] Sheikh, "CRS Report for Congress", CRS-10.
[69] Lewis, "The Evolving Process", 463.
[70] Ibid.
[71] U.S Department of Treasury, "Debt Restructuring Programs (FY2006)", accessed August 2, 2010, http://www.treas.gov/offices/international-affairs/intl/fy2006/tab14_tropical_forest.pdf.
[72] Leon, "Expanding the Scope", 152.

tropical conservation activities through local NGOs in the Philippines.[73] The Philippines agreed to apply in local currency the amount it will save in the debt-service repayments over the next 14 years to conservation activities over that period.[74] A board containing two representatives from each of the United States and Philippines governments and five representatives from local NGOs oversees the agreement. The agreement was signed with the intent to facilitate the protection of tropical and coastal forests areas in Luzon, Visayas and the Mananao regions.[75]

In 2004 a debt-for-nature agreement was signed with Colombia, which allowed US$20 million to be invested to protect tropical rainforests in that country over a period of 12 years. This agreement is managed by an oversight committee composed of representatives from the governments of Colombia and the United States, as well as the WWF, TNC and CI. Funds were invested in order to establish protected areas and reserves and to restore and maintain existing ones. The funds help protect rainforests covering some 4.5 million hectares across the Andes, Caribbean coast, the Ilanos and the plains along the Orinco River.[76]

In a 2006 TFCA agreement with Guatemala, the United States contributed US$15 million and the TNC and CI US$1 million each. The money is to be invested in NGO projects over 15 years, with a small amount invested in a conservation trust fund, to attract interest for further projects. Funded conservation projects, such as support for park rangers, sustainable development assistance and environmental monitoring, will concentrate on four regions: the Maya Biosphere reserve, the Cuchumantanes region, the Western Highlands Volcanic Chain and the Montagua/Polochic system.[77] Investment in preservation initiatives was conducted in the hope of halting illegal logging and drug trafficking.[78]

In 2006 an agreement was signed with Botswana – the first debt exchange with an African nation under the TFCA. The United States agreed to forgo US$7 million in debt repayments for much needed enhanced protection of the Okavango Delta and Chobe National Park, as surveys had

[73] U.S. Department of the Treasury Office of Public Affairs, "Factsheet: US–Philippines Debt-Reduction Agreement Under the Tropical Conservation Act (TFCA), TFCA Debt Swap Signing Ceremony with Philippines" (press release, September 19, 2002), accessed August 2, 2010, http://www.ustreas.gov/press/releases/reports/po34432.pdf.

[74] Ibid.

[75] Ibid.

[76] U.S. Department of Treasury, "Debt Restructuring Programs".

[77] Erik Ness, "Guatemala and US Agree on Debt Relief", *Frontiers in Ecology and the Environment* 4 (November 2006): 457.

[78] Marc Lacey, "U.S. to Cut Guatemala's Debt for Not Cutting Trees", *New York Times*, October 2, 2006.

indicated that the Okavango Delta is drying up due to increases in grazing, deforestation and tourism.[79]

Two agreements have been signed with Peru under the TFCA, the first being in 2002. TNC, WWF and CI contributed about US$1.1 million towards this agreement, in addition to the US$6.6 million forgiven by the United States. The first agreement specified 10 areas to become protected within the Peruvian National System of Protected Areas.[80] This allowed for the preservation of 27.5 million acres of rainforest.[81]

The second agreement was announced in late 2008 and provided for US$25 million of Peru's debt to be redirected into local funds to protect rainforests over the next seven years. With the execution of this agreement, Peru will become the largest beneficiary country under the TFCA, with more than US$35 million generated for conservation projects.[82] Funds generated through the project will be directed towards protecting tropical rainforests of the south-western Amazon Basin and dry forests of the central Andes and will be managed by Peruvian NGOs. The area is home to dense concentrations of birds, primates and other mammals, such as spectacled bears, giant otters and Amazon river dolphins. Conservation of the forests is also important because the river supplies water to many people living in the area.[83]

To date, 15 TFCA agreements have been entered into in 12 countries, which will generate more than US$218 million for tropical forest conservation.[84] The success of TFCA programs has led to recent expressions of interest from Brazil, Peru (again) and Kenya.[85] In 2007 Indonesia and the United States signed a joint statement that expressed their desire to work towards an agreement to implement a debt-for-nature exchange under the TFCA.[86] It is estimated that Indonesia has already lost 72% of its rainforests, and half of what

[79] USAID, Tropical Forest Conservation Act (TFCA) Program Descriptions, accessed February 17, 2010, http://www.usaid.gov/our_work/environment/forestry/tfca_descs.html.

[80] Ibid.

[81] The Nature Conservancy, "US–Peru Debt-for-Nature Swap", accessed February 17, 2010, http://www.nature.org/success/perudebt.html.

[82] Daniel Gorelick, "United States, Peru Announce Debt-for-Nature Agreement", *America.gov*, October 21, 2008.

[83] U.S. Department of Treasury, "Debt-for-Nature Agreement to Conserve Peru's Tropical Forest" (press release, October 21, 2008).

[84] Bangladesh, El Salvador, Belize, Peru, the Philippines, Panama, Colombia, Jamaica, Paraguay, Guatemala, Botswana, Costa Rica and Indonesia; U.S. Department of the Treasury, "U.S. Indonesia Begin Talks on Tropical Forest Conservation" (press release, January 15, 2010)

[85] U.S. Department of Treasury, "Debt Restructuring Programs".

[86] U.S. Embassy Jakarta, "US–Indonesia Debt-for-Nature Statement" (press release, December 11, 2007).

remains is threatened, either by commercial logging, fires or clearance for other plantations.[87] The Deputy Co-coordinating Minister for the Economy, Mahendra Siregar, has stated that he expects the debt exchange to be implemented in 2009.[88] An agreement was signed between the United States and Indonesia in June 2009 for the value of US$30 million over eight years. The funds available from the debt exchanges were provided by the US government and US$2 million by two environmental NGOs.[89] The funds generated by the debt exchange will be used to conserve about 7 million hectares of degraded forest.[90] Although this represents a small portion of Indonesia's debt, it has been heralded as 'one of the breakthroughs in conserving forests, as well as decreasing our national debt'.[91]

In early 2010 the United States and Indonesia began talks to implement a second debt-for-nature exchange under the TFCA. The Department of Treasury has provisionally set aside US$19 million for the treatment of eligible Indonesian debt with the aim of targeting the conservation of protected areas, improvement of natural resource management and fostering sustainable livelihoods.[92] In June 2010 the United States and Indonesia announced a US$301 million partnership on environment, climate change and education. The programs include US$119 million for science, oceans, land use, society and innovation. A debt-for-nature exchange under the TFCA is one program outlined along with a climate support project.[93]

D. The Future of the TFCA

The TFCA has been criticised for its limited scope, since the funding it provides for conservation initiatives is limited to areas of tropical forests. Certainly the sums involved have been notably small relative to those involved in more general debt-for-development exchanges. Efforts to use the model of the

---

[87] In 2007 Greenpeace applied to the *Guinness Book of World Records* to have Indonesia included for having the fastest rate of deforestation in the world between 2000 and 2005; Abdul Khalik, "U.S. Offers RI Debt-for-Nature Swap", *Jakarta Post*, July 4, 2007.

[88] "Government Secures Debt Swap with Italy", *Jakarta Post*, October 1, 2009.

[89] U.S. Department of State, "Signing of Debt-for-Nature Agreement with Indonesia" (press release, June 30, 2009).

[90] Adianto P. Simamora, "RI, US Negotiating Second Debt-for-Nature Deal", *Jakarta Post*, January 16, 2010.

[91] Queensland Yasen, "More Funds May Not Mean Better Forest Conservation", *Jakarta Post*, June 11, 2010.

[92] U.S. Department of Treasury, "U.S. Indonesia Begin Talks on Tropical Forest Conservation" (press release, January 15, 2010).

[93] Mustaqim Adamrah, "US Puts Up $301 Million for 'Partnership' with RI", *Jakarta Post*, June 29, 2010.

TFCA to extend conservation efforts beyond tropical forests have stalled each time. In 2001 the Coral Reef and Coastal Marine Conservation Act was passed by the US House of Representatives. Modelled on the TFCA, it approved US$10 million in annual appropriations each year from 2002 to 2005 for coral reef conservation.[94] Like the TFCA, it was to allow for concessional loans to be reduced through a debt reduction, debt-for-nature exchange or a debt buy-back, and also as in the case of the TFCA, the amounts involved are tiny. Under this arrangement, the money would have been invested in a Coral Reef and Other Coastal Marine Resources Fund.

Similarly, the EAI Board was to oversee the implementation, and reports made annually to Congress.[95] Following its passage through the House of Representatives, the proposed legislation was referred to the Senate Committee on Foreign Relations and was never brought to a vote in the Senate. The Bill met a similar fate when reintroduced in 2003.

The TFCA was reauthorised in 2001 and again in 2004 for the period through to 2007. Reauthorisation of the Act has since been blocked.[96] Since 2007, reauthorisation of the TFCA has been sought and has included the coral reef conservation initiative that failed to come to fruition as a separate initiative. In 2007 the Bill was passed by the House of Representatives and presented in the Senate, with an amendment to change the title to the Tropical Forest and Coral Reef Conservation Act and to extend the provisions of the TFCA to include coral reef protection.[97] The Bill was approved by the Senate Foreign Relations Committee in September 2007 but was not voted on by the full Senate.[98] It was reintroduced into the House in January 2009 and again referred to the committee stage. It has been considered by the House Committee on Foreign Affairs, which recommended the Bill be considered by the Senate as a whole. While it has been placed on the calendar of business, the time-frame in which it is to be considered is dictated by the majority leader. At the time of writing, the Bill has yet to be considered by the Senate.

[94] Leon, "Expanding the Scope", 149.
[95] The Library of Congress, "To Amend the Foreign Assistance Act of 1961 to Provide for Debt Relief to Developing Countries Who Take Action to Protect Critical Coral Reef Habitats", accessed August 2, 2010, http://thomas.loc.gov/cgi-bin/bdquery/z?d107:HR02272:@@@L&summ2=m&.
[96] U.S. Department of Treasury, "Treasury International Programs", 26.
[97] The National Oceanic and Atmospheric Administration estimated that 60% of the world's coral reefs may be destroyed by 2050 if degradation continues at the present rate. WWF, "Great Move on Bill to Protect Tropical Forests and Coral Reefs", accessed August 2, 2010, http://wwf.worldwildlife.org/site/PageServer?pagename=can_results_tropical_forest_act.
[98] Ibid.

In light of the present uncertainty surrounding the reauthorisation of the TFCA and its possible extension to coral reefs, there has been considerable scrutiny of its successes over the past decade. In 2007 the TFCA underwent a Program Assessment Rating Tool (PART) re-evaluation, undertaken by the Office of Management and Budget, and was rated as 'moderately effective'.[99] Funding under the TFCA has, however, never reached the levels envisioned at its conception, when US$325 million was authorised for the first three years of its operation.[100] From the date of enactment until February 2002, only US$24.8 million was given in debt reductions.

The need for yearly appropriations from Congress for funding has restricted the amounts made available under the TFCA.[101] In the 2009 budget requests, Treasury International Programs requested only US$20 million for the year for debt treatment under the TFCA. While US$141 million was requested for debt restructuring in total, the vast majority of this was earmarked for initiatives under the Highly Indebted Poor Countries (HIPC) Initiative.[102] In 2006 the Congressional Research Service, however, stated that while US$82.6 million had been used by the United States to restructure loan agreements, an estimated US$136.5 million in local currency would be generated in the following 26 years through the investment of interest payments in designated Tropical Forest Funds.[103] The potential for long-term financing is one of the benefits of bilateral debt exchanges.[104]

Under TFCA agreements, up to 2007, an estimated 136 million acres of tropical forests had been preserved.[105] The success of initiatives designed to ensure long-term funding of conservation of forests is difficult to measure in a short time-frame, and it has been suggested that it might not be possible to conduct a fair analysis until at least 10 years after the implementation of each transaction.[106] Under the Bush administration, it was assumed that the TFCA would continue to be reauthorised, given its role in White House

[99] Department of Treasury, "Treasury International Programs", 26.
[100] Lewis, "Land and Resource Management", 89.
[101] Kunich, "Losing Nemo", 117.
[102] U.S. Department of Treasury, "Treasury International Programs", 21.
[103] Sheikh, "CRS Report for Congress", i.
[104] William K. Reilly, "Using International Finance to Further Conservation: The First 15 Years of Debt-for-Nature Swaps", in *Sovereign Debt at the Crossroads*, eds. Chris Jochnick and Fraser A. Preston (Oxford: Oxford University Press, 2006), 203.
[105] Mark Steven Kirk, "Kirk Tropical Forest and Coral Conservation Act Passes the House" (press release, October 9, 2007), accessed August 2, 2010, http://www.house.gov/list/speech/il10_kirk/Kirk_Tropical_Forest.html.
[106] Sheikh, "CRS Report for Congress", CRS-16.

climate change policy.[107] With the advent of the Obama administration, such an assumption may need to be revisited.

Following the enactment of the EAI in 1991, Peter Passell wrote that 'the big question now is whether Washington, preoccupied with war in the Persian Gulf and recession at home, is sufficiently committed to the swap idea to plough through the political and financial obstacles'.[108] Nineteen years later, in a depressingly similar context, the same questions must now be asked of the future of the TFCA.

IV. CONCLUSION

In summary, as this brief survey has indicated, there is a broad array of US legislative mechanisms available for promoting debt-for-development initiatives. Their utilisation thus far has been both generally quite successful and limited. In terms of the overall amounts that have been devoted to the implementation of these techniques, the results are disappointing. Moreover, in the current financial climate, such initiatives are not a high priority – another question, postulated later, is whether they *should* be – and questions have been asked regarding their cost effectiveness and political sensitivity, particularly as they often involve 'conditionality' requirements, with accompanying political overtones.

In addition, although the US remains outside the context of the Kyoto Protocol, the discussions that have recently concluded in Copenhagen[109] appear to indicate that the priorities of the United States, as one of the main drivers of the 'Copenhagen Accord',[110] tend to support a market-driven approach to areas of climate change, including the question of deforestation and development issues. Whilst it is certainly too early to be writing an obituary for America's use of the traditional debt-for-development technique, this tendency to incorporate market-sensitive private industry into the environmental/developmental context within which the Kyoto Protocol and its successors will operate may mean that the legislative initiatives described will remain grossly underutilised by the United States.

[107] Ibid.
[108] Peter Passell, "Washington Offers Mountain of Debt to Save Forests", *New York Times*, January 22, 1991.
[109] See United Nations Framework Convention on Climate Change, Official Website of the United Nations Climate Change Conference in Copenhagen COP 15/CMP 5, December 7–18 2009, accessed August 2, 2010, http://unfccc.int/meetings/cop_15/items/5257.php.
[110] Copenhagen Accord of 18 December 2009, accessed August 2, 2010, http://unfccc.int/files/meetings/cop_15/application/pdf/cop15_cph_auv.pdf.

5

Italian Exchanges

Ross P. Buckley

I. INTRODUCTION

Italian debt exchanges are regulated by two pieces of legislation: the Measure for the Stabilisation of Public Finance (law 499/1977) and the Measure to Reduce External Debt of Lower Income and Highly Indebted Countries (law 209/2000).

For a country to be eligible for debt exchange under law 209/2000, the debtor nation must:

(i) have reached a 'multilateral understanding' with an organisation such as the Paris Club;
(ii) have made a commitment to respect human rights;
(iii) have renounced war as a means of solving controversy; and
(iv) be pursuing measures for social and human development, particularly the reduction of poverty.[1]

Under this law, funds liberated by a debt conversion can be utilised in four specified sectors: agriculture, health, education and infrastructure.[2] Within 90 days of entering into an agreement, the Italian Minister of Treasury, Budget and Economic Programs, in concert with the Minister of International Affairs, must issue criteria stipulating how the agreement will be carried out. Agreements may be suspended if funds are not being used for the purposes outlined in the agreement.[3] A report must be made annually to the Italian Parliament for each debt-for-development exchange agreement,

---

[1] Legge 28 luglio 2000, n 209 [henceforth, 209/2000], *Misure per la riduzione del debito estero dei Paesi a piu basso reddito e maggiormente indebitati*, art 1.
[2] 209/2000 art 3(3).
[3] 209/2000 art 4(1).

detailing, among other things, the costs, timing and progress of projects being implemented.[4]

Under article 5 of law 209/2000, the Italian government can authorise a debt exchange in cases of natural disasters and grave humanitarian crises to assist the people and nations affected by such events. Pursuant to this provision, Italy undertook a debt exchange with Indonesia in 2005. Italy agreed to exchange US$24.2 million and €5.7 million of loans previously rescheduled under the Paris Club. The funds were to be used in Aceh and northern Sumatra – areas devastated by the Boxing Day tsunami in late 2004.[5] A management committee including representatives of Indonesia and Italy was established to monitor the projects and ensure their transparency and accountability.[6] Between 2006 and 2008, a substantial portion of the funds was invested in 10 development projects. The terms of the final phase of the debt-for-development exchange were finally settled in early 2009 with an agreement that the remaining funds would be utilised for a range of development projects in Aceh. Seven projects will be financed for a total of US$13.6 million, including the construction of a fishing port, three irrigation systems and two roads. The remaining money will be used to support a government poverty alleviation scheme called the Hopeful Family Program.[7]

Under law 209/2000, Italy has participated in a sizeable number of other debt-for-development exchanges, including ones with Yemen, Pakistan and other countries.[8] However, Italy's largest debt-exchange programs to date have been with Kenya and Egypt, and it is these we will examine.

II. KENYA–ITALY DEBT-FOR-DEVELOPMENT PROGRAM

At the end of 2002, Kenya's external debt stood at US$5.1 billion, 32.2% of which was bilateral debt. The International Monetary Fund recommended that debt sustainability in Kenya be achieved by 'partial substitution of domestic debt by

---

[4]   209/2000 art 6(1).

[5]   "Italy Agrees to Carry Out Debt-Swap for Aceh Reconstruction", *Jakarta Post*, March 9, 2005.

[6]   Zakki P Hakim, "Post-Tsunami Deal on Debt Swap Signed", *Jakarta Post*, March 10, 2005.

[7]   "Government Secures Debt Swap with Italy", *Jakarta Post*, January 10, 2009.

[8]   In 2003 Italy signed a debt-exchange agreement with Yemen by which Italy agreed to allow US$15.9 million of bilateral debt owed by Yemen to be used to finance development projects under the framework of its Poverty Reduction Strategy. See "Italy and Yemen Finalize Debt-for-Development Agreement", *Yemen Times*, September 15, 2003. In 2008 Italy undertook a debt-for-development exchange with Pakistan for US$100 million focussed on rural development, poverty alleviation and education. A joint government monitoring body will assess and approve the specific projects to be undertaken. See "Pakistan: Italy Converts $100 million Debt into Aid", *Andkronos International*, April 4, 2008.

increased inflows of external grants and concessional loans' plus debt resched-uling.[9] Kenya was eligible to participate in a debt-for-development agreement with Italy following two debt-rescheduling agreements through the Paris Club in 2001 and 2004.

In October 2006, Italy and Kenya signed a debt-for-development agreement to the value of €44 million over 10 years. The program's objectives are to foster economic growth, increase employment and work towards poverty alleviation.[10] The agreement supports community-based projects, seeks to address the causes of poverty and promotes direct beneficiary participation in national poverty-reduction strategies in six designated regions in Kenya.[11] Four areas are earmarked for support under the debt-for-development agreement: water and irrigation, health, education and vocational training and the upgrading of slums. Designated funds are to be paid annually, in local currency, into an ad hoc counterpart fund of the Central Bank of Kenya.[12] Article II (6) of the agree-ment states that 'all amounts spent by selected projects shall be considered as cancelled by the Italian government'.[13] Therefore, under the agreement, Kenya in effect is able to repay the principal on its loans from Italy by spending the equivalent amount in local currency on national development projects.

The implementation of programs under this debt-for-development agree-ment is overseen by three interministerial bodies: the Steering Committee, the National Technical Committee and the Secretariat. The Steering Committee is composed of representatives of the Kenyan Ministry of Finance, the Kenyan Ministry of Planning and National Development and the Italian Embassy. It is responsible for defining the priority areas for intervention, approving initia-tives to be financed, supervising the implementation of initiatives and control-ling the management of the counterpart fund.[14]

The National Technical Committee draws its members from Kenyan national and local governments, from civil society and from the Italian

9 International Monetary Fund, *Kenya: Debt Sustainability Analysis* (Washington, DC: IMF, 2003), accessed August 2, 2010, http://www.kiddp.org/docs/Debt%20sustainability%20 kenya.pdf.
10 Kenya–Italy Debt for Development Program, "Introduction", accessed August 2, 2010, http://www.kiddp.org/intro.html.
11 Nirobi, Kilifi, Tharaka, Nyandyra, Suba and West Pokot.
12 Kenya–Italy Debt for Development Program, "Financing Procedures", accessed August 2, 2010, http://kiddp.prg/finan.html.
13 "Agreement on Debt-for-Development Swap Between the Government of the Italian Republic and the Government of the Republic of Kenya" (2006), accessed August 2, 2010, http://www.kiddp.org/docs.html.
14 "Regulation Scheme of the Agreement on Debt-for-Development Swap Between the Governments of Italy and Kenya" (2006), accessed August 2, 2010, http://www.kiddp.org/ docs.html.

Co-operation for Development.[15] Its role is to provide a technical assessment of proposed initiatives, which it presents to the Steering Committee with recommendations.[16] It also monitors the implementation of agreements.

The Secretariat is composed of a Kenyan director and an Italian appointed co-ordinator. It is in charge of the day-to-day running of the program. It implements resolutions, decisions and directives of the Steering Committee, and authorises the distribution of funds.[17] Suggestions for projects are made through District Development Committees, which also co-ordinate the implementation of approved projects.

In the area of education, funding from the Kenya–Italy Debt-for-Development Program (KIDDP) has focussed on the vocational training sector through Youth Polytechnics (vocational training centres). Polytechnics are regional facilities that focus on education for local requirements in areas such as carpentry, metal work and animal husbandry. KIDDP has aligned its priorities with those of the National Policy for Youth Polytechnics and the Vocational Training Sector Plan of the Ministry of State for Youth Affairs. The emphasis is on capacity building, curriculum implementation, provision of training equipment and rehabilitation of infrastructure. The aim is to improve the resources and teaching capacity of 50 polytechnics within the six designated regions and during the 10 years of the program.[18]

In the water sector, selected projects seek to increase access to safe water and sanitation services, particularly in rural areas. In the health sector, projects are aligned with the National Health Sector Strategic Plan. The aims are to increase access to health services in rural areas through community health projects and to improve the quality of those services through the provision of equipment and upgrading of health facilities. The training of community members is also a priority in order to create, train and equip a body of community health workers.[19]

The final priority sector is the upgrading of slums, particularly the Korogocho slum in Nairobi, with an estimated population of 120,000. The

[15] The Italian Co-operation for Development is an organisation within the Ministry of Foreign Affairs that works to alleviate poverty and support institutional growth within developing countries by supporting development programs globally through public–private partnerships. See Co-operazione Italiana allo Sviluppo, accessed August 2, 2010, http://www.cooperazioneallosvillupo.esteri.it.

[16] "Regulation Scheme of the Agreement on Debt-for-Development Swap Between the Governments of Italy and Kenya".

[17] Ibid.

[18] Kenya–Italy Debt for Development Program, "Kenya–Italy Debt-for-Development Programme Support towards the Kenya Vocational Training Sector", 10, accessed August 2, 2010, http://www.kiddp.org/docs.html.

[19] Kenya–Italy Debt for Development Program, Brochure (2008), 8, accessed August 2, 2010, http://www.kiddp.org/docs.html.

goal is to improve the quality of life in the slum and enhance welfare and security.[20] The objectives of the program are to gain a detailed appreciation of Korogocho, build the capacity of actors and institutions within the community, prepare a sustainable plan for upgrading, provide land tenure and implement visible improvements.[21] A Residents Committee was elected in August 2008 to represent the community. Consultations have since taken place between community organisations, faith-based organisations and government.[22] The boundaries of Korogocho and its eight villages have been mapped, a foot-bridge has been built to connect the slum with the neighbouring community and work has begun on a community office.[23]

In 2007 and 2008, seven water projects, seven education projects and three health care projects were implemented. One year into the program, Joseph Kinyua, Permanent Secretary of Treasury, said:

> I wish to encourage other development partners to borrow a leaf from the Government of Italy and consider this innovation, in order to release additional resources to find programmes that will enable us to achieve the MDGs [Millennium Development Goals].[24]

In general, the KIDDP has been directed towards significant areas of developmental need within Kenya and appears to have been well operated and generally effective. The selection of projects has tended to avoid those that provide high-profile photo opportunities for donors, in favour of those, such as enhancing access to water and upgrading of slums, that are more likely to make a real difference to the lives of local people. In addition, the governance arrangements in which, on a range of levels, Kenyan and Italian officials work closely together are well adapted to facilitate the transfer of knowledge and skills that can be an important collateral benefit of well-structured aid programs.

III. EGYPT–ITALY DEBT-FOR-DEVELOPMENT PROGRAM

In 2001 Italy signed a US$149 million debt-for-development agreement with Egypt, to be conducted over five years. This was the fourth debt-exchange arrangement Egypt had participated in, following agreements with France

---

[20] Korogoch Slum Upgrading Programme, "Goals and Objectives", accessed August 2, 2010, http://www.ksup.org/.
[21] Ibid.
[22] "Kenya–Italy Debt for Development Program", 19.
[23] Korogoch Slum Upgrading Programme, "Projects", accessed August 2, 2010, www.ksup.org/projects.php.
[24] "Kenya–Italy Debt for Development Program", i.

(1994), Switzerland (1995) and Germany (2001).[25] The Italian Co-operation for Development's willingness to enter into this agreement in terms of the significant relationship between the two nations: Italy is Egypt's second-largest export market and the fifth-largest source of imports into Egypt.[26] The Italy–Egypt Debt Swap Agreement (IEDSA) focussed on three objectives: human development, poverty alleviation and environmental protection. Applicants eligible for grants under the program were Egyptian public institutions, Egyptian nongovernmental organisations (NGOs), Italian NGOs and UN agencies.[27] The exchange simply redirected otherwise scheduled debt repayments away from Italy and into a special fund in the Bank of Egypt designated for mutually agreed upon development projects. In other words, under this agreement, there was no element of debt cancellation and Egypt still had to repay its debts, but the repayments were redirected in their entirety towards development projects within Egypt. The agreement was initially for 2002 to 2007, but the end-date was extended to December 2008 to allow for the completion of projects that had experienced delays.[28]

In total, 53 projects were financed by the IEDSA.[29] Project areas that received funding were the environment, water resources, rural development, poverty, youth and children, health, women's development and information, communication and technology (ICT). Preference was given to projects in areas in which Italy had conducted successful domestic programs, in order to exploit the creditor country's expertise. These areas included the promotion and protection of cultural assets, environmental management, education and small and medium enterprises.[30]

The IEDSA was overseen by a Management Committee and supported by a Technical Support Unit. The Management Committee comprised the Ambassador of Italy and the Egyptian Minister of International Co-operation, assisted by experts in development and representatives of Egyptian ministries and the Bank of Egypt.[31] The Management Committee was responsible for

[25]   Italian Co-operation in Egypt, "The Italian–Egyptian Debt-for-Development Swap", accessed August 2, 2010, http://www.utlcairo.org/english/progetti/progetti/16_debtswap_main.html.

[26]   Italian Co-operation in Egypt, "Italy and Egypt: Cooperation Between Two Ancient Civilizations" (February 2007), 1, accessed August 2, 2010, http://www.utlcairo.org/english/brochure%20en%20mar07.pdf.

[27]   Italian Co-operation in Egypt, "The Italian–Egyptian Debt-for-Development Swap".

[28]   Italy–Egyptian Debt-for-Development Swap Program (IEDSA), "Annual Report" (2008), 6, accessed August 2, 2010, http://www.utlcairo.org/stampa/DS1_final_report2008.pdf.

[29]   For further information on specific projects, see ibid.

[30]   Italian Co-operation in Egypt, "Italy and Egypt: Cooperation Between Two Ancient Civilizations", 3.

[31]   Samir Radwan, Sherif Kamel and Nivine El Oraby, "Partners for Development: The Experience of the Italian–Egyptian Debt Swap Program (2001–08)" (2008), 26, accessed August 2, 2010, http://www.utlcairo.org/stampa/Final%20study%20IEDS.pdf.

selecting programs, monitoring the implementation of the agreement and reviewing the results. The Technical Support Unit supported the Management Committee by monitoring and implementing the agreement and by transferring funds.[32] Development projects were undertaken throughout Egypt, with a specific focus on poor areas.[33]

Environmental and rural development projects received the highest level of funding. The projects undertaken were diverse, from the development of a sustainable area management plan to biodiversity research, solid waste management and management of protected areas.[34] The Wadi El Hitan Museum was established under the IEDSA and later nominated by UNESCO as a World Heritage natural site.[35] Funded rural development projects focussed on increasing productivity and access to markets, as well as fostering organic agriculture.[36]

Projects funded by the agreement in the area of ICT have been lauded as particularly successful.[37] ICT projects were funded not only to increase the availability of technology throughout the country, but also to provide the training required to use it. While only 5% of the IEDSA budget was spent on ICT, the programs have been heralded for supporting technological development across the country and increasing computer literacy.[38]

Egypt's projects also created new economic and social opportunities for underprivileged groups, such as women, low-wage and low-skill workers and those in rural communities. The Smart Schools Network Project and Mobile IT Club projects provided ICT access to members of rural communities,[39] and broader access to educational materials was achieved through the Electronic Library Project and the Community Portal Development Project.[40]

Overall, the IEDSA was considered a great success by both Egyptian and Italian officials. The Italian Ambassador to Egypt, His Excellency Claudio Pacifico, has claimed that the outcomes achieved validate the debt-exchange approach and that debt-for-development exchanges serve as a potent

---

[32] IEDSA, "Annual Report", 9.
[33] The Delta, Greater Cairo and Giza.
[34] Radwan, Kamel, El Oraby, "Partners for Development", 35–38.
[35] IEDSA, "Annual Report", 82–83.
[36] Radwan, Kamel and El Oraby, "Partners for Development", 41.
[37] Ibid., 13.
[38] Sherif Kamel and Eslandar A Tooma, *Exchanging Debt-for-Development: Lessons from Egypt's Debt-for-Development Swap Experience*, http://www.oei.es/deuda/FinalEng.pdf; article produced by the Economic Research Forum (ERF), with support from the Ministry of Communications and Information Technology (MCIT) and the Ministry of International Cooperation (MIC) (2005), 3.
[39] Radwan, Kamel and El Oraby, "Partners for Development", 44.
[40] Ibid., 47–48.

demonstration of a positive partnership in development.[41] There has, however, been criticism of some areas of the agreement, particularly of the failure to involve local communities at the project design stage and of bureaucratic delays in government procedures.[42]

However, on balance, the development programs appear to have been particularly successful in the areas of slum upgrading, community development and youth rights and in fostering ICT literacy. The implementation of the debt exchange has further illustrated the success of programs that are 'decentralized, participatory, and integrated'.[43] As with the Kenyan program, the general focus has been more on grassroots programs than on big-ticket photo-opportunity initiatives.

IV. CONCLUSION

The Italian Co-operation in Egypt stated that 'the Italian debt-for-development swap is considered as a model of co-operation, which is to be imitated and replicated'.[44] Since the conclusion of the first IEDSA, Italy has demonstrated its willingness to participate in further debt-for-development exchanges. In light of the positive outcomes of the first exchange agreement, a second debt-for-development agreement was signed with Egypt in 2007 for a four-year period, to the value of US$100 million. The focus is on developing export markets for Egyptian agricultural products, encouraging collaboration between the Egyptian and Italian private sectors, supporting the development of basic industries and enhancing the reforms in the ICT sector.[45]

Italy's debt exchanges in Kenya have been likewise well targeted and conducted. All of Italy's programs are characterised by a high degree of transparency in which the executed versions of all important documents are posted on the Italian government Web site and information generally is made freely available.

Given the success of the debt-for-development projects that have already been implemented, Italy is seeking to implement other agreements. In March 2010 the Italian Ambassador in Jordan announced that Italy intends to implement another debt-exchange agreement with Jordan to the value of €16 million.[46]

[41] Ibid., 11.
[42] Ibid., 61–62.
[43] Ibid., 62.
[44] Italian Co-operation for Development in Egypt, "Italy and Egypt: Cooperation Between Two Ancient Civilizations", 6.
[45] Radwan, Kamel and El Oraby, "Partners for Development", 26.
[46] "Jordan, Italy Discuss Debt-for-Development Swap", Jordan News Agency, March 23, 2010.

6

German Exchanges

Ross P. Buckley

I. OVERVIEW OF GERMAN DEBT EXCHANGES

Germany was one of the first countries to use debt exchanges to promote debt relief and development efforts, having done so since 1993. By the end of 2008, Germany had signed debt exchanges with 19 countries to a face value of €1.36 billion. In these agreements €737 million of bilateral debt was waived.[1]

The German Federal Ministry for Economic Co-operation and Development (BMZ) selects countries eligible for debt exchanges by looking at the urgency of the need for debt relief, the political conditions in the debtor nation, previous co-operation in debt management and the current educational initiatives and poverty-reduction measures of the debtor nation.[2] The BMZ's budget is allocated through German budgetary regulations, and the German government has to approve the debt to be exchanged.[3] Going forward from 2008 onwards, €150 million of bilateral debt has been earmarked for debt exchanges each year.

The BMZ states that 'funds released as a result of debt relief must be used to combat poverty and promote sustainable development'.[4] Sectors eligible for investment include environmental and resource protection, education and general poverty reduction.[5] German debt-for-development exchanges involve

---

[1] German Federal Ministry for Economic Cooperation and Development (BMZ), "Debt-for-Development Swaps", accessed August 2, 2010, http://www.bmz.de/en/issues/DebtRelief/instrumente/dept_swaps.html.

[2] Kathrin Berensmann, *Debt Swaps: An Appropriate Instrument for Development Policy? An Example of German Debt Swaps* (Bonn: German Development Institute: 2007), 15.

[3] Ibid., 14.

[4] German Federal Ministry for Economic Cooperation and Development, "Background: Debt Holds Back Development", accessed August 2, 2010, www.bmz.de/en/issues?DebtRelief/hintergrund/index.html.

[5] BMZ, "Debt-for-Development Swaps".

a substantial element of debt forgiveness, with typically only 20% to 50% of the debt cancelled being required to be invested in local currency in development projects.[6]

Germany has cancelled US$7.1 billion face value of debt under the extended Highly Indebted Poor Countries (HIPC) Initiative.[7] Given this extensive debt cancellation, debt exchanges are no longer required with HIPCs. However, the scope of debt exchanges that Germany may undertake has recently been expanded. Until 2008, only debt rescheduled by the Paris Club was eligible for German debt-for-development exchanges, but this rule has recently been amended to permit the exchange of non-restructured debt. This important legislative change allows debt exchanges to be undertaken with countries that are not defined as low- or lower-middle-income countries.[8]

Kathrin Berensmann attributes the success of German debt-for-development agreements, specifically in Jordan and Indonesia, to the way they have been developed in line with the national development strategies of debtor nations.[9] The first exchange between Germany and Indonesia was signed in 2002. Germany forgave €25.6 million on condition that 50% of the debt forgiven be invested in education. The funds were designated for improving facilities in primary schools in 17 provinces and reached approximately 33,000 schools.[10] Indonesia, although not an HIPC, had developed an interim Poverty Reduction Strategy Paper in order to qualify for preferential loans from the World Bank.[11] The debt exchange was undertaken in line with Indonesia's national development strategy, which defines education as a priority.[12]

Similar debt exchanges have been undertaken by Germany with Jordan to target sectors outlined in its national development strategy: water sanitation, education and poverty reduction. Between 1992 and April 2006, Germany signed debt-exchange agreements with Jordan amounting to €213.6 million. This represented 59% of Jordanian foreign currency denominated debt owed

---

[6]   Berensmann, *Debt Swaps*, 14.
[7]   German Federal Ministry for Economic Cooperation and Development, "The German Contribution to the HIPC Initiative", accessed August 2, 2010, http://www.bmz.de/en/issues/ DebtRelief/instrumente/hipc_initiative/taking_stock.html.
[8]   BMZ, "Debt-for-Development Swaps".
[9]   Berensmann, *Debt Swaps*, 17.
[10] German Federal Ministry for Economic Cooperation and Development, "Debt Swap Between Indonesia and KfW: Debt Release in Favour of Basic Education" (press 4elease, December 4, 2002), accessed August 2, 2010, http://www.kfw.de/EN_Home/Presse/PressArchiv/bis11.2005/ Pressemitteilung22335.jsp.
[11] German Federal Ministry for Economic Cooperation and Development, "Indonesia: Situation and Cooperation" (press release, October 2007), accessed August 2, 2010, www.bmz.de/en/ countries/partnercountries/indonesien/cooperation.html.
[12] Berensmann, *Debt Swaps*, 17.

to Germany at the end of 2005, thus having a significant impact on debt reduction (which is rare for debt-for-development exchanges).[13]

Germany has demonstrated its continued commitment to debt exchanges as a means of enhancing levels of international aid through its involvement in the Debt2Health initiative of the Global Fund to Fight Aids, Malaria and Tuberculosis. As discussed in Chapter 3, Germany was the first donor nation to participate in the program and has committed more than €200 million to projects in Indonesia and Pakistan. In addition to the above-mentioned debt-for-development exchanges, Germany has over the past two decades demonstrated a specific focus on environmental goals through numerous debt-for-nature agreements.

II. GERMAN DEBT-FOR-NATURE AGREEMENTS

In 1996 Germany signed a debt-for-nature agreement with the Philippines in which it agreed to cancel DM 12.8 million of bilateral debt in exchange for the Philippines investing 30% of the debt in local currency in a Community Forest Program.[14] Environmental conservation was similarly the focus of a debt exchange worth DM 10 million with Peru in 1999.[15] Germany has since expanded the notion of 'debt for nature' beyond environmental concerns, such as forest conservation to address needs in poor countries for water and sanitation.[16]

As discussed in Chapter 2, in 2003 Germany introduced Madagascar to bilateral debt-for-nature exchanges. Germany agreed to cancel €23.3 million in exchange for the equivalent of €13.8 being invested in local currency in environmental conservation over 20 years.[17] Under the debt-exchange agreement with Germany, the funds were invested in the Madagascar Foundation

---

[13] Ibid., 16. Berensmann cautions against the comparison of these figures because the terms of the current FC-related claims do not coincide with the terms of debt swapped, although she concludes that it 'does provide an indication of the significance of the debt swapped'; Ralf Maurer, *Evaluation of Swiss Debt Reduction Facility – Program Design* (2001).

[14] Amanda Lewis, "The Evolving Process of Swapping Debt for Nature", *Colorado Journal of International Environmental Law and Policy* 10 (1999): 442.

[15] Alberto Paniagua V, "Bilateral Debt-for-Nature Swaps: The Profonanpe Experience – Peru", Fifth World Parks Congress Sustainable Finance Stream (September 2003), Durban, South Africa, 5.

[16] William Reilly, "Using International Finance to Further Conservation: The First 15 Years of Debt-for-Nature Swaps", in *Sovereign Debt at the Crossroads*, eds. Chris Jochnick and Fraser A. Preston (Oxford: Oxford University Press, 2006), 211.

[17] Melissa Moye and Jean-Paul Paddak, *Madagascar's Experience with Swapping Debt for the Environment: Debt-for-Nature Swaps and Highly Indebted Poor Country (HIPC) Debt Relief* (Washington, DC: WWF Center for Conservation Finance, 2003), 5.

for Protected Areas and Biodiversity and the National Association for Management of Protected Areas.[18]

In 2001 Germany cancelled DM 60 million of debt owed to it by Peru in exchange for the equivalent of DM 24 million in local currency being invested by Peru to alleviate poverty in farming communities. Mutually agreed upon projects included the provision of seeds for planting and the enhancement of processing of agricultural products and the improvement of rural infrastructure. The aim was to encourage farmers into alternative revenue sources that were not dependent on illicit drug cultivation.[19] By 2004 Germany had engaged in similar debt-for-nature exchanges with Bolivia, Ecuador, Honduras, Jordan and Vietnam.[20]

Most recently, Germany has undertaken a number of debt exchanges with Indonesia. In 2004 Germany and Indonesia entered into a debt-for-environment agreement in which US$29.25 million of debt was cancelled.[21] A second exchange for environmental purposes was signed in 2006, with €6.25 million to be spent over a four-year period. The program aimed to increase Indonesian environmental quality through funding aid for micro and small businesses. The money was to be distributed through an environment soft-loan program, overseen by an Indonesian financial institution, PT Bank Syariah Mandiri.[22] All debt-for-development exchanges between Indonesia and Germany are monitored by the Jakarta branch of the German Development Bank (KfW).[23] Indonesia and Germany have suggested there may be further debt-exchange agreements to curtail the effects of climate change and limit the level of deforestation,[24] and in early 2009 the Deputy to the Co-ordinating Minister for the Economy, Mehendraw Siregar, confirmed that Indonesia was in negotiation with Germany for a €20 million debt exchange.[25]

Germany's debt-exchange programs appear to have been well targeted and effectively administered. However, information on the programs is not easy

---

[18] Ibid.

[19] KfW, "KfW and Peru Sign Agreement on Debt Conversion" (press release, 1 March, 2001), accessed February 17, 2010, http://www.kfw.de/EN_Home/Presse/PressArchiv/bis11.2005/Pressemitteilung22291.jspp.

[20] Matthias von Bechtolsheim, "Promotion of Developing Countries: Debt for Nature Swaps in German Financial Co-operation" (Frankfurt: KfW, 2004), accessed August 2, 2010, http://www.cbd.int/doc/external/germany/germany-kfw-en.pdf.

[21] Tony Hotland, "RI, Germany Agree US$29.25 Debt Swap Deal", *Jakarta Post*, May 15, 2004.

[22] Republic of Indonesia, "Debt-for-Nature Swap Program on Environmental Investment for Micro and Small Businesses" (press release, October 3, 2006).

[23] Hotland, "RI, Germany Agree".

[24] Tony Hotland, "RI–Germany Eye Cooperation Around Renewable Energy Sources", *Jakarta Post*, February 28, 2008.

[25] "Government Secures Debt Swap with Italy", *Jakarta Post*, January 10, 2009.

to obtain, and the German government does not appear to be committed to conducting the programs in a transparent manner. It is almost as if Germany believes these programs are the business only of itself and the recipient government. A greater commitment to transparency, like Italy's, would at the least allow other nations to benefit from Germany's experience, as well as serve as a useful check against potential abuses or inefficiencies in its programs. This is not to suggest that there have been abuses or inefficiencies, nor is there any evidence of the same. However, there is much to be said for the adage that underpinned the design of US securities regulation in the 1930s and that the US financial system, to its great detriment, moved away from in the years leading up to the recent global financial crisis: that 'sunlight is the best disinfectant'.

III. CONCLUSION

Germany has committed itself to achieving the Millennium Development Goals (MDGs) in its Program of Action 2015. Its support for the Debt2Health initiative is explained as a measure to fulfil this commitment.[26] The use of debt exchanges in the designated sectors of the environment, education and poverty reduction are in line with a commitment to meet the MDGs and expand debt relief beyond the HIPCs to reach lower- to middle-income countries. At the International Conference on Financing for Development in 2002, in Monterrey, Mexico, developed countries examined how to mobilise the necessary resources to meet the MDGs with the resultant Monterrey Consensus on a pledge to increase official development assistance (ODA).[27] In line with the Consensus, Germany has set a timetable to achieve an increase in ODA as a proportion of gross national income to 0.7% by 2015.[28] Debt exchanges can thus be seen as an initiative of the German government in line with these commitments and as measures to increase aid effectiveness.

In 2008 the BMZ highlighted the adoption of budget support as a tool for increasing aid, whereby the funds would be channelled directly to the national budget of partner countries, with payments contingent upon the fulfilment of agreed-upon disbursements.[29] Budget support aims to reduce the costs of

---

[26] German Federal Ministry for Economic Cooperation and Development, "Debt Conversion Initiative Launched to Fund Health Programs" (press release, October 26, 2007).

[27] German Federal Ministry for Economic Cooperation and Development, "Summary of the 12th Development Report" (May 2005), 7, accessed August 2, 2010, http://www.bmz.de/en/service/infothek/fach/materialien/materialie149.pdf.

[28] Ibid., 19.

[29] German Federal Ministry for Economic Cooperation and Development, "Budget Support in German Development Policy: A Contribution to Increase Aid Effectiveness" (2008), 6, accessed August 2, 2010, http://www.bmz.de/en/service/infothek/buerger/Budgethilfe.pdf.

project-based financing, facilitate increased public spending and improve the level of joint policy dialogue.[30] The BMZ noted that the use of budget support as a development tool represents a contribution to the achievement of MDGs and is in line with the Paris Declaration on Aid Effectiveness of 2005.[31] The Paris Declaration established five key principles for enhancing aid effectiveness: ownership, harmonisation, alignment, results and mutual accountability. Budget support is perceived as a measure specifically designed to strengthen partner country ownership.[32] In an assessment of German debt exchanges, Berensmann advocated an increase in their scope and noted the potential to move beyond funding of individual projects to the use of debt exchanges as a tool for budgetary support, much along the lines advocated by John Langmore in Chapter 17 of this volume.[33] The expansion of debt exchanges in this way would certainly assist Germany in meeting its development commitments. In 2010 Germany failed to meet its own targets in increased development aid, falling €3.5 billion short of the 0.51% of GDP target.[34] In such a context, debt-for-development exchanges may provide an important source of funds for development projects.

[30] Ibid., 2.
[31] Ibid., 19.
[32] Ibid., 8.
[33] Berensmann, *Debt Swaps*, 21–22.
[34] "Germany Will Miss 2010 Development Aid Target", *BW-World.DE*, July 3, 2010, accessed August 2, 2010, http://www.dw-world.de/dw/article/0,,5329562,00.html.

7

French Exchanges

Ross P. Buckley

I. OVERVIEW

France was involved in numerous debt exchanges in the 1990s. The largest debt exchanges were a debt-for-equity exchange with Morocco to the value of FF 600 million that sought to foster economic and social development through increased French investment[1] and a debt-for-development exchange with Egypt worth FF 58 million in 1993.[2] More recent debt exchanges have included agreements with Jordan for US$15.3 million to be invested in poverty-reduction programs[3] and with Madagascar for US$20 million to be invested in the Madagascar Foundation for Protected Areas and Biodiversity in 2008.[4]

However, of late France has routinely used debt exchange primarily as a mechanism to meet additional commitments undertaken as part of the Paris Club for debt relief to highly indebted poor countries (HIPCs).[5] The enhanced HIPC will provide $39.4 billion in debt relief to highly indebted countries in present-value terms,[6] to reduce debt in HIPC countries by 49% and their debt service by 56%.[7]

---

[1] Melissa Moye, *Overview of Debt Conversion* (London: Debt Relief International, 2001), 11.
[2] Sherif Kamel and Eskandar A Tooma, "Exchanging Debt-for-Development: Lessons from Egypt's Debt-for-Development Swap Experience" (2005), 17, accessed August 2, 2010, http://www.oei.es/deuda/FinalEng.pdf.
[3] Rana Awwad, "France Signs Debt-Swap Agreement with Jordan", *Jordan Times*, March 7, 2002.
[4] WWF, "Monumental French Debt-for-Nature Swap" (press release, June 13, 2008).
[5] In January 2000, all G7 countries agreed to cancel all bilateral debt to the HIPCs. See France-Diplomatie, "The C2Ds, a Funding Instrument under the APSFs", accessed August 2, 2010, http://www.diplomatie.gouv.fr/en/france-priorities_1/governance_6058/financial-governance_6397/the-c2ds-funding-instrument-under-the-apsfs_11332.html.
[6] The present value of debt is calculated using the cost of borrowing export credits from OECD governments. See Matthew Martin, "Assessing the HIPC Initiative: The Key Policy Debates", in *HIPC Debt Relief: Myths and Reality*, eds. Jan Joost Teuissen and Age Akherman (The Hague: Fondad, 2004), 12–14.
[7] Ibid.

Under France's scheme of Debt Cancellation and Development Contracts (C2Ds), the debtor nation still repays the debt to France, but the money is then reinvested in the debtor country through grants allocated to projects that have been agreed upon by both countries. With the aim of reducing poverty, potential beneficiary sectors are primary education and vocational training, health and the fight against major epidemics, the decentralisation of infrastructure and the management of natural resources.[8]

Three French government ministries manage C2Ds. The Ministry of Economics, Finance and Industry and the Ministry of Foreign Affairs oversee the financial transactions and the negotiations with the debtor country. The implementation of the C2D is managed by the French Agency for Development (AFD).[9] The French and the debtor governments negotiate the C2D, but the French government retains substantial influence.[10] In order to better align the partnership around the national strategies of the debtor nation to combat poverty, Partnership Framework documents have been entered into since 2004, with all debtor nations undertaking C2Ds to define the agreed-upon strategy and to be signed by both governments and published.[11]

The C2D mechanism is described by the French government as a 'donation-based refinancing mechanism' with an approach that 'lays emphasis on ownership by the relevant country and partnership by combining civil society participation with effective and foreseeable aid'.[12] The AFD states that the benefits of C2Ds lie in the 'meaningful dialogue' they facilitate with debtor nations about poverty reduction and the greater accountability they provide to the French Parliament about aid funding.[13]

Twenty-two countries are eligible for C2Ds, with the total debt eligible for refinancing estimated at US$4.6 billion.[14] The C2D is carried out when the nation reaches the completion point of the HIPC process. To date, C2Ds have

---

[8]   Coumba Fall Gueye, Michael Vaugeois, Matthew Martin and Alison Johnson, *Negotiating Debt Reduction in the HIPC Initiative and Beyond* (London: Debt Relief International, 2007), 26.

[9]   Danny Cassiman and Joe Vaessen, *Linking Debt Relief to Microfinance: An Issues Paper* (Geneva: International Labour Office, 2006), 10.

[10] Ibid.

[11] France Diplomatie, "Framework Partnership Document – Congo (2008–2012)", accessed August 2, 2010, http://www.diplomatie.gouv.fr/en/country-files_156/congo_201/france-and-congo_5882/cultural-scientific-and-technical-cooperation_6291/framework-partnership-document-france-congo-2008–2012_11773.html.

[12] Ibid.

[13] Agence Française de Développment, "Debt Reduction – Development Contracts", accessed August 2, 2010, www.afd.fr/jahia/Jahia/site/afd/lang/en/pid/1163.

[14] WWF, "Central Africa's First Debt-for-Nature Swap Helps Tropical Forests in Cameroon" (press release, June 22, 2006).

been signed with nine countries. Mozambique reached its HIPC completion point in 2001, and France agreed to a 100% bilateral debt cancellation of €95 million to be undertaken in two C2D agreements from 2001 to 2004 and 2005 to 2007.[15] France has continued to use conditional financing for projects in Mozambique, following the Absolute Poverty Reduction Strategy paper for 2006–2010, with €14 million financed through C2D in 2010.[16] Uganda, Bolivia, Tanzania, Mauritania, Ghana, Madagascar, Nicaragua and Cameroon have also signed C2Ds with France. In Mauritania, Tanzania and Nicaragua, special focus was on using the funds to support the development of the education sector.[17] In mid-2010 France signalled an intention to sign a C2D with Congo. In March the International Monetary Fund, World Bank, Paris creditor countries and Brazil cancelled US$2.4 billion. France is planning to sign an agreement to the value of €30 million per year for five years.[18]

II. C2D IN ACTION: PARTNERSHIP WITH CAMEROON

In 2006 France and Cameroon signed a C2D for €537 million over five years, the largest foreign public development program ever signed by France. The agreement earmarked four sectors for investment: education, health, infrastructure and natural resources.[19] The agreement was the first C2D to allocate funds for the protection of natural resources, with US$25 million allocated over five years to protect parts of the Congo Basin, the world's second-largest tropical forest. The money will be contributed to the Forest and Environment Sector Program,[20] with the funds earmarked for investment in the environmental management of forest activities, community resource management, training and research and the sustainable management of resources.[21]

The Organisation of Economic Co-operation and Development (OECD) had criticised early C2Ds as providing an uncertain role for participation by

---

[15] Cassiman and Vaessen, *Linking Debt Relief to Microfinance*, 10.

[16] AFD, "AFD in Mozambique", accessed August 2, 2010, http://www.afd.fr/jahia/Jahia/lang/en/home/Qui-Sommes-Nous/Filiales-et-reseau/reseau/PortailMozambique/pid/759.

[17] Working Group on Debt Swaps for Education, "Draft Report for the Director-General of UNESCO" (August 2007), 5–6, accessed August 2, 2010, http://www.unesco.org/education/EFAWGSDE/WGDSE_2nd_draftreportforDG_EN.pdf.

[18] "Towards a Compete Debt Cancellation for Congo Brazzaville", *Afrique Avenir*, April 15, 2010.

[19] AFD, "AFD in Cameroon: Implementation of Debt-Reduction Development Contract (C2D)" (December 2007), accessed August 2, 2010, http://www.afd.fr/jahia/webdav/site/afd/users/administrateur/public/pdf/AFD_Cameroun_GB.pdf.

[20] The Cameroon government's Department for Forest Policy.

[21] AFD, "AFD in Cameroon".

nongovernmental organisations (NGOs).[22] The agreement with Cameroon addressed this criticism through the creation of a Steering and Monitoring Committee, composed of representatives of both governments, as well as members of civil society and NGOs. This body allocates the resources and monitors the results. The meetings are co-chaired by the French Ambassador to Cameroon and the Cameroon Ministers of Economy and Finance. The meetings are also attended by the European Union Commission's delegation in Cameroon.[23]

Oversight of the agreement is undertaken by two additional administrative bodies. The Bilateral Technical Committee oversees technical and administrative monitoring. It examines the projects and programs proposed and evaluates the research and feasibility. The committee is composed of representatives of the President of Cameroon and the Minister of Finance, and the Chair of the Technical Committee for Program Monitoring. From France there are representatives of AFD and of the Economic and Cooperation services of the French Embassy in Cameroon. In France there is also a permanent Technical Secretariat for Program Implementation that reports to the Minister of Economics and Finance, and centralises and consolidates budget and accounting information relating to C2D implementation.[24]

The agreement contains a number of provisions intended to enhance the perception of ownership in Cameroon. All procurement procedures are aligned with national procedures, and there is a minimum level for participation of local subcontractors. The funds are allocated over five years, with a focus on improving living conditions, reducing poverty and enhancing education, the fight against AIDS, health care and infrastructure. All contracts relating to the implementation of the agreements contain provisions relating to social and environmental responsibility.[25]

Seventy-four per cent of the allocated funds under the 2006–2011 agreement had been paid as of April 2010. Infrastructure has received 50% of the funding, 20% has gone to health care and another 20% to education, and the remaining has gone to agricultural projects. The Bilateral Technical Committee has reported that there has been widespread participation of national companies in the funded projects.[26]

[22] Development Assistance Committee, *DAC Peer Review: France* (Paris: OECD, 2004) 15.
[23] AFD, "AFD in Cameroon".
[24] Ibid.
[25] Ibid.
[26] "C2D: Pass Mark for Project Engagement", *All Africa*, April 13, 2010.

III. CONCLUSION

In contrast to Germany's commitment to debt-for-development exchanges as a tool for debt relief as well as the promotion of development, France's use of Debt Cancellation and Development Contracts reflects a deep unease with debt forgiveness. Using debt exchange to meet HIPC commitments rather than to increase debt forgiveness makes it an instrument to add further conditions to pre-existing debt-relief commitments instead of a means to generate additional debt relief and increased aid flows to debtor nations. Conceived as a tool to encourage dialogue with debtor nations and foster the participation of civil society, C2Ds offer no additional debt-relief forgiveness for countries with unsustainable debt levels but redirect debt repayments into development projects.[27] The OECD has also criticised C2Ds, quite justifiably, because of the high costs associated with their complex management systems.[28]

In summary, C2Ds stand out as the pre-eminent example of how to misuse the debt-for-development mechanism. In France's hands, debt-for-development exchanges have become a way to reduce the sovereignty of developing countries. C2Ds give France control over how the savings will be spent from debt cancellation that France, as a member of the G7 nations and the Paris Club, has already committed to extending. It is to be hoped that no other developed nations follow France's example and misuse this mechanism in this way.

---

[27] Richard Moncrieff, *French Development Aid and the Reforms of 1998–2002*, PhD thesis, School of Humanities, University of Southampton, December 2004, 128.

[28] Development Assistance Committee, *DAC Peer Review*, 15.

8

Other Donor Nations' Exchanges

Ross P. Buckley

The countries mentioned in the preceding chapters – namely the United States, Italy, Germany and France – have the largest national programs for utilising debt exchanges for multiple purposes, whether as an arm of environmental policy, as a way to enhance aid levels or (regrettably) as a means of meeting international commitments to forgive developing country debt. Other donor countries have similar programs. This chapter looks at the bilateral debt exchanges entered into by Switzerland, Spain and Norway.

I. SWISS DEBT-FOR-DEVELOPMENT EXCHANGES

As debt-for-development exchanges became more widely used in the 1990s, Switzerland was the first donor country to use such exchanges as an integral part of its national development program.[1] In March 1991 the establishment of the Swiss Debt Reduction Facility (SDRF) was announced at the parliamentary session celebrating the 700th anniversary of the Swiss Confederation. Its creation was the result of a sustained campaign by local nongovernmental organisations (NGOs), whose petition, 'Debt Needs Debt Reduction', had garnered 250,000 signatures in support of a comprehensive debt-reduction program.[2] The SDRF was established with the objective of cancelling all official bilateral and commercial debt owed to Switzerland by highly indebted poor countries (HIPCs). Debt relief was channelled through the establishment of counterpart funds to invest in poverty-reduction schemes, income generation and environmental projects. The SDRF has been credited with 'piloting' debt-for-development conversions and the techniques of counterpart funding.[3]

---

[1]   Ralf Maurer, *Evaluation of Swiss Debt Reduction Facility – Program Design* (2001), 5.
[2]   Ibid., 9.
[3]   Ibid., 5.

The SDRF was established with an endowment fund of CHF 500 million. The State Secretariat for Economic Affairs managed the program, and the Swiss Agency for Development Co-operation was responsible for the utilisation of local currency resources generated by the debt-for-development exchanges. To be eligible for debt reductions, debtor countries had to have either:

(i) a low annual per capita income of less than US$700 per year;
(ii) had debt renegotiated with the Paris Club with favourable results; or
(iii) had its debt rescheduled with the Swiss Development Co-operation but not at the favourable rate granted for the poorest nations.[4]

To be eligible, countries also had to demonstrate that they had sought to implement economic and social reforms within the country and had developed coherent debt-relief management strategies.[5] Debt reductions took place under the SDRF from 1991 to 1995, with the Fund thereafter being utilised as a 'financing window' for the HIPC Initiative.[6] Nineteen countries benefitted from debt reductions under the program, with counterpart funds established in 12 countries.[7] The nominal debt reduced was slightly more than CHF 1 billion, which was converted into CHF 267 million in local currencies, which in turn was placed in trust funds and used to fund development programs.[8]

Accordingly, the early exchanges under the SDRF allowed for large measures of debt cancellation, approaching 75% of the debt on average. This contrasts, most favourably, with many debt exchanges by the United States, and all French ones, which were done at face value (with no debt cancellation involved), and even with German-initiated exchanges, in which, typically, half of the debt is cancelled and the balance converted and applied in local currency.

In 1995 Switzerland agreed to a debt-reduction agreement with Egypt, where CHF 150.3 million of Egypt's debt was reduced by 40%. The debt utilised in the agreement was rescheduled and came from commercial transactions. The remaining 60% of the debt not forgiven was deposited in local currency in the Egyptian–Swiss Development Fund, established under the agreement,

4 State Secretariat for Economic Affairs (SECO), "The Swiss Debt Reduction Program 1991–2001: Achievements, Perspectives", 10, accessed August 2, 2010, www.seco.admin.ch.
5 Ibid.
6 Maurer, *Evaluation of Swiss Debt Reduction Facility*, 11.
7 Bolivia, Honduras, Jordan, Tanzania, Peru, Zambia, Ivory Coast, Ecuador, Egypt, Guinea, Philippines and Senegal. Other nations that received debt relief did not establish counterpart funds, as the debt forgiven was of a much smaller proportion. See SECO, "The Swiss Debt Reduction Program", 16–17.
8 Maurer, *Evaluation of Swiss Debt Reduction Facility*, 10; SECO, "The Swiss Debt Reduction Program", 5.

to provide financing for poverty-reduction programs.[9] The priority areas of
the agreement were job creation, environment/natural resources and social
services.[10] The size of counterpart funds in donor nations in other instances
ranged from CHF 1 million in Guinea to CHF 90 million in Egypt. The use
of counterpart funds and the general administration of the Swiss exchange
programs appear to have been highly effective and transparent.

The endowment fund was depleted by 2001.[11] Further debt reduction was
not extended under the program, as it was decided to channel all remaining
debt relief through the HIPC Initiative.[12] Therefore, Switzerland, after pioneering the technique in Europe, no longer participates in debt-for-development
exchanges. However, Spain and Norway (along with Germany, France and
Italy, the activities of which we've already considered) continue to use debt
exchanges.[13]

II. SPANISH DEBT-FOR-EDUCATION EXCHANGES

In 2004 the Spanish President announced that Spain's commitment to debt
relief extended beyond the HIPC Initiative and committed it to be 'actively
involved in debt swap operations for social development, especially in the
area of primary education'.[14] In 2005 the Spanish Minister for Foreign Affairs
reiterated Spain's commitment 'to find innovative and additional sources of
financing of development'. He announced Spain was 'working on a plan to
swap debt for public investment in key areas for human development in Latin
American countries'.[15] Spain has implemented this commitment through
debt-for-education exchanges.

Whilst Germany and France are active in the field of debt-for-
education exchanges, the UNESCO working group on debt-for-education

[9] Sherif Kamel and Eskandar A. Tooma, "Exchanging Debt-for-Development: Lessons from
Egypt's Debt-for-Development Swap Experience" (2005), 15, accessed August 2, 2010, http://
www.oei.es/deuda/FinalEng.pdf.
[10] SECO, "The Swiss Debt Reduction Program", 55.
[11] Ibid., 4.
[12] Mauer, *Evaluation of Swiss Debt Reduction Facility*, 6.
[13] Marta Ruiz, "Debt Swaps For Development: Creative Solution or Smoke Screen?" (2007),
5 (European Network on Debt and Development, October 2007), accessed August 2, 2010,
http://www.eurodad.org/uploadedFiles/Whats_New/Reports/Debt_swaps_ENG(2).pdf.
[14] Working Group on Debt Swaps for Education, "Draft Report for the Director-General of
UNESCO" (August 2007) 10, accessed August 2, 2010, http://www.unesco.org/education/
EFAWGSDE/WGDSE_2nd_draftreportforDG_EN.pdf.
[15] Speech by the Spanish Minister of Foreign Affairs and Cooperation at the 60th Period of
Sessions of the United Nations General Assembly, New York, United Nations, 2 September 2005,
accessed August 2, 2010, http://www.pnac.es/IDIOMAS/en-GB/AboutTheAoC/Statements/
mae20050920en.htm.

exchanges has modelled its best-practice guide for debt exchanges on those undertaken by Spain.[16]

In 2005 Spain signed a four-year debt-for-education exchange of US$100 million with Argentina. The funds exchanged under the agreement were transferred to the Education Ministry with the stipulation that they be in addition to the annual education budget.[17] An oversight committee, with representation from both governments, undertakes the supervision, monitoring and evaluation of the agreement.[18] The funds from the agreement were allocated to two existing scholarship schemes for students of impoverished families to complete lower–secondary education. The funds provided textbooks and teaching materials, as well as additional income to families of poor students.[19] Whilst the amount of debt cancelled by the agreement was negligible in comparison with Argentina's total external debt of US$190 billion, the funds represented an extraordinary 10% of public expenditure on nonsalary components of public education.[20]

In 2005 Spain also signed debt-for-education agreements with Ecuador for US$50 million and with El Salvador for US$10 million. The funds in El Salvador were directed towards the purchase of educational materials and the construction and renovation of facilities in impoverished regions.[21] Since then, Spain has entered into debt-for-education exchanges with Honduras for US$138.3 million, Bolivia for US$72 million and Peru for US$11 million and €6 million.[22] In 2007 Spain signed an agreement with Paraguay to exchange US$10 million of debt for investment in education. These funds were included in the 2009 Budget of the Ministry of Education and Culture. Some of the funds will go towards the government's planned investment in education infrastructure.[23]

Spain's initial debt exchanges were solely with Latin American countries, but it has recently signed an agreement with Ghana. In March 2009 Spain and Ghana entered into a debt-for-education exchange for US$46.36 million over a seven-year period. The money will be deposited in

[16] UNESCO Working Group on Debt Swaps for Education, "Draft Report", 7.
[17] Carlos Aggio, "A Case Study on Debt Conversion: Spain and Argentina", Background paper prepared for the Education for All Global Monitoring Report (2005), 3, accessed August 2, 2010, http://www.oei.es/deuda/145999e.pdf.
[18] Ibid., 4–5.
[19] Ibid., 4.
[20] Ibid., 5.
[21] "What Are Debt-for-Education Swaps?" Working paper for the UNESCO Working Group on Debt Swaps for Education (2007), 16 (copy on file with author).
[22] UNESCO Working Group on Debt Swaps for Education, "Draft Report", 5.
[23] Natalia Ruiz Dias, "Paraguay Debt-for-Education" (2009).

a debt-for-development exchange trust fund. A joint government committee will be established to determine which sectors will benefit from the funds diverted by the agreement.[24]

Spain's debt-exchange activities have been targeted towards promoting education and generally have been conducted efficiently and transparently. They can serve as a useful model for the structuring and implementation of debt-for-education exchanges for other donor nations interested in promoting education.

III. NORWAY

Norway has long been a leader within Europe in debt relief for developing nations. In 1998 it developed a plan of action on debt relief for developing countries and was the first OECD country to urge 100% debt cancellation for HIPCs.[25] In its 2004 "Debt Relief for Development: A Plan of Action", Norway indicated it would 'pursue the Norwegian proposal for bilateral creditors to undertake multilaterally co-ordinated debt-for-development swaps'.[26] An attempt to arrange a debt exchange with Ecuador in 2004 was, however, met with protests from civil society organisations in both countries, which claimed that this debt was 'illegitimate', as the money was lent for an irresponsible purpose. Norway lent to Ecuador as part of the Norwegian Ship Export Campaign of 1976 to 1980, which sought to secure employment for the failing domestic ship-building industry, at the expense of the needs of the debtor nation.[27] In 2006 Norway responded to these criticisms by cancelling the debt to Ecuador, which had been loaned to purchase vessels built in Norway. The debt was cancelled in recognition that the loans were made by Norway out of self-interest, not responsibly to aid Ecuador's development.[28]

Norway has cancelled US$80 million of debt with Ecuador, Egypt, Peru, Jamaica and Sierra Leone,[29] all of which arose out of export credit for Norway's ship-building industry. Burma and Sudan also hold debt to Norway from the Norwegian Ship Export campaign; however, Norway has declined to cancel

[24] David Adaevoh, "Spain to Provide $46.36 million Debt-Relief to Ghana", *Modern Ghana News*, March 9, 2009.
[25] Royal Norwegian Ministry of Foreign Affairs, "Debt Relief for Development: A Plan of Action" (press release, April 16, 2004), accessed August 2, 2010, <ttp://www.regjeringen.no/en/dep/ud/Documents/veiledninger/2004/Debt-Relief-for-Development.html?id=419443.
[26] Ibid.
[27] Jubilee USA, "Recent Developments on Odious and Illegitimate Debt", Briefing Note 5, April 2008, 2.
[28] Ruiz, "Debt Swaps For Development", 9.
[29] Ibid., 16.

any debt until the internal situation changes in these two nations.[30] In cancelling these debts, Norway has not used the labels 'illegitimate' or 'odious' debt,[31] but has recognised these debts as a failure of development policy.[32] Debt cancellation has been undertaken as a means to bring to an end 'a dark chapter in the history of Norwegian development cooperation'.[33] Norway was criticised within the Paris Club for breaking creditor solidarity in the unprecedented move of cancelling this debt; however, the Norwegian Minister for International Development, Erik Solheim, indicated that in cancelling illegitimate debt, Norway hoped 'to see more active debate on the creditor countries' political responsibility towards poor countries'.[34] To this end, Norway provided funding to both the United Nations Conference on Trade and Development and the World Bank to research the concept of odious debt in international law.[35] There has been increased public debate on the issue of odious debt, and Ecuador was the first country to convene an official debt audit commission to assess the legitimacy of loans to the country.[36] However, NGOs and international financial institutions have not thus far been successful in agreeing on how to define or tackle the problem of illegitimate and odious debt.[37]

Norway did undertake a debt-for-development exchange in 2006. Debt exchanges were used by the Asian Development Bank (ADB) as a tool to raise funds for the Pakistan Earthquake Fund. The earthquake in Pakistan in 2005 killed 80,000 people and left 200,000 injured and more than 2.6 million without shelter. The ADB and the World Bank estimated that US$5.2 billion would

---

[30] Norwegian Campaign for Debt Cancellation, "Norway Cancel Illegitimate Debt and Take Co-responsibility for Failed Development Policy" (press release, October 2, 2006).

[31] Alexander Sack in 1927 defined odious debt as debt contracted against the interests of a population without their consent, accompanied by full awareness of the creditor nation. The concept of illegitimate debt is broader, encapsulating debt resulting from the loss of war, irresponsible lending and lending without transparency or participation. See Jubilee USA, "Recent Developments", 2.

[32] Norwegian Ministry of Foreign Affairs, "Norwegian Development Assistance in 2008: Priority Areas", accessed August 2, 2010, http://www.regjeringen.no/en/dep/ud/selected-topics/development_cooperation/norwegian-development-assistance-in-2008.html?id=493308.

[33] Norwegian Ministry of Foreign Affairs, "Norway Defends Unilateral Debt Cancellation in the Paris Club" (press release, October 2, 2006).

[34] Ibid.

[35] Both papers were published in 2007, and their findings differed considerably. The UNTCA paper by Robert Howse concluded that odious debt was a concept grounded in public international law, whilst the World Bank paper asserted that public international law provides no foundation for the repudiation of debts on the basis of their 'odious nature'. See Jubilee USA, "Recent Developments", 4.

[36] Ibid., 2.

[37] Alex Wilks, "World Bank, NGOs Clash at Roundtable on Odious Debt", *Bretton Woods Project*, September 26, 2008.

be necessary to provide aid to the area.[38] Norway contributed US$20 million in November 2006 through a debt-for-development exchange. The funds were committed to the specific target of reconstructing primary schools.[39]

IV. CONCLUSION

European nations, with the exception of France, have led the way in the use of debt-for-development mechanisms in the past decade. This is consistent with the greater concern they have displayed for the debt burdens under which many developing countries labour. For instance, when the United States argued strongly for the total cancellation of Iraq's debt to Paris Club creditors in the aftermath of the Iraq war, France and Germany insisted that it also support total debt cancellation for HIPCs and that debt relief for the much richer Iraq be capped at 80%.[40] This stance of the leading European powers led to the resolution of the G8 nations in 2005 that the International Monetary Fund, the concessional lending arm of the World Bank and the African Development Fund, should totally cancel all of their debts to poor countries that comply with the requirements of the World Bank's debt-relief program, the HIPC Initiative. This resolution became known as the Multilateral Debt Reduction Initiative (MDRI). This total cancellation of debt will certainly assist those nations that receive it, but only 24 nations currently qualify for it, and only a further 17 can potentially become eligible in the future.[41] The exclusion of so many heavily indebted nations from HIPC status makes the debt cancellation offered by debt-for-development exchanges for such nations even more important.

Debt-for-development exchanges have made a significant contribution to date to development programs. The debt burden on developing countries has severely curtailed spending on health, education and other social programs, and the need to raise exports to service the debt has often damaged the environment in those countries. Debt-for-development exchanges have been important because they have gone some small way towards redressing these damaging social and environmental impacts of external debt.

---

[38] Asian Development Bank, "Belgium in EURO 10 Million Debt Swap for Pakistan Earthquake Reconstruction" (press release, January 31, 2007).

[39] Norwegian Ministry of Foreign Affairs, "Norway to Undertake Debt-for-Development Swap with Pakistan" (press release, November 3, 2006). In January 2007 Belgium similarly committed to a debt swap to fund the earthquake relief, to the value of €10 million; ibid.

[40] Ross P. Buckley, "Iraqi Sovereign Debt and Its Curious Global Implications", in *Beyond the Iraq War: The Promises, Perils and Pitfalls of External Interventionism*, eds. Michael Heazle and Iyanatul Islam (London: Edward Elgar, 2006), 141.

[41] International Monetary Fund, "A Factsheet: Multilateral Debt Relief Initiative" (January 2009), accessed August 2, 2010, www.imf.org/external/np/exr/facts/mdri.htm.

9

Debt-for-Development Exchanges in Australia: Past, Present and Future

Adele Webb and Luke Fletcher

I. INTRODUCTION

This chapter is an attempt to write the eight-year history of Australia's first debt-for-development exchange. This is a story not just about the benevolence of Australia, sacrificing money owed to it in order to assist poor Indonesian children suffering from tuberculosis. It is also a story about the consequences of rich-country policies that are designed to make their exporters competitive in a global marketplace, for these export finance policies and the debt accumulation of less developed countries are inherently linked. The relationship between a competitive trade policy and the accumulation of debt runs as a constant theme throughout this contribution.

The chapter is written from a perspective that is critical of what may be called the 'debt-dependent development model'. This is not the simplistic belief that debt is always bad: many countries, such as Australia in the late 19th and early 20th centuries and, more recently, South Korea, have become development success stories, despite borrowing heavily in key periods. Rather, it is the more nuanced position that borrowing to facilitate development should be done selectively and with great caution, lest it lock one into a subordinate relationship to richer countries and financial institutions; and that unless the borrowing regime is a mature democracy (or an extremely enlightened autocracy) with a functioning development model, the borrowing will almost certainly produce more problems than solutions. It is unfortunate that the occasional blindness of economic theory has combined with the common self-centredness of wealthy nations' foreign policy to exploit and at times even create these problems. Critical civil society and movements like the international Jubilee network see themselves as existing to redress these imbalances.

Much more could be written about these broader development issues, but there is not the space to do so here. Rather it is better to turn to the task at hand: that of telling the tale of the origins, development and implementation of, and future possibilities for, Australian debt-for-development exchanges.[1] To this end, this chapter first looks at the mechanisms by which Australia has become a creditor nation; Section III then looks specifically at the nature of Indonesian debts still owed to Australia; Section IV tells the story of civil society advocacy for debt exchanges; Section V discusses the challenges and processes by which Australia's first debt exchange, Debt2Health, was brokered; and the final section suggests where the best opportunities lie for future debt exchanges.

II. AUSTRALIA AS A CREDITOR NATION

Notwithstanding its membership in international lending agencies, including the World Bank and International Monetary Fund (IMF), Australia is a relatively small player when it comes to the debt of the two-thirds world.[2] Compared with countries like the United States, Japan, the United Kingdom and Germany, Australia is a minor creditor with little outstanding bilateral debt. This is in part because of the way that Australian development assistance has been delivered. With a couple of notable exceptions,[3] the Australian aid program has provided bilateral assistance only in the form of grants.

Despite a relatively minor role as a lender to the two-thirds world, the Australian government joined with the other creditor countries in supporting the 1996 introduction of the Highly Indebted Poor Country (HIPC) Initiative, an official debt-relief scheme co-ordinated by the World Bank and the IMF. The HIPC Initiative and the subsequent 1999 Enhanced HIPC Initiative were a response to the calls of Jubilee 2000 campaigners worldwide for the cancellation of the 'unpayable[4] debts of the poorest countries by the year 2000 and a

---

[1]   Although the term 'debt swap' is sometimes used to describe this mechanism, throughout this chapter the term 'debt-for-development exchange' or simply 'debt exchange' is preferred.

[2]   A note on terminology: the term 'two-thirds world' is preferred here to the more prevalent terms 'third world' and 'developing world', because of the many assumptions and judgements built into the latter terms; moreover, the term 'two-thirds world' better represents the inequalities in global wealth, with the majority of the world's population living in circumstances starkly different from those of the top one-third. The term 'impoverished countries' is also preferred to the more commonly used 'poor countries'.

[3]   These are, first, the now-defunct Development Import and Finance Facility (or DIFF scheme) and, second, the A$1 billion 2005 post-tsunami reconstruction package (Australian–Indonesian Partnership for Reconstruction and Development), half of which was in the form of tied loans. Both will be discussed at length later in the chapter.

[4]   Jubilee campaigns around the world interpreted the word 'unpayable' in different ways. For many campaigns in the Global North it meant reducing debt to a 'sustainable' level, while for most Global South campaigns it meant going beyond the search for a 'sustainable' level, to seeking cancellation as a matter of justice. At the first international meeting of the Jubilee

reaction by G7/G8 creditors to the growing fear that an unprecedented rise in the incidence of sovereign debt defaults could destabilise the world economy. In 1998 the Australian government announced A$30.5 million[5] in additional aid funding as a contribution to the HIPC Initiative. Then in April 2000, influenced by the announcements made by the G8 and the public pressure exerted by Australian Jubilee 2000 campaigners,[6] Australian Treasurer Peter Costello announced that the government would provide 100% bilateral debt forgiveness to those countries that met the HIPC requirements.[7]

As of March 1999 Australia was owed an estimated total of A$4 billion in sovereign debt by less developed countries. Of the 41 countries deemed eligible for possible debt relief under the HIPC Initiative, Australia was owed money by four – Vietnam, Ethiopia, Nicaragua and Laos.[8] Given the aforementioned grant-based nature of the Australian aid program, this A$90 million of debt was almost exclusively generated through export finance loans and insurance by the Export Finance and Insurance Corporation (EFIC). EFIC is the wholly government-owned entity established to provide finance and insurance products to Australian exporters where they cannot be sourced through commercial channels.[9] Vietnam's A$67.6 million debt consisted of 11 EFIC

movement in Rome 1998, participants struggled to find a definition of 'unpayable' that represented their diversity of interpretations. 'The Jubilee Call for Debt Cancellation' that was issued linked four kinds of debts to the word 'unpayable': (1) debt that could not be serviced without placing a burden on impoverished people; (2) debt that in real terms has already been paid; (3) debt for improperly designed projects and programs; (4) odious debt and debt incurred by repressive regimes.

5   All dollar currencies refer to Australian dollars unless otherwise stated.
6   The Australian government was handed the Jubilee 2000 petition with the signatures of 385,000 Australians. In December 1999, the report of the Joint Standing Committee on Foreign Affairs, Defence and Trade entitled "World Debt: A Report on the Proceedings of a Seminar" was presented to the Senate; a motion passed by Senator Ferguson stated that the Jubilee 2000 petition demonstrated 'the depth of feeling in the community about the debt issue'. Accessed August 29, 2010, http://parlinfo.aph.gov.au/parlInfo/search/display/display.w3p;adv=;db=;group=;holdingType=;id=;orderBy=;page=0;query=hon%20kathy%20sullivan%20hipc;querytype=;rec=2;resCount=Default.
7   Answers to Questions on Notice (Question 1425, May 29, 2000), Australian House of Representatives Hansard, accessed August 29, 2010, http://parlinfo.aph.gov.au/parlInfo/genpdf/chamber/hansardr/2000–05–29/0180/hansard_frag.pdf;fileType%3Dapplication%2Fpdf. In the previous year the government had stated in Parliament that retiring the debt of the four HIPCs would not have a significant impact on the Australian economy in overall macroeconomic terms. Answers to Questions on Notice (Question 604, February 11, 1999), Australian Senate Hansard, accessed August 29, 2010, http://parlinfo.aph.gov.au/parlInfo/genpdf/chamber/hansards/1999–05–11/0175/hansard_frag.pdf;fileType%3Dapplication%2Fpdf.
8   AusAID Memorandum on DAC, 1999, accessed August 29, 2010, http://www.ausaid.gov.au/publications/pdf/dac_memorandum1999.pdf.
9   For more information about EFIC as an institution see Jubilee Australia, "Risky Business: Shining a Spotlight on Australia's Export Credit Agency" (December 2009), 12–14, http://www.jubileeaustralia.org/resources/reports.

loans, including those related to a fruit and vegetable processing plant, an abattoir, a coal processing plant, metallic telephone cabling, a sugar refining plant, sugar-cane milling equipment and a digital automatic data processing machine.[10] Ethiopia's A\$15.3 million debt was incurred through a loan written in 1990–1991 for sugar-cane milling equipment.[11] The A\$5.7 million owed by Nicaragua arose from a 1986 EFIC loan for sugar-cane harvesting equipment.[12] Vietnam was removed from the HIPC Initiative when the World Bank determined that its debt was sustainable and Laos declined to participate in HIPC; this left only Ethiopia and Nicaragua as the only countries eligible for full bilateral debt cancellation by Australia. Having met their HIPC requirements, the two countries finally had their debt retired by the Australian government in 2004.[13]

The government, however, remained reluctant to extend debt relief to countries outside the HIPC umbrella. Why was this? The HIPC Initiative required that countries eligible for debt relief not only be fiscally poor (and indebted), but also have demonstrated a track record of implementing structural and policy reforms mandated by the IMF and the World Bank. This framework was firmly supported by the Australian government: in 1999 Senator Robert Hill, in response to a parliamentary question on the issue, declared that 'debt relief without true adjustment would be wasted'. Unconditional cancellation, he said, would encourage unsustainable debts

[10]   Answers to Questions on Notice (Question 604, February 11, 1999), Australian Senate Hansard, accessed August 29, 2010, http://parlinfo.aph.gov.au/parlInfo/genpdf/chamber/hansards/1999–05–11/0175/hansard_frag.pdf;fileType%3Dapplication%2Fpdf.

[11]   This loan was provided under the DIFF scheme, a program managed by both AusAID and EFIC to provide goods and services to aid-recipient countries through a mix of tied aid and export credit; the nature of this scheme is discussed later in this chapter.

[12]   This debt was rescheduled in 1991. In negotiations at the Paris Club (discussed later) at that time, Australia extended the term to 25 years and agreed to a grace period of 14 years. As a result, the first instalment of principal on this debt is not due until 2007. In addition; at a meeting of the Paris Club on December 9, 1998, all creditors agreed to defer all repayments of debt – including interest – owed by Nicaragua (and Honduras) until 2001, when there will be further discussion of the issue. Answers to Questions on Notice (Question 604, February 11, 1999), Australian Senate Hansard, accessed August 29, 2010, http://parlinfo.aph.gov.au/parlInfo/genpdf/chamber/hansards/1999–05–11/0175/hansard_frag.pdf;fileType%3Dapplication%2Fpdf.

[13]   Nicaragua's debt was officially cancelled on April 15, 2004. See "Australia Does the Right Thing on Debt", *ACFID Media Release* (April 22, 2004), accessed August 29, 2010, http://www.acfid.asn.au/news-media/docs_media-releases/docs_2004-releases/0304_debt.pdf. Ethiopia's A\$7.9 million bilateral debt was cancelled in November the same year; see "Australia Forgives Ethiopia's Debt" (joint press release, Treasurer, Minister for Foreign Affairs and Trade and Minister for Trade, November 15, 2004), accessed August 29, 2010, http://www.treasurer.gov.au/DisplayDocs.aspx?pageID=&doc=pressreleases/2004/098.htm&min=phc.

by rewarding weak economic performance and shielding governments from their responsibilities.[14]

It is worth pointing out that, in making these statements, the government was simply echoing the position of the international community of creditors that structural adjustment under IMF and World Bank programs was a necessary condition of debt relief to ensure sound economic policies in indebted countries. While predictable, this position does not match up with the realities of international development. More than 20 years of structural adjustment programs yielded no proof of their success in reducing poverty, accumulating wealth and strengthening economies. Senator Hill's statement on behalf of the government that such reforms were necessary to avoid 'weak economic performance' was particularly unfortunate given that the less developed countries that have been most successful in recent years (the Asian Tigers, China, India, not to mention Thailand, with its comparatively successful recovery from the Asian financial crisis) are those that have deliberately avoided the policy prescriptions of the IMF and the World Bank.[15] Furthermore, the debt owed to Australia arose from loans given to promote trade[16] rather than money extended for more altruistic purposes, as is often assumed. The Australian economy had already benefitted from enhanced export sales, and it is therefore questionable whether it should have the right to expect, by virtue of the remaining debt, to be able to leverage additional control over the structural reform policies of recipient countries.

The other multilateral forum offering an avenue for less developed countries facing debt distress is the Paris Club, an informal grouping of the largest 19 lending countries, including Australia. Though nonbinding and operating without a legal basis, this club of creditors finds it in its interests to take co-ordinated action when renegotiating the repayment of debts.[17] Through these meetings the Australian government has agreed to reschedule or partially cancel sovereign debts owed by a number of less developed countries. For example, on

---

[14] Answers to Questions on Notice (Question 604, February 11, 1999), Australian Senate Hansard, accessed August 29, 2010, http://parlinfo.aph.gov.au/parlInfo/genpdf/chamber/hansards/1999–05–11/0175/hansard_frag.pdf;fileType%3Dapplication%2Fpdf.

[15] See Ross Buckley, "Beyond the Multilateralised Chang Mai Initiative: The Asian Monetary Fund", in R. Buckley, R. Hu and D. Arner, eds., *East Asian Integration: Finance, Law and Trade* (London: Edward Elgar, forthcoming).

[16] EFIC is refreshingly explicit about its primary purpose being to support domestic business; many other export credit agencies still persist with the pretence that the development needs of the recipient countries are equally important. See Jubilee Australia, "Risky Business", 12–14, accessed August 29, 2010, http://www.jubileeaustralia.org/resources/reports.

[17] The Paris Club has been criticised for being a partial body where creditors act as both judge and jury, protecting their own interests first and foremost.

three occasions the Australian government rescheduled EFIC loans to the Indonesian government covering payments originally due between 1998 and 2003.[18] In addition, following the December 2004 tsunami, the government agreed through the Paris Club to put a moratorium on Indonesia's debt repayments due in 2005. Through a Paris Club agreement, Australia also retired A$195 million of Egypt's debt in 1991 as part of a co-ordinated action by creditors thought to be in response to the country's support to allies during the first Gulf war. Perhaps most well publicised was the agreement negotiated between Iraq and the Paris Club group of creditors in 2004, with Australia announcing it would cancel US$850.7 million as its part of the international effort to forgive 80% of the US$38.9 billion of Iraqi government debt owed to these countries.[19] In order to reconcile EFIC accounts, the money was counted as part of official development assistance (ODA).

Outside of the existing multilateral debt-relief initiatives and Paris Club negotiations, debt relief by creditors can take three other forms: first, unilateral partial or complete cancellation, such as the action of the Norwegian government in 2006;[20] debt buy-backs, that is, the purchase of the debt by the country itself, usually at a discount, from its creditors; and third, debt-for-development exchanges. The magnitude of Indonesia's debt problem, the origins and nature of loans from Australia and the reason for its being a suitable counterpart in an Australian debt-for-development exchange are discussed in the next section.

III. INDONESIA: AUSTRALIA'S LARGEST DEBTOR

Along with that of its neighbour, the Philippines, Indonesia's economy is dominated by the spiral of debt – continuous repayments constantly financed by new borrowings. The 1997 Asian financial crisis decimated the country's

---

[18] Rescheduling agreements with Indonesia: 1998, 2000, 2002.

[19] Media release from the Department of Foreign Affairs and Trade, "Australia in International Agreement to Forgive Iraq's Debt" (November 22, 2004), accessed August 29, 2010, http://www.dfat.gov.au/media/releases/department/d017_04.html. The United States used its influence to see that other members of the Paris Club, including Australia, took actions similar to its own in writing off large proportions of Iraq's sovereign debt after the country's invasion. Also see Ross Buckley, "Iraqi Sovereign Debt and Its Curious Global Implications", in Michael Heazle and Iyanatul Islam, eds., *Beyond the Iraq War: The Promises, Perils and Pitfalls of External Interventionism* (London: Edward Elgar, 2006), 141–155.

[20] In 2006, following a successful public campaign, the Norwegian government made the unilateral decision to stop collecting payment of bilateral debts of five less developed countries, cancelling a total of US$80 million without condition. The Norwegian government acknowledged that it "shared responsibility" for the debts, since the exports were made primarily to promote its own ship-building industry, which was in crisis at the time.

economy, as did the policy requirements of the IMF's 'bailout' package. Devaluation of the currency and the transfer of private debt to the public sector saw Indonesia's debt burden double in four years.[21] Despite consistent economic growth through the early and middle 2000s, Indonesia remains a country with deep impoverishment, severe inequality and a stifling debt overhang. In the national budget of 2009, debt servicing represented expenditure 11 times greater than that on health, a bleeding of national income that is patently costly in a nation with a severe disease burden and unacceptably high poverty levels.[22]

Despite the punitive annual repayments and the fact that almost half the population is mired in poverty, Indonesia, as a 'middle-income country', has not been eligible for the World Bank/IMF-mandated debt-relief programs. This is ostensibly due to the country's comparatively strong export profile led by its performance in primary commodity exports: according to the World Bank Debt Sustainability Framework, the resulting debt-to-export ratio makes Indonesia's debt burden 'sustainable'. Such a judgement is in itself an indictment of the Framework, though it is beyond the scope of this chapter to address the issue further.[23] The contradiction between punitive debt repayments and a massive shortfall in social spending has unfortunately not tended to trouble important sections of the Indonesian government, which are averse to any characterisation of Indonesia as unable to pay its debts.[24] The fear is that calling attention to Indonesia's debt situation would have implications for Indonesia's ability to raise funds on the private capital markets, especially bond markets. (Government bonds are, of course, another form of debt, which hardly makes bond markets a sustainable solution to the problem.) It is through this particular constellation of forces and interests that Indonesia has

---

[21] See R. Buckley, "Re-embedding the Market: Reforming International Financial Governance", in K. Macdonald and S. Marshall (eds.), *New Visions for Market Governance: Crisis and Renewal* (Oxford: Routledge, 2011); Joseph Stiglitz, *Globalisation and Its Discontents*, Ch. 4, "The East Asia Crisis: How IMF Policies Brought the World to the Verge of a Global Meltdown" (New York: W. W. Norton), 89–132; Ann Pettifor, "Dirty Debt: Rich Countries Share Responsibility for Indonesia's Impossible Debt Burden", *Inside Indonesia* 69 (January–March 2002): 5.

[22] Almost 50% of Indonesian's live on less than US$2 per day. See AusAID country overview, accessed August 29, 2010, http://www.ausaid.gov.au/country/indonesia.cfm.

[23] For a comprehensive critique of the problems of the Debt Sustainability Framework, see the EURODAD report "Still Missing the Point: Unpacking the New World Bank/IMF Debt Sustainability Framework" (September 2005), accessed September 6, 2010, http://www.eurodad.org/debt/report.aspx?id=118&item=0708.

[24] For more on this see Ross Buckley, "Why Are Developing Nations So Slow to Play the Default Card in Renegotiation Their Sovereign Indebtedness?" *Chicago Journal of International Law* 6(1) (2005): 345–360.

been rendered ineligible for HIPC debt relief. The government of Indonesia has instead relied on rescheduling by the Paris Club when facing difficulty meeting its debt servicing obligations.

Debts of the Indonesian government owed to Australia are small compared with both its total obligations and its obligations to other major lenders (such as Japan, the Asian Development Bank, the World Bank and the IMF).[25] As of June 2009, Indonesia owed Australia an estimated A\$845 million, up slightly from A\$830 million in June 2008. Indonesia's debt to EFIC has been around the A\$1 billion mark for the best part of one and a half decades, rising occasionally to as much as A\$1.5 billion. This differs from the case of most other sovereign governments that may have owed EFIC amounts in the hundreds of millions at any one time but that have tended to pay off the debts rather quickly.

More than 97% of the money owed by Indonesia to Australia was loaned during the 1980s and early 1990s as part of the Development Import Finance Facility (DIFF) scheme.[26] A policy of the Australian Department of Foreign Affairs and Trade, DIFF was intended to open up new foreign markets for Australian exporters while at the same time assisting the 'development needs' of importing countries. Recipient governments were offered EFIC loans partially supported by aid grants to fund the import of goods and services from Australian companies. As we discuss in more detail Section IV, Indonesia received the bulk of the DIFF loans during the 16-year period of the scheme.[27] DIFF was contentious and heavily criticised for misusing the overseas development assistance program to promote Australian exports. In 1996 the policy was discontinued following a change of government and a subsequent Senate enquiry into the scheme's effectiveness. The new Treasurer, Peter Costello, reportedly described DIFF as a 'subsidy paid to domestic business'.[28]

The importance of Indonesia as a recipient of Australian credit extends beyond its signal role in the DIFF scheme; it is the only country in recent decades to which Australia has loaned aid money. The A\$1 billion assistance package to Indonesia in the immediate wake of the 2004 Boxing Day tsunami

[25] See International NGO Forum on Indonesian Development, *Debt Swaps for Indonesia: A Proposal for Improving Their Effectiveness* (2007), 5, www.infid.org.
[26] According to the 2009 annual report of EFIC, as of that time Indonesia's exposure on the National Interest Account was A\$826 million (all accrued through DIFF), as compared with A\$21 million on the Commercial Account.
[27] DIFF operated between 1980 and 1996 before being discontinued.
[28] Peter Costello's characterisation was described by New South Wales parliamentarian Sandra Nori. See NSW Legislative Assembly Hansard, "Development Import Finance Facility Abolition" (October 30, 1996), accessed August 29, 2010, http://www.parliament.nsw.gov.au/prod/PARLMENT/hansart.nsf/V3Key/LA19961030034.

consisted of 50% grant-based assistance and 50% loans. Though highly concessional, with zero interest and a grace period on repayment of principle until
2015, the A$500 million worth of loans will nevertheless add to Indonesia's
total national debt. The belief was expressed at the time, both inside and outside the Australian Parliament, that the program should have been delivered
entirely through grants, consistent with Australia's other development assistance programs. Further, no requirement was made that a percentage of the
funds be devoted to tsunami assistance activities; in fact, much of the loaned
money may end up going to contracts for projects outside of Aceh.[29] It is also
worth noting that the initial package required that contracts be awarded exclusively to Australian and New Zealand firms, though this was later amended to
allow Indonesian companies to bid for work.[30]

IV. LOBBYING FOR DEBT EXCHANGES IN AUSTRALIA

Early advocacy efforts by Jubilee Australia to lobby for a debt-for-development
exchange as an innovative approach to Indonesia's outstanding debt made
little progress. To the best of the authors' knowledge, the first time that a debt-
for-development exchange was proposed in Australia was in October 2002,
when in a submission to the parliamentary enquiry into Australia's relations
with Indonesia, Jubilee Australia proposed that the government consider a
'debt-for-poverty-reduction' exchange, pointing to the recent conclusion by
Germany of its first such debt-exchange agreement.[31] Around the same time,
the Indonesian government had begun to formally request that Australia consider a debt-for-development exchange 'as a way of addressing the bilateral
debt between the two countries'.[32]

In 2004 Jubilee representatives stepped up their lobbying for debt-for-development exchange. Recommendations for an exchange were made in a number

---

[29] In 2009 Indonesia expert Peter McCawley said, 'Even the most superficial examination of the
Australian Government's decision indicated that important foreign policy considerations lay
behind the announcement', pointing to the government's own research note, which went so
far as to note that '[i]t is quite possible that most of the grant aid and loan component will be
spent on projects outside Aceh'. "Foreign Aid: What's It For?" *The Interpreter*, Lowy Institute
for International Policy, July 10, 2009, accessed August 29, 2010, http://www.lowyinterpreter.
org/post/2009/07/10/Foreign-aid-Whats-it-for.aspx.

[30] Ibid.

[31] Jubilee Australia, Inquiry into Australia's Relations with Indonesia, Submission No. 37
(October 31, 2002), accessed September 6, 2010, http://web.archive.org/web/20060920113352/
www.aph.gov.au/house/committee/jfadt/indonesia/subs/subindo37.pdf.

[32] Indonesia reiterated the request to the Australian government to 'consider a debt swap
program' during the Sixth Indonesia–Australia Ministerial Forum in Jakarta, March 2003.
See http://202.148.132.171/wnew/jministo30311e.htm, accessed September 6, 2010.

of meetings with parliamentarians and Treasury officials.[33] In the same year, most likely as a result of this lobbying, the key Australian interparliamentary committee on foreign affairs, the Joint Standing Committee on Defence, Foreign Affairs and Trade, endorsed a debt-for-development exchange on the grounds that Indonesia was ineligible for further Paris Club rescheduling and that such an exchange would be consistent with the Australian aid program.[34] In 2005, as the tsunami aid package was announced, Jubilee Australia's public statements continued to emphasise debt conversion as preferable to aid loans as a way of assisting Indonesia in response to this crisis.

Nevertheless, resistance to the concept continued among Australian policy makers. When AusAID sought public submissions in response to the 2006 White Paper on the future of the Australian aid program, Jubilee Australia entered a proposal for debt-for-development exchanges and even took this position directly to officials during the public consultation process of September 2005. In the final version of the 2006 White Paper[35] the recommendation was not taken up, and informal discussions with Australian Treasury officials over this period revealed the sentiment that any mechanism for reducing Indonesia's debt to Australia was unnecessary, given that the debt was 'sustainable' and Indonesia was meeting its payment obligations.[36]

Towards the end of 2006 further discouraging signals were received from another source. Heading into the November 2006 G20 Finance Ministers Meeting in Melbourne, the Make Poverty History Coalition, working closely with Jubilee Australia, adopted an Australian–Indonesian debt-for-development exchange as one of its key policy requests.[37] Although the issue was somewhat swamped by the attention given to the campaign's platform for more foreign aid, it received some focus at this time, including some mention in the press.[38] Nevertheless, discussions with the Treasurer's senior ministerial

[33] Meeting between Jubilee Australia representatives (accompanied by colleagues from ACFID [the Australian Council for International Development] and TEAR [Transformation · Empowerment · Advocacy · Relief] Australia) and MPs, March 2004; meeting between Jubilee Australia Sydney Working Group and Opposition MP Laurie Ferguson, July 2004.
[34] Joint Standing Committee on Foreign Affairs, Defence and Trade, "2004 Report on Australia's relationship with Indonesia", 4.39 and 4.40.
[35] AusAID, "Australian Aid: Promoting Growth and Stability – White Paper on the Australian Government's Overseas Aid Program" (April 2006), accessed August 29, 2010, http://www.ausaid.gov.au/publications/pubout.cfm?Id=6184_6346_7334_4045_8043.
[36] Information here and in the following four paragraphs has been drawn from the personal experience of the authors.
[37] The Australian Make Poverty History Coalition at the time had a tripartite focus on aid, trade and debt, and the adoption of a debt-for-development exchange with Indonesia was the campaign's principle policy target for the third area.
[38] See, e.g., Ross Buckley, "Transparency Helps Narrow the Gap", *Australian Financial Review*, November 16, 2006, 63. Ross Buckley also made a presentation on debt-for-development

advisors suggested that the government was not disposed to look favourably on debt-for-development exchanges.[39] (At this stage, very little engagement had been made with the then opposition party, the Australian Labor Party, ALP.) With the idea being rejected by the Treasurer's office, Treasury and AusAID, prospects for any adoption of the debt-conversion idea appeared dim.

Not long after, however, Jubilee Australia hosted a delegation from the Innovative Financing team of the Global Fund to Fight HIV/AIDS, Tuberculosis and Malaria on its visit to Australia.[40] Since its creation in 2002, the Global Fund has become the dominant financier of programs to fight the three diseases, with approved funding of US$19.3 billion for more than 600 programs in 145 countries. To date, programs supported by the Global Fund have saved 4.9 million lives by providing AIDS treatment for 2.7 million people, antituberculosis treatment for 7 million people and the distribution of 122 million insecticide-treated bed nets for the prevention of malaria.[41] Following positive negotiations with the German government, the Global Fund was looking for a second creditor country to participate in its innovative financing mechanism called Debt2Health. Through this mechanism, the Global Fund facilitates debt-conversion agreements between creditor and debtor countries and in so doing raises extra financial resources for its programs in affected countries. The Global Fund considered Indonesia to be a country particularly suitable to the program due to its large debt burden and its need for more resources to fight disease, particularly tuberculosis. Australia, given its proximity to Indonesia and its outstanding debt claims on Indonesia, was considered by the Global Fund to be a good potential participant from the creditor side.

At first, it appeared as if the Global Fund's visit might have been in vain, when the delegation received a lukewarm response in meetings organised by Jubilee Australia in late November 2006. Government officials from Treasury, DFAT and AusAID expressed little interest in debt-for-development exchanges or in participation in the Debt2Health initiative. However, the visit would prove to be instrumental since, energised by its engagement with this new and influential ally, Jubilee Australia, in partnership with the Make Poverty History policy team, stepped up its advocacy efforts in Parliament House. Assisting Jubilee

exchanges at the Make Poverty History G20 Forum in Melbourne Town Hall, early November 2006.
[39] Meeting in October 2006 between an advisor to the Treasurer, Peter Costello and Make Poverty History/Jubilee Australia representatives.
[40] The team included the Global Fund's Director of Innovative Financing, Robert Fillip, and, on secondment, the Coordinator of Erlassjahr.de, the equivalent campaign to Jubilee Australia in Germany.
[41] Figures from the Global Fund's Web site: http://theglobalfund.org, accessed on 10 August 2010.

Australia and Make Poverty History in this effort were RESULTS Australia and the Lowy Institute for International Policy, both supporters of the Global Fund. Although the government parliamentarians remained noncommittal, the proposal piqued the interest of key opposition MPs, among them the newly appointed Shadow Parliamentary Secretary for Overseas Development Assistance, Bob McMullan.

At the beginning of 2007, the tide seemed to be turning in favour of debt-for-development exchange. In an attempt to capitalise on this shift of momentum, Jubilee Australia undertook to produce a longer policy document explaining the need for a debt exchange with Indonesia and championing the Global Fund Debt2Health scheme as the perfect vehicle to pilot it. The paper,[42] published in April 2007, drew heavily on the success of the debt-for-education exchanges between the German and Indonesian governments that had funded a number of new school facilities. Although the government continued to reject the idea, officially ruling out support for the proposed Debt2Health exchange in Parliament in May,[43] the likelihood of a change of government in the elections scheduled for the end of 2007 was becoming increasingly clear. In June the aforementioned Bob McMullan, who had made warm remarks about a debt-for-development exchange with Indonesia at a Jubilee Australia event in April,[44] officially announced that if elected his party would implement such an agreement along the lines proposed by Jubilee Australia and the Global Fund. When, as expected, the ALP won the subsequent election on November 24, 2007, implementing Debt2Health became official government policy.

V. THE IMPLEMENTATION OF THE DEBT2HEALTH PROJECT

It is probably fair to say that the involvement of the Global Fund was crucial in selling Debt2Health to the ALP. The Global Fund has a rigorous process for partnering with local civil society not only to determine areas of need, but also to ensure that resources are delivered to the right places and to maintain a standard of absolute intolerance for misuse of its funds. On a number of occasions, financing for programs has been suspended in response to the

---

[42] Jubilee Australia, "A Debt-for-Development Swap with Indonesia" (April 2007), accessed August 29, 2010, http://www.jubileeaustralia.org/resources/reports.

[43] Answer to a Question on Notice (Question No. 3067) by Senator Allison to the Minister representing the Minister for Foreign Affairs, Australian Parliamentary Hansard (May 8, 2007), accessed August 29, 2010, http://www.aph.gov.au/hansard/senate/dailys/ds080507.pdf.

[44] Jubilee Australia's event at the Fringe Program of the ALP National Conference, which was entitled "Is Australia a Responsible Lender?" April 2007.

Global Fund's concerns about the accountability and transparency of local groups managing the funds.[45] Furthermore, the Australian government is a donor to the Global Fund and respects it as an effective institution of service delivery. In this context, the Debt2Health agreement could be seen as not only addressing Indonesia's debt problems, but also providing a new revenue stream for existing development programs with an established modus operandi and built-in checks and balances.

The Global Fund's involvement also spared the Australian government from having to make decisions about the type of project to target through a debt-for-development exchange, along with the potentially complicated discussions with Indonesian ministries about design and implementation. In addition, Australia was to some extent treading some well-worn ground, in that Debt2Health negotiations had been under way for some time between the German and Indonesian governments (the agreement finalised between Germany and Indonesia in 2008 was the Global Fund's first Debt2Health contract). Finally, that the project would provide a much needed injection of resources into Global Fund programs fighting the tuberculosis epidemic – Indonesia has the third-highest rate of tuberculosis in the world, with more than 90,000 Indonesians dying from the disease every year – was another powerful rationale for enlisting the support of AusAID.

This is not to say that the lead up to the 2010 signing of the Debt2Health agreement was straightforward. A small hiccup occurred early in the process when doubt arose about the functioning of the Global Fund's programs in Indonesia. The Indonesian civil society groups that were overseeing the Global Fund's operations in Indonesia (collectively known as the Country Coordinating Mechanism, CCM) chose not to submit a proposal for a subsequent funding round, which led some officials to worry whether the Global Fund programs in Indonesia had become compromised. As it turned out, however, the CCM was in fact investing time to tighten its processes, and these concerns were very quickly put to rest. The project also created extra administrative burdens, and although Australian bureaucrats were spared the task of having to design a new aid project, they were nonetheless required to expand their comprehension of an institution with which they had had little prior involvement. While this might not seem a major obstacle, it is the understanding of the authors that, for AusAID officials in Canberra and Jakarta, Debt2Health did present an extra challenge.

---

[45] The Global Fund has suspended payments to nonperforming countries, including those to Zambia (2009), Mauritania (2009), Philippines (2009) and Myanmar (2005).

The signing of the final agreement between the Australian Minister for Foreign Affairs and Trade and his counterpart in the government of Indonesia was announced on July 15, 2010[46] – more than two and a half years after the ALP came to power (and coincidentally just when this chapter was being completed). There was never any suggestion that an agreement would not be reached: repeated assurances were given by the Australian side that the deal would eventually be struck once the necessary details had been ironed out. The time lag between the ALP assuming power and the conclusion of the debt-for-development exchange agreement most likely had more to do with the intricate financial details of the deal as well as the unfamiliarity amongst the various officials with the process. It appears, for example, that it took some time for the negotiation process to take off and that there was a long period of discussion necessary to determine which contracts were to be exchanged and on what terms. Given that the authors were not privy to these internal government processes, these comments are only speculation.

A. *The Issue of Illegitimacy*

The most serious point of contention regarding the implementation of Debt2Health has been the nature of the loan contracts chosen for use in the exchange. At the same time the debt-exchange policy was coming into being, Jubilee Australia was undertaking its own investigations into the nature of Indonesian debt to Australia and was becoming increasingly aware that issues of illegitimacy might arise over some of the original loans. Its public positions on this issue in 2007 reflected this growing concern.[47] In-depth treatments of how the problem of illegitimate debt intersects with the use of debt-for-development exchanges are to be found in Chapter 10 by Julia Roy and Chapter 11 by Jürgen Kaiser in this volume. However, a fundamental agreement of the international debt movement[48] is that debts found to be illegitimate should be

---

[46] Australia, "Indonesia and the Global Fund Debt Swap Agreement to Increase Tuberculosis Services in Indonesia", Joint Media Release of the Global Fund and Governments of Indonesia and Australia, July 15, 2010.

[47] In its 2007 policy paper advocating for the debt exchange, Jubilee Australia included a section on the origins of Indonesia's debt to Australia; it concluded that it was highly possible that some of Australia's debt claims on Indonesia were illegitimate and that 'all debts found to be illegitimate should be cancelled immediately and without conditions'. When the ALP announced in June that, if elected, it would seek a debt exchange with Indonesia, Jubilee Australia welcomed the announcement but warned that the Australian government should ensure that none of the loan contracts to be used in the exchange were associated with illegitimate lending practices. Jubilee Australia, "A Debt-for-Development Swap with Indonesia" (April 2007), accessed September 6, 2010, http://www.jubileeaustralia.org/resources/reports.

[48] The international debt movement is a collection of regional and country networks and campaigns that work on the issue of debt and its impact on development. Groups tend to be

cancelled immediately and without conditions.[49] Such a position arises from the movement's contention that those governments and institutions lending to less developed countries, often in the name of 'development', should share responsibility for self-interested or poorly conceived loans and should pay the outstanding costs of the illegitimate debts created. Norway is still the only country that has acknowledged this principle in practice by cancelling debts shown to have arisen from loans that were made more for the purpose of boosting domestic exports than to serve the development needs of the recipient country.[50]

It is arguably the case, however, that many of Indonesia's debts to Australia may be said to fall into the same category as the Norwegian loans. As described earlier in the chapter, more than 95% of the loans to Indonesia originated from the DIFF program. Although DIFF loans were made to a variety of countries, Indonesian-based exporters received the bulk of the big-ticket loans. Over the nine-year period between 1984 and 1993, Australian construction company Transfield received the benefit of approximately one-third of the taxpayer-raised DIFF funds to pursue a joint venture with Indonesian trading partner PT Bakrie & Brothers, building around 2,500 prefabricated steel bridges in the country.[51] The latter company was owned by Aburizal Bakrie, a controversial Indonesian government figure and one of Indonesia's richest men, who secured his fortune through his close links to the Suharto regime but who has since been implicated in serious charges of corruption, tax evasion and maladministration.[52] In 2010 more than 50% of these loans remain unpaid. These preliminary findings warrant further investigation, including a proper audit of the existence, locations and development purpose of these bridges. It seems

linked most formally in regional blocks, such as the Jubilee South Asia–Pacific Movement on Debt and Development (Jubilee Australia, as a Northern country, is an associate member of JSAPMDD). Global meetings where Southern and Northern networks and campaigns meet for consultation and the setting of strategy occur approximately every three years; however, there is constant interaction and dialogue among the groups.

[49] See Jubilee South Declaration on Illegitimate Debt, 2007 World Social Forum, accessed August 29, 2010, http://www.jubileesouth.org/index.php?option=com_content&task=view&id=79&Itemid=2.

[50] In 2006 Norway set the precedent on dealing with 'illegitimate' debt when it acknowledged that it 'shared responsibility' and cancelled the debts of five developing countries (Ecuador, Egypt, Jamaica, Peru and Sierra Leone) totalling US$80 million, because the exports were made primarily to promote its own ship-building industry, which was in crisis at the time.

[51] Calculations based on analyses of EFIC annual reports.

[52] See, e.g., "Bakrie Denies Latest Tax-Dodging, Corruption Allegations", *Jakarta Globe*, June 4, 2010, accessed August 29, 2010, http://www.thejakartaglobe.com/home/bakrie-denies-latest-tax-dodging-corruption-allegations/378735; "Mud Flung at Minister in Wake of Java disaster", *Sydney Morning Herald*, June 23, 2006, accessed August 29, 2010, http://www.smh.com.au/news/world/mud-flung-at-minister-in-wake-of-java-disaster/2006/06/22/1150845316233.html.

that there did exist within AusAID documentation that included more information about the bridges, but these records may have since been destroyed as part of the routine sorting process of government agencies, which makes an audit from the Australian side challenging.[53] However, unless such an audit is undertaken, questions will remain about whether these bridges served genuine development needs in the country and, therefore, whether it is appropriate that the debt be kept on the books.

Because of the ongoing questions about the nature of export credit loans to Indonesia, Jubilee Australia and its Indonesian civil society counterpart proposed that the comparatively untainted tsunami aid loan be used for the exchange instead.[54] However, this suggestion was not taken up by either side.[55] (It is always possible, given the unprecedented nature of the tsunami loan package, that the Australian government will not seek repayment when it begins to fall due in 2015.) Furthermore, the Australian government insisted on adhering to nonbinding Paris Club rules to use the rescheduled portion of Indonesia's debt in the exchange. Rescheduling agreements make it difficult to identify which original loan contracts are being repaid in any particular year.

Why is all this important? In the past, exchanges have tended to use the debts arising from overseas development assistance (ODA) rather than those generated by export credit agencies (ECAs). For example, all German debt exchanges to date have used ODA loans. ECA-backed projects have often been financed in an atmosphere of corruption,[56] and as we have seen, export credit finance is primarily about supporting domestic business. Thus by exchanging export credit–generated debt before completing a proper audit of it, Australia is potentially setting a worrisome precedent. Such a practice discourages full scrutiny of the original loans and doesn't allow decisions to be made about what to do with the debt (whether it should be partially or completely forgiven,

---

[53] Conversations between Jubilee Australia and officials from the Trade Finance Section of the Department of Foreign Affairs and Trade, February 5 and August 2, 2010.

[54] Jubilee Australia and INFID – the International NGO Forum on Indonesian Development – proposed this in a joint letter to the Australian Prime Minister on February 6, 2009. This was after INFID wrote to the Prime Minister, Kevin Rudd, asking him to pay attention to the relationship between these export credit loans and the support of the Suharto dictatorship.

[55] Australian officials demurred at this suggestion because payments on the tsunami loans will not fall due until 2015 and because they believed that the Indonesian government would prefer nonconcessional ECA debt cancelled rather than debt on highly concessional terms, like the tsunami loan.

[56] See Berne Declaration et al., "A Race to the Bottom: Creating Risk, Generating Debt and Guaranteeing Environmental Destruction: A Compilation of Export Credit & Investment Insurance Agency Case Studies" (March 1999), accessed August 29, 2010, www.ecawatch.org/eca/race_bottom.pdf.

subject to an exchange or collected in full). The best solution to this dilemma would be for the Australian government to actively assist civil society in carrying out a proper audit of any questionable loans – especially those that have been extended to a corrupt regime – before making a decision about doing any sort of debt exchange. This is the only way to ensure that matters of transparency in sovereign lending and borrowing are respected and the move to a fairer and more just financial system is promoted.

VI. NEW OPPORTUNITIES

Along with Indonesia, there are a number of low- and middle-income countries represented on Australia's debt list: Egypt, Zambia, Philippines, Sri Lanka and Vietnam are among them. Assuming that the Debt2Health exchange progresses successfully, there is no reason that Australia could not again participate in a similar exchange with other owing countries. Ideally, however, debt exchanges require three ingredients: a significant enough debt exposure; a supportive government and civil society in the host country; and a plausible mechanism or program to absorb the funds. On these grounds, the best candidates for a debt-for-development exchange – after Indonesia – are Egypt and Zambia.

A. *Egypt*

Egypt may not seem to be the most obvious candidate for the next debt-for-development exchange with Australia, but there are a number of reasons it should be considered. First, like Indonesia's, Egypt's debts owing to Australia have been on the books for a long time and have interesting origins. During the 1980s the Egyptian government had been borrowing money from the Australian Wheat Board (AWB) in order to purchase Australian wheat. To protect itself from the risk of nonpayment, the AWB secured EFIC insurance for the loans. Sure enough, things turned sour for Egypt in the late 1980s, with the government facing negative economic growth, skyrocketing unemployment and one of the highest debt-to-GNP ratios in the world. Things took another turn for the worse when the Gulf war effectively shut down trade for the country in the early 1990s. When the Egyptian government could not pay its creditors, the AWB made a claim to EFIC on its credit insurance, resulting in EFIC assuming Egypt's wheat debts. Australia agreed to reschedule the payments of these wheat debts at Paris Club meetings in 1987 and 1991, and as mentioned earlier, Paris Club creditors even agreed to partial cancellation of Egypt's debt, arguably a reward for the country's alliance during the Gulf war. Yet today, the balance of these rescheduled credit insurance debt is still significant at A$111 million.[57] The debts are repayable by 2016.

The second point of note in support of an Australian exchange with Egypt is the country's successful history of debt-for-development exchanges, having concluded many of them with the governments of France (1994), Switzerland (1995), Germany (2001) and Italy (2001). Egypt has a system whereby it deposits revenues from debt-exchange agreements into a counterpart fund, which is then used for development projects in the country. Organisations including the Egyptian government agencies, Egyptian civil society groups and UN bodies are then entitled to apply for the counterpart funds, which are used to finance projects in human development, poverty alleviation and environmental protection. The Italian–Egypt debt-exchange program helped finance 53 projects between 2001 and 2008, details of which have been written up in a report of the two bodies.[58]

B. *Zambia*

Landlocked Zambia in southern Africa has had significant external debt obligations written off since 2005 through the HIPC Initiative. Although Zambia is no longer in the debt trap it once was, domestic and external forces are still hampering the government's ability to meet its human development challenges. The fiscal reprieve offered as a result of debt relief has undoubtedly had a positive impact on the lives of the poor, with the injection of new funds seeing stronger poverty reduction in government social policy. For example, the country scrapped the prohibitive fee HIV positive citizens had to pay in order to receive antiretroviral treatment.[59] Yet HIPC debt relief is no perfect remedy: not only are the resources freed up simply not enough for Zambia, the 30th-poorest country in the world, to achieve the Millennium Development Goals (MDGs),[60] but Zambia's major dependence on copper exports for the majority of its income leaves the economy just as vulnerable post-HIPC.

---

[57] According to EFIC Annual Report 2009, A$24 million on the Commercial Account, with the balance on the National Interest Account.

[58] "Italian–Egypt Debt for Development Swap Program: Annual Report 2008", Italian Embassy in Cairo and Arab Republic of Egypt, accessed August 29, 2010, http://www.utlcairo.org/stampa/DS1_final_report2008.pdf.

[59] UNDP Africa Viewpoint, "Deriving Maximum Social Benefits from Debt Relief: A Case of Zambia", *Monthly Policy Brief*, Issue No. 9, June 2009, http://www.undp.org/africa/africaviewpoint/2009-june.pdf.

[60] The average Zambian lives on US$3.72 dollars per day (this is calculated from US$1,548 per year and is adjusted for purchasing power parity; from UNDP 2009 Human Development Indicators database, using 2007 data, accessed August 29, 2010, http://hdrstats.undp.org/en/

As a fragile post-HIPC economy, Zambia is not immune to the risk of new debt distress. The country was not spared the fiscal impacts of the recent crisis, including a 40% drop in the value of the kwacha by March 2009 as a consequence of the drop in copper prices.[61] Zambia was also the victim of an unscrupulous 'vulture fund' in 2006, which sued the country in court for debt it acquired on the secondary market, increasing Zambia's debt burden. By 2009 its debt stock had risen again to US$2 billion after falling from US$4 billion to US$500 million following the debt relief granted in 2005. The United Nations Development Programme has recommended that the Zambian government take care that new loan contracts entered into be relevant and beneficial to the poorest segments of the country.[62]

Though contributing to economic growth, Zambia's mining-led growth path has failed to utilise the main economic asset of the poor – their labour – and as such has not fostered enough poverty alleviation, particularly for the 70% of the poor who reside in rural areas.[63] In 2006 EFIC facilitated a very large private-sector mining investment in Zambia, the Lumwana mine.[64] In support of Australian resource company Equinox Minerals, EFIC contributed debt finance of A$54.5 million (US$43 million) to the US$584 million financing for the project in 2006–2007, which it repeated in 2008–2009 with another project loan of A$11.4 million. All of this has left Zambia with a debt to EFIC of A$71.7 million as of 2009.[65]

Should EFIC collect repayment from the Zambian government on its A$71.7 million loan? While the mining venture is claiming to offer substantial social investment in the country, the truth is that the public good derived from a private investment of this nature is relatively small, limited to the creation of a

---

countries/country_fact_sheets/cty_fs_ZMB.html), life expectancy is 44.5 years and almost 20% of children do not reach the age of five (Global Fund grant portfolio for Zambia, accessed August 29, 2010, http://portfolio.theglobalfund.org/Country/Index/ZAM?lang=en).

[61]　"Towards a Renewed Debt Crisis? Risk Profiles of the Poorest Countries in the Light of the Global Economic Slowdown", Dialogue on Globalization, Jürgen Kaiser, Irene Knoke and Hartmut Kowsky, June 2009, 64, http://library.fes.de/pdf-files/iez/global/06444.pdf.

[62]　UNDP Africa Viewpoint, "Deriving Maximum Social Benefits".

[63]　It was estimated that if the country continues with this mining-led growth path, overall (head count) poverty will decline only marginally to 62.3% by 2010 (from 68% in 2004). This will clearly be insufficient for making progress towards halving the 1990 poverty of 70% 10 level by 2015. UNDP, "Zambia: MDG Progress Report 2008", 5, accessed September 6, 2010, http://www.undp.org.zm/joomla/attachments/005_Zambia%20MDGs%20Progress%20Report%20Zambia%202008.pdf.

[64]　The mine is located 220 kilometres west of the Zambian Copperbelt and 65 kilometres from the regional centre of Solwezi.

[65]　2007 EFIC Annual Report, accessed August 29, 2010, http://www.efic.gov.au/corp-responsibility/Documents/Full%20Annual%20Report%202007.pdf.

maximum of 2,500 jobs, a new school and project-related infrastructure in the mine area. Being the largest open-pit copper mine in Africa, the project will no doubt generate lucrative profits for Equinox Minerals and other foreign contractors and, of course, government revenue and foreign exchange. But generous tax incentives and tax breaks to foreign mining outfits will mean that Zambia's earnings will be less than they could be. Moreover, the Zambian government will need all the revenues it can find to fight its crippling HIV/AIDS epidemic. According to UNAIDS 15% of the adult population (1.1 million out of a total population of 12.6 million) is living with HIV/AIDS.[66] The Global Fund estimates that a staggering 330,000 Zambians are in need of antiretroviral therapy.[67] A case could be made for the Australian government to cancel Zambia's debt outright. At the very least, a debt-for-poverty or a debt-for-health exchange should be considered for Zambia to help raise funds for its HIV epidemic. The Global Fund has a presence in Zambia, having approved more than US$600 million worth of loans, around half of which have been disbursed, the result of which is almost a quarter of a million Zambians on antiretroviral therapy and 6 million malaria nets distributed. Although the Global fund has tended not to use Debt2Health funding in HIPCs, it is open to doing so. Australia might, then, consider approaching Zambia and the Global Fund about Zambia's participation in the Debt2Health program.

VII. CONCLUSION

What conclusions might reflecting on the history of debt-for-development exchanges in Australia bring us? One would be the importance of perseverance in attempts to effect policy change. Advocates, whether within civil society, academia or government, will have noted from reading Section III that, as much as anything else, it was sustained argument and engagement that won the day in having debt exchanges accepted as official policy. This might seem an obvious comment to make about advocacy and policy change, but it is a poignant one, nonetheless. As for the support for the policy in the wider community, it was interesting that, in conversations with the apocryphal 'ordinary Australians' about debt exchanges, people said they liked the idea of having some control over what they saw as the spending of 'their money'.

[66] "Annex: HIV and AIDS Estimates and Data, 2001 and 2007", *2008 Report on the Global AIDS Epidemic*, UNAIDS, accessed August 29, 2010, http://www.unaids.org/en/KnowledgeCentre/HIVData/GlobalReport/2008/2008_Global_report.asp.
[67] Currently the Global Fund finances antiretroviral treatment for 250,000 of these, but a shortfall still exists. Global Fund grant portfolio for Zambia, accessed August 29, 2010, http://portfolio.theglobalfund.org/Country/Index/ZAM?lang=en.

Thus, although the case for unconditional cancellation of at least some of this debt remains strong, for now it seems that many people do not share this view. The narrative of illegitimacy is still very challenging to many people both inside and outside government, and much of the work surrounding the debt crisis remains very sensitive. People's default assumption seems to still mirror the story projected by many in government: that the debt crisis is the fault of corrupt and venal third world officials and that, in contrast, industrialised nations have been generally well intentioned in their dealings with developing countries.

However, as this chapter has shown, there is much more to the story of the 'debt crisis' than the simplistic interpretation of rich-country charity being subsequently wasted. Corruption and waste in the two-thirds world have regularly left a well-worn trail back to institutions and actors in industrialised countries like Australia. It is hoped that, in this telling of the tale of Australia's debt claims, the case has been made that trade policy and national interest considerations play an important role in producing and perpetuating the debt trap in less developed countries. It would seem, then, that debt-for-development exchanges can be of benefit above and beyond the inherent good they do in helping reduce foreign debt and bringing positive development outcomes. They in fact can have the additional benefit of exposing the links that undoubtedly exist between trade, foreign policy and debt, a story that bears continual retelling.

PART III

Critiques of Exchanges

10

Debt Audits: A Necessary Precondition
to Credible Exchanges

Julia Roy

A sovereign debt 'exchange' is not a simple charitable gift, but a conversion of an original financial or trade transaction that benefits both debtor and creditor. There is evidence that some originating transactions gave rise to sovereign debt that is odious or illegitimate.[1] If the debt is illegitimate, any future transactions that deal with the debt – including exchanges – may also be illegitimate. Allegations of illegitimacy cannot be confirmed or denied without access to the details of the debts' originating transactions. Therefore, in order to assess the legitimacy of a proposed debt exchange, the debts' originating transactions must first be examined and deemed legitimate, in a public debt audit.

In order to conduct a public debt audit, the information disclosed must be sufficient to answer four questions: how much is owed, by whom is it owed, for what is it owed, and is it really owed (i.e., is it legitimately owed)?[2] Answering the final question requires the most information. This includes the essential terms of the contract and/or rescheduling, such as rates of interest, and off-balance sheet conditions, such as buy-back agreements;[3] the benefit received by the foreign population; evidence of due diligence, in particular whether the capacity of the future debtor was examined[4] and the content of

---

[1] See, e.g., Jubilee USA, "Recent Developments on Odious and Illegitimate Debt", accessed August 2, 2010, www.jubileeusa.org/?id=111.

[2] AAJ, ATTAC (Uruguay), CADTM, CETIM, COTMEC, Auditoria Cidada Da Divida (Brazil), Emmaus International, Eurodad, Jubilee South Centre, eds., *Let's Launch an Enquiry into the Debt! A Manual on How to Organise Audits on Third World Debts* (Geneva: CETIM, 2006), 62.

[3] For example, a transaction that finances the building of a power station may include a condition that the government enter into a future contract to purchase the power from the foreign corporation that built, owns and controls the station. This can represent billions of dollars of net financial flows out of the developing country that are not reflected on the ECA's balance sheet.

[4] AAJ et al., eds., *Let's Launch an Enquiry*, 79.

any environmental impact statements;[5] and the intended and actual use of funds to show that they were not used to bribe foreign officials. This information is needed to determine the character of the contracting parties at the time the contract was concluded, if procedural irregularities can be detected, if a lack of consent can be detected and if other sources of illegitimacy can be determined.[6]

There is no legal definition of legitimacy or any international law that prohibits collecting interest and repayments on 'illegitimate' sovereign debt. This chapter will not argue that there is or should be (this has been done elsewhere).[7] Rather, this chapter builds on those works and argues that if it is accepted there should be a measure of illegitimacy or odiousness of sovereign debt, and debt that crosses a certain threshold of illegitimacy should be cancelled; there should also be corresponding limitations on future dealings with illegitimate sovereign debt, which the 'charitable' clothing of a debt exchange does not avoid. This thesis rests on three arguments: that legitimacy can be measured, that debt exchanges are financial transactions benefiting both creditor and debtor and not simple charity and that details of sovereign debt should not be secret. This chapter will also dispel the myths that exchanges do not benefit creditor countries, that sovereign debt is created solely by national governments and that public disclosure of the details of a debt's originating transactions would have adverse commercial and international relations consequences.

I. LEGITIMACY

This chapter will not canvass the many definitions of, and arguments for and against, criteria of legitimacy. Instead, it will demonstrate that, at the least, legitimacy can be measured, and it will establish a working definition of legitimacy.

---

[5] On the environmental devastation caused by EFIC-backed transactions see especially Scott Hickey, "Risky Business", *UNSW Law Journal* 32(2) (2009): 587.

[6] AAJ et al., eds., *Let's Launch an Enquiry*, 70–77.

[7] See, e.g., Lee Buchheit and Mitu Gulati, "Odious Debts and Nation Building: When the Incubus Departs", *Maine Law Review* 60 (2008): 2478; James Feinerman, "Odious Debt, Old and New: The Legal Intellectual History of an Idea", *Law and Contemporary Problems* 70 (2007): 193; Robert Rasmussen, "Sovereign Debt Restructuring, Odious Debt, and the Politics of Debt Relief", *Law and Contemporary Problems* 70(2) (2007): 251; and Patricia Adams, "Chapter 17: The Doctrine of Odious Debts", in *Odious Debt: Loose Lending, Corruption, and the Third World's Environmental Legacy* (Toronto: Probe International, 1991), accessed August 2, 2010, http://www.eprf.ca/probeint/OdiousDebts/OdiousDebts/chapter17.html.

If under the domestic laws of the creditor country a sovereign debt would be unenforceable, it should be deemed illegitimate.[8] Technically, the domestic laws that govern lending do apply to the international transactions that fall within their jurisdiction. For example, the laws of the United States and United Kingdom (which have jurisdiction over the majority of international sovereign debts) will not enforce an agreement that involved unconscionable conduct or that facilitated illegal behaviour like corruption.[9] However, while these laws can and should apply to sovereign debt, traditionally they have been applied only to domestic transactions – for example, dealings between a mortgagor and bank or a vendor and purchaser. As it happens, unconscionability and corruption are common grounds on which many advocates argue sovereign debt should be deemed illegitimate and cancelled (there are many others that also find parallels in domestic laws). Therefore, the domestic laws that could be, but are not currently, used to find international transactions legally invalid can at the least provide suitable criteria for determining the legitimacy of sovereign debt for the purpose of a debt audit.[10]

II. CHARITY?

It is important not to lose sight of the fact that debt exchanges *are* sovereign debt transactions. A debt exchange is not simple debt cancellation (although it typically will involve an element of debt cancellation), nor is it true overseas aid. It is a modification of pre-existing sovereign debt agreements. If the existing debt is illegitimate, then future transactions that effectively 'trade' on that debt – even if the trade is for a development objective – are also illegitimate.

Those who argue for a doctrine of illegitimate or odious debt believe that such debt is, in legal terms, voidable or void. That is, either it should be cancelled at the option of the debtor when the illegitimacy is revealed or it never legally existed as debt in the first place. Any funds transferred in repayment of the debt were transferred in error and should be refunded. Either way, the effect for those who argue this doctrine is that illegitimate debt has no value. Therefore, it is not something that can be validly traded. This is worth

---

[8] I have developed this definition and argued for its practical application elsewhere. See Julia Roy, "A Domestic Law Approach to International Illegitimate and Odious Debt", forthcoming (copy on file with author).

[9] On unconscionable conduct see *Williams v Walker-Thomas Furniture Co.*, 350 F.2d 445 (D.C. Cir. 1965) and *Lloyds Bank Ltd v Bundy* [1975] QB 326. On corruption see *World Duty Free Co v Republic of Kenya* (ICSID Case No Arb/oo/7, 4 Oct. 2006).

[10] See also Chapter 3, Section IV, this volume.

repeating: illegitimate debt has no value, and so cannot be validly traded for anything – even for development assistance.

Borrowing from common law rules of contract – the laws of the United States and United Kingdom – an agreement requires valuable consideration to become a legally enforceable contract. Certain things are incapable of constituting valuable consideration, including the promise to do something already required by law or to not do something already prohibited by law.[11] If debt is illegitimate (according to the definition given earlier), it should not be legally enforceable. Therefore, the promise not to enforce a debt cannot be valid consideration, and the agreement fails to form a binding contract.

To put this another way, from the perspective of a debt-relief campaigner, if in a debt-exchange agreement the debt being 'traded' or 'reassigned' to a development project is illegitimate, then the creditor country is not contributing anything.[12] It had no legitimate entitlement to collect the debt, and so is giving nothing by agreeing not to take it. The creditor country does receive a benefit in the debt exchange, however. In many cases, the exchanged debt is called 'overseas development assistance' and is counted towards the creditor country's annual overseas development budget. The size of a government's or opposition party's pledged overseas development budget (large or small) is often an important feature in its election campaign. By 'exchanging' illegitimate debt and counting this amount towards its pledged overseas development budget, it actually *gains* the exchanged amount in its annual budget.

For example, if the creditor country forgives 50 million dollars of debt in exchange for the debtor country's promise to spend 25 million dollars on an agreed-upon development project, but the debts originating transaction was illegitimate, then the creditor country is agreeing not to collect 50 million dollars to which it had no legitimate entitlement and in exchange is gaining credit for 25 million dollars of overseas development assistance that it did not have to spend. The debtor country funds its own aid and gains only foreign instructions on how to spend it, and the creditor country gains 25 million dollars in its annual budget.

It follows that by public auditing of the debt to be exchanged, only debts to which the creditor country is legitimately entitled will be used. Debts found to be illegitimate may be cancelled. The debt-exchange transaction will then be what it is meant to be and what the creditor country is gaining credit for: a

---

[11]   *Collins v Godefroy* [1831] 1 BAd 950.
[12]   See by contrast the quote in Chapter 1, Section II, this volume, reflecting the more common perception that creditor countries give everything and receive nothing in debt exchanges.

transaction in which the creditor country is using its wealth and advantage to assist the development of a poor debtor country.

This is the technical and theoretical argument for mandatory debt audits. Unfortunately, it is of little practical use. It is based on the presumption that illegitimate debt should not be collected, that developing debtor countries should not be told how to spend their own money and that 'charity' should be scrutinised to ensure that it is and does as advertised. Such assumptions are not widely accepted. In the real world, illegitimate debt that is arguably legally void or voidable is never treated as such and is very rarely cancelled. Even if the debt is illegitimate, the debtor country is still sending repayments to the creditor country and getting no benefit in return. Unaudited debt exchanges are certainly an improvement on this situation.[13] So why persevere with a call for debt audits? There are a few good reasons.

III. AVOIDING THE AD HOC SOLUTION

The first is that debt exchanges are a way of answering public concern over unsustainable sovereign debt, without fixing the way sovereign debt works. In the same way that the Highly Indebted Poor Countries (HIPC) Initiative placated the huge global movement that arose around Jubilee 2000 – because on paper the debt relief offered sounded good to lay campaigners but in practice did not make much or enough of a difference to the vast majority of debtor countries with unsustainable debt levels – so debt exchanges sound like a great answer to unsustainable debt but neither acknowledge nor address the real source of the problem.

Creditor countries love ad hoc solutions: the Paris Club, the HIPC Initiative and now debt exchanges. Ad hoc solutions are cheap and controllable, and do not involve real change. The reality is that debt transactions are measured in billions while individual debt exchanges are measured in millions: they are not going to solve the debt problem. Certainly, a project does not have to solve a global program to still be useful to some. However, such a piecemeal approach can be used to legitimise the current sovereign lending system by appearing to offer a sustainable solution that avoids reform.

Insisting that the details of a debt exchange's originating transactions be disclosed before a debt exchange proceeds at the least ensures that the exchange is not propagating an unsound system. At the best, the exchange may become

---

[13] See, e.g., Chapter 11 by Jürgen Kaiser, this volume, which argues for a pragmatic approach to debt exchanges.

a vehicle for change by introducing legitimacy as a condition for any future dealings with sovereign debt.

IV. SECRECY AND EXPORT CREDIT

The second good reason for insisting on a debt audit is the role that export credit plays in creating sovereign debt, and so inevitably the role it plays in sovereign debt exchanges.

Almost every country in the world now has an Export Credit Agency (ECA). Despite playing a critical role, these agencies are largely unknown. Few textbooks on international trade and finance give them more than a passing mention. Yet ECA lending exceeds all multilateral development bank (MDB) and overseas development agency lending, has an impact on almost every international trade decision and *directly* finances at least one in every eight dollars of world trade.[14]

The ECA's primary role is to fill a gap in the market by providing insurance and finance to support and promote its country's exports in circumstances where the risk in the transaction is too high for commercial insurance or finance.[15] ECAs are also a mechanism through which some developed countries distribute loans and development assistance overseas.[16] Decisions made by and implemented through a nation's ECA are key components of that country's foreign relations and international trade policy.[17]

Export credit and insurance often create sovereign debt. ECAs may insure or lend to both the domestic exporter and foreign importer in a transaction or reinsure the private institution that provided these services in the first instance.[18] As a precondition, ECAs often insist that the importer government provide a counter-guarantee. If and when either party defaults, the ECA pays out the claim or loses the value of the loan repayments, and this amount becomes debt owed by the importing country's government.[19] In this way, *a transaction between two private entities is transformed into bilateral public debt.*

Export credit is incredibly secretive. ECAs are usually underwritten by taxpayer dollars, while being given extensive protections from standard public disclosure laws like freedom of information legislation. Sovereign debt-relief

[14] Delio E. Gianturco, *Export Credit Agencies: The Unsung Giants of International Trade and Finance* (Westport: Quorum Books, 2001), 1.
[15] Ibid., 2.
[16] See generally "Tied Aid Credits" in ibid., 33–34.
[17] Ibid., 1–2.
[18] Ibid., 2–3.
[19] Ibid., 116–117.

campaigners believe that loans underwritten by national governments and owed to the state are matters of public concern and that their essential details should be available for public scrutiny. They believe this is especially important given that the private commercial arena in which export credit transactions originate lends itself to conduct that would not as easily occur in the more heavily scrutinised arenas of public office. Most export credit agencies disagree, but there are legal arguments in favour of disclosure found in the existing common law of creditor countries like the United States and United Kingdom.

For example, the principle of responsible government, a hallmark of the Westminster System, 'necessarily impl[ies] a limitation on legislative and executive power to deny the electors and their representatives information concerning the conduct of the executive branch of government throughout the life of a federal parliament'.[20] Similar sentiments can be found in the broader American principles of representative government, and government for, by and of the people. Whether a country or its ECA is collecting repayments on or exchanging debts that would be deemed odious or illegitimate is arguably 'relevant information' required by the electorate to properly exercise its democratic oversight by freely electing representatives with 'relevant information about the functioning of government'.[21]

A. *Export Finance and Insurance Corporation*

Take, for example, Australia's export credit agency, Export Finance and Insurance Corporation (EFIC). Australia shares much of its common law traditions with the United States and United Kingdom, and so provides a suitable case for examination. EFIC has existed in various forms for more than 50 years and was established in its current form under the Export Finance and Insurance Corporation Act 1991 (Cth). Like many ECAs, EFIC occupies the grey legal area of a hybrid public–private body. It is wholly owned by the Commonwealth government and is underwritten by the Consolidated Revenue Fund but operates as a 'self-funded', statutory corporation.

EFIC's primary mission is to 'support the growth of Australian businesses internationally'.[22] It does this with two distinct accounts. The commercial account underwrites risks as a corporation and operates at a profit.[23] EFIC

[20] *Lange v Australian Broadcasting Corporation ('Lange')*, 145 ALR 96, 107.
[21] Ibid., 106.
[22] EFIC, "Our Mission and Values", accessed August 2, 2010, http://www.efic.gov.au/about/Pages/ourvisionmissionandvalues.aspx.
[23] EFIC, "Governance", accessed August 2, 2010, http://www.efic.gov.au/about/governance/Pages/EFICact.aspx.

lauds this as a reflection of strong risk management policy.[24] However, this is also a basic requirement of an ECA under the rules of the World Trade Organization.[25] If an ECA operates at a deficit or is otherwise unviable without government assistance that is 'inconsistent' or 'incomparable' with commercial available packages, it becomes a prohibited and/or actionable trade subsidy.[26]

The national interest account (NIA) is the means by which trade and development policy objectives, too risky for EFIC's commercial account, are achieved. The Minister for Trade may direct EFIC to enter the NIA into transactions considered to be in the national interest.[27] Any losses that result are indemnified by the Commonwealth,[28] and approximately one in three transactions supported by the NIA results in a claim.[29]

The NIA's current exposure is A$1.1 billion.[30] Details of this debt's originating transactions are secret.[31] This is controversial for a number of reasons. EFIC is indemnified by taxpayer dollars and is under the portfolio of a government minister. Also, what little *is* known of the transactions is suspect. Seventy-seven per cent of the A$1.1 billion exposure is owed by Indonesia.[32] These were loans supported by aid dollars under the now-defunct Development Import Finance Facility (DIFF) scheme[33] and were made at the time of the dictator, Suharto. Jubilee Australia and the International NGO Forum on Indonesian Development (INFID) have reason to believe that some transactions under

[24] Ibid.
[25] Rodney Short, "Export Credit Agencies, Project Finance, and Commercial Risk: Whose Risk Is It Anyway?" *Fordham International Law Journal* 24 (2004): 1371, 1372.
[26] "Agreement on Subsidies and Countervailing Measures", Annex 1A to the Marrakesh Agreement Establishing the World Trade Organisation, opened for signature April 15, 1994, 1867 UNTS 3 (entered into force January 1, 1995), Article 14: "Calculation of the Amount of a Subsidy in Terms of the Benefit to the Recipient, for the Purposes of Determining 'Benefit' within the Meaning of Articles 1: Definition of a Subsidy", Part II: "Prohibited Subsidies" and Part III: "Actionable Subsidies".
[27] EFIC, "Principal Accountabilities", accessed June 21, 2010, http://www.efic.gov.au/about/governance/framework/Pages/principalaccountabilities.aspx.
[28] Export Credit and Insurance Corporation Act 1991 (Cth) (EFIC Act), s 65.
[29] Department of Foreign Affairs and Trade (DFAT), *Annual Report* (2006–2007); DFAT, *Annual Report* (2005–2006); DFAT, *Annual Report* (2004–2005); and DFAT *Annual Report* (2003–2004). This figure is based on the value of exports supported on EFIC's NIA to value of claims paid on National Interest Account Business: 2006–2007, 46.2:14.7; 2005–2006, 20.7:6.7; 2004–2005, 30.3:10.7; 2003–2004, 20.2:9.1.
[30] EFIC, *Annual Report* (2008), 29, 19.
[31] EFIC has an exemption to the Freedom of Information Act 1982 (Cth) Sch 2, which it exercises fully.
[32] EFIC, *Annual Report* (2008), 19.
[33] Ibid.

the DIFF scheme were made for the wrong purpose, without due diligence, and/or may have involved or facilitated corruption in the Suharto regime.[34]

Like the debts recently cancelled by Norway,[35] the DIFF scheme was an aid and development program that tried to support the creditor's national industry. It did this by extending credit to aid recipients so that they could purchase Australian products for their programs. However, unlike Norway, Australia still collects payments for these projects from the aid recipients.

Of course, just because something is secret does not mean it is necessarily illegitimate. However, when Australian export credit is placed within its real world context, there is sufficient reason to expect that some of it facilitated or enabled official corruption. If the veil of secrecy were to be lifted from NIA transactions, there would be no need for this type of speculation. It seems uncontroversial to argue that Australian taxpayers have a right to know what has been done with their money.

B. Australia and Indonesia

Indonesia still owes Australia approximately A$800 million from export credit transactions entered into at the time of Suharto. Many of these were overseen or signed on the Indonesian side by ministers and officials with notoriously suspect records – and not all of the Australian companies involved have clean hands either.[36]

It is, of course, most unlikely that all or even the majority of export credit transactions between Australia and Indonesia at the time of Suharto were illegitimate because of corruption. But a few easily could have been. Certainly, A$75 million worth could have been. And A$75 million is the amount of debt Australia is forgiving in exchange for Indonesia's promise to spend A$37.5 million on health initiatives.[37] This is not to suggest an international sovereign debt conspiracy. Rather, this highlights that debt exchanges may be an attractive vehicle for quietly disposing of debts arising from transactions that would fall below the standards of equity and due diligence expected by the creditor and debtor country electorates should their details be made public.

---

[34] See, e.g., Jubilee Australia, "Illegitimate Debt", accessed June 24, 2010, http://www.jubilee-australia.org/illegitimate_debt.

[35] See Chapter 8, this volume.

[36] The Australian Wheat Board was among tens of Australian corporations that lodged affidavits stating that disclosure of details of the debts owed by Indonesia to Australia would reveal commercially sensitive information and negatively affect its commercial relationships.

[37] See Chapter 9, this volume.

V. BEST FOOT FORWARD

This leads to the final reason for insisting on debt audits as a precondition to legitimate debt exchanges, which is also the simplest. What is the harm in continuing the use of debt exchanges with the best foot forward, of implementing a best-practice model? The answer, for some, is that conducting a public audit will require disclosing commercially and internationally sensitive information, and that this will indeed cause harm.

In many countries, a freedom of information application will be the first step in beginning a citizen's audit of sovereign debt (including debt that may be exchanged). A recent application in Australia was rejected by EFIC on multiple grounds, including most prominently the fact that publicly disclosing the originating transactions of debts owed to Australia would compromise Australia's international relationships and reveal commercially sensitive information. Tens of Australian corporations that have benefited from ECA-backed transactions lodged supporting affidavits stating that disclosing details of transactions from as many as 20 or more years ago would reveal commercially sensitive information. The corporations listed undue advantage to competitors and interference with ongoing negotiations as the major detrimental consequences of disclosing this information.

On the one hand, it is arguable that a private corporation receiving insurance or finance from a government entity should be held publicly responsible to the extent that it has drawn on public funds (and in an export credit–backed transaction, only funds that have been drawn on will create sovereign debt). On the other hand, accepting the alleged right to commercial confidence, there is little evidence that if certain transaction details, from many years ago, were publicly disclosed it would result in the consequences outlined here.

It would be easy to prescribe measures that would limit any commercial interference from disclosure of the necessary information. For example, a *short-term* disclosure exemption of 4 or more years would prevent undue advantage to competitors or interference with ongoing negotiations. Provided a disclosure exemption is limited to only a few years, the governments and ECA would still be held accountable by an eventual audit. And a debt exchange, which is unlikely to be 'exchanging' debt less than 4 years old (usually it is at least 10 or 20 years old), could still be effectively audited.

Moreover, public disclosure of the details of older transactions is unlikely to have a negative impact on the international trade of individual banks and trading corporations or the international relations of creditor countries, unless the disclosed details reveal irresponsible lending practices, a lack of due diligence or the presence of corruption. In short, the only remaining answer to 'what is the harm of mandating an audit of debts prior to a debt exchange?' is that doing so may reveal illegitimate (and embarrassing) debts.

VI. CONCLUSION

Only legitimate debts should be traded or made the subject of future transactions. If debts are not legitimate, they should not be exchanged, and a debt audit is necessary to determining their legitimacy. But even in the 'real world', where the legitimacy of debt is rarely a factor in its repayment or exchange, there are many good reasons for conducting a public audit of debt to be exchanged: audits will prevent the use of exchanges to legitimate an unsound sovereign lending system and to hide embarrassing debts; they will shine a spotlight on the largely overlooked private export credit transactions that create much sovereign debt and whose secrecy lends itself to unsavoury practices; and they will ensure that debt exchanges are 'as advertised' – genuine development assistance in which benefit flows from wealthy developed countries to poorer developing countries.

Even simpler than this, what is there to lose by implementing a best-practice approach to debt exchanges? Performing basic due diligence and verifying that the sovereign debt transaction to be modified was legitimate and valid will only improve future lending practices and help introduce legitimacy as a criterion of acceptable lending and debt collection. It is not very much to ask.

11

How to Deal with Debt Illegitimacy in Relation to Debt Conversion: Reflections on an All-Too-Real Case

Jürgen Kaiser

Debt-relief campaigners have been looking at the instrument of debt exchanges with some mistrust. The reason behind this distrust is the very real danger that exchanges may be used to legitimise or even launder claims that have been found to be illegitimate and should therefore be cancelled without any further consideration of their sustainability or alternative uses.[1]

The proposition that illegitimate debt should not be eligible for a debt-for-development exchange is clear-cut and has a lot of common sense on its side, yet this chapter analyses it from the perspective of a debt-relief campaign that has been arguing for the cancellation of a clearly illegitimate debt. The case is about a (remaining) debt of some €200 million owed by Indonesia to Germany for the sale and refurbishment of 39 warships of the former German Democratic Republic navy between 1992 and 2003.[2]

I. WARSHIPS FOR INDONESIA, 1992–2004

In 1993 a large section of the navy of the former German Democratic Republic (GDR) was sold to Indonesia. In total, 39 corvettes, minesweepers, troop supply ships and landing crafts were sold for 20 million deutsche marks (DM) (€10 million/US$13 million), slightly more than their scrap value. Due to the bad condition of the vessels, the German government felt it was appropriate to also

---

[1] This has been summarized best by Marta Ruiz, "Debt Swaps for Development: Creative Solution or Smoke Screen?" (European Network on Debt and Development, October 2007), accessed August 2, 2010, http://www.eurodad.org/uploadedFiles/Whats_New/Reports/Debt_swaps_ENG(2).pdf.

[2] J. Kaiser and H. Kowsky, "German Claims on Indonesia", in *Skeletons in the Cupboard: Illegitimate Debt Claims of the G7*, European Network on Debt and Development, February 8, 2007, http://www.eurodad.org/uploadedFiles/Whats_New/Reports/Eurodad%20SkeletonsCupboardG7Report.pdf.

sell the modernisation of the vessels by German companies as well as the restoration of relevant navy infrastructure in Indonesia as part of the package. The restoration in Germany alone cost almost DM 475 million (€243 million/US$316 million). The deal was insured for a total of DM 700 million (€358 million/US$466 million) by Hermes AG, the German export credit agency.

In 2001 and 2003, Hermes AG granted further cover in connection with the sale of the vessels. In reply to a parliamentary question from the Socialist Party (PDS), the government stated that 'the overhaul of eight corvettes' motors came with two export guarantees (Hermes guarantees) of €24.2 million in total'. In order to finalise the transaction, which was controversial both in Germany and in Indonesia, a private agreement was made between the German and Indonesian Defence Ministries. This stated that 'the buyer undertakes to use the objects of the agreement solely for coastal protection, the safeguarding of the sea route and to combat smuggling'. This agreement was broken by the Indonesian side. There is reason to assume that the agreement was breached during the presidency of Suharto. Well-documented evidence, however, exists only for breaches during the reign of his successors Habibie, Wahid and Megawati Sukarnoputri. The vessels have been used in all major internal armed conflicts of the Archipelago.

In the summer of 1999, former East German Military (NVA) landing craft were used in the massacre in East Timor by Indonesian army-supported militia. In January 2000, four former NVA vessels took part in the sea blockade of the Maluku Islands. Parts of the Indonesian army worked closely with extremists, and their blockade allowed hundreds of thousands of people to be driven from their villages. In March 2000 a landing craft brought soldiers from the Kostrad Infantry battalions 515 and the Elite Kopassus unit to the contested province of Papua and to the offshore island of Biak. The same vessel had already brought troops to the island in July 1998; on July 6, 1998, these troops killed at least 8 and injured 37 people in a bloody suppression of a demonstration by unarmed civilians. In May 2003 another vessel landed troops and tanks in the vicinity of the port of Lhokseumawe in the civil war-ridden province of Aceh. In a raid, the troops killed 10 villagers, including a 12-year-old boy.

These Hermes insurances were granted after the terms of payments for the already existing Indonesian debts to the bilateral creditors of the Paris Club were restructured. Normally any real or rumoured insolvency excludes the granting of a Hermes insurance. This suggests that the interest in the lucrative order for the Mannheim Motorenwerke and MTU Friedrichshafen was so large that this regulation was ignored.

The servicing and restructuring of individual export credits and guarantees are not published in Germany. Therefore, the following account can give only a broad idea of the extent of the outstanding debt on this dubious transaction. We can assume that from 1993 until 1998 this debt was serviced in accordance with the German Development Cooperation's (KfW) normal financing terms and conditions. We can also assume that during this period less than one-third of the outstanding debt was paid off. In 1998, following the Asian financial crisis, Indonesia temporarily ceased payments on its bilateral foreign liabilities. In the same year – and then again in 2000 and 2002 – Indonesia restructured its debts at the Paris Club. In 2005, following the devastating impact of the tsunami disaster, Indonesia was able to achieve a temporary stay of payment on its external debt, which came to an end in late 2007 and further prolonged the repayment of the German claim. It can therefore be assumed that Germany is still owed at least €200 million of the original debt. This forms part of the total known nonconcessional German claims on Indonesia of €493 million at the end of 2007.

II. WHAT IS AN ILLEGITIMATE DEBT?

Indonesian and German nongovernmental organisations (NGOs) have jointly called upon the German government to cancel at least the portion of the debt that is still outstanding. The loans would in fact already have been paid back in full by Indonesia were not it for the three rounds of debt renegotiations that Indonesia underwent in the Paris Club in the aftermath of the Asian crisis of 1998–2002. However, this call met with two very distinct types of problems, which ultimately led the involved NGOs, erlassjahr.de and the International NGO Forum on Indonesian Development (INFID), to refine their respective demands in ways that make the case relevant to the present volume.

Ahead of a vibrant debate over sovereign debt illegitimacy in the German Parliament's development committee, erlassjahr.de had commissioned research into the case. The legal paper was based on the applicability of the classical 'odious debts' doctrine and was prepared by the Vienna law professor August Reinisch.[3] The doctrine had been developed by the Russian scholar Alexander Nahum Sack and taken up by modern authors such as Patricia Adams and Jeff King.[4] Its key elements are that a debt must be considered a

[3] August Reinisch, *Analysis of the Export of Warships from the Former GDR Navy to Indonesia between 1992–2004 in Terms of the Legitimacy of the German Entitlement ot Payment* (Vienna: erlassjahr.de, 2008).

[4] Alexander Nahum Sack, *Les effets des transformations des états sur leurs dettes publiques et autres obligations financièrs* (Paris: Recueil Sirey, 1927); Patricia Adams, *Odious Debts: Loose Lending, Corruption and the Third World's Environmental Legacy* (Toronto: Earthscan, 1991); J. King, "Odious Debt: The Terms of the Debate", *North Carolina Journal of International and Commercial Regulation* 32 (2007): 605–667.

personal debt of the respective rulers rather than the contracting state, if three conditions are met:

1. The debt must not have benefited the population of the debtor country.
2. There must have been a lack of informed consent by the population to the taking out of the loan (which would regularly happen through a due constitutional process).
3. The creditor must have been aware of both these factors at the time of signing the loan contract or must have deliberately ignored the obvious.

The doctrine is one of the narrowest concepts of debt illegitimacy presently under consideration. Other concepts put the bar far lower and start to consider a claim illegitimate, and hence unrecoverable, if just certain aspects of the project or the financing process have been dubious.[5] The reason for selecting the odious-debts doctrine lay in the immediate political need to exert as much pressure as possible on creditors to force a cancellation of this debt. This would hardly have been achievable on the basis of a more voluntary and loosely defined concept.

Professor Reinisch's paper concluded that the doctrine was indeed applicable to the present case and provided a basis for a unilateral cancellation of the German claim. However, dialogues with the German government and arguments brought forward in its defence indicated that there was no way to substantially threaten the creditor with a legal process that would ultimately void the German claims. This was due to the fact that the odious-debts doctrine is not a binding legal doctrine, as well as the questionable applicability of some of its criteria. For instance, it was unclear whether the Suharto regime was indeed unconstitutional and that therefore there was no informed consensus of the Indonesian people as required by the doctrine.

As a consequence, further arguments regarding the case focused on the violation of *ius cogens*, compelling norms of international law. *Ius cogens* refers to norms that have to be respected anywhere on the globe as undeniable

---

[5] See, e.g., J. Hanlon, *Defining Illegitimate Debt: Understanding the Issues* (Oslo: Norwegian Church Aid, 2002). Hanlon sets up a veritable laundry list of issues that may have gone wrong with a loan, concluding that irrespective of creditors' individual responsibilities in each case, they all could make a claim. Ben-Shahr and Gulati in turn try to translate the de factor shared responsibility among debtors and creditors into a quantitative benchmark for debt cancellation according to each side's level of responsibilities for such misuses. See Omri Ben-Shahar and G. Mitu Gulati, "Partially Odious Debts? A Framework for an Optimal Liability Regime", *Law & Contemporary Problems* 70, No. 4 (2007): 47–81.

principles of peaceful coexistence among peoples and states. *Ius cogens* again is a very narrow norm, which includes only very few principles:

- prohibition of wars of aggression;
- prohibition of torture;
- prohibition of crimes against humanity; and
- the right of peoples to self-determination.

It is being discussed among international law scholars and policy makers whether other norms, for instance, the UN's human rights charter, should also be considered in its entirety as *ius cogens* norms. In the present case, Germany evidently supported a war of aggression by Indonesia against the people of East Timor, which at the time of the sale was still officially considered by Germany to be a territory of Portugal, a member of the European Union. This argument was considered irrefutable by German authorities. However, despite the clear-cut legal case, neither the German nor the Indonesian NGOs were in any position to take the German government to court in that case, which is the second problem: that even with a clear-cut case, the cancellation of illegitimate debt may not be achieved by any legal means.

III. CANCELLATION OF ILLEGITIMATE DEBT BY LEGAL MEANS

In the context of global financial relations, the cancellation of illegitimate debt has been confined to very few cases in history. In reality the key actors in a process that would question creditors' claims are the governments of the affected countries. Those governments, however, either out of ignorance or due to political pressure from rich creditors/donors, do not tend to engage in litigation. Consequently, civil society organisations, which had an interest in stopping the Indonesian people from paying for the bullets that had been fired at them, had to engage in politicking on an issue they consider a legal and ethical one. But how to do that in any meaningful way? Is there any way forward, other than pointing time and again to the scandalous nature of the debt?

NGOs had to accept that even the most compelling legal arguments would not ground an effective claim and be reminded that sovereign debt cancellation is almost never a legal issue and nearly always a political one. An institution like the Paris Club, which handles sovereign debt owed to governments, has no legal foundation at all. The Club, as well as the World Bank and the International Monetary Fund, as masters and commanders of the global debt-relief Highly Indebted Poor Country and Multilateral Debt Relief Initiatives, deal with individual countries according to self-determined rules (and at times beyond the rules) and according to the institutions' or Paris Club members' political preferences.[6]

In order for the claim to be advanced, it had to be negotiated. As Germany has a broad range of experiences in exchanging claims with Indonesia, a debt exchange of this particular claim was suggested by both sides, the NGOs as well as (albeit timidly) the German Ministry of Development Co-operation. This was for both sides a difficult endeavour: NGOs would have to work around their principle of not accepting any illegitimate debt exchanges. The Ministry would be heading towards confrontation with the German Treasury, because nonconcessional claims had so far been excluded from the German debt-for-development conversion program.[7]

For the NGOs, however, while developing a strong conversion proposal, it became clear that a debt exchange might not be just the unavoidable realpolitik compromise it first appeared to be, but rather be preferable to the straight cancellation of the debt. The call for the cancellation of an illegitimate debt treats the state, the government and the people of an indebted country as an entity: whatever benefits one is assumed to benefit all. However, in places like Indonesia the reality is slightly more complex: when erlassjahr.de discussed the present cancellation with NGOs working on human rights issues in Indonesia, they were originally opposed to the idea. These NGOs believed that there was a real danger that cancellation of those claims would merely add insult to injury for the victims of the atrocities committed with the help of the former German warships by the Indonesian military. The country had undergone a very piecemeal regime change since the end of the Suharto dictatorship. Many of the military commanders were still in power and would thus profit from a unilateral cancellation of the German claim. The Indonesian military budget and the financing of the state security apparatus at large are not transparent. Any substantive control by Germany or any third party over the use of the resources freed by the debt cancellation was extremely unlikely. In short, on top of German complicity in committing the atrocities, the cancellation would ultimately mean the perpetrators had got the weapons for

---

[6] J. Kaiser, "Debt Management á la Louis XVI: A Short Promenade Through Program and Practice of the Paris Club", accessed August 2, 2010, http://www.erlassjahr.de/english/debt-management-a-la-louis-xiv518.html.

[7] Germany has had an ambitious debt-conversion program since 1993. Funded at present with an annual €200m, it allows for the cancellation of claims due from German development co-operation loans, provided that the debtor government invests between 50% and 100% of the cancelled amount into mutually agreed-upon development projects. For details see http://bmz.bund.de.

free. As a result, erlassjahr.de drafted a proposal for a debt exchange to fund a 'Reconstruction and Reconciliation Fund', with or without a relief element.

IV. GERMAN–INDONESIAN RECONCILIATION FUND FOR VICTIMS OF VIOLENCE UNDER THE DICTATORSHIP

A. *Background*

During most of their existence, the Republic of Indonesia and the Federal Republic of Germany have developed strong political, economic and cultural linkages. Very often co-operation has been fruitful, at times even setting standards for North–South co-operation. Other aspects of the relationship appear in a more critical light. The proposal for a Reconstruction and Reconciliation Fund aims to harness one of those mechanisms and experiences of positive co-operation and turn it into an investment in a better future for Indonesians in a democratised society.

B. *The Proposal*

Instead of continued repayment to Germany, the government of Indonesia shall stop the outstanding payments on the warship sale. This will allow the Indonesian government to rather make the outstanding annual instalments towards a newly created Reconciliation Fund.

This proposed debt exchange follows the concept of earlier concessional debt-exchange experiences between Germany and Indonesia. Those debt exchanges have involved governmental as well as nongovernmental entities and most recently even an independent agency, namely the Global Fund to Fight Aids, Malaria and Tuberculosis under its Debt2Health program, as discussed in Chapter 3.

The Reconciliation Fund shall receive the regular instalments, including interest on outstanding principal on the (rescheduled) German claims related to the warship sale. It shall be administered by an Administrative Committee, composed of one representative each of the government of Indonesia, the German Embassy in Jakarta, Indonesian human rights organisations and German or international human rights organisations.

Members will be nominated by the two governments based on proposals made by respective NGOs. The Committee decides by majority on the financing of projects, which serve to:

(a) provide damage compensation to civilian victims of civil strife and repression between 1992 and 2000 in Indonesia, in cases where no compensation has yet taken place; and

(b) support projects of non-governmental entities which aim at reconciliation after the years of conflict and at improving harmony in a multi-ethnic society; specific emphasis will be on post-traumatic support and legal support to victims where appropriate.

Support will be given in the form of grants under normal procedures as applicable by the German development co-operation. Eligible for application are:

(1) individuals, public entities, such as municipalities or communities of individuals, which can demonstrate to have been affected by human rights violations during the times of armed conflict; and
(2) non-governmental institutions, Indonesian or International, which are running programs in support of purpose line (b).

C. Precedence

While the proposal would be pioneering in making conversion funds available for victims of civil strife, the cancellation of questionable claims because of assumed creditor co-responsibility is not without precedence. In 2006 the Norwegian government unilaterally, and unrelated to any existing debt-relief scheme, decided to cancel claims on five countries because of evident creditor co-responsibility for failed project financing.[8] Norway's move has been highly praised by civil society, as well as the parties involved, and has served to strengthen amicable relationships between the debtor and creditor countries.

V. CONCLUSION

The Reconciliation Fund so far has not moved beyond the status of a civil society organisation proposal, despite the promising start of talks with Germany. The reason for this has firstly, and primarily, been the inability of Indonesian NGOs to formally engage the Indonesian government in a debate over a possible debt exchange. INFID put a lot of effort into organising a conference on the issue in April 2009 in Jakarta, in order to clearly demonstrate all the detrimental aspects of the sale. However, members of the government largely abstained from attending. Treasury officials, who were subsequently contacted by INFID and German NGOs, requested that the initiative for such an innovative solution come from the German side. Even for German debt campaigners who have been working to exert pressure on German governments for

---

[8] For details see K. Abildsnes, *Why Norway Took Creditor Responsibility: The Case of the Ship Export Campaign* (Oslo: Norwegian Debt Campaign, 2007).

decades, this seemed overly ambitious. Reluctance to act on the part of the Indonesian officials was additionally fuelled by the fairly comfortable fiscal situation of the Indonesian government, even in the context of the global financial crisis.

Secondly, progress was stalled by the change of government in Germany in the autumn of 2009. The new centre–right government consists of exactly the same party coalition that was in power when the warships were sold. Thus, the willingness of the former Development Minister, who had been a prominent critic of the boat sale in the early 1990s, to reopen the case could no longer be relied upon. Such are the practical challenges facing the proposal.

This approach is even less likely than 'normal' debt-exchange programs to ever lead to large-scale debt reductions. While debt conversion is necessarily a narrow and focussed instrument, as shown elsewhere in this volume, the conversion of illegitimate debt is even more so, due to the necessarily narrow definition of illegitimate debt.

The proposal implies an undeniable interference with the debtors' sovereignty, based as it is on a debt that proponents themselves consider illegitimate. Particularly in Latin America the debate over debt illegitimacy has provided an astonishing revival of sovereignty-based and isolationist concepts,[9] and the proposal goes exactly the opposite way. It is a product of the commitment of external NGOs to defend the interests of the victims of human rights abuses against the legitimate government of the indebted country. This raises a broad range of questions on state philosophy and sovereignty, which have all been brushed aside by the proponents of the Reconciliation Fund for very pragmatic reasons, particularly the fact that the illegitimate debt will simply continue to be serviced in the absence of an innovative political initiative, as well as the deliberate rejection of the identity between state and people, which is a cornerstone of the above-mentioned sovereignty-based approaches to debt illegitimacy.

The proposal pays regard to the very real distinction between the interests of the people, who have been victimised, and their government. It is the first knowing attempt to put the intrinsic potential of this debt-conversion approach to use for dealing with an illegitimate debt.

The proposal allows elements like a tailor-made redemption rate for the consideration of the shared responsibility for debt illegitimacy between debtors

[9] As an example see the report of the Ecuadorean debt audit commissions, Internal Auditing Commission for the Public Credit of Ecuador (CAIC), "Final Report of the Integral Auditing of Ecuadorian Debt" (Quito, 2008), accessed August 2, 2010, http://www.eurodad.org/upload-edFiles/Newsletters/Resumen_Ejecutivo-ENGLISH%20VERSION%20RELACIONES%20EXTERIORES%20(2).pdf.

and creditors, as well as the debtor's capacity to pay. While the simple and straightforward call for a cancellation of illegitimate debt allows only for the acceptance or rejection of debt illegitimacy, the quantitative considerations, which are part and parcel of any debt conversion, allow for an appropriate balanced solution regarding a given loan. It may lead to a nearly complete cancellation with just a symbolic payment being made by the debtor, which would ultimately allow the creditor government to maintain that it came to a negotiated solution accepting its co-responsibility for any misuse of the funds, without accepting sole and outright responsibility – and any consequential legal consequences. At the other end of the spectrum, a debt exchange's redemption rate could be 100% (and therefore the debt-cancellation element of an exchange could be zero); this would allow creditors to claim that they had not accepted any charge of misbehaviour on their part (or their predecessors'), while the debt exchange as such would still have a huge and visible impact on repairing damage that had been caused by the creditors' money in the first place.[10]

The proposal allows for a face-saving consideration and a practical way of dealing with an illegitimate debt. It should be recalled that debt illegitimacy, despite all efforts by academics and civil society, has regularly been ignored by creditor as well as borrower governments keen to cover up the sins of the past. This again has had far-reaching consequences for present and future borrowing and lending policies: if all sides assume that nobody will reveal the responsibilities for failed, corrupt and misused loans, more responsible lending will not become the norm. Given the huge amounts of new lending to be provided to Southern governments through the rescue packages agreed upon by the G20, this is all the more worrisome. Any demonstration – be it through sanctioning or negotiated settlements – of lenders having to assume responsibility for the quality of their lending to low- and middle-income countries is badly needed if we are to avoid a repetition of the past debt crisis of the 1980s and 1990s. Eliminating illegitimate claims through debt conversion can be one small stepping stone on this road.

---

[10] It should be recalled that even in its pioneering unilateral cancellation of claims out of its failed ship export campaign in 2006, the Norwegian government never accepted that those claims had ultimately been 'illegitimate'. Instead it accepted its co-responsibility as a creditor for the failed financing.

12

The Human Rights Dimension in Exchanges

Gillian Moon

There are two principal aspects to the human rights dimension in debt-for-development exchanges. The first relates to the beneficial potential of the exchanges: they can be a useful mechanism to enhance the realisation of human rights, especially economic and social rights. The second arises when a particular development project or the broader scheme under which it operates has an adverse impact on some human rights in the debtor country.

Development is a variable and contested concept. That said, improving people's social and economic situation, by moving towards higher levels of human health, education, employment and standards of living generally, constitutes a large part of the process of development under most definitions. Likewise, improvements in systems of law and governance, such as greater participation in government, guarantees of free and fair elections and impartial systems of law enforcement, form a large part of most conceptualisations of development. These understandings of development focus on improvements in human well-being, as distinct from, say, narrower notions of industrial or technological development.

Human development goals of this kind are also guaranteed human rights under international law. Indeed, there is a high level of interaction and interdependence between the process of development and the realisation of human rights. This chapter considers debt-for-development exchanges from this perspective. It looks, first, at the human rights obligations of states in the context of development and at what is meant by the term 'development'. It then explores the capacity for debt-for-development exchanges to support or undermine human rights and considers whether the human rights–based approach to development might give useful guidance to parties negotiating exchanges.

I. HUMAN RIGHTS OBLIGATIONS OF STATES IN THE CONTEXT OF DEVELOPMENT

As with any activity, countries embarking on development initiatives under debt exchanges must comply with the obligations imposed on them under the human rights treaties to which they are signatories. The principal sources of states' international human rights obligations are the International Covenant on Economic, Social and Cultural Rights (ICESCR) and the International Covenant on Civil and Political Rights (ICCPR). The human rights guaranteed under ICESCR include the rights to education, the highest possible standard of physical and mental health, an adequate standard of living (including adequate food, water and shelter), work and social security and cultural expression.[1] The corresponding obligation imposed on states under ICESCR is to take progressive steps towards the realisation of these rights, to the maximum of available resources.[2] Although this seems a somewhat inchoate and deferrable obligation, the ICESCR does include some immediate obligations too. A state cannot be passive: at all times, it must actively take expeditious, deliberate, concrete and targeted steps to improve realisation of the rights.[3] The state must also ensure that whatever realisation of rights is occurring takes place on a nondiscriminatory basis.[4] Finally, a state must not take retrogressive steps regarding rights, except in the most dire circumstances and temporarily.[5]

By contrast, states' obligations under ICCPR are expressed in terms that are immediate and absolute ('states shall'), without any express deference to resource constraints. The human rights that must be ensured include the right to life, to freedom of movement, to freedom of thought, conscience, religion and expression, to associate and form trades unions and to take part in public affairs, for example by voting.[6] The ICCPR also guarantees a number of freedoms, including freedom from slavery, torture, arbitrary arrest and incitement

---

[1] International Covenant on Economic, Social and Cultural Rights 1966 (ICESCR), articles 13, 12, 11, 6–8, 9 and 15.

[2] ICESCR, article 2(1).

[3] UN Committee on Economic, Social and Cultural Rights, General Comment No. 3, "The Nature of States Parties' Obligations", para. 2.

[4] ICESCR, article 2(2). The unlawful grounds are 'race, colour, sex, language, religion, political or other opinion, national or social origin, property, birth or other status'. A further ground is disability.

[5] UN Committee on Economic, Social and Cultural Rights, General Comment No. 3, para. 9.

[6] International Covenant on Civil and Political Rights 1966 (ICCPR), articles 6, 12, 18–19, 22 and 25.

to racial hatred.[7] Like the ICESCR, the ICCPR stipulates that states carry out their obligations in a nondiscriminatory manner.[8]

A glance through existing debt-for-development schemes reveals that they concern themselves almost exclusively with social and economic development, as opposed to political or governance-related development. The two exceptions are schemes that exclude from participation debtor countries which have not made commitments to protect human rights or are engaging in gross violations of human rights[9] – usually unlawful state killings, torture and the like – and schemes intended to show support for a way of life that facilitates democratic, political and civil freedoms.[10]

Debtor countries negotiating debt-for-development exchanges will ordinarily be signatories to ICESCR and ICCPR. With the focus of most debt-for-development schemes being on key economic and social fields like health, education, poverty reduction and rural livelihoods, debtor countries bring to the negotiations legal obligations to move forward, without retrogression, in the realisation of economic, social and cultural rights and to do so in a way that is not discriminatory.

In the current context, this latter requirement of nondiscrimination is intended to ensure that the benefits of new initiatives are not restricted by gender, race, religion or other irrelevant difference. It also has the important purpose of ensuring that historically disadvantaged groups, typically women and minorities, are not *indirectly* excluded from the benefits.[11] In fact, the non-discrimination obligation in the principal conventions extends to a requirement that states take positive steps to ensure that historically disadvantaged groups are not left behind the more privileged sectors of the population in the process of progressive realisation of rights.[12] The obligations are especially

---

[7]   ICCPR, articles 8, 7, 9 and 20.
[8]   ICCPR, article 2(1). The unlawful grounds are the same as those under ICESCR.
[9]   Examples include the Italian Measure for the Stabilisation of Public Finance 1977 and Measure to Reduce External Debt of Lower Income and Highly-Indebted Countries 2000; the US Tropical Forests Conservation Act 1998 (TFCA).
[10] See, e.g., the 1991 'debt-for-democracy' exchange by Paris Club countries of a large amount of Poland's debt; S. Freeland and R. Buckley, "Debt-for-Development Exchanges: Using External Debt to Mitigate Environmental Damage in Developing Countries", University of New South Wales Faculty of Law Research Series, Year 2010, Paper 14, 10.
[11] The prohibition on discrimination in the ICCPR and ICESCR has been interpreted to include a prohibition on indirect discrimination.
[12] There is an obligation on states to take positive action to correct historical discrimination. This is explicit in the Convention on the Elimination of All Forms of Racial Discrimination 1966 (CERD) and the Convention on the Elimination of All Forms of Discrimination Against Women 1976 (CEDAW), each convention anticipating that states will introduce temporary special measures for the purpose of securing advancement of certain groups and aimed at accelerating de facto equality; CERD, article 1(4), and CEDAW, article 4.

strong in international law in relation to racial discrimination, the prohibition on which is widely considered to be a peremptory norm.[13]

A. *The Right to Development*

The often-cited 'right to development' is not expressly recognised in the ICCPR or ICESCR as a human right, or as a clear legal obligation imposed on states.[14] Although a resolution adopting the Declaration on the Right to Development was passed by the United Nations General Assembly in 1986,[15] the Declaration has not progressed to treaty stage and seems unlikely to do so in the near future. In part, this is because it is unclear what the precise meaning of the right would be and, as a matter of law, who the right bearers and the obligation holders would be, if such a right were to be expressly recognised in international law. A further reason the Declaration is unlikely to become a treaty is that there is much disagreement as to what is meant by the term 'development' as a process or, more precisely, what steps ought to be taken in order to achieve development as an outcome.

B. *Differing Ideas about Development*

Development is a contested and politicised field. What Bjorn Hettne and Robert Potter call 'development thinking'[16] has been dominated for at least the past quarter-century by market-oriented thinking focussed on development as primarily an economic process, measured by rates of economic growth. Development economists favouring this approach seek to improve welfare in developing countries through their fuller integration into the global economy. The influence of this approach does not appear to have been particularly strong

---

[13] The predominant view is that the prohibition on sex discrimination has not yet acquired the status of a peremptory norm of internal law. Moreover, a large number of reservations have been entered by signatory countries to CEDAW, significantly reducing its reach in practice.

[14] The African Charter on Human and Peoples' Rights 1981 is the only instrument that expressly recognises a right to development; article 22.

[15] United Nations General Assembly, Declaration on the Right to Development (A/RES/41/128) (1986). The United States was the only UN member country to vote against its adoption by the General Assembly.

[16] The study of development became a discipline in its own right after the Second World War, and today there are many perspectives on how to stimulate and advance development, an area of enquiry that Bjorn Hettne and Robert Potter have named 'development thinking'. See B. Hettne, *Development Theory and the Three Worlds: Towards an International Political Economy of Development* (Essex: Longman Group Ltd, 1995); R. Potter, "Theories, Strategies and Ideologies of Development", in *The Companion to Development Studies*, eds. V. Desai and R. B. Potter (London: Hodder Arnold, 2002), 61–62.

in the selection of development projects negotiated in debt exchanges to date, possibly because the majority have focussed more on environmental protection and conservation than on traditional development activities. Some more recent debt-for-development exchanges do, however, display the influence of this type of development thinking. For example, the US Tropical Forests Conservation Act 1998 (TFCA) sets out eligibility criteria that relate to the economic policies of the debtor countries, including having established a relatively open investment regime.[17] The 2006 Italy–Kenya debt-for-development scheme seeks to foster economic growth and increase employment, amongst other goals.[18]

Nongovernmental international aid agencies and the development community overall have opposed the dominance of the narrow, economically focussed approach that has long guided the provision of official development and financial assistance by the industrialised countries and international agencies. They have fought to substitute, instead, an approach that views development as a broader social and cultural process, in which economic development is but one part and in which there is an emphasis on equitable distribution of the benefits of development. The human rights community has stood beside the aid and development community in this struggle. Indeed, the 1986 Development Declaration can be seen as a political move by the United Nations to place an expansive, equality-focussed definition of development in the key international instrument:

> [Development is] a comprehensive economic, social, cultural and political process, which aims at the constant improvement of the well-being of the entire population and of all individuals on the basis of their active, free and meaningful participation in development and in the fair distribution of benefits resulting therefrom.[19]

This definition presents development as a broad process extending well beyond the economic sphere to include beneficial change in society, culture and the political realm. The definition leaves relatively open the question of what steps should be taken to achieve development as an outcome, but it does suggest norms that should guide whatever is done, such as that it be participatory, inclusive and equitable.

[17] US Tropical Forests Conservation Act 1998, para. 805(a)(2).
[18] See Co-operazione Italiana allo Sviluppo, accessed August 2, 2010, http://www.cooperazioneallosvilluppo.esteri.it.
[19] Preamble to Declaration on the Right to Development. The preamble further states that 'the human person is the central subject of the development process and that development policy should therefore make the human being the main participant and beneficiary of development'.

With this Declaration, the UN also intended to tie the development process tightly to the realisation of human rights. Article 1(1) declares an inalienable human right to development. It also adds to the definition that, through the right to development, 'every human person and all peoples are entitled to ... [a form of] development in which all human rights and fundamental freedoms can be fully realized'. Thus, the Development Declaration both identifies development as a human right in itself and defines it as a broad, participatory, inclusive and equitable process through which all people can claim the realisation of their human rights and fundamental freedoms.

Debt-for-development negotiations cannot avoid taking place in the context of this political struggle over how development should be defined and approached – a struggle that is ongoing in development theory, policy and practice. They also cannot avoid taking place in the context of the very close relationship between the process of development and the realisation of human rights, particularly in the operational sense. To date, debt-for-development exchanges have varied in their human rights impacts.

II. THE POTENTIAL FOR DEBT EXCHANGES TO ENHANCE HUMAN RIGHTS

Debt exchanges can divert government funds into human rights–enhancing development initiatives, such as building public schools or medical services, thus supplementing national public expenditure and official aid funding in these sectors. A great improvement would be the automatic exclusion of 'odious debt'[20]; such debt should be written off, releasing funds for general public expenditure by developing country governments *in addition to* any funds released through debt exchanges. Debt exchanges may also be beneficial when they are developed in line with well-designed, human rights–supporting national development programs of debtor nations, such as the German debt-for-development exchanges in Jordan and Indonesia.[21] Debt-for-development exchanges also promote human rights–enhancing development when funding favours initiatives which *expressly* support the realisation of human rights.

Some debt-for-development schemes impose rights-supporting prior conditions for any negotiation of exchanges. For example, the Italian scheme requires that a prospective recipient nation be actively working towards enhanced social and human development, particularly poverty reduction,

---

[20] The term 'odious debt' is used here to refer to debt that is incurred not for the benefit of a country as a whole and its people but for that of a despotic regime.

[21] See Kathrin Berensmann, *Debt Swaps: An Appropriate Instrument for Development Policy? An Example of German Debt Swaps* (Bonn: German Development Institute, 2007).

that it has made significant commitments towards human rights protection, presumably including signing and ratifying the principal human rights
treaties, and that it has renounced war as a means of solving controversy.[22]
Similarly, the US TFCA requires that an eligible developing country have a
democratically elected government, a track record of co-operation in the elimination of international drug trafficking and international terrorism and not
be a gross or consistent violator of human rights.[23]

Clearly, debt-for-development exchanges, particularly those that require a
track record of reasonable human rights compliance or that direct funds to
projects which positively support the realisation of human rights, have the
potential to be beneficial. So why do debt-for-development schemes sometimes work against the realisation of rights? What pitfalls and traps might
cause otherwise beneficial debt exchanges to affect human rights adversely?

III. THE POTENTIAL FOR DEBT EXCHANGES TO
ADVERSELY AFFECT HUMAN RIGHTS

It is highly unlikely that a debt-for-development scheme would be framed
so as deliberately and directly to negate human rights. On the other hand,
not many schemes expressly support the realisation of human rights either.
Where human rights are mentioned in the terms of a negotiated exchange,
it is usually in the context of excluding countries with records of egregious
human rights violations from schemes. For example, the US Enterprise for the
Americas Initiative 1991 (EAI) imposes a prior condition that debtor countries
'not engage in a consistent pattern of gross violations of internationally recognized human rights'.[24]

Even those schemes that are evidently intended to support the realisation
of social rights, such as exchanges tying project funding to education and
health initiatives, may have some adverse rights consequences. Projects may,
for example, incidentally entrench existing discrimination and disadvantage
by exacerbating economic and social disparities. Where discrimination and
inequality are entrenched, there is the likelihood that new initiatives will,
so to speak, build on the same grid unless they are deliberately and carefully
structured so as not to do so.

Moreover, adverse human rights consequences may result from prior
conditions applied in some debt-exchange schemes, particularly where

---

[22] See note 9 of this chapter.
[23] TFCA, para 805(a)(1), referring to para 703(a)(1)–(5) and (7) of the US Foreign Assistance
      Act 1961.
[24] Enterprise for the Americas Initiative, 22 U.S.C. § 2430b(a)(4).

the conditions are directed more towards advancing aspects of the creditor country's own external affairs policies or commercial interests than advancing human rights in the debtor country. Both the US TFCA and the US EAI, for example, require that a developing country has instituted 'major investment reform' or has made 'significant progress towards an open investment regime' before a debt exchange will be considered.[25] While the United States will no doubt benefit from this condition, a developing country deregulating and liberalising its investment laws in order to qualify for a debt exchange may experience adverse human rights consequences from the adjustment that it is not in a financial or regulatory position to constrain.

This is not to suggest that requiring investment reform as a prior condition will necessarily affect human rights adversely. The UN High Commissioner for Human Rights has noted:

> It is difficult to generalise the effects of investment [reform] on the enjoyment of human rights.... Today, most developing countries seek investment as a means of promoting development.... From a human rights perspective, it is important ... to attract investment and promote national development.[26]

She added, however, that it is equally important 'to achieve economic, social, cultural and political development in which all human rights and fundamental freedoms can be fully realised'.[27] She also warned that, while

> well-managed investment has the potential to promote and protect human rights, [a] human rights approach emphasises that [investment reform] ... should not go so far as to compromise state action and policy to promote and protect human rights. To the extent that investment agreements concern human rights issues, *states have a duty to regulate.*[28] [emphasis added]

The duty, she explained, requires that states retain the capacity to regulate some forms of investment, 'particularly short-term and volatile investments' with the capacity to 'reduce the available resources needed to promote human rights,' and that they retain the flexibility to use certain economic development measures, to withdraw deregulation commitments in the light of experience and to introduce new regulations to promote and protect human rights.[29]

---

[25] Enterprise for the Americas Initiative, 7 USC § 1738 (1994), § 1738b(a)(3); TFCA, para 805(a)(2).

[26] Report of the UN High Commissioner for Human Rights, "Human Rights, Trade and Investment", E/CN.4/Sub.2/2003/9, 2 July 2003, 2, 8 para. 6, accessed August 2, 2010, http://www.unhchr.ch/Huridocda/Huridoca.nsf/e06a5300f90fa0238025668700518ca4/9b2b4fed82c88ee2c1256d7b002e47da/$FILE/G0314847.pdf.

[27] Ibid.

[28] Ibid., 3.

[29] Ibid., 3–4.

While it is unclear exactly what investment reforms are required under the TFCA and the EAI, either scheme could potentially trigger adverse human rights consequences in a developing country seeking debt relief through an exchange.

A. *Economic, Social and Cultural Rights*

In addition to the foregoing general concern about the regulatory impact of investment reforms required under debt exchanges, a particular concern arises regarding essential services following deregulation and liberalisation of investment. Most economic and social rights are 'delivered' through the medium of services, including health, education, water and sanitation, and income safety nets. Investment liberalisation often results in at least partial privatisation of such services, where they have previously been government owned, frequently using the structure of public–private partnerships. Human rights concerns arise when newly privatised essential services are operated on a more commercial basis than in the past. The introduction or raising of fees and/or eroding of universal service obligations that often follow privatisation may make essential services less accessible to the poor (the majority of whom in developing countries are women and minorities) or to those in remote areas and may have adverse human rights consequences. Project designers need to be aware that regulatory changes can result in new barriers to access arising. Indeed, it may be that relatively simpler projects, which reduce access barriers for *existing* essential services, would deliver greater development gains than schemes that, while increasing the overall quantity of essential service provision through greater private participation, end up pricing the most vulnerable consumers out of the market.

B. *Civil and Political Rights*

It is unlikely that a debt-for-development scheme would be structured so as to violate civil or political rights directly. More likely is that a scheme would simply not concern itself either with the human rights impacts of its projects or with whether the debtor state intended to pay appropriate attention to compliance with its ICCPR obligations in implementing those projects. An example might be development projects that adversely affect people who were not adequately consulted. ICCPR article 25 requires that citizens 'shall have the right and the opportunity [without discrimination] and without unreasonable restrictions, ... to take part in the conduct of public affairs, directly or through freely chosen representatives'. This article has been interpreted to include, if not a right to participate *directly* in *all* public affairs (which includes local decision making concerning, e.g., development infrastructure and employment projects), then at least a right to participatory state practices that are not in contrast or conflict with article 25.[30] Either way, debtor states are obliged to respect and protect this right, including when they are negotiating and implementing debt-for-development projects.

C. Indigenous Rights

A problem may arise when a development project interferes with the customary practices or statutory entitlements of the indigenous peoples of an area. Probably the starkest example of this occurred in connection with the 1987 debt-for-conservation exchange involving the Beni Biosphere Reserve in Bolivia and a US-based nongovernmental organisation, Conservation International, the negotiations for which failed to include the local indigenous people. The exchange extinguished any statutory opportunity for the Moxo Indians to claim legal recognition of their traditional land rights over the Chiamese Forest.[31]

Under the various domestic laws currently in place, many indigenous peoples enjoy a procedural right to be consulted, which may extend from a mere right of notification to a right of veto. In some formulations, the right could ensure traditional owners a high degree of control over the outcome of negotiations over debt-for-development proposals that might affect them. For example, the Australian Native Title Act 1993 recognises and protects a right to negotiate, held by traditional owners as defined under that Act.[32] In this sense, indigenous peoples may enjoy a more strongly defined right than others in a community to participate in public affairs affecting them, a fact of which debtor country governments should be fully aware in negotiating debt-for-development exchanges.

Under international law, however, both the status of many other rights asserted by indigenous peoples and the nature of states' obligations with respect to them are not particularly clear or are contested. For example, while 'all peoples have the right of self-determination',[33] it is by no means certain that indigenous peoples within a sovereign state possess this right

---

[30] C. Dommen, "The WTO, International Trade, and Human Rights", in *Mainstreaming Human Rights in Multilateral Institutions*, ed. Michael Windfuhr, accessed August 2, 2010, http://www.3dthree.org/pdf_3D/WTOmainstreamingHR.

[31] See Chapter 2, this volume.

[32] Native Title Act 1993, subdivision P.

[33] ICESCR and ICCPR, common article 1(1).

independently. The right is asserted in article 3 of the Declaration on the Rights of Indigenous Peoples, a 2007 resolution of the UN General Assembly, but is not (yet) expressed in treaty form as binding law. It has also been stated that indigenous peoples possess 'sovereignty' rights.[34] While such rights may be correctly asserted from the traditional perspective of the indigenous people themselves, international law has yet to recognise a separate indigenous right to sovereignty.

Failure to respect and protect the different cultural and customary law heritage of indigenous peoples might be unlawful where it constitutes racial discrimination, which is prohibited under multiple international law instruments and under customary international law.[35] The Convention on the Elimination of All Forms of Racial Discrimination (CERD) prohibits racial discrimination with regard to participation in political and public life[36] (as well as in relation to the other human rights and freedoms guaranteed under the covenants, including any property-related rights). The legal basis for many references to the rights of indigenous peoples (as distinct from human rights generally) will be found in equality concepts and guarantees of nondiscrimination.

IV. A HUMAN RIGHTS–SUPPORTING APPROACH TO DEBT FOR DEVELOPMENT?

It is clear that developing countries have human rights obligations that accompany them in their negotiations over the broad focus and finer details of debt-for-development exchanges. It is also clear that the process of development and the realisation of human rights are intricately connected. Debt-for-development schemes ought to support the realisation of human rights, as should any development initiative. At the very least, they ought not to have retrogressive effects on rights.

The concept of a human rights–supporting approach to development has been operationalised in recent years, principally by the United Nations in its work on the human rights–based approach to development (HRBAD). Building on the work of Amartya Sen and Mahbub ul Haq,[37] the United

---

[34] See, e.g., David M. Leon, "Expanding the Scope of the Tropical Forest Conservation Act: Exchanging Foreign Debt for Sustainable Development", *University of Miami International & Comparative Law Review* 11 (2003): 141; Amanda Lewis, "Swapping Debt for Nature", *Colorado Journal of International Environmental Law and Policy* 10 (1999): 436.

[35] The international instruments include ICESCR, article 2(2); ICCPR, article 2(1); and CERD.

[36] CERD, article 5.

[37] In 1990, led by Amartya Sen and Mahbub ul Haq, the United Nations Development Programme introduced the notion of development as 'human development', measured by

Nations has taken steps to incorporate into its development work new understanding and knowledge about how the process of development can be steered to facilitate the realisation of human rights and freedoms for all. From the late 1990s, many UN agencies attempted to adopt a human rights–based approach to their development co-operation work, but each 'tended to have its own interpretation of approach and how it should be operationalised'.[38] In 2004 the UN Statement of Common Understanding on a Human Rights–Based Approach to Development Cooperation and Programming drew them together in a relatively consistent approach. Under the Common Understanding, all UN programs of development co-operation and assistance must aim to 'contribute directly to the realization of one or several human rights'.[39] The United Nations Development Group has observed that the human rights–based approach to development

> leads to better and more sustainable outcomes by analyzing and addressing the inequalities, discriminatory practices and unjust power relations which are often at the heart of development problems. It puts the international human rights entitlements and claims of the people and the corresponding obligations of the State in the centre of the national development debate.[40]

In light of the brief survey in this chapter of human rights–related traps and pitfalls for debt exchanges, could the Common Understanding provide guidance for negotiating countries seeking to avoid adverse human rights outcomes? One possibility might be for domestic legislation authorising debt exchanges, or the terms of exchanges individually, to include a reference to guidance provided by the human rights principles set out in the Common Understanding:

> Human rights are universal and inalienable … indivisible … interdependent and interrelated…. All individuals are equal [and] … are entitled to their human rights without discrimination…. Every person and all peoples are entitled to … participation [in development] in which human rights … can

human indicators, in contrast to the dominant, but more limited notion of development as economic development, measured by economic growth. Their ideas grew into a concept of human development that fully accepts an indivisible relationship between itself and human rights. See R. B. Potter, T. Binns, J. A. Elliott and D. Smith, *Geographies of Development* (Essex: Pearson / Prentice Hall, 2004), 12.

38 United Nations, "The Human Rights Based Approach to Development Cooperation: Towards a Common Understanding among UN Agencies", 2004, accessed August 2, 2010, http://www.undg.org/archive_docs/3069-Common_understanding_of_a_rights-based_approach.doc.

39 Ibid., para. 1.

40 United Nations Development Group, "Human Rights–Based Approach to Development Programming", accessed August 2, 2010, http://www.undg.org/index.cfm?P=221.

be realised.... States and other duty-bearers are answerable for the observance of human rights.[41]

These principles provide guidance for the respect of human rights in development projects. They are open to being used for violation avoidance, exhorting respect for human rights without turning debt-for-development schemes into human rights programs. They give guidance on avoiding traps, such as underestimating the interrelated and interdependent nature of rights, or implementing development projects that are insufficiently participatory or discriminatory in their effects. They also remind states that their human rights obligations apply to all their activities. If a reference to these principles were, say, adopted as a standard for Paris Club agreements, it could be phrased as a simple statement:

> The human rights principles set out in paragraph 2 of the United Nations' Human Rights Based Approach to Development Cooperation: Common Understanding guide all development programming funded under debt exchanges.

An alternative path might be to encourage the channelling of funds through a third party with its own operational principles and systems that are respectful of human rights principles. An example is the Debt2Health initiative of the Global Fund, established to enable debt exchanges to free up domestic resources for investment in Global Fund programs to fight HIV/AIDS, malaria and tuberculosis. While the Global Fund is 'a financing institution [that] does not provide normative guidance, ... [nor is it] an implementing agency', it has developed a gender equality strategy to guide its funding decision making. The Fund believes that it can act as a useful catalyst in this way, 'supporting countries' efforts to take the gender dimensions of the three epidemics into account in their proposals and subsequent programme implementation'.[42] The Fund has justified the taking of this step by pointing out that

> [i]n the majority of countries applying for funding, ... the government has committed to realising gender equality and women's empowerment through the adoption of various human rights instruments, including the Convention on the Elimination of All Forms of Discrimination Against Women (CEDAW).[43]

---

[41] UN, United Nations, "The Human Rights Based Approach", para. 2.
[42] The Global Fund Strategy for Ensuring Gender Equality in the Response to HIV/AIDS, Tuberculosis and Malaria, Part 1, para. 2, accessed August 2, 2010, http://www.theglobalfund.org/documents/strategy/TheGenderEqualityStrategy_en.pdf
[43] Ibid., Part 1 para. 1.

The Global Fund also applies general principles to its work and funding decisions that broadly support human rights principles, including strengthening community participation in the development of proposals, poverty reduction, nondiscrimination and adherence to international law obligations.[44]

There is, of course, a risk that creating operational links between debt exchanges and human rights would discourage countries from negotiating exchanges at all. This would be a damaging development, as the number of debt-for-development exchanges is even now too small. Although some have criticised his view,[45] the UN Independent Expert on Debt and Human Rights considers (human rights–supporting) debt-for-development exchanges to be largely beneficial and has called for more, as one partial solution to developing countries' heavy debt burdens.[46] While some debt-for-development exchanges do adversely affect human rights and while there is considerable underutilisation of their human rights–promoting potential, any human rights statement or linkage that might have a chilling effect on this sector should be very carefully considered.

---

[44] Framework Document of the Global Fund, Section III: Principles, accessed August 2, 2010, http://www.theglobalfund.org/documents/TGF_Framework.pdf.

[45] See, e.g., Melik Özden, Europe–Third World Centre (CETIM), "Debt and Human Rights: Consequences for Human Rights of the Debt of the Countries of the South and the Current State of Its Treatment within the United Nations Bodies", 18.

[46] Statement of Mr Bernards Mudho, Independent Expert of the Commission on Human Rights, on the effects of economic reform policies and foreign debt on the full enjoyment of all human rights, United Nations General Assembly, Sixty-first Session, Third Committee, New York, October 25, 2006, para. 10, accessed August 2, 2010, http://webcache.googleusercontent.com/search?q=cache:6WzE4iAgaLcJ:www2.ohchr.org/english/bodies/chr/special/docs/foreigndebtAG2006.doc+swaps+independent+expert+on+the+effects+of+Foreign+Debt+on+the+Full+Enjoyment+of+all+Human+Rights,&cd=2&hl=en&ct=clnk&gl=au.

13

Bangladesh's Experience with Exchanges: Liability to Potential

M. D. Shamsuddoha

I. INTRODUCTION

Bangladesh has long been considered a 'test case' for the International Financial Institutions' 'economic medicine' – the neoclassical development theories that basically nullify a country's sovereign development planning and implement World Bank–International Monetary Fund (IMF) reform theories. These economic reform theories, in fact, contribute to reinforcing a 'rentier economy' controlled by the national elites and international development brokers, and made the country largely dependent on foreign trade and the recycling of aid money.

Aside from the World Bank and IMF policies, the 'aid consortium' that was established by the aid agencies in 1974 imposed cross-conditionality on policy reform, progressively taking control of the public finances, supervision of fund allocation and setting of development priorities. All these mechanisms, combined with IMF–World Bank's policy-based lending under the structural adjustment program, created favoured ground for enlarging outstanding debt, which now amounts to US$23.6 billion, 21% of the country's gross domestic product (GDP). This gives rise to a debt servicing liability of US$2 billion in the 2010–2011 financial year, almost double the annual budgetary allocation to the health and agriculture sectors. The increasingly higher debt repayments represent an 'outflow' of potential resources that could be invested in essential services to reduce human poverty. Though cancellation of outstanding debt owed by Bangladesh would help the country to translate its debt-service 'liabilities' into development 'potentials', unfortunately Bangladesh has failed to qualify for 'debt cancellation' under the Highly Indebted Poor Country (HIPC) Initiative and the Multilateral Debt Relief Initiative (MDRI) of the World Bank and IMF.

Although it is one of the poorest countries in the world, Bangladesh has seen a steady increase in its economy and some success in attaining the

Millennium Development Goals (MDGs). However, the increasing cost of debt servicing and the undue economic burden caused by climate change are becoming major challenges in the fight against poverty. In this context a debt-for-development exchange aimed at countering the effects of climate change would provide a valuable opportunity to increase developmental funding and limit the resources that leave Bangladesh each year in debt-service repayments.

II. HISTORY OF INDEBTEDNESS: BANGLADESH, A LABORATORY OF EXPERIMENTING NEOCLASSICAL THEORIES

Since the liberation of Bangladesh from Pakistan in 1971, the country has suffered several major economic convulsions during successive fragile political regimes. Following the liberation, the early attempts to radically restructure the economy and socialise the means of production failed. These reforms between 1971 and 1975, supported by large-scale nationalisation of industries, rigid wage–price controls, foreign exchange controls and a highly regulated external trade regime were a major change from the economic policies of the pre-independence period and hence resulted in a major macroeconomic shock. Furthermore, a massive loss of natural resources during the liberation war severely aggravated the macroeconomic situation. Such circumstances also exacerbated social and political unrest.

Bangladesh joined the International Financial Institutions (IFIs), the World Bank and the IMF in August 1972, but in the years between 1972 and 1975, despite facing an economic crisis, it did not receive structural adjustment loans from the IFIs. In March 1973, during the country's first policy dialogue with the IMF, the IMF raised doubts about the external value of the Bangladesh taka and advised a 'devaluation' of the taka. The Fund's argument was that in 1973 Pakistan devalued its currency (the rupee), and in 1971 the value of the Bangladeshi taka and Pakistani rupee were the same. Bangladesh, however, resisted the need for devaluation.

In the later part of 1973, Bangladesh's fiscal and monetary situation further deteriorated; foreign exchange reserves shrank, while setbacks in agricultural output had increased the demand for imports. Disbursement of foreign assistance went down and import prices rose. This led the country to further negotiate with the IMF with a view to drawing the first and the second tranches of its quota of special drawing rights (SDR) to the IMF. The SDR is an international reserve asset, created by the IMF in 1969 to supplement its member countries' official reserves. Under its Articles of Agreement, the IMF may allocate SDRs to members in proportion to their IMF quotas. Such an allocation provides each member with a low-cost asset. To qualify for assistance from the IMF, Bangladesh proposed adopting a set of fiscal measures for price sta-bilisation and domestic resource mobilisation. The IMF disagreed with the Bangladesh proposal and further emphasised the need for devaluation. It was said that devaluation would provide a unique opportunity to mobilise domes-tic resources by the simple device of export taxes on jute and jute manufac-tures, which constituted 90% of exports. Until early 1974, the government of Bangladesh was not willing to consider devaluation; it was, however, willing to accept IMF directives to reduce inflation by improvements in budgetary and public sector performance, to raise interest rates, to restrict credit, to tax imports and to remove subsidies on food and agricultural inputs. By the mid-dle of 1974, famine, lack of food aid and lack of foreign currency reserves to buy food pushed Bangladesh to approach the IMF again. The IMF argued that the devaluation of the currency in conjunction with a uniform exchange rate, as well as appropriate fiscal and credit policies, was the only way open for Bangladesh to have access to the new credit tranches.[1] The Aid Consortium was established by the aid agencies in Bangladesh in 1974. Since its inaugu-ration and until 2004, it met annually in Paris. The Bangladesh government was usually invited to send observers to the meeting. Prior to the Bangladesh Aid Consortia Meeting in October 1974, the international donor community supported the position of the IFIs, that if Bangladesh devalued its currency, there would be a large flow of food assistance to the country.

Given this mounting pressure, Bangladesh devalued the exchange rate by 58%, and the country obtained credit of US$75 million from two credit tranches of the IMF. A set of conditions were also imposed on monetary and fiscal policies, which were, among others, (1) gradually reducing subsidies on food grains and eventual terminating subsidies on agricultural inputs, (2) imposing export taxes on raw jute and jute manufactures, (3) liberalising import regulation, (4) limiting additional credit to the public enterprises, (5) reducing the role of the Trading Corporation of Bangladesh (TCB), the state trading organisation accounting for a substantial part of the country's imports other than food grains and (6) abolishing the minimum price of jute and leaving it to market forces.

The government's willingness to undertake adjustment measures associated with the support from the International Development Agency (IDA) and IMF ensured the availability of assistance from these institutions and other donor

---

[1]   Nurul Islam, "Economic Policy Reforms and the IMF Bangladesh Experience in the early 1970s", in Rehman Sobhan, ed., *Structural Adjustment Policies in the Third World: Design and Experience* (Bangladesh: University Press Limited, 1991), 250.

countries. By the end of financial year 1974–1975, donors had pledged nearly US$880 million in food aid and commodity lending, and disbursed close to US$670 million. The total aid commitment that year exceeded US$1,250 million, which was nearly two and half times than that of 1973–1974.[2]

While the country was experiencing major economic policy reforms, in August 1975 a military coup d'état overthrew the Awami League government. The military-backed government started a hasty retreat from the pre-1975 policies and undertook massive denationalisation, which resulted in financial and fiscal turmoil and constituted another set of shocks to the macroeconomy. The scale and magnitude of denationalisation and privatisation accelerated. While reduced foreign aid dependency has been an explicit objective of successive political regimes in Bangladesh, the attainment of even a moderate degree of self-reliance remained a distant dream. Given the high degree of external dependence, it was only expected that Bangladesh would turn to the IFIs for financial assistance.[3] While the IMF–World Bank loans are soft with respect to low interest rates and repayment terms, they require adherence to a set of stringent conditions. The Extended Fund Facility (EFF) was an IMF lending facility established in 1974 to assist member countries in overcoming balance-of-payments problems that stem largely from structural problems and require a longer period of adjustment than is possible under a stand-by arrangement. The loan agreement with the IMF under its EFF in December 1980 was revoked in July 1981, after six months and disbursement of only SDR 20 million out of SDR 800 million, as Bangladesh was unable to adhere to the limits imposed on the fiscal deficit. Following the suspension of the EFF, Bangladesh again approached the IMF for funding under the Compensatory Financing Facility (CFF), which was introduced in 1963 to mitigate the adverse effect of export instability on the balance of payments of countries that export primary commodities, to deal with the severe decline in trade and rising cost of food grain imports. Meanwhile, in 1983 Bangladesh negotiated for a stand-by arrangement for Fund support of SDR 68 million after agreeing to establish a benchmark for a real effective exchange rate. The suspension of EFF also made the country turn to external commercial sources with high interest.

Up until 1985, although there was no financing arrangement with the IMF, Bangladesh continued to receive support from the annual Import Programme

---

[2] M. Syeduzzaman, "Bangladesh Experience with Adjustment Policies", in Rehman Sobhan, ed., *Structural Adjustment Policies in the Third World: Design and Experience* (Bangladesh: University Press Limited, 1991), 264–284.

[3] Sultan Hafeez Rahman, "Structural Adjustment: The Design of Policies, Relevant Issues and a Framework of Monitoring", in Rehman Sobhan, ed., *Structural Adjustment Policies in the Third World: Design and Experience* (Bangladesh: University Press Limited, 1991), 203–215.

Credit (IPC) of the World Bank (IDA). While the first three credits were aimed at rehabilitation of the war-ravaged economy, from the 4th IPC onwards the IDA began to address various issues pertaining to economic efficiency and policy reforms. For instance, the 4th IPC focussed on reform in the jute and textile industries, which continued through the 5th and 6th credits; the 7th and 8th IPCs focussed on export development and the restructuring of the leather and chemical industries and the 9th and 10th IPCs shifted focus to the agriculture sector with reforms to reduce subsidies on food, fertilizer and irrigation, as well as pressure to privatise the distribution of agricultural inputs. Similarly, the 11th IPC, negotiated in 1982, focussed on the policy reforms in the field of trade and industry, while the 13th IPC placed considerable emphasis on trade and industrial policy reforms – in particular, reform of tariff structure for selected industries. Throughout the 1980s, the Bank and the IMF were increasingly focussing upon policy prescriptions as conditions of lending, and processing of IPC/nonproject loans and credits from IDA became contingent upon having a program/arrangement with the IMF on macroeconomic policies.[4] From 1972, Bangladesh contracted 13 Import Programme Credits (IPCs) amounting to a total of US$1,165 million. IPCs were phased out after the 13th IPC in 1986, as the World Bank felt the necessity of 'more extended dialogue and in-depth sector work'. Though IPCs were subsequently phased out, the trade and industrial policy reforms, along with financial sector reforms, were pursued under Industrial Sector Credits. The Industrial Sector Credit was intended to be the first of a series of adjustment credits to help Bangladesh undertake structural reforms. It followed a long list of sector credits and import program credits. A credit of US$190 million became effective on June 30, 1987. The second tranche was released on June 28, 1988. It was fully disbursed and closed on May 11, 1989.[5]

Given the backdrop of huge economic loss caused by flood in 1984–1985, Bangladesh approached the IMF again and secured a 19-month stand-by arrangement for more than US$200 million. To qualify for this fund, the government initiated a set of reform measures to reduce expenditure, tighten credit and restore international competitiveness. The processing of the 13th IPC of the IDA, which was under discussion at that time, adopted the IMF's conditionalities. In many respects, Bangladesh was a test case in the implementation of IMF conditions.[6]

---

[4] Syeduzzaman, "Bangladesh Experience with Adjustment Policies".
[5] Project Performance Assessment Report No. 13252, Independent Evaluation Group (IEG) 06/30/1994.
[6] Michael Chossudovska, *The Globalization of Poverty and the New World Order* (Ontario: Global Outlook, 2003), 160–166.

During the following years, after the introduction of policy reform stipulations of the World Bank and IMF in the 1980s, Bangladesh contracted a loan under the Structural Adjustment Facility, established in 1986 to provide assistance on concessional terms to low-income nations facing protracted balance-of-payment problems. It also received funding from the Extended Structural Adjustment Facility (ESAF) in 1990. Both loans imposed rigorous conditions that included opening the country's market for foreign goods and services and policy reform for attracting foreign direct investment (FDI). The country undertook the first phase of trade openness from 1982 to 1986 under the World Bank's policy-based lending, which had continued at a higher pace under the IMF's Structural Adjustment Facility loan contract from 1987 to 1991 and the IMF's Enhanced Structural Adjustment Facility loan contract from 1992 to 1995. These reforms resulted in substantially lower quantitative restrictions, opened up trade in many restricted items, rationalised and lessened import tariffs and created a more liberalised foreign exchange regime.[7]

IFI-Mandated policy reforms ware undertaken in Bangladesh from 1982, and even earlier since import liberalisation was among the conditionalities associated with the second stand-by arrangement signed with the IMF in 1975. The Bank required policy prescriptions with respect to structural adjustment – trade and financial liberalisation, openness, deregulation, privatisation and so on – and greater reliance on global market mechanisms led to poor economic performance.

III. AID POLITICS AND INDEBTEDNESS: CROSS-CONDITIONALITIES BY THE DEVELOPMENT PARTNERS IN BANGLADESH

Aside from the policy prescriptions made by the World Bank and IMF, conditions were imposed on loans granted to Bangladesh by other multilateral and bilateral donors. For instance, during the structural adjustment program implementation period the Asian Development Bank (ADB) provided a US$2.46 billion loan and US$47 million in technical assistance with the stipulation that the World Bank–IMF structural adjustment conditionalities be fulfilled. USAID and Japan also followed the same lending strategy in their co-financing programs.

The policy prescriptions from international lenders created mounting pressure for Bangladesh to devalue its currency in the middle of 1974. In fact, to

7 A. Razzaque, B. H. Khondker, N. Ahmed and M. K. Mujeri, "Trade Liberalization and Economic Growth: Empirical Evidence on Bangladesh", MIMAP-Bangladesh Focus Study 03, 2003, BIDS, Dhaka.

firmly implant the macroeconomic restructuring, in 1974 Bangladesh's international creditors had demanded formation of the Aid Consortium under the leadership of the World Bank. During this period, in the context of famine that was compounded by a lack of foreign exchange to buy food, Bangladesh agreed to appear before the Aid Consortia Meeting in October 1974.

Following the Aid Consortia Meeting, Bangladesh received substantial commitments of food aid and loans from the IFIs, which were conditional upon devaluation. In fact, the aid politics of the international donor communities forced the country to implement most of the essential ingredients of the structural adjustment program by the mid-1970s. The Aid Consortium had taken control of the public finances and started direct supervision of the allocation of funds, setting of development priorities and reform of the banking system. Against an unstable political background, with military regimes from 1975 to 1981 and from 1982 to 1990, the IFIs and aid agencies succeeded in maintaining substantial control over the country's development policies. While the donor agencies established control over economic policies, the military engaged in massive corruption and exploited the country's resources.

IV. DEBT PROFILE OF BANGLADESH: A FIVEFOLD INCREASE IN EXTERNAL DEBT SINCE THE 1980S

The debt burden of Bangladesh has increased steadily since the early 1980s, despite the various rescheduling, restructuring and debt conversion schemes put forward by creditors. The lending policy of the World Bank and IMF has also shifted since 1980 from short-term macroeconomic adjustment problems to policies aimed at changing the structure of incentives to achieve productive efficiency and institutional reforms. In fact, these procedures, combined with IMF–World Bank policy-based lending under the structural adjustment program encouraged greater accumulation of debt, while prompt reimbursement of interest payments was still required. The policies imposed by the IFIs covered virtually every aspect of the economy, such as public expenditures, interest rates, exchange rate, credit ceilings, tax and tariff regimes, market structures, pricing policies in agriculture, industry, trade, public enterprises and enhancing the role of the private sector.

Between 1980 and 2004 foreign debt in Bangladesh increased around fivefold, from US$3.9 billion in 1980 to US$20.3 billion in 2004,[8] and now amounts to US$23.6 billion (2010), which is 21% of the country's GDP. The cumulative increase of the country's debt burden is due mainly to the increase of

[8] Data from World Bank Global Development Finance, 2005 and 2006.

multilateral debt from US$1.7 billion in 2004 to US$23.6 billion in 2010. The IDA, the soft-loan window of the World Bank, is the main multilateral creditor. Since Bangladesh joined the World Bank in 1972, the World Bank has financed 209 operations with credit totalling US$17.2 billion. Debt-service liabilities are owed 48% to the World Bank, 26% to the ADB, 13% to the Japanese government, 11% to the IMF and other donors and 2% to the US government.

V. REPAYMENT OF DEBT-SERVICE LIABILITY: LESS MONEY FOR THE ESSENTIAL SERVICE SECTORS

Despite the fact that the country paid US$1 billion in debt service in 2007 and 2008, 50% of the population still lives in extreme poverty (less than US$1.25 a day), and 48% of five-year-olds are underweight, the worst percentage of any country in the world. Overall Bangladesh ranks 112 out of 135 in the human poverty index compiled by the United Nations.[9] Such an appalling scenario of underdevelopment indicates that Bangladesh does not have adequate resources to finance its development; however, it was still required to spend around US$2 billion in the 2010–2011 financial year on foreign debt servicing, 11.1% of its budget. The domestic debt burden has also been increasing steadily as the government has been resorting to domestic borrowing to fill the budget deficit. In 2010 domestic debt accounted for around US$18 billion, while foreign debt is US$23.6 billion.[10]

In the past few years, Bangladesh has been spending more on external debt servicing than on public service sectors like education or health. In 2007 the country had to pay US$1,551.3 million for external debt servicing, which is 18% of total government expenditure. In the same year, public spending on education and health were 16.5% and 7.4% of total expenditure, respectively. In the 2010–2011 financial year, the budgetary allocation for debt servicing liability was around US$2 billion, which is almost double the allocation to the health and agriculture sectors, which are US$1.1 billion and US$1.08 billion, respectively.[11]

Spending on debt service has increased steadily, and debt repayments outstrip the inflow of grant aid. There will be a sharp increase in debt servicing

9   UNDP, *Human Development Index* (Geneva: United Nations, 2007).
10 Calculated on the basis of the proposed annual budget of FY 2010–2011.
11 In fiscal year 2010–2011 the total annual budget allocation is around US$18.85 billion, while allocation to the education sector is US$2.5 billion (13.9%), that to the health sector is US$1.1 billion (6.2%) and that to the agriculture sector is US$1.08 billion (5.7%). See Government of Bangladesh (2009), "Millennium Development Goals Need Assessment and Costing 2009–2015, Bangladesh", country report 2009.

in coming years due to the commencement of repayment of the IMF's Poverty Reduction Growth Facilities (PRGF) loan of US$590.7 million. In this context a Jubilee Netherlands study in 2006 showed that for every dollar in grant aid received, Bangladesh paid back at least US$1.5 in debt repayment.[12] One dollar spent on debt service means a dollar less in the development budget, resulting in less money for the essential service sectors.

VI. DEBT CANCELLATION INITIATIVES: THE ARBITRARY NATURE OF 'DEBT-TO-EXPORT RATIO' CRITERIA

As a result of campaigning by millions of people around the world, some of the debts of the poorest countries in the world have been cancelled under the HIPC Initiative and the MDRI. The HIPC program was initiated by the IMF and the World Bank in 1996, following extensive lobbying. It provides debt relief and low-interest loans to cancel or reduce external debt repayments to sustainable levels. However, assistance is conditional on the national governments of these countries meeting a range of economic management and performance targets. As of September 2009, the HIPC program had identified 40 countries (29 of which are in sub-Saharan Africa) as potentially eligible to receive debt relief. The MDRI was introduced in September 2005 to operationalise the outcome of deliberations at the G8 summit in Gleneagles in July of that year. The MDRI is to provide 100% cancellation of eligible debt owed by eligible countries to four multilateral financial institutions, including the World Bank and IMF.

There is clear and mounting evidence that debt cancellation is among the most effective forms of financing poverty reduction in the developing world, and to date nearly £100 billion of debt of 40 eligible countries has been cancelled. This does not include Bangladesh. The calculation of a country's 'debt sustainability' on the basis of arbitrary indicators like its 'debt-to-export ratio' made Bangladesh ineligible for the HIPC Initiative and the MDRI. According to World Bank and IMF calculations, the debt-to-export ratio for Bangladesh stands at 146%, which is below the official threshold of 150%. The HIPC Initiative generally leads to a reduction of debt to the level of 150% of export income. It also paves the way for debt reduction under the new MDRI: countries that reach the completion point of the HIPC Initiative are also eligible for the MDRI. The MDRI provides for cancellation of debt outstanding as of the end of 2003 and IMF debt outstanding as of the end of 2004. Ironically, as

[12] SUPRO, "External Debt Serving, Essential Services and MDGs in Bangladesh", Dhaka, 2007.

Bangladesh didn't meet the debt cancellation criteria set by the World Bank and IMF for the HIPCs, it also didn't qualify for the debt cancellation under the MDRI, notwithstanding the fact that Bangladesh complied with two other criteria of attaining macroeconomic stability and developing a poverty-reduction strategy. Bangladesh has regularly paid its debts, and expanded its exports, and is now being punished for this success.

One of the central problems that exist within the aid system established by the Bretton Woods institutions is that debt relief is not aligned with the MDGs; rather, it is based on arbitrary indicators of debt-to-export ratios.[13] Jeffrey Sachs proposed that 'debt sustainability' should be redefined as 'the level of debt' consistent with achieving the MDGs by 2015 without a new debt overhang. Similarly, former Secretary General of the United Nations, Kofi Annan, has said that

> to move forward, we should redefine debt sustainability as the level of debt that allows a country to achieve the MDGs and reach 2015 without an increase in debt ratios. For most HIPC countries, this will require exclusively grant based finance and 100% debt cancellation, while for more heavily indebted non-HIPC and middle-income countries it will require significantly more debt reduction than has yet been on offer.[14]

If debt sustainability is redefined based on the amount of finance needed for achievement of the MDGs, Bangladesh may well be able to claim full debt cancellation.

VII. DEBT CANCELLATION: FREEING UP MONEY FOR ATTAINING MDGS

Despite a huge poverty burden, inflationary pressure, natural disasters, political instability and the world financial crisis, Bangladesh has consistently averaged 5.5% growth in its GDP over the past 10 years.[15] Bangladesh has made significant progress in reducing poverty over the past 20 years, with several models of development that have received global attention and are being replicated in many other parts of the world. However, poverty remains widespread; 41.2% of the population is living below the poverty line − 31.9% in poverty

---

[13] Jeffery Sachs, *Investing in Development: A Practical Plan to Achieve the Millennium Development Goals* (London: Earthscam, 2005).

[14] "In Larger Freedom: Towards Development, Security and Human Rights for All", Report of the Secretary-General, United Nations, March 21, 2005.

[15] European Commission, "Country Strategy Paper: Bangladesh 2002–2006", accessed September 6, 2010, http://eeas.europa.eu/bangladesh/csp/02_06_en.pdf>.

and 9.3% in extreme poverty. Another 34.1% is living in situations of extreme vulnerability and is at risk of falling below the poverty line.[16] Nutrition levels are very poor; child malnutrition is among the highest in the world and remains more severe than in most other developing countries, including those in sub-Saharan Africa. One in every three babies is born with low weight, and 48.6% of children below the age of five have stunted growth. Half of all children below the age of five suffer from malnutrition.[17] On the other hand, poor incentives for attending school combined with acute poverty contribute to low attendance and a high drop-out rate: 47% of primary school students do not complete their primary education.[18] A large number of people lack basic services, and instances of human rights violations remain prevalent, especially among women. If progress were to continue at the levels achieved in the 1990s, the MDGs would be partially met by 2015. The extreme poverty goal would be reached (but 16 million would still live on less than US$1 a day, and 40 million would be below the upper poverty line); universal primary education would be achieved but with grave doubts about its quality; the gender equality goal in primary education has already been reached (but on most other measures of gender equality – higher secondary education, literacy, labour force participation – women will fare worse than men); but child mortality reduction targets would not be met.

The prospects for continued progress towards achieving the MDGs in Bangladesh depend on securing adequate and predictable financing. According to the MDGs Needs Assessment and Costing Report 2009–2015, Bangladesh, to achieve the MDGs within the projected time line, has to increase development funding to the following extents:

- US$4.83 billion for agricultural and rural development, including employment generation and road infrastructure for MDG 1;
- US$2.27 billion for education including pre-primary, primary, secondary and nonformal education for MDG 2;
- US$0.59 billion for gender parity;

[16] Bangladesh Bureau of Statistics, "Report on Welfare Monitoring Survey 2009", accessed September 6, 2010, www.bbs.gov.bd/project/welfaresurvey_09.pdf.
[17] Selim Jahan, "Financing Millennium Development Goals: An Issues Note", Prepared for an International Seminar on Staying Poor: Chronic Poverty and Development Policy, Manchester, United Kingdom, April 7–9, 2003, accessed September 6, 2010, www.undg.org/archive_docs/5634-Financing_MDGs__An_Issues_Note.pdf.
[18] Integrated Regional Information Networks (IRIN), "Bangladesh: Primary-School Dropout Rate Rises to 47 Percent", November 4, 2007, accessed September 6, 2010, www.irinnews.org/Report.aspx?ReportId=75139.

- US$1.63 billion for health systems, including health infrastructure for MDGs 4, 5 and 6; and
- US$0.26 billion for the environment, US$1.88 billion for energy and US$2.02 billion for water supply and sanitation for MDG 7.

The grand total of additional financing needed for each year from 2009 to 2015 amounts to US$14.88 billion. The net annual requirement of external support is US$7.5 billion, four times more than the present foreign aid Bangladesh receives.

Since the financing for the attainment of MDGs is largely inadequate and unpredictable, full or at least partial debt cancellation for Bangladesh is necessary to free up money for development. For example, debt cancellation in Mali freed up money to provide salaries to 5,000 community teachers.[19] In Mauritania funds from debt relief were directed towards improving health care. Before debt relief, only around 40% of births were attended by a health professional – now the figure is nearly 60%.[20] Thus, debt relief to debt-constrained nations, which are not eligible for relief under the HIPC Initiative, enables those countries to concentrate more on developmental issues.

Though Bangladesh has neither negotiated any agreements with the Paris Club for debt cancellation nor become eligible for HIPC debt cancellation, cancellation of bilateral debt has been granted by several countries in the past. For instance, in 1991 the United States cancelled US$292 million of official development assistance debt,[21] and in 1999 Canada cancelled US$0.6 million of outstanding debt. Japan cancelled around US$2.2 billion and US$1.46 billion, respectively, in 2003 and 2004.[22] However, cancellation often means limited relief with a lot of policy conditions attached – forcing countries to restructure their economies in ways that are often unhelpful and always undemocratic. For example, in Afghanistan, the World Bank has attached conditions that forced the country to undertake privatisations, especially in the banking sector, and many other countries have been forced to privatise vital state industries in order to receive debt cancellation.

[19] K. Hinchcliffe, quoted in *Do the Deal. Do the Deal* (CAFOD ActionAid, Oxfam, February 2005).

[20] K. Hinchcliffe, "Notes on the Impact of the HIPC Initiative on Education and Public Health Expenditures in African Countries" (2004), accessed August 2, 2010, http://siteresources.worldbank.org/INTAFRICA/Resources/HIPC_Impact_04.pdf.

[21] "US Debt Reduction Activities, FY 1990 through FY 1999", Report to US Congress (February 2000), accessed September 2, 2010, http://treas.gov/press/releases/reports/debtreduct.pdf.

[22] Ministry of Foreign Affairs Japan, "Outline of Japan's Aid to Bangladesh" (June 2009), accessed September 2, 2010, http://www.mofa.go.jp/region/asia-paci/bangladesh/index.html.

While it is important to cancel current debts, it is equally important to make sure that the debt-cancellation process is fair and transparent. In the current debt-relief processes, power is in the hands of the creditors and they share no responsibility for bad lending decisions.

VIII. DEBT-FOR-DEVELOPMENT EXCHANGES: COUNTERING CLIMATE CHANGE

Climate change is an unfolding phenomenon with very drastic adverse environmental, economic, social and human consequences, particularly for Bangladesh. Although developed countries and economic policy instruments are largely responsible for the climate crisis, the impacts are affecting poor countries disproportionately. The fourth IPCC report described the impacts of climate change in different regions of the globe. The report demonstrated that in Bangladesh the effects of higher temperatures, more variable precipitation, more extreme weather events and rising sea level will most likely continue to intensify. These changes are already having an impact on the lives and livelihoods of millions of poor people who remain exposed to climate risks. It is a question of national survival for such a low-lying coastal country that is located only a few metres above sea level.

In Bangladesh the geographical distribution, frequency and intensity of climatic hazards are already being altered significantly by climate change. The UN International Strategy for Disaster Reduction estimates that 9 of every 10 disasters are climate related. In Bangladesh, an increasing incidence of disasters that have clear links with climate change has been observed. These disasters are causing huge financial loss to the country and impeding the county's economic growth. In 2007 Bangladesh faced two devastating disasters: consecutive monsoon floods in July and a category 4 supercyclone, Sidr, in November. Monsoon floods in June and August 2007 caused extensive agricultural production losses and destruction totalling nearly US$1.1 billion. And cyclone Sidr in November 2007 caused 3,500 deaths, along with extensive damage of resources totalling US$1.7 billion – roughly 2.8 % of GDP. But Bangladesh received only US$400 millions as loans and grants from development partners in response to these disasters.

The occurrence of these events in close succession is a reminder of the country's extreme vulnerability to frequent hydro-meteorological hazards, which stand to be exacerbated by climate change. Losses and damage resulting from frequent and intense disasters caused by climate change are causing billions of dollars of economic loss annually, again making the country more indebted to the IFIs.

A 1- to 2-metre sea level rise would inundate 18% of Bangladesh's total land, directly affecting 11% of the country's population. Saltwater intrusion from a rise of sea level in low-lying agricultural plains, along with other hazards, could lead to a 40% decrease in food grain production and displace 30 million people.[23]

The unprecedented effects of climate change will also have an adverse impact on the pursuit of the MDGs. The goals of eradicating poverty, combating communicable diseases and ensuring environmental sustainability are already in jeopardy. Major incidents that affect poverty-reduction strategies and MDG achievement are (1) inundation or submersion of low-lying coastal areas due to a rise in sea level and a huge displacement of the population; (2) incremental cost for disaster risk reduction and financial loss due to an increased level of disasters; (3) intrusion of salinity and consequential scarcity of drinking water; (4) reduction in crop production of around 30% and (5) increasing health hazards. Thus, the country would require new, additional and incremental financial resources for adaptation and for undertaking clean development paths. In this regard, the Bali Action Plan refers to the need of 'improved access to adequate, predictable and sustainable financial resources and … a provision of new and additional resources' and 'innovative means of funding to assist developing country parties that are particularly vulnerable to the adverse impacts of climate change in meeting the cost of adaptation'.

The adaptation financing required to build social and economic capital in order to absorb shocks now and in the future include climate proofing development and economic growth, climate proofing of existing infrastructure, additional investments for new infrastructure, costs on community level/community-based adaptation, capacity building, restoration of ecosystem services, addressing mass displacement and mainstreaming adaptation into poverty-reduction strategies and other relevant government policies and programs.[24]

In the past three decades the Bangladeshi government has invested more than US$10 billion to make the country more climate resilient and less vulnerable to natural disasters. In recent years, in the context of frequent and intense hydro-meteorological disasters caused by climate change, Bangladesh has been facing enormous economic loss, which has burdened the country with more debt, as humanitarian responses to the disasters are quite inadequate.

---

[23] Z. Karim, S. G. Hussain, and A. U. Ahmed, "Climate Change Vulnerability of Crop Agriculture", in S. Huq, Z. Karim, M. Asaduzzaman and F. Mahtab (eds.), *Vulnerability and Adaptation to Climate Change for Bangladesh* (Dordrecht: Kluwer, 1999).

[24] Benito Muller, "International Adaptation Finance: The Need for an Innovative and Strategic Approach" (June 2008), accessed September 6, 2010, http://www.oxfordenergy.org/pdfs/EV42.pdf.

The government of Bangladesh examined its vulnerability to climatic change and formulated its Climate Change Strategy and Action Plan (CCSAP) and identified a number of projects in six major categories: food security, social safety and health, comprehensive disaster management, infrastructure, research and knowledge management, mitigation and low carbon development and capacity building. The implementation of the Bangladesh Climate Change Strategy and Action Plan (BCCSAP) would require approximately US$5billion in a year. But in the context of uncertainty and inadequacy of adaptation finance from the multilateral mechanisms, as well as difficulty in accessing the funds from bilateral sources, the government of Bangladesh has taken the initiative to finance climate change adaptation measures from its own revenue income. In the 2009–2010 financial year, the government allocated around US$100 million to a trust fund, Bangladesh Climate Change Trust Fund, for undertaking climate change adaptation measures. Since the government has established the Trust Fund, it has had to sacrifice the same amount of investment in other important sectors such as health, sanitation, education and poverty reduction.

IX. CONCLUSION

In this context a debt-for-development exchange that would enable debt repayments to be diverted into the Trust Fund would provide much needed financing, while at the same time addressing Bangladesh's debt burden. The redirecting of outstanding debt to climate financing should not be treated as 'new and additional' funds from developed countries and also should not be tied with conditions of co-financing. Furthermore, this financing should not result in further impoverishment, disempowerment and discrimination of marginalised people and communities in the South, or cause destruction of the environment.

14

The Philippines' Experience with Exchanges

Joffre Balce

An account of debt-for-development exchanges in the Philippines provides a good demonstration of the evolution of the technique itself, evolving from a commercially driven transaction to one focussed on development projects and proposed by creditor countries. The Philippine experience sheds light on both the strengths and weaknesses of the debt-exchange technique and illuminates the opportunities and potential pitfalls in applying debt-for-development exchanges in the future. This chapter uncovers the manner in which debt-for-development exchanges can help developing countries overcome their dependence on external debt and harness their own resources for their developmental ends.

I. DEBT-FOR-DEVELOPMENT EXCHANGE FOR RURAL BANK REHABILITATION

In 1990 a World Bank team packaging a US$100 million agricultural loan identified a shortfall of capital in more than 800 rural banks in the Philippines that totalled about US$50million. It was estimated that the Philippine Deposit Insurance Corporation had a risk exposure of up to US$250 million of insured deposits in those banks. These banks also owed the Central Bank of the Philippines about US$75 million, which brought the total potential loss for the government to US$335 million should the banks fail. However, at the same time, they saw an opportunity because other banks had capital of about US$75 million in excess of the prescribed levels. Hence, the system had more than enough resources collectively to solve its problem. To effectively manage the funds from the World Bank loan, a merger of the rural banking system was identified as necessary. What was needed was an incentive program in the rural banking industry to attract capital. Considering the available and potential

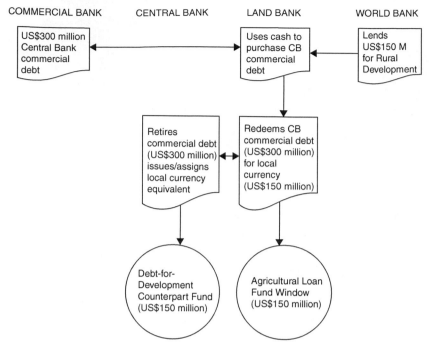

FIGURE 14.1. Proposed debt-for-rural bank capital strengthening.

benefits of strengthening rural banking, the World Bank team recommended increasing the system's capital by a further US$50 million.

A team of Filipino technocrats from three government departments proposed a debt-for-development exchange whereby the Philippine government would be allowed to use the funds from the World Bank loan to purchase Central Bank commercial debt in the international market, which was trading at around a 50% discount at the time. This meant that the government could buy back US$300 million of its own borrowings, on condition that the Central Bank release the equivalent of US$150 million in local currency to the Land Bank of the Philippines for wholesale lending facilities in the countryside. Furthermore, a US$150 million counterpart fund was created with local currency to finance debt-to-equity exchanges in the Philippines (see Figure 14.1). It was decided that local debt-to-equity exchange transactions for the rural banks would work as follows (see Figure 14.2):

1. A rural bank with increased liquidity can buy its debt from the Central Bank at a 50% discount and capitalise on the discounts earned to enhance its capital base. This doubles the rural bank's capital brought in by the original investment.

CENTRAL BANK   RURAL BANKING SYSTEM

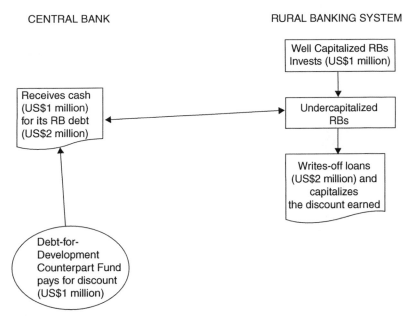

FIGURE 14.2. Proposed debt-to-equity conversion mechanics.

2. The Central Bank can then afford to shoulder the burden of the discount from its rural bank debts with its discounts earned from the buyback of its debt in the international commercial markets.

There was, however, an area of concern. If the discounts on Philippine debt in the international commercial debt markets were below 50%, then there was a potential for the Philippine government to suffer a financial loss if the rural bank investors claimed a higher discount from retiring their debts than the Central Bank of the Philippines could afford to shoulder. To address that issue, the debt-to-equity exchange mechanism was tweaked in the following manner to include two other government financial institutional stakeholders (see Figure 14.3):

1. Fresh investments in the rural bank could be used to purchase a seven-year negotiable promissory note (NPN) from the Land Bank of the Philippines that doubles upon maturity.
2. The rural bank would then exchange the NPN based on its future value for its debts with the Central Bank at the book value.
3. To enhance the value of the NPN, the Philippine Deposit Insurance Corporation assigned its subrogated deposit claims from the liquidators of past closed banks to guarantee the NPNs.

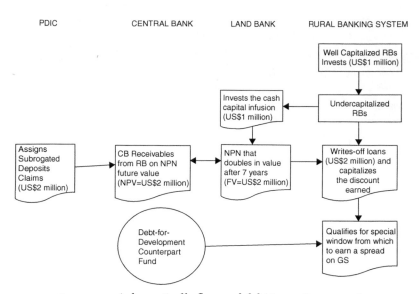

FIGURE 14.3. A domestically financed debt-to-equity conversion.

4. The rural bank was then able to write off its debts from the commercial bank and capitalise the discounts earned. Thus, the rural bank's net worth increases twofold on the investment it has infused into the bank.

5. Depending on the size of the investment, the rural bank is able to utilise the funds from a counterpart fund. The fund was formed with the money earned by the Central Bank of the Philippines after redeeming its debt from the international market. This enabled the rural banks to borrow at rates below the prevailing government securities and thereby further enhance their capital base.

Strict conditions were attached to participants in the program, such as allowing only fresh cash investments and restricting dividend declarations in order to preserve the extra capital strength acquired.

This commercial market–driven debt-for-development exchange – which involved buying Philippine debt from the international market at marked-to-market prices – initiated a paradigm shift, for the following reasons:

1. A World Bank loan – not donations or endowment funds – was used to purchase sovereign debt from the market.

2. Debt-for-equity exchanges in the rural banking system were devised independently using domestic resources among local players.

3. No extraordinary legislation was required – it was a co-operative effort between government and stakeholders.
4. Market-based approaches fostered developmental approaches, especially where all parties had something to gain at no one's expense or disadvantage.

II. DEBT-FOR-DEVELOPMENT EXCHANGE
FOR SUSTAINABLE DEVELOPMENT

The Foundation for a Sustainable Society, Inc. (FSSI), is another interesting model that highlights the active participation of nongovernmental organisations (NGOs) from both creditor and debtor countries in debt-for-development exchanges. Swiss NGOs encouraged their government to pursue avenues of forgiving debt owed by poor indebted countries and supported it in doing so. As discussed in Chapter 8, the Swiss Debt Reduction Facility (SDRF) was the result of NGOs' successful petitions to form a SFr 700 million fund – in honour of the 700th anniversary of the Swiss Confederation in 1989 – to write off debts of underdeveloped economies owed to the government and commercial institutions. Although the management of the funds was placed in government hands, the Swiss NGOs were active in policy consultations, oversight and assessment of the programs implemented under the SDRF. Swiss NGOs were also important government partners in proposing prospective participants in the SDRF. Their connection with the NGOs in the Philippines was essential to the creation of the FSSI.[1]

The Swiss government's Debt for Development Unit (DDU) and the Philippine office of the Swiss NGO Helvetas formed a relationship with the Coalition of Development NGOS (CODE-NGO). It then conducted due diligence concerning the potential management of a Swiss–Philippine debt exchange based upon an evaluation of previous debt-for-development exchanges with the United States, working within the parameters of the SDRF. Unlike the Swiss NGOs, which were limited largely to an advocacy role, CODE-NGO and other affiliated NGOs had a stake in addressing the debt problems and pursuing sustainable development, and they assumed a lead role in the management of the counterpart fund formed under the debt exchange. All parties also agreed that – in the spirit of transparency – the

---

[1] Carmel V. Abao, "Building the Foundations of a Sustainable Society: The Philippine Experience at Creative Debt Relief" (2006), 11, accessed September 7, 2010, http://www.fssi.com.ph/index.php?option=com_docman&task=doc.

governance and management of the fund would be undertaken in close partnership with the Philippine government, the Swiss government and civil society. All parties, the Swiss government and NGOs as well as their Philippine
counterparts, agreed that a new NGO should be formed to manage the counterpart fund. The FSSI was created to fulfil the developmental purposes and
objectives of the SDRF – to address poverty and support socioeconomic development projects in a substantial, far-reaching and sustainable manner. The
FSSI was created by Philippine NGOs, whose representatives were actively
involved in bringing the debt-for-development exchange to life. The fund was
also overseen by Swiss government representatives and a representative of the
Philippine Department of Finance. They acted as advisors to the Board of
Trustees, which was composed of representatives of the founding NGOs that
met annually.[2]

On August 11, 1995, the Philippine and Swiss governments finally signed
the bilateral agreement to cancel the export credit loans of Switzerland to
the Philippines, which amounted to Sfr 42,436,000.00. The Philippine government then converted 50% of the face value of this debt into a counterpart
fund in government securities worth PHP 454,822,597.00. This amount was
entrusted to the management of the FSSI, which was incorporated by the 25
NGOs and coalitions involved in the design and negotiations. The endowment fund was created to support high social impact programs and projects
of NGOs, co-operatives, grassroots community-based enterprises, people's
organisations and similar private organisations (the process is mapped out
in Figure 14.4).[3]

As with many debt-for-development exchanges, the creditor country was
concerned to ensure good governance of the endowment fund. For this
exchange the challenges were twofold: ensuring that the funds were invested
in a manner that served the developmental needs of the Philippines into the
future and ensuring that the funds were used to tackle developmental goals
and not wasted by the trustees. The first six years were challenging due to
lacklustre returns on investments of the endowment fund, due in part to the
falling value of the Philippine peso and in part to wasted funding in implementing development projects. In 2002 the management and staff of the FSSI
embarked on a review of its institutional strategies.

Firstly, investments made by FSSI were reviewed. Financial institutions
were given strict instructions to invest the core funds conservatively rather
than pursuing promises of higher returns, regardless of past performance.

[2] Ibid., 16–17.
[3] Ibid., 10.

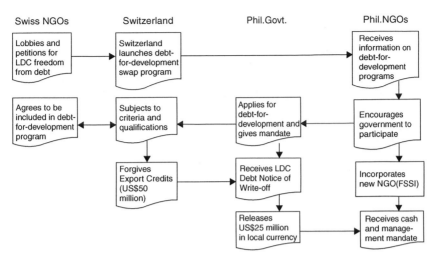

FIGURE 14.4. Close co-operation between government and civil society.

This also opened the gate for smaller banks, credit unions and microfinance institutions to bid for and qualify as depositories of the FSSI's principal funds. This not only worked in finding a safe investment haven for the funds, but also mobilised funds to support smaller institutions.

Secondly, the disbursement of the counterpart funds was examined. The prudent management of counterpart funds is essential to the success of any exchange. A primary benefit of debt-for-development exchanges is the potential to create a means of long-term financing of development goals. To best manage operational and administrative expenses, only one main office was established, with a small staff. To keep project appraisal costs minimal, FSSI prioritised projects of NGOs that were willing to shoulder counterpart costs in their respective communities. Furthermore, to manage default risks arising from moral hazard (i.e., pursuing riskier economic behaviour because another party bears the risk of financial losses), the FSSI preferred projects that were willing to provide counterpart equity or capital – either directly or by a third party – with the result that the proponent stood to lose if the venture failed.

Finally, technical and financial appraisals included an assessment of the proper financial needs of each project – be it a grant, a bridge loan, a donor campaign or technical assistance provided by a partner NGO. Support was no longer limited to lending or investment.

In the review of FSSI its governance procedures were strictly monitored. The NGO members of the FSSI agreed that projects affiliated with them or referred by them had to pass the same criteria as nonaffiliated or independent projects. Furthermore, membership was opened to other NGOs willing to abide by the same principles. Lastly, FSSI committed itself to abiding by professional financial principles that were compatible with principles of developmental finance.

With the approval of the Swiss government representative for the new strategic directions in 2003, the Swiss government announced its willingness to entrust the governance of FSSI to Philippine stakeholders. The Philippine Department of Finance retained a Philippine government presence within the fund to act as observer and adviser.[4]

In summary, the following features made the SDRF and FSSI experience different from most debt-for-development exchanges:

1. the close co-operation of NGOs from both creditor and debtor nations with their respective governments in facilitating the transaction – from inception to implementation – and in ensuring a transparent process; and

2. the full management of the counterpart fund by NGOs, which is possible if, and only if, the withdrawal by the government is conditional on the NGOs committing to a policy and practice of safe, sound and prudent financial management and abiding by principles of good corporate governance.

III. ATTEMPTED DEBT-FOR-DEVELOPMENT EXCHANGE PROGRAM INITIATED BY POLITICIANS

In 2003, at a Philippine congressional hearing, NGOs from the Freedom from Debt Coalition (FDC) participated in a discussion about the growing problem of external debt (which was beyond the ability of the country to repay). Debt servicing constituted more than 40% of the annual budget, and debt repayments were taking priority over expenditures on development needs. In light of this dilemma, the FDC representative suggested the vigorous pursuit of debt-for-development exchanges building on previous Philippine experience. Congressional leadership seized on the idea.

In 2005 the Speaker of the House, Jose De Venecia, announced a Debt-for-Equity in Millennium Development Goals (MDGs) Investments Plan. The plan was endorsed by both the United Nations and creditor countries committed to achieving the MDGs by 2015. The proposal was a systemic, wholesale

---

[4] Foundation for a Sustainable Society, Inc., Web site, "History", accessed September 7, 2010, http://www.fssi.com.ph/index.php?option=com_content&task=view&id=14&Itemid=96.

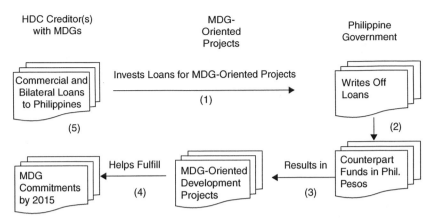

FIGURE 14.5. The De Venecia debt-for-MDG development proposal.

approach to debt reduction similar to the SDRF, but with the initiative coming from the debtor's side. The plan offered commercial and sovereign creditors of the Philippines a direct social investment stake in a smorgasbord of projects in areas such as poverty reduction, environment preservation, health, education and basic services (see Figure 14.5).[5]

This differed from the SDRF in several respects. Firstly, the program did not provide any discount on the debt, just a straight conversion. Secondly, this was primarily an initiative of politicians rather than a program driven by the lobbying efforts of NGOs. The result was that it was greeted with suspicion and apprehension by Philippine civil society. The first criticism was that it was not a debt-for-development exchange but a debt-to-equity conversion whereby the government would convert debt into local currency, bringing a host of other systemic risks (such as inflation) that could cause more harm than good to the economy and development. Thirdly, there was the risk of legitimising debts that many believed should not be paid in the first place, absolving creditors from any responsibility for questionable lending practices. These issues are considered in Chapters 10 and 11 of this volume. In this respect, De Venecia's proposal ran contrary to the international Jubilee campaign calling for the cancellation of unjust and illegitimate debts.[6]

The United Nations and the Paris Club had two general responses to the Philippines proposal. The first was to insist upon the rules of the Paris Club being followed, that is, to use the Evian approach, which requires an analysis

---

[5] State of the Nation Address, 13th Philippine Congress, July 25, 2005, 3–5.
[6] Mong Palatino, "Commentary: Debt Conversion and the Philippine Experience", UPI Asia. com., October 29, 2007.

of debt sustainability by the International Monetary Fund, and to negotiate a new restructuring with the Paris Club. The second was to drop this idea altogether, since it would have a negative impact on the creditworthiness of the Philippines.[7] Partly as a result, the proposal has not been pursued, but neither has it been entirely discarded.

This proposal may well be revived under a new presidency in 2010. If it isn't, at the least the proposal (1) reminded Philippine policy makers of the complexities involved in formulating a general program given the international frameworks set by creditors and (2) called attention to the need to establish the legitimacy of loans proposed for use in debt exchanges. There can be no authentic development without justice and that applies to debt-for-development transactions as well.

IV. PROSPECTIVE APPLICATIONS OF LESSONS LEARNED

Given the lessons learned from these past experiences, future debt-for-development exchanges will be best pursued with the following principles in mind:

1. Mobilising local resources for debt-for-development exchanges is possible and has enormous potential as a means of achieving development goals.

2. Co-operation among government and private sector stakeholders, in both creditor and debtor countries, not only facilitates debt-for-development negotiations, but also improves the design of the transactions and its systems of governance. Debtor governments that pursue debt-for-development exchanges without engaging civil society will reduce the chance of success of the project and also raise questions, doubts and apprehensions about the project.

3. Professional financial management principles and good corporate governance are necessary for the sustainability and continued growth of the counterpart fund, which otherwise might be misconstrued as another government dole-out for simple distribution to beneficiaries. There must be a strong obligation upon beneficiaries not to deplete the funds but to safeguard and enhance their value so that they provide an ongoing financing mechanism.

[7] Joseph Lim, "Towards Financing the Medium Term Development Goals of the Philippines", Discussion Paper Series 2006–23 (Makati City, Philippines: Philippine Institute for Development Studies, December 2006), 98–103.

With such lessons in mind, debt-for-development exchange approaches should be considered in a number of areas, which are discussed in the following sections.

A. *Debt for Rural Investment in Power Enhancement*

Debt-for-equity exchanges have been used to privatise state enterprises such as electricity, telecommunications and water. However, this strategy has not made inroads into alleviating debt dependency. Political influence and power that were concentrated in the government were merely transferred to private corporations. Privatisation has been seen as a way to satisfy the advocates of free-enterprise doctrines, but it has not generally improved service delivery in the Philippines. Co-operative enterprises claim to have a far better track record of delivering results. The United States has models of electricity and telephone co-operatives as proven ways of responding to rural communities' needs when private enterprise found it unprofitable to do so.[8] The Philippines replicated these models in its rural program of electricity development and has managed to provide electricity broadly to the countryside.[9] However, when the private corporate sector found these franchise areas eventually becoming profitable after more than 20 years of co-operative supplied power, they demanded taking over supplying power from the electricity co-ops. The pursuit of privatisation has contributed to widening socioeconomic disparities as the economic benefits have become concentrated in the hands of a few corporations and families. These inequalities have been aggravated by the monopolistic practices of the new owners. This is supported by deregulation policies that enable them to charge market-based utility rates. Far preferable would be mechanisms that ensure a wider base of ownership and governance of such essential enterprises (see Figure 14.6).

The proposed debt-for-development exchange for electric co-op strengthening would work like a debt-to-equity exchange. Current subscribers can offer to buy out the electric co-ops debts to the government at a discount. The government in turn owes foreign creditors and aid agencies and could repay these debts with what the subscribers pay them. It can be assumed that foreign creditors whose intention in financing power generation networks was to spur countryside economic development will be willing to accept an early

---

[8] National Rural Electric Cooperatives Association Web site, accessed September 7, 2010, http://www.nreca.org/AboutUs/Overview.htm.
[9] National Electrification Administration Web site, accessed September 7, 2010, http://www. nea.gov.ph/.

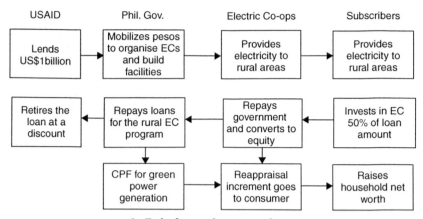

FIGURE 14.6. Debt for rural power and empowerment.

repayment of their loan at a discount. In this case, the government can agree to form a counterpart fund from the savings in paying the loan in full for projects such as investments in green power in the countryside. The subscribers, in turn, are able to raise the value of their investments in the electric co-ops, the shares in which may be credited by electronic scrip to the subscribers' pension funds instead of issuing them as printed paper certificates. With financial independence from the government will come political independence for the co-ops, which will then need to install the policies, procedures and systems of good corporate governance to ensure success.

B. *Debt-for-Microfinance Development Exchange*

Microlending is the provision of tiny loans (microcredit) to poor people to help them engage in productive activities or develop very small businesses. Instead of using collateral to ensure repayment, microlenders harness social pressure within the borrower's community. Because of more vigorous and reliable collection methods, many microlending institutions are able keep default rates well below 5%. With the growing success of this method, the volume of microloans is steadily increasing and attracting the attention of commercial institutions. The more general term, 'microfinance', covers a broader range of services, including credit, savings and insurance.[10]

The conventional approach has been for high-income countries to extend assistance for the formation of microfinance institutions (MFIs) as a

[10] ACCION International Web site, accessed September 7, 2010, http://www.accion.org/.

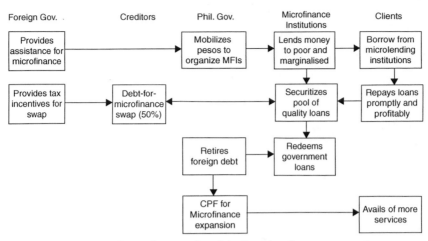

FIGURE 14.7. From direct aid to debt-for-microfinance expansion.

poverty-alleviation strategy. Debt-for-development exchanges can be designed, using the principles already mentioned, to provide ongoing funding sources for these institutions. Microloans can be securitised and used to back issued bonds, which will then be exchanged for government debt at a premium of say US$1 million of microloan-backed bonds to be exchanged for $2 million of government debt. The government will thus be able to form a $1 million counterpart fund in local currency for expanded microfinance services.

If countries like the Philippines are able to generate a volume of loans feasible for securitisation[11] – the technique of pooling specified assets, in this case microloans, and using their cash flow to back an issue of bonds – debt-for-development exchanges may even be used for exchanging the higher value microfinance-backed securities with the debtor's country's lower-rated loans for a premium. Highly developed countries' governments can provide tax incentives for foreign commercial banks to engage in the exchange, complementing or acting as an alternative to extending microfinance assistance to the governments of less developed countries and NGOs. Microfinance institutions that then hold the country's debts can go to the government and redeem the loans, share the gains from the discounts earned, generate more local currency for more microfinance activities and venture into larger loans for co-operative ventures, housing and insurance (see Figure 14.7).

[11] Andrew Davidson, *Securitization: Structuring and Investment Analysis* (Hoboken, NJ: Wiley and Sons, 2003), 3.

C. *Debt-for-Pension-Funds Enhancement Program*

Pension funds in the Philippines – the Social Security System (SSS) for private workers and the Government Social Insurance System (GSIS) for government employees – have many times been used as a source of political capital. Corporations have utilised these funds by borrowing in the money markets and investing in the capital markets. Government has also at times resorted to a form of gimmickry by raising membership coverage and pension benefits to levels that are unaffordable, for short-term political reasons. The great majority of overseas Filipino workers, the most important contributors of foreign exchange to the government, do not enjoy coverage and membership in the SSS. Making matters worse are the high fees that remittance firms and commercial banks and institutions charge, which directly deplete the remittances received by Filipino families.

Debt-for-development exchange mechanisms have the potential of correcting this market distortion that disadvantages ordinary working Filipinos. Pension funds could start purchasing government debt from foreign creditors after conducting due diligence on the legality of the loans. In particular, overseas Filipino workers could organise themselves into a co-operative pension fund and use their foreign exchange to buy back Philippine government debt, making the government accountable to them and not to foreign creditors. Any gains from the purchases of Philippine government loans when the pension funds redeemed them from the government could form a counterpart fund that could potentially make available capital for overseas workers so that if one day these workers returned to the Philippines and reunited with their families, there would be a source of capital available to them to start small businesses.

This will take an enormous amount of organising and co-ordinating, and is much easier said than done. However, all strategies begin this way, and the potential of reducing fees on remittances from abroad, and multiplying the value of such remittances through debt exchanges, is in the Philippines context very significant indeed.

V. CONCLUSION

This brief discussion of the Philippine experience opens the very real possibility of a paradigm shift in debt-for-development exchanges by encouraging communities to co-operate and respond to mutual needs. From this perspective, the major obstacle is not the lack of resources but the absence of political will to explore these new opportunities. The question remains whether governments and NGOs will be willing to invest in communities and ordinary citizens, raise the counterpart resources from debt-for-development exchanges and raise the awareness that the resources to develop their economies are available within them. This paradigm shift may in time diminish the influence of the traditional politics of patronage and dependence and thus meet strong resistance. However, it will also increase the participation levels of citizens beyond elections and, for those with faith in the democratic process, is a promising way forward.

PART IV

Innovative Applications of Exchanges

15

Farmer-Managed Natural Regeneration: A Land Rehabilitation Technique Well Adapted to Funding by Exchanges

Tony Rinaudo

I. INTRODUCTION AND BACKGROUND

Many developing countries' problems are compounded by severe environmental damage, including deforestation, soil erosion and biodiversity loss. Deforestation continues at an alarmingly high rate – about 13 million hectares per year – although the net loss in forest area in the period 2000–2005 is estimated at 7.3 million hectares per year.[1] Seventy-four percent of rangelands and 61% of rain-fed croplands in Africa's drier regions are damaged by moderate to very severe desertification.[2] In some African countries, deforestation rates exceed planting rates by 3,000%.[3] The area of the globe affected by water erosion is roughly 11 million square kilometres and the area affected by wind erosion is around 5.5 million square kilometres.[4] Combined, this equates to an eroded area some 241 times the size of Tasmania. With species extinctions running at about 1,000 times the 'background' rate, some biologists contend that we are in the middle of the earth's sixth great extinction.[5]

For many years in Sahelian countries, conventional Western forestry methods were applied to solving desertification and deforestation problems, and exotic tree species were typically favoured over indigenous species. Large

---

[1] Global Forest Resources Assessment, 2005 15 *Key Findings* (FAO, 2005). However, much of the replanting is of monoculture stands of trees, which are no real compensation for the loss of old-growth, biologically diverse forests.

[2] M. K. Tolba, O. A. El-Kholy, D. F. McMichael and R. E. Munn (eds.), *The World Environment, 1972–1992: Two Decades of Challenge* (New York: United Nations Environment Program / Chapman & Hall, 1993).

[3] S. C. Nana-Sinkam, *Land and Environmental Degradation and Desertification in Africa: The Magnitude of the Problem* (1995), Retrieved November 26, 2007, from FAO Corporate Document Repository.

[4] "Soil Erosion Site", last modified February 13, 2008, http://soilerosion.net/.

[5] Richard Black, "World's Biodiversity 'Crisis' Needs Action Says UN", accessed September 6, 2010, http://news.bbc.co.uk/2/hi/8449506.stm.

and small tree-planting projects were commissioned to curtail the southward movement of the Sahara Desert, but few made any lasting impression. Little thought was given to the appropriateness of this approach. Existing, indigenous vegetation was generally dismissed as 'useless bush'. In the name of aforestation, many projects even cleared existing woody vegetation in order to make way for exotic species. Often exotic tree species were simply planted in fields containing living and sprouting stumps of indigenous vegetation, the presence of which was barely acknowledged, let alone seen as important.

This was an enormous oversight. In fact, these living tree stumps are so numerous they constitute a vast 'underground forest', just waiting for a little care to grow and provide multiple benefits at little or no cost. The live tree stumps may produce between 10 and 30 stems each. During the process of traditional land preparation, farmers saw the stems as weeds and slashed and burnt them before sowing their food crops. Under this management system, stems rarely grew beyond 1.5 metres tall before being slashed again the following season. The net result was a barren landscape for much of the year, with few mature trees remaining. To the casual observer, the land appeared to be turning to desert; most concluded that there were no trees present and that the only way to reverse the problem was by planting trees.

Farmer-managed natural regeneration (FMNR) is the systematic regeneration of this 'underground forest'. In its basic form, desired tree stumps are selected in a field. For each stump, a decision is made as to how many stems will be chosen for growth. The tallest and straightest stems are then selected, and side branches are removed to roughly half the height of the stem. The remaining stems are then culled. The best results are achieved when the farmer returns regularly to prune any unwanted new stems and side branches as they appear. In reality, there is no fixed way of practicing FMNR, and farmers are free to choose which species they will leave, the density of trees they prefer and the timing and method of pruning. In addition, the practice of FMNR is not confined to farmland. It is being practised on degraded communal forest and grazing lands as well.

FMNR has become a catalyst for large-scale people-led environmental restoration, and communities and individuals are benefiting from its impact on poverty alleviation, enhanced food security and development of governance structures. In the 27 years since being introduced in Niger Republic, FMNR has spread to more than 50% (5 million hectares)[6] of the nation's farmland with little intervention by nongovernmental organisations (NGOs)

---

[6] World Resources Institute (WRI), "Turning Back the Desert: How Farmers Have Transformed Niger's Landscapes and Livelihoods", in *World Resources, 2008: Roots of Resilience – Growing the Wealth of the Poor* (Washington, DC: WRI, 2008).

Left: Typical Niger farm scene in the early 1980s, Maradi region.
Right: By 2007, farmers in the Maradi region were leaving up to 150 trees per hectare on once barren land.

 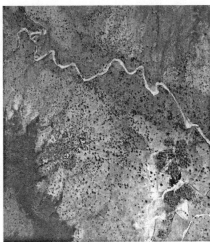

Comparison of tree cover in 1975 (left) and 2003 (right), Galma, Niger Republic. The black spots are trees, indicating a greatly enhanced level of tree cover. *Source*: U.S. Geological Survey.

or government. Building on Niger's success, today FMNR is being promoted in a number of African countries through a loose coalition of NGOs, including World Vision, which met in 2007 to form the Sahel Regreening Initiative, whose original intention was to promote FMNR in four West African countries.

II. THE INNOVATIVE ASPECTS OF FMNR

FMNR is a modern-day application of the centuries-old practices of coppicing and pollarding, the significance of which seems to have been lost by some

Demonstration of FMNR in Ghana. Notice original tree stump (centre) surrounded by multiple stems which have had side branches pruned to approximately two-thirds of their height.

forestry experts in regard to indigenous vegetation. Coppicing is a traditional method of woodland management in which young tree stems are repeatedly cut down to nearly ground level, and pollarding is a pruning system in which the tree stem or minor branches are removed 2 or 3 metres above ground level every year. FMNR is innovative in that it challenges the common assumptions about deforestation and desertification and conventional approaches to tackling them.

Conventional approaches to reforestation are costly, time-consuming and top-down. They require external skills and resources and have been largely ineffective in sub-Saharan Africa. The assumed causes of deforestation and desertification include extended drought, goats and population growth resulting in accelerated tree destruction. These factors certainly contribute to the problem but don't completely explain it, as drought, goats and population growth do not automatically lead to loss of trees.

Conventional approaches to reversing desertification, such as funding tree planting, rarely spread beyond the project boundary once external funding is withdrawn. By comparison, FMNR is cheap, rapid, locally led and implemented, uses local skills and resources and has been highly successful. FMNR uses nothing new, is so simple and cheap that the poorest farmer can learn by observation and teach her neighbour and thus can be done at scale without ongoing government or NGO intervention. Given an enabling environment, or at least the absence of a 'disabling' environment, FMNR can and does spread well beyond the original target area without project or government help.

Prior to the introduction of FMNR in the Niger Republic, government antidesertification activities were often top-down and favoured policing techniques over participation and community responsibility. Too often there was conflict between forestry staff and communities. Restoration techniques involved raising tree seedlings in nurseries and transplanting them. These techniques are costly and slow and, in the harsh environmental conditions of West Africa, generally have a low success rate. In fact, despite the millions of dollars spent on nurseries and planting, weeding, fencing and guarding seedlings, few projects have made any lasting impression. In Niger it is estimated that some 60 million trees were planted in a 12-year period and that less than 20% survived.[7]

While tree planting is important and can make a significant contribution, FMNR by contrast has the potential to spread rapidly across a region at a fraction of the cost and time it would take to implement a conventional reforestation project. Many people do not realise the enormous regenerative capacity of this regrowth and think that environmental restoration can take place only through tree planting. Others are prejudiced, believing that indigenous tree species are slow growing and of less value than exotic species. In fact, coppiced and pollarded trees can grow very rapidly, and the species being managed have multiple uses for traditional societies.

As with other activities, though, farmers need an incentive for practising FMNR – an incentive not in terms of a subsidy or cash payment, but in terms of assurances that they will benefit from their labour. Giving farmers either outright ownership of the trees they protect or tree user rights has made it possible for large-scale farmer-led reforestation to take place.

Tentative steps to introduce FMNR in Niger commenced in 1983, in the south-central Maradi region. Almost three decades on, FMNR has spread to more than half the farmland in Niger. A social rather than a technical breakthrough was achieved. The greatest barriers to reforestation were neither the absence of an exotic super tree nor ignorance of best-practice nursery and tree husbandry techniques. The greatest barriers were the collective mind set that saw trees on farmland as 'weeds' needing to be cleared and inappropriate laws that put responsibility for and ownership of trees in the hands of the government and not in the hands of the people whose livelihoods depended on them. Not having any control over the trees on their own land and having no hope of legally benefiting from them, many farmers opted to remove them from their fields altogether.

7 Personal communication, C. Reij, consultant, VU University, Amsterdam.

The effects of FMNR in Niger include the following:

- Reforestation: In Niger, over a 20-year period, more than 5 million hectares of previously cleared farmland now has perennial vegetation, in some cases in excess of 150 trees per hectare, but more typically 40 to 60 trees per hectare, equating to more than 200 million trees.[8]
- Increased incomes: Some estimates put additional household income at around $200 per person per year, and for the Maradi region alone a conservative estimate puts additional income for the region attributable to FMNR at US$17 million to $23 million per year.[9]
- Increased food security: Farmers in Niger are producing an additional 500,000 tons of grain per year because of FMNR, meeting the requirements of 2.5 million people.[10] In 2004 the then National Director of World Vision in Senegal wrote that despite the severe famine in Niger induced by drought and locust attack, farmers practising FMNR in the Aguie Department did not need food assistance because they were able to meet their own needs by selling firewood and nontimber forest products.[11]

III. SUSTAINABILITY OF FMNR

A. *Self-Sustainability and Replicability of FMNR*

FMNR has spread beyond project boundaries in Niger Republic largely from farmer to farmer and without project intervention or government involvement. Hence, once started, the movement is maintained and spread utilising local resources and initiative. This means that donor nations in a debt exchange should be able to anticipate very substantial returns on their 'investment' in FMNR.

B. *Social and Financial Sustainability*

FMNR has made rural areas more financially viable, improved physical living conditions and enhanced food security and livelihoods. For farmers who have

[8] WRI, "Turning Back the Desert"; C. Reij, G. Tappan and M Smale, "Agroenvironmental Transformation in the Sahel: Another Kind of 'Green Revolution'", IFPRI Discussion Paper, International Food Policy Research Institute, 2009.

[9] Mickey Leyland, "Assessing the Impacts of FMNR in the Sahel: A Case Study of Maradi Region, Niger", 2009 (unpublished paper).

[10] C. Reij, G. Tappan and M. Smale, "Re-Greening the Sahel Farmer–Led Innovation in Burkina Faso and Niger", in *IFPI Millions Fed: Proven Successes in Agricultural Development* (2009), accessed September 6, 2010, http://www.ifpri.org/publication/millions-fed.

[11] Eric Toumieux, *Niger Trip Report* (World Vision Senegal document, 2004).

fully adopted FMNR into their land management, FMNR has increased average household income by around $200 per annum. There is less pressure on men to leave Niger during the dry season and seek work elsewhere – a common practice that places large strains on families and their health. Women and children spend less time collecting firewood and have more time for productive activities and education.

C. *Environmental Sustainability*

Before FMNR was introduced, very few trees were left on farmlands across southern Niger. Crops and livestock were exposed to strong, sand-laden winds, and young crops were often sand-blasted or buried outright, causing farmers to replant up to five or six times in a season. Biodiversity was greatly reduced. For eight months of the year, fields were completely bare and windswept, showing no vegetative cover or only the regrowth from living tree stumps, which was slashed and burnt from January to March. Reflecting the vegetation loss, wildlife and birds also left the area. In the rainy season, only annual crops such as millet, sorghum, peanuts and cowpea were grown. Today, farmers leave an average of 3 perennial tree species on their farms and, in some cases, in excess of 10 species and they nurture up to 150 trees per hectare on once-barren land. This has also created a habitat for some wildlife and birds.

IV. GLOBAL POTENTIAL OF FMNR

Since 2004, the practice of FMNR has spread across Niger to Senegal, Mali, Ghana, Chad, Ethiopia and Uganda through World Vision. Other organisations, such as the Sahel Regreening Initiative, have been actively promoting FMNR in the West African Sahel and Ethiopia and facilitating alliances between donors and implementers. There are also numerous 'spontaneous' examples of one or other form of FMNR occurring without known contact with outside influences – for example, in Burkina Faso and Mali. FMNR is possible wherever suitable root, tree stump and soil seed banks have the capacity to regenerate and the community and individuals are willing to practise it. Vast areas of cleared land around the globe retain tree roots, stumps and/or seed, which have the capacity to regenerate under the right conditions.

In that very little of African agriculture is mechanised and vegetation has not been completely removed, the roots, stumps and seeds of trees can still be found over large areas of land. Many of the species within these vegetation types have the ability to grow new stems (suckers), once cut. Similar situations where FMNR is possible occur in temperate, semiarid, subtropical and tropical regions around the world.

V. CRITICAL SUCCESS FACTORS

Experience has proved a number of factors to be central to the success of
FMNR adoption:

1. Community-felt need: FMNR is more likely to be adopted when com-
    munities acknowledge their situation and the need to take action. This
    perception of need can be supported by educational activities that show
    graphically to farmers the potential that the nurturance of native trees
    on their land offers them.

2. The building of capacity either spontaneously (through farmers teach-
    ing farmers) or through an outside agency: In order for communities to
    adopt FMNR, it may be necessary to counter entrenched beliefs about
    the unimportance of trees and to give pointers on tree management
    techniques. For example, farmers commonly believe that having trees
    in fields is detrimental to crop yields and livestock productivity, and
    few realise the enormous financial benefits that can be derived from
    trees. Such misconceptions need to be countered. Similarly, farmers
    may not know the best time of year to prune, which stems and branches
    to prune or the importance of using sharp implements and minimising
    damage to the tree. Building capacity to better manage trees can greatly
    enhance the speed of revegetation and increase the benefits.

3. The establishment of organisational structures with locally devised
    by-laws or regulations: The establishment of organisational structures
    (e.g., co-operatives) or strengthening existing structures (e.g., traditional
    hierarchies or development committees) provides an enabling environ-
    ment for FMNR promotion and adoption. Along with this, the crea-
    tion of mutually agreed upon regulations to protect tree regrowth and
    to institutionalise respect for others' property, being trees, gives people
    the necessary confidence to practice FMNR. Having such local insti-
    tutional support builds confidence in those wanting to practice FMNR
    in that tree management rules and consequences for infringements are
    public knowledge and there is a structured way of providing justice.

4. Favourable policy environment: There must be an assurance that if
    individuals and the community protect trees, they will have the right
    to benefit from their work. Many national forestry codes exclude people
    who rely on natural resources for their livelihoods from benefiting from
    trees, and the end result is that over time whole districts are deforested.
    By granting user rights or outright ownership rights, people have con-
    fidence that if they make the effort to protect trees, they will have the

right to use and/or sell wood and nontimber forest products. Ironically, as the Niger example shows, the net effect of this assurance is an overwhelming net gain in protected and sustainably managed trees.

5. Access to markets: Wood and nontimber forest products are a readily traded and valuable commodity across much of the developing world. When farmers can legally sell wood and nontimber forest products, interest in FMNR is stimulated.

6. Broad spectrum buy-in: The creation of a critical mass of FMNR adopters and stakeholder support is important. People do not like to act alone or to be different from the majority. Gaining peer group acceptance and wide stakeholder support is very important for rapid adoption. As far as possible, various levels of government, departments of agriculture and forestry, universities, researchers, private enterprises, NGOs, sedentary and nomadic farmers, men, women and youth should be well informed and supportive of the value of FMNR.

7. Long-term nature of the intervention: Any innovation will take time to be adopted, and problems will inevitably be encountered along the way. It is critical that a project take a long-term view and be available for encouragement, consultation and support for at least five years, and perhaps up to eight years. This does not mean projects should run the same activities year after year, but they should fade into a more background presence, ready to assist as issues arise.

VI. HOW DEBT EXCHANGES CAN INCREASE THE SPREAD OF FMNR

A. *Unfunded Activities*

Debt exchanges can play a pivotal role in the spread of FMNR through funding the following activities:

- Creating awareness of the potential of FMNR: Despite FMNR's enormous impact in Niger Republic, it is still relatively unknown and there is an urgent need to bring it to the attention of decision makers.
- Advocacy and political debate for policy change regarding control of natural resources: Natural resource laws in many countries do not provide the necessary enabling environment for FMNR to flourish. There is a need to fund advocacy campaigns for appropriate policy change.
- Training for all stakeholders (communities, local, regional and national authorities, departments of agriculture and forestry, NGOs, etc.): Training and exchange visits are crucial elements for the spread of FMNR.

- Follow-up and monitoring of farmers practising FMNR: Any new initiative takes time to become established. In the formative years, adequate follow-up and monitoring of practitioners is essential for success.
- Formation of co-operatives or strengthening of existing organisational structures such as village committees: Having an organisational structure gives legitimacy to FMNR and defines boundaries, obligations and benefits to both practitioners and nonpractitioners alike.
- Formalisation of FMNR into agriculture and forestry departmental procedures: Currently FMNR is not an officially recognised or sanctioned activity in many countries. Promotion and adoption are greatly enhanced once it becomes an officially sanctioned activity.
- Formation of certified markets for wood and nontimber forest products: Peoples' motivation to practice FMNR is accelerated when they benefit financially through legitimate markets.

B. *Obstacles and Incentive*

The focus of debt exchanges should be on tackling the following obstacles:

- Lack of awareness of the potential of FMNR: This is a big obstacle, as many decision makers simply do not know about FMNR.
- Dominance of the 'tree-planting paradigm' amongst professionals for solving desertification and deforestation problems: Because of their training and work experience, most decision makers and technical experts think in terms of expensive tree nursery and planting-out operations. An example of this is the widespread endorsement of the 'Green Wall Against the Sahara' tree planting initiative at a cost of US$911 million.[12] Even though Niger Republic (which is included in this scheme) has realised such a spectacular reversal in desertification without planting a single tree, no mention of FMNR is made in the proposal.
- Unwillingness on the part of government agencies to 'trust' communities to care for the environment: There is a historical mistrust between government agencies, which see themselves as protectors of the forest, and communities, which are seen as destroyers of the forest. These barriers that have built up over generations are real, and they need to be dismantled before FMNR can flourish.
- Unfavourable landownership and user rights laws: Individuals and communities act out of self-interest. If there is no prospect of benefiting from

[12] "GEF Backs Great Green Wall with 119 Million US Dollars", June 18, 2010, accessed September 18, 2010, http://news.theage.com.au/breaking-news-world/gef-backs-great-green-wall-with-119-million-us-dollars-20100618-yk4z.html.

their activities in pruning and protecting trees, most see no reason for doing so.

- Perceived lack of revenues to government departments through FMNR: Whereas government-managed, large-scale forestry projects can be seen as revenue-raising ventures, it is harder for some to see the benefit of individually managed, small-scale interventions. In fact, through regulating markets, governments can create revenue streams from FMNR.
- Farmers' fears that trees will reduce crop yields and attract pests: Almost universally, farmers clear trees from farmland because of perceived competition with crops and pastures. In fact, with the right balance of trees and with appropriate pruning methods, both fodder production and crop yields can be increased.
- Farmers' suspicion that they will not benefit from their labours by being able to use and/or sell the wood and nontimber forest products: Initially it is necessary to invest in extension services and build trust so that farmers' fears can be allayed and prejudices overcome.
- Absence of acknowledgement or promotion of FMNR by government departments of agriculture or forestry: Currently, FMNR is not known to be officially sanctioned or promoted by any government department.

The incentives for practising FMNR are based on the fact that it is an effective, low-cost means of:

- meeting commitments to the Millennium Development Goals, especially MDG 1 (eradication of extreme poverty and hunger) and MDG 7 (ensuring environmental sustainability);
- meeting commitments to UN conventions such as the convention on biodiversity and the convention on desertification;
- meeting greenhouse gas reduction targets;
- boosting national food security and increasing community resilience to environmental shocks;
- increasing government revenues made possible from increased FMNR-generated income; and
- reducing the damage bill from violent storms, flooding and drought.

C. *Costs of an FMNR Program*

Table 15.1 presents a very rough estimate of costs (in US dollars) of a comprehensive FMNR promotion and implementation program in a single imaginary district in one country.

TABLE 15.1. *Costs of an FMNR program*

		Cost per district Year 1	Year 2	Year 3	Year 4
FMNR awareness creation	One-week visit to country where FMNR is practised (10 male and female farmers and government officials) Accom. per diem: 10 × $50/day × 7 days = $3,500 Airfares: 10 × $2,500 = $25,000 In-country travel accommodation = $10,000 Leaders' workshop = $10,000	$48,500	$0	$0	$0
FMNR workshops	In-country workshops per village cluster or watershed, say 20 clusters × $5,000 Training in FMNR and a forum to help overcome fears of officials (losing control, revenue) and fears of farmers (reduced crop yields, not benefiting from their labours) Follow-up/ progress meetings	$100,000	$100,000	$50,000	$50,000
Change of national laws on access to and use of natural resources (especially land and trees)	Advocacy, forums, legal assistance, etc.	$100,000	$50,000	$10,000	$10,000
District-wide departmental adoption and promotion of FMNR	Two vehicles: $100,000 Two motor bikes: 2 × $3,000 = $6,000 Travel/maintenance costs, $20,000 × 2 = $40,000 Two staff + per diems: $16,000/year = $32,000 Two staff + per diems: $12,000/year = $24,000 Office and incidentals: $20,000	$106,000 $116,000	$121,800	$127,890	$134,285
Establishment of certified markets for wood and nontimber forest products	20 markets at $10,000 Auditing and follow-up	$200,000	$20,000	$5,000	$5,000
Formation of co-operatives	With internal by-laws, revenue-raising ability, governance skills: 20 co-operatives @ $5,000 Auditing and follow-up	$100,000	$20,000	$5,000	$5,000
		$770,500	$311,800	$197,890	$204,285

The costs for the first four years, for one district, is $1,484,475. For an eight-year program, add vehicle replacement ($120,000) and four-year running costs ($880,000), for a total cost of $2,484,475. This initial investment is proportionally greater than subsequent investments in other districts once a favourable policy environment has been created and farmers have experience in practising FMNR. The considerable savings on offer include the following:

- Once accomplished, there will be no ongoing requirement to invest in policy change.
- Travel to another country will be unnecessary, as there will be local examples to visit, greatly reducing expenses and the time required.
- Farmers will largely teach farmers. Rather than depending on paid staff, where there is an enabling environment and once farmers understand and begin practising FMNR, they will learn from each other and the method will spread largely without external inputs.

D. Potential Problems

Potential problems in funding FMNR programs through government and ensuring that funding is additional are as follows:

- Accountability issues that are normal for all government-to-government financial transactions need to be identified and dealt with appropriately.
- Lack of third-party recipients of cash flow for FMNR programs means accountability issues are heightened.
- FMNR is not part of standard agriculture or forestry curricula and therefore is neither widely known nor a mainstream activity.
- Technical services such as forestry and agriculture departments are largely unfamiliar with FMNR, and it is not in the suite of practices they promote.
- In that FMNR is currently not a standard practice or promoted by government departments, it would automatically be an additional activity, finding space for which within current budgets is likely to be very difficult.

The following measures should be put in place to ensure that these problems are addressed:

- Standard accounting procedures with regular audits should be followed.
- Ideally, reputable and well-established NGOs and community-based organisations already working in the agriculture and forestry sectors

should collaborate and become recipients of cash flows for FMNR promotion.

- When FMNR workshops are held, key academic and technical services staff should be invited.
- FMNR resource materials should be made available for incorporation into university and technical school curricula and technical notes used by agriculture and forestry departments.

There are no insurmountable obstacles to including FMNR in debt-exchange programs, and no issues have been identified that are outside the range already experienced and that have already been adequately dealt with in existing debt-exchange programs. In fact, given that FMNR is relatively cheap and rapid and has potentially very large positive impacts on poverty reduction and the attainment of food security, it is an excellent candidate for inclusion in debt-exchange programs.

VII. CONCLUSION

The scale of land degradation, deforestation and desertification in many indebted countries is enormous, and the impact on local populations has reached critical levels. FMNR is a low-cost, rapid and effective method of reforestation with demonstrated enormous untapped potential for large-scale environmental restoration. FMNR is also a proven tool in alleviating poverty, enhancing food security and fostering good governance.

FMNR programs can be easily adapted to meet requirements for funding through debt exchanges. No incompatibility issues have been identified that would be an impediment to including FMNR in debt-exchange programs.

16

Restoring Mangroves in the Philippines

Ross P. Buckley

I. INTRODUCTION

The Philippines' economic situation is quite bleak. Its total external debt was US$65.8 billion at the end of 2008, up from US$58 billion in 2000.[1] Poverty has increased in the past 30 years, with 45% of the population living on less than US$2 per day.[2] The Philippines owed Australia A$66.6 million in 2009,[3] down significantly from A$493 million in 2003.[4] Most of this debt was incurred more than 10 years ago as a result of the Development Import Finance Facility (DIFF) scheme. DIFF was a soft-loan scheme to fund purchases from Australian companies by recipient governments and has been criticised by Australia's former Treasurer, Peter Costello, as a 'subsidy paid to domestic businesses'.[5] The Australian economy has thus already benefited from the enhanced exports.[6]

In the mid-2000s the Philippines took substantial steps to reduce its external sovereign debt. President Arroyo implemented fiscal and monetary policies that helped to control inflation and lift the nation's debt rating. These included raising the Value Added Tax (VAT) from 10% to 12% in February 2006, which was intended to bring in additional revenue of PHP 75 billion

[1] Asian Development Bank, *Key Indicators for Asia and the Pacific* (Philippines: Asian Development Bank, 2009).
[2] Ibid., 158.
[3] Public sector debt (loans and export finance guarantee only) owed to EFIC (National Interest and Commercial Account), in 2009, EFIC Annual Report.
[4] Ibid.
[5] Quoted by Ms. Nori, New South Wales Legislative Assembly Hansard, "Development Import Finance Facility Abolition" (October 30, 1996), accessed August 2, 2010, http://www.parliament.nsw.gov.au/prod/PARLMENT/hansart.nsf/V3Key/LA19961030034.
[6] Ibid.

in 2006,[7] and extending the VAT to energy products in November 2005.[8] The VAT was intended to lift the ratio of tax to gross domestic product (GDP) and provide greater revenue for the government. This ratio reached a peak of 17% in 1997 but later fell, and the increase in tax rates in 2006 lifted national tax income to only 14.3% of GDP.[9] With debt burdens remaining high and tax revenue low, economic growth has been stymied and the debt burden has not been eased. Tax reform remains a pressing issue for the newly elected President Aqutio.[10]

The Philippines continues to struggle with limited budgetary resources, massive levels of foreign debt and a rapidly growing population. Although remittances from abroad do assist, it is clear that without further assistance Filipinos have a long road ahead of them before they see material benefits from the sacrifices they have made. The economic growth in the decade following the Asian economic crisis was spurred by private consumption and was highly dependent on net exports for growth.[11] Private consumption was fuelled by remittances, with about 9 to 11 million Filipinos working overseas and with remittances representing 10% of GDP. Although gross national savings increased in the early years of the new century, such funds were not used to foster investment, and the inherent structural weaknesses became very clear in the wake of the global financial crisis (GFC).[12] Following the GFC, the growth rate in the Philippines dropped to 3.8% in 2008 compared with 7.1% a year earlier, and inflation rose from 2.8% to 9.3%. The violent shock to the economy in the aftermath of the crisis revealed the inherent instability of the factors driving growth in the Philippines. In response to the GFC the Filipino government ran a fiscal deficit of 3.5% of GDP in 2009.[13]

Current poverty levels in the Philippines will cause long-term damage to the nation's human capital and make economic reform significantly more difficult in the future.[14] The Philippines is facing a number of serious threats to

---

[7] "Philippines: Market Strategy – Improving Local Debt Outlook", *Emerging Markets Monitor* 11 (2006): 9.

[8] IMF, "IMF Executive Board Concludes 2005 Article IV Consultation with the Philippines", Public Information Notice (PIN) No. 06/25, March 6, 2006.

[9] Joseph Anthony Lim, *The Impact of the Global Financial Crisis and Economic Turmoil on the Philippines: National Responses and Recommendations to Address the Crisis* (Penang, Malaysia: Third World Network, 2010), 11.

[10] AusAid, "Philippines", accessed August 2, 2010, http://www.ausaid.gov.au/country/country.cfm?CountryId=31.

[11] Lim, *The Impact of the Global Financial Crisis*, 2.

[12] Ibid., 9.

[13] AusAID, "Philippines".

[14] Commonwealth, *Philippines Australia Development Cooperation Strategy, 2004–2008* (Canberra: Australian Government and AusAID, 2004), 2.

its continued progress, including poverty, political instability, security concerns, natural disasters and avian flu.

This chapter first examines the manner in which poverty threatens economic development in the Philippines and proposes and analyses a debt-for-development project between the Australian and Philippine governments as a means for Australia to enhance greatly the effectiveness of its debt relief and aid efforts for the Philippines.

II. LEVELS OF POVERTY

Poverty is a major threat to stability in the Philippines. For poverty levels to be reduced, the Philippines must achieve sustainable broad-based economic growth. If the current poverty levels are allowed to continue, the long-term effects on health and education will frustrate economic development in the future.[15] The Philippines has one of the highest levels of income inequality in Asia.[16] The wealthiest 20% of the population receive 50% of national income, the poorest 20% less than 5% of national income. While levels of poverty have dropped from 30% in 1990, the number of those below the poverty line is greater than it was two decades ago.[17] Poverty is most severe in the rural communities and specifically on the island of Mindanao, with 47% of the population there living below the poverty line.[18] More than half the islanders live on less than US$0.60 a day (well below the global level for extreme poverty); 30% of children under the age of five are stunted as a result of chronic malnutrition, and only one-third of children finish primary school.[19] Decades of conflict on the island have contributed to poor agricultural productivity, a lack of investment in infrastructure, unequal land and income distribution and poor social services.[20]

Australia's Development Program objectives for the Philippines in 2007 state that 'Poverty Reduction in Philippines depends primarily on sustaining and improving on the current higher rates of economic growth'.[21] This has clearly been hampered in the past few years. In the aftermath of the GFC it became apparent that the Philippines is highly unlikely to achieve a number

[15] Ibid.
[16] Ibid., 17.
[17] AusAID, "Philippines".
[18] Commonwealth, *Philippines–Australia Development Assistant Strategy, 2007–11* (Canberra: Australian Government and AusAID, 2007), 3.
[19] United Nations News Service, "UN Food Agency Supports Peace Effort in Philippines' Island of Mindanao", *UN Daily News*, April 6, 2006.
[20] *Philippines–Australia Development Assistant Strategy, 2007–11*, 1.
[21] Ibid., 9.

of the Millennium Development Goals, namely maternal mortality ratios, contraceptive prevalence rates and a number of education targets.[22] The development indicators are significantly lower in Mindano, where life expectancy is 10 years below the national average and where the rates of maternal and infant mortality are 80% and 30%, respectively, higher than the national average.[23] The Philippines also lags behind other countries in the region in terms of poverty, with 13.2% of the population living on less than a dollar per day, compared with 7.7% in Indonesia and 8.4% in Vietnam.[24]

Australia has shown its concern for poverty in the Philippines through the Medium-Term Philippines Development Plans for 2001–2004 and 2004–2010, and the 2002 ministerial statement, Australian Aid: Investing in Growth, Stability and Prosperity.[25] The Australian government has a new four-year strategy: the Australia–Philippines Development Assistance Strategy 2007–2011. In 2010–2011 Australia will give just over A$100 million in overseas development aid to the Philippines.[26] The development program has three pillars: economic growth, basic education and national stability and human security.[27] The goal of the strategy is to increase levels of aid to the Philippines over five years.[28] Currently, aid represents only 0.5% of Philippine national income, and Australian aid makes up less than 10% of total Philippines overseas development aid.[29]

Poverty in the Philippines is a complex problem that deserves more of Australia's attention. Because poverty-reduction efforts are already funded by several sources, Australia's role in alleviating poverty must be precise and calculated not to interfere or overlap with other projects. It should target the root of the problem through programs that encourage self-sufficient, long-term economic and social development in the poorest communities.

[22] Hyewon Kang, *The Philippines' Absorptive Capacity for Foreign Aid* (Makati City: Philippine Institute for Development Studies, 2010), 10–11.
[23] Commonwealth, *Philippines–Australia Development Assistant Strategy, 2007–11*, 4.
[24] Kang, *The Philippines' Absorptive Capacity*, 1.
[25] Commonwealth, *Medium-Term Philippines Development Plan (MTPDP) for 2001–2004* (Canberra: Australian Government and AusAID, 2001; Commonwealth, *Medium-Term Philippines Development Plan (MTPDP) for 2004–2010* (Canberra: Australian Government and AusAID) (the report can be found at http://www.neda.gov.ph/ads/mtpdp/MTPDP2004–2010/PDF/MTPDP2004–2010.html, and while it does not state the year of publication, it makes reference throughout to 2003 as though that year has finished, e.g., it mentions GDP for 2003); Alexander Downer, "Australian Aid: Investing in Growth, Stability and Prosperity", Eleventh Statement to Parliament on Australia's Development Cooperation Program (2002); Commonwealth, *Philippines–Australia Development Assistant Strategy, 2007–11*.
[26] AusAID, "Philippines".
[27] Commonwealth, *Philippines–Australia Development Assistant Strategy, 2007–11*, 14.
[28] Ibid., 14.
[29] Ibid., 2.

III. ADVANTAGES OF A BILATERAL DEBT EXCHANGE

The Philippine government is open to entering into debt-for-development exchanges with Australia, and Australia has much to gain and little to lose from such agreements. No outlays would be required from the Australian government because all funding would come from the conversion of existing debt into Philippine pesos. While the amounts involved would not be large, as the Philippines' remaining debt to Australia is small, the effects of these exchanges could nonetheless be significant. The negotiation, implementation and supervision of these exchanges will also provide the opportunity to strengthen the relationship between the two governments.

The Philippines is in Australia's backyard, and Australia is in the Philippines'. Their interdependence is highlighted by Australia's vulnerability to avian influenza, which in turn is dependent on poultry-raising practices in Indonesia and the Philippines. Australia ranks among the top three bilateral aid donors (along with the United States and Japan) to the Philippines and has shown its continued concern through the Medium-Term Philippines Development Plan.

It is in the interests of the Australian and the Philippines governments to agree to convert some part of the bilateral debt owed by the Philippines to Australia into funding for debt-for-development projects. A relatively modest initial sum of A$25 million to A$40 million could be made available, with the balance of the debt to become available upon the successful implementation of the initial project. Both governments would have an active role in structuring the transaction and selecting the projects. The structure of the transaction would afford complete transparency and accountability and the implementation of the projects would be closely monitored by both governments.

The primary objectives of an exchange would be to reduce poverty and improve economic development, and thus serve to assist the Philippines in achieving its Millennium Development Goals, because, as already noted, the Philippines is behind its targets in a number of areas.[30] Any exchange should support and complement the Philippines' national development plans.

The choice of debt-for-development projects must be a joint decision of the debtor and creditor governments. Recent research suggests that donors overlook at their peril the expertise resident in developing countries about what their country needs.[31] In other words, if the Australian government wishes to

[30] World Bank Group, "Millennium Development Goals for the Philippines", accessed August 2, 2010, http://ddp-ext.worldbank.org.
[31] See Ross Buckley, "Why the Policy Development Capacity of Some Developing Countries Exceeds That of the International Monetary Fund", *Tulane Journal of International and Comparative Law* 15 (2006): 121.

get the most bang for its debt-relief buck, it needs to give careful attention to the projects suggested by the Philippine government.

IV. MANGROVES

Mangrove forests protect coastlines, improve fish yields and provide forest resources. Mangroves provide protection from storms, hurricanes and tsunamis by absorbing the energy of wind and waves and stabilising the shoreline, thus protecting villages from tidal surges.[32] They trap sediment, filter pollution, improve the supply of nutrients and provide habitats for marine life. With a coastline of 36,300 kilometres, mangroves are of central importance in coastal resource management in the Philippines. Rural Filipino communities use mangrove trees for timber, to thatch roofs and to make medicines. Apart from the ecological value, mangroves provide approximately US$83million per year for the Philippines through fish and sustainable wood harvest.[33] At the turn of the century, mangroves in the Philippines covered around 450,000 hectares. Overexploitation and conversion to agriculture, salt ponds, industry and settlements saw the decline of mangrove forests to only 120,000 hectares in 1994–1995.[34]

Intensive shrimp farming has been largely responsible for the more recent destruction of mangrove forests in the Philippines. Half the area covered by mangroves was developed into aquaculture ponds up until the mid-1980s, with 95% of Philippine water pond being derived from mangroves.[35] Shrimp farms require the complete removal of mangroves, yet have a productive life of only about five years. After that time, yields decline dramatically, and pollution and disease rise. At this point shrimp-farm investors move on, to clear another mangrove forest.[36] Mangroves around the region have been cleared for such a purpose, with estimates that as early as 1997 the Philippines had lost 60% of its mangrove forests, Thailand 55%, Vietnam 37%, and Malaysia 12%.[37]

---

[32] According to the Harbor Department of the Ministry of Communications and Transport, there is severe erosion of the shoreline in several areas where there are no mangroves. The cost of constructing breakwaters to prevent such erosion is estimated to be around US$875 per metre of coastline. Suthawan Sathirathai and Edward Barbier, "Valuing Mangrove Conservation in Southern Thailand", *Western Economic Association International* 19 (2001): 116.

[33] See http://www.bohol-philippines.com/mangrove-forests.html. Accessed August 2, 2010.

[34] J. H. Primavera and J. M. A. Easteban, "A Review of Mangrove Rehabilitation in the Philippines: Successes, Failures and Future Prospects", *Wetlands Ecology and Management* 16 (2008): 346.

[35] Coralie Thornton, Mike Shanahan and Juliette Williams, "From Wetlands to Wastelands: Impacts of Shrimp Farming", *SWS Bulletin* (March 2003): 48.

[36] Sathirathai and Barbier, "Valuing Mangrove Conservation", 110.

[37] Roy R. Lewis III, "Mangrove Restoration and Benefits of Successful Ecological Restoration", Paper presented at the Mangrove Valuation Workshop, Beijer International Institute of Ecological Economics, Stockholm, Sweden, April 8, 2001, 4.

In order to minimise the damage to the mangrove forests, a 1983 report by the ICUN Commission on Ecology suggested that the conversion of mangrove forest into fishpond not exceed one hectare of ponds for three hectares of mangroves left untouched. However, conversion has proceeded apace, so that only one-half a hectare of mangroves remains to one hectare of pond. The impetus for this ecological disaster has been the increase in fish/shrimp culture ponds.[38]

Shrimp farming is lucrative business and has been actively promoted by the Philippine government for economic reasons. However, intensive shrimp farming is not economically beneficial once all of its costs are factored in, including declines in fishing revenue and loss of coastline protection.[39] This would remain true even if shrimp farmers were required to reinstate the mangroves, and did so successfully, after the five-year life span of their farms, which, of course, they are not. One hectare of mangroves in the Philippines can yield 400 kilos of local fish and seafood annually, and help feed a further 400 kilos of fish and 75 kilos of seafood that mature elsewhere.[40] The removal of one hectare of mangroves thus costs fisheries between US$200 and US$700 per annum. The cost of restoring mangroves is therefore recoverable from the value generated for local fisheries within a few years.[41]

Local rural communities often see little returns from shrimp farms in their region. Intensive shrimp farming is capital intensive and thus beyond the capacity of local small-scale farmers. The loss of mangroves is detrimental to the lifestyle and livelihoods of local communities and yet the local rewards are few. Furthermore, mangroves in the Philippines are considered public property, and thus communities must rely on the Royal Forestry Department (RFD) to enforce mangrove protection.[42]

In 1976 the National Mangrove Committee was formed with the task of designing a comprehensive program that would rationalise mangrove planning.[43] In the 1980s there were further moves towards an integrated mangrove management plan for the Philippines, with the passage of various laws for the purpose. Mangrove management falls under the jurisdiction of the

---

[38] Primavera and Easteban, "A Review of Mangrove Rehabilitation", 346.

[39] Lewis, "Mangrove Restoration".

[40] Ibid., 4–5.

[41] Edward Barbier, "Valuing the Environment as an Input: Review of Applications to Mangrove–Fishery Linkages", *Ecological Economics* 35 (2000): 47; Edward Barbier, Ivan Strand and Suthawan Sathirathai, "Do Open Access Conditions Affect the Valuation of an Externality? Estimating the Welfare Effect of Mangrove–Fishery Linkages in Thailand", *Environmental and Resource Economics* 21 (2002): 343.

[42] See, e.g., Barbier, Strand and Sathirathai, "Do Open Access Conditions Affect the Valuation of an Externality?"

[43] Primavera and Easteban, "A Review of Mangrove Rehabilitation", 347.

Department of Environment and Natural Resources.[44] The first government-sponsored plan of reforestation was put into place in the mid-1980s in the islands of Marungas. It was, however, the contributions of international development assistance programs that spurred reforestation programs.[45] For example, two loans from the Asian Development Bank for US$80 million were used to fund a seven-year Fisheries Sector Program (FSP) from 1990. One target of the program was to plant 30,000 hectares of mangroves. However, due to bad weather and a lack of qualified staff to manage the project, only 7,000 hectares were planted.[46] In 1999 a Community Bases Resource Management Project was implemented by the Department of Finance under a US$38 million loan from the World Bank. The aim was to address problems of rural poverty, environmental degradation and natural resource depletion. Projects included the rehabilitation of 5,302 hectares of degraded mangrove forest and new planting of a further 2,074 hectares.[47]

Despite the large scale of funds injected into the reforestation effort and the planting of an estimated 44,000 hectares of mangrove seedlings, the results have been underwhelming. The failure has stemmed in part from a basic misunderstanding of where to plant the mangrove seeds, with seedlings perishing in mudlands, sandflats and seagrass meadow.[48] Recently, some communities have drafted local rules to protect mangroves and reserve their use for local communities.[49] Since 2005, Yadfon, a nongovernmental organisation, has worked to assist 20 communities to manage their own mangroves.[50]

The ecological as well as economic threat to coastal communities has been noted internationally. In the past 25 years Africa has lost about 500,000 hectares of mangroves.[51] Internationally several types of programs have been undertaken to restore and protect mangrove forests. Bangladesh currently employs villagers to plant mangroves on coastal mudflats.[52] More than 100,000 hectares have

[44] Ronald J. Maliao and Bernice B. Polohan, "Evaluating the Impacts of Mangrove Rehabilitation in Cogtong Bay, Philippines", *Environmental Management* 41 (2008): 415.
[45] Primavera and Easteban, "A Review of Mangrove Rehabilitation", 358.
[46] Ibid., 349.
[47] Ibid., 352.
[48] David Malakoff, "Massive Mangrove Reforestation Backfires: The Philippines" (July 15, 2008), accessed August 2, 2010, http://mangroveactionproject.org/news/current_headlines/massive-mangrove-restoration-backfires-the-philippines.
[49] Sathirathai and Barbier, "Valuing Mangrove Conservation".
[50] John Parr, "Natural Coastal Defence Barriers: Ecosystems Can Benefit from Public Participation", *Bangkok Post* (Thailand), February 21, 2005.
[51] See F. Borjana (ed.), *The Relevance of Mangrove Forests to African Fisheries, Wildlife and Water Resources* (Accra, Ghana: UN Food and Agriculture Association, 2009).
[52] See M. S. Iftekhar and M. R. Islam, "Managing Mangroves in Bangladesh: A Strategy Analysis", *Journal of Coastal Conservation* 10 (2004): 139–146.

been planted for relatively little expense. Ecuador has discouraged the further destruction of its mangroves by giving shrimp farmers incentives to restore mangroves.[53] In Tanzania, community initiatives have had some success, with community consultation and awareness raising in Zanzibar undertaken by the government. Cutting of mangrove wood by nonvillagers has been banned, and traditional methods of rotational harvesting have been promoted.[54]

The cost of successfully restoring mangrove forests varies widely and depends upon whether excavation or fill is required before planting. Many mangrove restoration projects have failed because they have moved directly into the planting phase without first re-establishing a suitable environment for the mangroves. Mangroves are a naturally recovering species; therefore, if natural recovery is not occurring there is generally a reason, and this reason must be addressed first. In the Philippines, large-scale mangrove planting projects have had success rates that vary from 0% to 66%.[55] The average success rate has been between 10% and 20%.[56]

The lessons of the past two decades of mangrove management projects have been, firstly, that overseas assistance is helpful in providing the expertise as to how the environment should be prepared to receive mangroves and, secondly, that local management is necessary to foster success. The low level of success of mangrove reforestation projects in the past two decades in the Philippines can be attributed in large part to the weak role given to local government units in co-ordination with national bodies. Local participation in design, implementation and monitoring is crucial in producing results, and participatory approaches are viewed as crucial for enhancing forest management.[57] The necessity of community participation has been recognised by the World Bank through the Global Competitive Marketplace grant program, which rewards community initiatives to combat climate change. In late 2009 the World Bank gave a grant to the Filipino Development Foundation in northern Sumar to replant mangroves in a coastal village of 2,000 people.[58]

---

[53]   American Association for the Advancement of Science, "Mangroves and Estuaries", *Atlas of Population & Environment*, accessed August 2, 2010, http://atlas.aaas.org.

[54]   I. Thompson and T. Christopherson (eds.), *Cross-Sectional Toolkit for the Conservation and Sustainable Management of Forest Biodiversity* (Montreal: Secretariat of the Convention on Biological Diversity, 2008).

[55]   Lewis, "Mangrove Restoration", 4–5.

[56]   Primavera and Easteban, "A Review of Mangrove Rehabilitation", 356.

[57]   Manicar S. Samson and Rene N. Rollon, "Growth Performance of Planted Mangroves in the Philippines: Revisiting Forest Management Strategy", *Ambio* 37(4) (2008): 239; Primavera and Easteban, "A Review of Mangrove Rehabilitation", 356.

[58]   World Bank, "Four Philippine CSOs Win Grants in 9th Global Development Marketplace in Washington DC" (press release, November 16, 2009).

Debt-for-development exchanges discussed in previous chapters have been heralded as a success when the implementation has been directed and co-managed with local communities, and this will similarly be the key for any debt-for-development exchange with the Philippines in the area of mangrove reforestation and preservation.

The debt-for-development exchange could financially support local projects to restore and protect mangroves. These local projects could provide employment and training for local communities, reduce the risk of conflict between communities and limit damage from natural disasters. This project could also support government efforts to give communities control over local mangrove forests.

V. CONCLUSION

Australia can do more than it is today to assist the Philippines' development. A debt-for-development exchange program with the Philippines has much to offer both countries, at a very small cost to Australia. The re-establishment of mangrove forests is a highly suitable target project for such an exchange, as the expertise Australia could contribute to the project would greatly enhance its effectiveness and the long-term returns from effective mangrove restoration are massive, given that mangroves, when mature, provide a critical fish breeding habitat, timber for local villagers and protection from tsunamis and cyclones. In addition, working together to structure and implement such projects will strengthen the bilateral relationship between Australia and the Philippines at the political and administrative levels.

17

Poverty Reduction through Social Protection: A Potential Form of Debt-for-Development Exchange

John Langmore

In June 2000 the 23rd Special Session of the UN General Assembly agreed to set a global goal for poverty reduction of halving severe poverty by 2015, the first time a global target for poverty reduction had been adopted by a global conference. Three months later, this target was reiterated by the UN Millennium Summit, and in 2001 the goal of reducing extreme poverty to half its 1990 level by 2015 became the first of the Millennium Development Goals (MDGs). Most countries adopted the MDGs quickly; others were more reluctant, amongst them the governments at the time of the United States and Australia. However, with changes of government, they too have joined the rest of UN member states, so that now nearly all countries and international institutions are committed to the goal.

The World Bank projects that the proportion of the total population of developing countries living on US$1.25 a day or less (which has been used as the standard measure of severe poverty since 2008) in 2015 is likely to be 15%, considerably less than half the proportion in 1990 of 42%.[1] This would mean that about 920 million people would be living under the international poverty line in 2015, about half the number in 1990. This dramatic improvement is principally because of the estimated fall in poverty in China, but declines are also under way in other East Asian countries, in Latin America and the Caribbean and in South Asia. However, sub-Saharan Africa, Europe and Central Asia are expected to miss the target. The global financial crisis is expected to add 64 million more people to the number of those who live in poverty than would have been so in the absence of the crisis. Progress in reducing poverty below US$2 a day is expected to be slower: about 2 billion people are expected to be living on US$2 or less per day in 2015.

[1] World Bank, *Global Economic Prospects 2010: Crisis, Finance and Growth* (Washington, DC: World Bank, 2010), 41–42.

These figures mean that despite significant economic growth in many countries, a huge number of people will remain oppressed by deprivation in the near future. *Even if the MDG target is achieved, that will still leave nearly a billion people living in severe poverty.* Stronger, equitable economic and social development is essential and so too are additional means of poverty reduction.

Poverty is multidimensional, manifested through malnutrition, inadequate housing or water, poor sanitation and lack of access to health services or education and in gender disparities as well as income deprivation. Addressing the links between inadequate income, unemployment, overcrowded accommodation, hunger, disease, constrained access to health services, schools, safety and social protection, let alone human rights and gender equity, is complex and demanding. Yet improving any of these will influence the capacity to influence others: improving employment opportunities, education, health, housing, water supplies, waste disposal and so on will contribute to easing other symptoms of poverty. One mechanism that Australians concerned about development commonly forget is the possibility of establishing or strengthening social protection as a means of directly reducing income poverty.

Yet the right to social protection has been widely recognised for decades and advocated as a cost-effective method of strengthening economic security. Article 22 of the 1948 Universal Declaration of Human Rights states that 'everyone, as a member of society, has the right to social security', and Article 25 articulates that more fully as 'the right to security in the event of unemployment, sickness, disability, widowhood, old age or other lack of livelihood in circumstances beyond his control'. Sixty years after its adoption by the UN General Assembly, this right is no more than an aspiration for 80% of the global population who still do not have access to social security. Governments, including Australia's, committed themselves at the World Summit for Social Development held in Copenhagen in 1995 to 'to develop and implement policies to ensure that all people have adequate economic and social protection during unemployment, ill health, maternity, child rearing, widowhood, disability and old age'. The Pittsburgh G20 Summit in September 2009 promised to 'continue to provide income, social protection, and training support for the unemployed and those most in risk of unemployment' and asked Labour Ministers to meet early in 2010 to consider whether further measures are desirable in relation to social protection, amongst other major themes.[2]

---

[2]   Leaders' Statement: The Pittsburgh Summit, September 25, 2009, para. 46.

The International Labour Organization (ILO) is currently advocating the following:

> The international community should not just repair the problems identified by the crisis in global financial, monetary and economic systems, but should be advocating and supporting the development of a social protection floor to protect people during the crisis, and thereafter. A social protection floor could consist of two main elements that help to realize respective human rights: *essential services*: ensuring the availability, continuity, and access to public services (such as water and sanitation, health, education, and family-focused social work support); and *social transfers*: a basic set of essential social transfers, in cash and in kind, paid to the poor and vulnerable to enhance food security and nutrition and provide a minimum income security.[3]

In crisis conditions, social security benefits, public health and nutrition programs and social services act as social, health and economic stabilisers, thereby curtailing the potential social and economic depth of the recession, by avoiding or reducing poverty, ensuring continuity in services and stabilising aggregate demand.

The terms 'social security' and 'social protection' are often used interchangeably, though 'social security' generally relates to formal financial support from governments and 'social protection' has wider connotations, including various community-based and voluntary forms of support in cash and kind. The ILO writes, 'The objective of most social security schemes is to provide access to health care and income security, i.e. minimum income for those in need and a reasonable replacement income for those who have contributed in proportion to their level of income'.[4] The World Bank has in the past used the very limited concept of social safety nets, but the inadequacies of that approach are now widely recognised. Authors experienced in developing countries advocate that social security also include such policies as access to productive assets, employment guarantees, minimum wages and food security. The ILO uses the broader concept of social protection, which covers not only social security but also nonstatutory schemes. The European Union includes in its measure of social protection such social services as crèches and home help. '[T]he distinctiveness of social protection lies in its emphasis on risks and vulnerability as the main factors behind poverty and deprivation', write two experts.[5]

---

[3]   ILO Briefing Note on the Global Financial Crisis: UN System Joint Initiatives, 2009.
[4]   ILO, *Social Security: A New Consensus* (Geneva: International Labour Organization, 2001) 38.
[5]   Armando Barrientos and Peter Lloyd-Sherlock, 'Non-contributory Pensions and Social Protection', Annex 2, *Welcome to the ILO's 5 Euro Project*, Geneva, September 2002, 80.

There can be no doubt about the benefits of social protection. It can prevent or alleviate poverty and reduce inequality and injustice. The net costs of starting social protection mechanisms are likely to be offset in due course by a better motivated, nourished, educated and healthier workforce. A reduction of inequality and despair reduces social tensions. The benefits of national social security schemes are shown by their universal use in successful developed countries, so they are naturally an aspiration of developing countries.

Obviously there are large differences in the capacity of countries to provide social protection, yet it is inhuman to expect anyone to have to live in perpetual deprivation and insecurity. The contemporary world has unprecedented technical and economic capacity to ensure at least minimum levels of economic security for all people. Poverty eradication is principally a matter for national economic and social policies. However, it is clear that there are many countries with average incomes per head below, say, a thousand US dollars a year that have no hope of generating the income and services to escape the imprisonment of generalised poverty without external assistance. It is essential to aim to reduce poverty faster than economic growth alone will permit. The aim of extending social protection is to leap-frog the natural restraints on such progress.

Poverty reduction is generally discussed as a matter of increasing investment, improving access to credit at reasonable interest rates, strengthening education, improving health and extending infrastructure, and each of those and other policies are vital means for building employment and opportunities for self-help. But national social protection systems ranging from the Brazilian Bolsa Familia – 'Family Grant' or 'Family Allowance' – and the Indian employment guarantee to pensions and health care schemes can be powerful means for alleviating poverty. These schemes contribute to both poverty reduction and to an increase in human capital.

One consequence of global interdependence is that all residents of rich countries can be aware of the enormity of the disparities, and most respond by wanting to make some contribution to relieving hardship. A degree of altruism is common – on condition that there is confidence that assistance will be effectively used. Provided that there is evidence of humane and efficient social protection being planned and, better still, starting to be delivered, it is likely that voters in rich countries might well be supportive of an exchange of 'debt for social protection' to inaugurate or extend a process of direct attempts to counteract poverty.

Initial contributions could be used to cover start-up costs for various forms of social protection, including social security such as a pension scheme or social insurance. The start-up costs would be likely to include establishing administration and public education. Employers and local and provincial governments might well be responsible for some of this, depending on the type of scheme. Contributory schemes become self-supporting over a period of years, so initial external assistance can be vital in quickly establishing a major scheme. This is particularly so in many developing countries where social security schemes fail to reach much of the informal sector. This is a particular difficulty for voluntary and especially micro-insurance schemes for which the availability of an initial subsidy can be a necessary condition for an effective foundation.

A recent paper from the ILO about whether low-income countries can afford basic social protection evaluates a package that includes four elements: universal basic old-age and disability pensions, basic child benefits, universal access to essential health care and social assistance like the Indian National Rural Employment Guarantee Scheme.[6]

A number of middle- and low-income countries, including Brazil, Botswana, India, Mauritius, Lesotho, Namibia, Nepal and South Africa, already have noncontributory old-age pensions. The evidence shows that these programs are of benefit not only to elderly people but also to their families and notably children. Cash benefit programs for children are in operation in some Latin American countries, where they are conditional on school attendance. They have been found to be most effective when combined with after-school activities. There are concerns, though, about the transferability of such schemes to countries in which education and health care are poorly developed, which is one indicator of the importance of building them up within a social protection system. The Indian Guarantee of Employment Act guarantees 100 days of unskilled work per rural household to adults or an unemployment allowance if no work can be offered. One researcher comments that the advantage of this type of scheme is that the beneficiaries select themselves: the non-poor do not participate because of the nature of the work and the low wages.[7]

The ILO has prepared detailed costing estimates for such schemes and concluded that 'low-income countries not only should but also can have social security systems that provide a basic package of health services to everybody, basic cash benefits to the elderly and to families with children and social assistance to a proportion of the unemployed.... A basic social protection package is demonstrably affordable ... on condition that the package is implemented through the joint efforts of the low-income countries themselves ... and of the

---

[6] ILO, *Social Security Policy Briefings Paper 3: Can Low-Income Countries Afford Basic Social Security?* (Geneva: Social Security Department, International Labour Organization, 2008).

[7] All information and comments are from ibid.

international donor community'.[8] Steps towards developing such programs are already under way in additional countries such as Tanzania, Zambia, Mozambique and Nepal, and other countries are expected to start soon.

Professor Anthony Clunies-Ross has prepared independent (and previously unpublished) estimates of 'the apparent cost in dollars of foreign exchange that would be required to fill the estimated "gap" for the year 2005 by which the household incomes (or expenditures) of people in low-income and lower-middle-income countries whose household incomes (or expenditures) per head were below the internationally accepted extreme-poverty borderline figure of US$1.25 PPP dollars per head a day'. That is, he tests whether the costs of social protection schemes such as those envisaged by the ILO are a theoretically feasible approach to a major reduction of poverty. His aggregate estimates for all low- and lower-middle-income countries, which had a total population of 4.8 billion people in 2005, are presented in an appendix, which appears at the end of this chapter. He concludes that the total cost would be around $94 billion. He comments:

> This total is well within the range of high-income OECD donors' aid in some recent years (including 2005 and 2006), and, even added to existing aid, would still be well within the range of what these donors *would be giving* annually if they fulfilled the pledge to transfer in aid 0.7% of their own incomes (about $224.5 billion in 2005 at prices of that year when actual aid given was $106.8 billion)[9]. Measured by the scale of rich countries' budgets these are far from astronomical figures. Making these calculations is not intended to imply that the best way of distributing the costs of meeting these very elemental needs of the 1.4 billion people estimated to be below the (1.25 PPP dollars a day) extreme-poverty line is for them all to be provided by the rich OECD countries. Both how they *should* be met and how realistically in the political context they *might* actually be met are further and separate issues; but the cost of meeting them from rich-OECD countries' resources must surely be of some interest and some relevance to these other questions.

Such estimates are far beyond the capacity of debt-for-social-protection schemes to finance. The point of including these figures is to show the overall feasibility of using social protection as a major means of poverty reduction and therefore to indicate that there are high-priority and cost-effective opportunities for using such an approach in planning debt exchanges.

[8]   Ibid., 17
[9]   A. I. Clunies-Ross, D. J. C. Forsyth and M. M. Huq, *Development Economics* (New York: McGraw-Hill, 2009), 589; tables based on OECD, Development Assistance Committee, International Development Statistics Online, accessed August 2, 2010, http://www.oecd/dac/stats, consulted June-August 2009.

Nevertheless, a debt-for-social-protection exchange could play a role in inaugurating or capitalising a new scheme. By increasing financial resources for a government at one point, such an exchange could contribute to over-coming initial financial constraints. Another possible means of playing a role would be for debt exchanges to be phased over a period of years, say 10, so as to contribute to the funds needed for early disbursement to members. Many social security schemes depend on building up assets through member contri-butions, so to have a starting grant or grants for the early years would assist in enabling payment to be made to members from the start.

A third possibility would be for the funds from a debt exchange to reduce debt-service payments, which could be used for a social protection scheme. For example, if a donor country forgave a debt of US$500 million, the recip-ient country could allocate the savings from the no longer required debt service to social security. Depending on the interest rate, this could gen-erate between $25 million and $50 million a year. This is a small amount, but it could nevertheless be useful in facilitating the early years of a social protection program.

Whether or not social protection is taken seriously as an option for the use of debt-for-development exchanges, it is imperative that it become a focus of Australian aid for poverty-reduction programs.

APPENDIX: COST OF FILLING THE EXTREME POVERTY GAP FROM
ABROAD: AN ARITHMETIC EXERCISE WITH AGENDA

Professor Anthony Clunies-Ross

Magnitude in Foreign-Exchange of the Aggregate (Extreme) Total Poverty Gap

This is an exercise with very modest objectives. It aims simply to show the apparent cost in dollars of foreign exchange that would be required to fill the estimated 'gap' for the year 2005 by which the household incomes (or expenditures) of people in low-income and lower-middle-income countries whose household incomes (or expenditures) per head were *below the interna-tionally accepted extreme-poverty borderline figure of 1.25 PPP dollars per head a day* did *in total* fall short of that figure.

Another way of expressing this is to say that the intention is to estimate the (extreme) *total poverty gap* in those countries for the year and to convert it into dollars of foreign exchange.

The data used are entirely World Bank figures published in issues of the World Bank's *World Development Report* (*WDR*) and *World Development Indicators* (*WDI*), together with the 'Poverty data' supplement to *World Development Indicators* 2008.[10]

There was a major revision of World Bank national-income and poverty figures for developing countries based on price surveys in 2005 that had been greatly improved. The results of this revision were embodied in the 2008 edition of *World Development Indicators* and its 'Poverty data' supplement. There were often big differences between the poverty figures reported then and those that had been published earlier, and correspondingly different estimates of PPP equivalences of currencies.

Though the calculations are related to the year 2005, the figures used to indicate the extent of poverty for various countries (expressed as *proportions of population* failing to reach the relevant poverty lines) are based on surveys conducted at various times. Where there is a choice I use those from as close to 2005 as possible.

The 2008 *WDI* and its 'Poverty data' supplement give, for each country, implied 'exchange-rates' between US dollars of foreign exchange and that country's PPP dollars. For almost all of the developing countries these figures imply that each actual US dollar will buy goods and services equal in that country to considerably more than one PPP dollar (generally between 2 and 4 PPP dollars). It seems perfectly legitimate to treat these figures as exchange-rates. They have been used here to convert *total poverty gaps* expressed in PPP dollars into US dollars of foreign exchange.

The 'poverty gap' figures given as percentages in *WDI* and *WDR* statistics are what are called *normalized poverty gaps* (NPGs). In relation to a particular poverty line such as 1.25 PPP dollars a day, a country's NPG expresses the percentage that its total poverty gap (TPG) – the aggregate amount by which some of its residents fall short of the poverty-line income – bears to what the population's total income would be if everyone received exactly the poverty-line income.

$$\text{So: } NPG = TPG_{PPP} / N.y_a$$

where N is the total population and
  y_a is the income per head at poverty-line a in PPP dollars *p.a.*
  TPG_{PPP} is the total poverty gap in PPP dollars *p.a.*

Hence $TPG_{PPP} = NPG.N.y_a$

---

[10] http://siteresources.worldbank.org/DATASTATISTICS/Resources/WDI08supplement 1216.pdf.

$$\text{and } TPG_{\$US} = NPG.N.y_a. \; E_{\$US/PPP}$$

where $TPG_{\$US}$ is the total poverty gap in $US *p.a.*

$E_{\$US/PPP}$ is the exchange-rate $US per PPP dollar

Where the poverty-line is 1.25 PPP dollars a day, $y_a = 1.25^*365.2425 = 456.553$

Where it is 2.00 PPP dollars a day, $y_a = 2.00^*365.2425 = 730.485$

This is of course because there are 365.2425 days on average in a year in the Gregorian Calendar.

The countries *covered by poverty-gap estimates* here are, as far as we can see, all the low-income and lower-middle-income countries for which the World Bank gives recent poverty figures. With others listed in the tables [presented in this appendix], they appear to cover all low-income and lower-middle-income countries except for some tiny states with less than half a million people each. The 2007 WDR gives the total population in these two income categories in 2005 as 4,828 million. This is 1.06 times the 4552 million for which we have poverty data here. To raise the 66,833.3 million US dollars (which as indicated is a *maximum* needed for filling the TPGs considered in these calculations) in that proportion would require $70,843.3 million. To allow arbitrarily an addition of a third for administrative costs[11] and wastage of any scheme designed actually to fill the gaps, together with a certain amount of over-filling that would inevitably be required in practice in order to go reasonably close to filling it completely, would bring it altogether to around $94.4 billion. This total is well within the range of high-income OECD donors' aid in some recent years (including 2005 and 2006), and, even added to existing aid, would still be well within the range of what these donors *would be giving* annually if they fulfilled the pledge to transfer in aid 0.7 % of their own incomes (about $224.5 billion in 2005 at prices of that year when actual aid given was $106.8 billion).[12] Measured by the scale of rich countries' budgets these are far from astronomical figures.

Making these calculations is not intended to imply that the best way of distributing the costs of meeting these very elemental needs of the 1.4 billion people estimated to be below the (1.25 PPP dollars a day) extreme-poverty line is for them all to be provided by the rich OECD countries. Both how they *should* be met and how realistically in the political context they *might* actually be met are further and separate issues; but the cost of meeting them from rich-OECD countries' resources must surely be of some interest and some relevance to these other questions.

---

[11]   ILO, *Social Security Policy Briefings Paper* 3, adds, for administrative costs alone, 15% of the direct amounts of transfers to persons under the scheme it examines.

[12]   See Clunies-Ross, Forsyth and Huq, *Development Economics*, 589.

TABLE 17.1. *Low-income countries: total extreme-poverty gaps in $US millions per year*

Country name	(1) Population 2005, m.	(2) NPG 2005, %	$(3) = (1)^*$ $[(2)/100]$ $^*456.553$ $TPG_{\$PPP}$ 2005, m.	$(4)\ E_{\$US/PPP}$	$(5) = (3)^*(4)$ $TPG_{\$US}$ 2005, m.
Afghanistan	n.a.				n.a.
Bangladesh	142	13.1	8492.8	0.37	3142.3
Benin	8	15.7	573.4	0.42	240.8
Bhutan	0.918	7.0	109.8	0.36	39.5
Burkina Faso	13	20.3	1204.8	0.38	457.8
Burundi	8	36.4	1329.5	0.32	425.4
Cambodia	14	11.3	722.3	0.31	223.9
Central African Republic	4	28.3	516.8	0.50	258.4
Chad	10	25.6	1168.8	0.39	455.8
Comoros	0.6	20.8	57.0	0.57	32.5
Congo Dem. Rep.	58	25.3	6699.5	0.45	3014.8
Cote d'Ivoire	18	6.8	558.8	0.55	307.3
Eritrea	4				n.a.
Ethiopia	71	9.6	3111.9	0.26	809.1
Gambia	1.5	12.1	82.9	0.26	21.5
Ghana	22	10.5	1054.6	0.41	432.4
Guinea	9	32.2	1323.1	0.33	436.6
Guinea-Bissau	1.6	16.5	120.5	0.41	49.4
Haiti	9	28.2	1158.7	n.a.	n.a.
India	1095	10.8	53992.0	0.33	17817.4
Kenya	34	6.1	946.9	0.39	369.3
Korea Dem. Rep.	22				n.a.
Kyrgyz Republic	5	4.4	100.4	0.28	28.1
Laos	6	12.1	331.5	0.28	92.8
Liberia	3	40.8	558.8	0.49	273.8
Madagascar	19	26.5	2298.7	0.32	735.6
Malawi	13	32.3	1917.1	0.33	632.6
Mali	14	18.8	1201.7	0.46	552.8
Mauritania	3	5.7	78.1	0.37	28.9
Mongolia	3	3.6	49.3	0.35	17.3
Mozambique	20	35.4	3232.4	0.37	1196.0
Myanmar	51				n.a.
Nepal	27	19.7	2428.4	0.31	752.8

Country name	(1) Population 2005, m.	(2) NPG 2005, %	(3) = (1)* [(2)/100] *456.553 $TPG_{\$PPP}$ 2005, m.	(4) $E_{\$US/PPP}$	(5) = (3)*(4) $TPG_{\$US}$ 2005, m.
Niger	14	28.1	1796.1	0.43	772.3
Nigeria	132	29.6	17838.4	0.46	8205.7
Pakistan	156	4.4	3133.8	0.32	1002.8
Papua New Guinea	6				n.a.
Rwanda	9	38.2	1569.6	0.33	518.0
Sao Tome & Principe	0.2			0.53	n.a.
Senegal	12	10.8	591.7	0.48	284.0
Sierra Leone	6	20.3	556.1	0.37	205.8
Solomon Islands	0.5				n.a.
Somalia	8				n.a.
Sudan	36				n.a.
Tajikistan	7	5.1	163.0	0.24	39.1
Tanzania	38	46.8	8119.3	0.35	2841.8
Timor Leste	1.0	19.1	87.2		n.a.
Togo	6	11.4	312.3	0.46	143.6
Uganda	29	19.1	2528.8	0.36	910.4
Uzbekistan	27	15.0	1849.0		n.a.
Vietnam	83	4.6	1743.1	0.30	522.9
Yemen Republic	21	4.2	402.7	0.36	145.0
Zambia	12	32.8	1797.0	0.54	970.4
Zimbabwe	13			1.48	n.a.
Totals with full data	2149				49406.7
Totals with population data (all except Afghanistan)	2326				

TABLE 17.2. *Lower-middle-income countries: total extreme-poverty gaps in \$US millions per year*

Country Name	(1) Population 2005, m.	(2) NPG 2005, %	(3) = (1)*[(2)/100] *456.553 $TPG_{\$PPP}$ 2005, m.	(4) $E_{\$US/PPP}$ 2005	(5) = (3)*(4) $TPG_{\$US}$ 2005, m.
Albania	3	<0.5	<6.8	0.49	<3.4
Algeria	33	1.4	210.9	0.43	90.7
Angola	16	29.9	2184.1	0.51	1113.9
Armenia	3	1.9	26.0	0.39	10.1
Azerbaijan	8	<0.5	<18.3	0.35	<6.4
Belarus	10	<0.5	<22.8	0.36	<8.2
Bolivia	9	9.7	398.6	0.28	111.6
Bosnia & Herzegovina	4	<0.5	<9.1	0.46	<4.2
Brazil	186	1.6	1358.7	0.56	760.9
Bulgaria	8	<0.5	18.3	0.38	6.9
Cameroon	16	10.2	745.1	0.48	357.6
Cape Verde	0.507	5.9	13.7	0.78	10.7
China	1305	4.0	23832.1	0.42	10009.5
Colombia	46	6.1	1281.1	0.47	602.1
Congo Republic	4	22.8	416.4	0.51	212.4
Cuba	11				n.a.
Djibouti	0.793	5.3	19.2	0.48	9.2
Dominican Republic	9	0.9	37.0	0.57	21.1
Ecuador	13	3.2	189.9	0.42	79.8
Egypt	74	<0.5	<168.9	0.27	<45.6
El Salvador	7	6.7	214.1	0.50	107.1
Georgia	4	4.4	80.4	0.41	32.9
Guatemala	13	3.8	225.5	0.53	119.5
Guyana	0.751	3.9	13.4	0.44	5.9
Honduras	7	10.2	326.0	0.43	140.2
Indonesia	221	4.6	4641.3	0.41	1902.9
Iran	68	<0.5	<155.2	0.30	<46.6
Iraq	n.a.				n.a.
Jamaica	3	<0.5	<6.8	0.60	<4.1
Jordan	5	<0.5	<11.4	0.54	<6.2
Kazakhstan	15	<0.5	<34.2	0.43	<14.7
Lesotho	1.795	20.8	170.5	0.55	93.8
Macedonia	2	<0.5	<4.6	0.39	<1.8
Moldova	4	1.7	31.0	0.35	10.9
Morocco	30	0.5	68.5	0.55	37.7
Namibia	2	24.6	224.6	0.67	150.5

Country Name	(1) Population 2005, m.	(2) NPG 2005, %	(3) = (1)* [(2)/100] *456.553 TPG$_{\$PPP}$ 2005, m.	(4) E$_{\$US/PPP}$ 2005	(5) = (3)*(4) TPG$_{\$US}$ 2005, m.
Nicaragua	5	5.2	118.7	0.38	45.1
Paraguay	6	3.4	93.1	0.32	29.8
Peru	28	2.0	255.7	0.45	115.1
Philippines	83	5.5	2084.2	0.39	812.8
Sri Lanka	20	2.6	237.4	0.35	83.1
Suriname	0.449	5.9	12.1	0.59	7.1
Swaziland	1.131	29.4	151.8	0.52	78.9
Thailand	64	<0.5	<146.1	0.40	<58.4
Trinidad	1.305	1.1	6.6	0.61	4.0
Tunisia	10	<0.5	<22.8	0.45	10.3
Turkmenistan	5	7.0	159.8	0.36	57.5
Ukraine	47	<0.5	<107.3	0.33	35.4
Total with full data (all except Cuba and Iraq)	2403				<17476.6
Total with population figures (all except Iraq)	2414				

TABLE 17.3. *Low-income and lower-middle-income countries combined: sum of total extreme-poverty gaps in $US millions per year*

Countries	(1) Population 2005, m.	(2) NPG 2005, %	(3) = (1)* [(2)/100] *456.553 TPG$_{\$PPP}$ 2005, m.	(4) E$_{\$US/PPP}$	(5) = (3)*(4) TPG$_{\$US}$ 2005, m.
Total with full data	2149 + 2403 = 4552				49406.7 + <17476.6 = <66883.3
Total with population figures (all except Iraq and Afghanistan)	2326 + 2414 = 4740				

These results have the encouraging implication that, whatever the political and administrative obstacles, the actual costs of the transfers required, combined with those of the projected health-service provision, and hence of doing much of the job of protecting people across the poorest quarter to a half say of the world's population from extreme destitution, are not outside the realm of financial possibility.

18

Climate Change Adaptation Exchanges: An Exploration of the Possibilities and Risks

Philip Ireland

I. INTRODUCTION

This chapter explores the potential role of debt-for-development exchanges in the context of climate change adaptation. This is a timely contribution. It has become apparent that the sums of money required for adaptation are outside the capacity of existing sources. This context demands innovative thinking about potential mechanisms for financing adaptation to climate change in the coming years. The present chapter has two key purposes. The first, as the title suggests, is to consider the opportunities and risks involved in supporting adaptation through the model of debt-for-development exchange. The second is to explore and interrogate contemporary notions of adaptation through the lens of debt-for-development exchanges.

Adaptation to climate change has received increasing attention over the past few years.[1] It is widely accepted that climate change is already having an impact on vulnerable communities around the globe through adverse weather events and gradual changes.[2] A range of stakeholders now recognise that there is a need to establish financial flows that support adaptation.[3]

---

[1] Neil Adger and Jon Barnett, "Four Reasons for Concern About Adaptation to Climate Change", *Environment and Planning* 41 (2009): 2800–2805; Steven Dovers, "Normalising Adaptation", *Global Environmental Change* 19 (2009): 4–6.

[2] Intergovernmental Panel on Climate Change (IPCC), *Climate Change, 2007: Impacts, Adaptation and Vulnerability – Contribution of Working Group II to the Fourth Assessment Report of the Intergovernmental Panel on Climate Change* (Cambridge: Cambridge University Press, 2007); World Bank, *World Development Report, 2010: Development and Climate Change* (Washington, DC: World Bank, 2010).

[3] Asa Persson, Richard Klein, Clarisse Kehler Siebert, Aaron Atteridge, Benito Muller, Juan Hoffmaister, Michael Lazarus and Takeshi Takama, *Adaptation Finance under a Copenhagen Agreed Outcome* (Stockholm: Stockholm Environment Institute, 2009); Martin Parry, Nigel Arnell, Pam Berry, David Dodman, Samual Fankhauser, Chris Hope, Sari Kovats, Roberts Nicholls, Savud Satterthwaite, Richard Tiffin and Tim Wheeler, *Assessing*

In the lead up to the Copenhagen United Nations Framework Convention on Climate Change (UNFCCC) negotiations in December 2009, considerable effort was applied to calculating potential costs for adaptation to climate change. Both government and nongovernmental organisations (NGOs) attempted to estimate what would be required to fund adaptation in the developing world. Estimates ranged from a few billion US dollars per year to more than a hundred billion per year.[4] Under the Copenhagen Accord, the outcome of the Copenhagen negotiations, 'developed countries'[5] are committed to providing US$30 billion over the period 2010–2012 and US$100 billion per year by 2020 to support mitigation, technology transfer, capacity building, reducing deforestation and adaptation in developing countries.[6]

Whilst these financing commitments are significant, there are several apparent problems that demonstrate key issues in the broader debate. Firstly, the Copenhagen Accord is not legally binding. This reduces the likelihood that the commitments will be met. Secondly, adaptation will receive only a portion of this funding, which will be less than current estimates of what is required. Thirdly, and perhaps most significantly, it is not clear at this point how these funds will be raised. Whilst the Copenhagen Accord may be superseded by new agreements in the coming years, it effectively reflects the gap that exists between the recognition of what is required and the means to achieve it. This is the context in which this chapter explores debt-for-adaptation exchanges.

Debt-for-adaptation exchanges offer a potential mechanism for the generation of adaptation financing whilst simultaneously reducing debt in developing countries. This chapter begins by exploring the literature concerning adaptation to climate change and debt exchanges in order to establish a theoretical framework. This is followed by an analysis of three conceptual models, each of which utilises different framings of adaptation. The chapter then assesses some of the key potential objections to these exchanges through the lens of advocacy NGOs. With careful and critical consideration, debt-for-adaptation exchanges offer an opportunity to provide much needed adaptation financing whilst at the same time reducing the developing world debt burden.

the Costs of Adaptation to Climate Change: A Review of the UNFCCC and Other Recent Estimates (London: International Institute for Environment and Development, 2009).

[4] Martin Parry et al., *Assessing the Costs*; World Bank, *World Development Report*, 257–260.

[5] I use the terms 'developed' and 'developing', as this is the language used by the Copenhagen Accord and the UNFCCC. I would like to note that I use these terms hesitantly, as they reinforce the idea of developmentalism in the development discourse. For an exploration of the issues related to this discourse see Jan Nederveeen Pieterse, *Development Theory* (London: Sage Publications, 2010).

[6] Copenhagen Accord, 2009, United Nations Framework Convention on Climate Change.

II. BACKGROUND AND FRAMING

A. *Adaptation to Climate Change*

Adaptation to climate change is a contested concept. It is intrinsically linked to development theory and is subject to a range of understandings. The IPCC (2007) defines adaptation to climate change as an 'adjustment in natural or human systems in response to actual or expected climatic stimuli or their effects, which moderates harm or exploits beneficial opportunities'.[7] This definition is interpreted in a variety of ways due to different understandings of climate predictions, risk and development pathways. The literature has increasingly drawn attention to these challenges, associated with both theory and practice.[8]

A recent commentary by Adger and Barnett identifies several reasons for concern about adaptation to climate change.[9] These include the dramatic scale of climate change, the interconnectedness of impacts, emerging trends of maladaptation and the complex contexts in which adaptation must occur. They state that their concerns are grounded in what they perceive to be 'a widespread belief that adaptation will be smooth, cheap and easy to implement' when 'the reality may be that adaptation to climate risks may be punctuated, messy, more costly than we are willing to pay'.[10] These concerns reflect the complexity that exists for both the reality and perception of climate change adaptation.

Several authors have attempted to consolidate the diversity of views of adaptation by designing consolidating frameworks. Figure 18.1 shows one such framework that was published by McGray, Hammill and Bradley for the World Resources Institute.[11] A similar framework has also appeared in Persson et al.[12] Figure 18.1 presents adaptation as a continuum of activities that focus

---

[7] IPCC, *Climate Change*, 2007.

[8] Adger and Barnett, "Four Reasons for Concern"; Neil Adger, S. Dessai, M. Goulden, M. Hulme, I. Lorenzoni, D. R. Nelson, L. O. Naess, J. Wolf, and A. Wreford, "Are There Social Limits to Adaptation to Climate Change?" *Climatic Change* 93(3–4) (2009): 335–354; Susanne Moser, "Whether Our Levers Are Long Enough and the Fulcrum Strong? Exploring the Soft Underbelly of Adaptation Decisions and Actions", in *Adapting to Climate Change*, eds. Neil Adger, Irene Lorenzoni and Karen O'Brian (Cambridge: Cambridge University Press, 2009), pp. 313–334.

[9] Adger and Barnett, "Four Reasons for Concern", pp. 2800–2805.

[10] Ibid., 2803–2804.

[11] Heather McGray, Anne Hammill, and Rob Bradley, *Weathering the Storm: Options for Framing Adaptation and Development* (Washington, DC: World Resources Institute, 2007).

[12] Asa Persson et al., *Adaptation Finance*.

1. Addressing Drivers of Vulnerability	2. Building Response Capacity	3. Managing Climate Risk	4. Confronting Climate Change
Bangladesh: Diversification of livelihood strategies in areas vulnerable to flooding	**Brazil:** Participatory reforestation in Rio de Janeiro's hillside favelas to combat flood induced landslides	**Tanzania:** Monitoring salinisation of drinking water and drilling new wells to replace those that are no longer useable	**Indonesia:** Managing coral reefs in response to widespread coral bleaching
Cuba: Vaccination program to eradicate diseases in low-income areas	**Mongolia:** Reinstating pastoral networks to foster appropriate rangeland management practices in arid regions	**Mali:** Teaching farmers to collect climate data and integrate it into other planting decisions	**Nepal:** Reducing the risk of glacial lake outburst floods from Tsho Rolpa Lake

◄——— Vulnerability focus   **Adaptation continuum**   Impacts focus ———►

FIGURE 18.1. A continuum of adaptation and development.
Source: Heather McGray, Anne Hammill and Rob Bradley, *Weathering the Storm: Options for Framing Adaptation and Development* (Washington, DC: World Resources Institute, 2007).

on different aspects of adaptation. The exploration in this chapter utilises this framework by exploring debt-for-adaptation exchanges from some of the different perspectives presented.

Figure 18.1 represents adaptation as a continuum with a diverse range of associated actions. On the two ends of this spectrum are the 'impacts focus' and the 'vulnerability focus'. The impacts focus, on the right-hand side, represents a common understanding of adaptation to climate change by actors such as the Intergovernmental Panel on Climate Change (IPCC).[13] In this category adaptation activities respond to specific and measurable climate change impacts that are clearly outside natural variability – for example, reducing community risk to glacial lake outburst floods in Nepal. These floods are caused by glaciers that are melting rapidly and have critical outflow events that threaten communities living in the valleys below. Adaptation interventions in these communities might involve the construction of protective barriers or relocation of parts of the community.

Alternatively, the vulnerability focus within this framework asserts that the reduction of general vulnerability can play a role in enhancing the capacity to adapt to climate change. This focus recognises that vulnerability is caused by different drivers. These might include conflict, the economy, trade and social contexts. These factors, whilst not directly related to the environment,

[13] IPCC, *Climate Change*, 2007.

can have a negative impact on individual and community capacity to respond and adapt to climate change. This end of the spectrum is conceptually more difficult, as it potentially includes a large range of measures that do not have a direct link to climate change. For example, the diversification of livelihood strategies is more commonly associated with poverty reduction. Whilst this might seem like a stretch theoretically, this conceptualisation is present in other places in the academic and policy discourse.[14]

In recent years it has become increasingly clear that a range of vulnerability reducing methods are applicable in the realm of climate change adaptation. For example, I explored the emergence of the description of disaster risk reduction (DRR) as 'no-regrets adaptation'.[15] I asserted that this language was being used to justify the use of pre-existing vulnerability reduction strategies as adaptive measures and posed the question: How might debt relief or conversion be considered 'no regrets adaptation'? By posing this question, I sought to understand how more general activities such as debt relief might enhance the capacity to adapt to climate change. This chapter broadens this enquiry by exploring several ways that debt-for-adaptation exchanges might be conceptualised.

B. *Proposals for Climate Financing and the Precedent of REDD*

There are many proposals for financing both climate change adaptation and mitigation. In the lead up to Copenhagen, a number of publications outlined a range of ideas.[16] An overwhelming conclusion of these reports was that an insufficient amount of financing is currently pledged and that it will require a variety of pre-existing and new mechanisms to reach what is perceived as required.

Within current models of climate change financing, there is some precedent for debt-for-development exchanges related to the conservation of forests. These proposals are generally being discussed within the framework of reducing emissions from deforestation and degradation (REDD). An example of

---

[14] Lisa Schipper, "Meeting at the Crossroads? Exploring the Linkages between Climate Change Adaptation and Disaster Risk Reduction", *Climate and Development* 1 (2009): 16–30; UN/International Strategy for Disaster Reduction (ISDR), "Linking Disaster Risk Reduction and Poverty Reduction: Good Practices and Lessons Learned" (Geneva: UN/ISDR, 2008).

[15] P. Ireland, (2010) "Climate Change Adaptation and Disaster Risk Reduction: Contested Spaces and Emerging Opportunities in Development Theory and Practice" *Climate and Development* 2(4) (2010): 332–345.

[16] See Charlie Parker, Jessica Brown, Jonathan Pickering, Emily Roynestad, Niki Mardas and Andrew Mitchell, *The Little Climate Finance Book* (Oxford: Global Canopy Programme, 2009); Asa Persson et al., *Adaptation Finance*.

such an exchange is the US government's REDD debt-for-nature exchange in Aceh, Indonesia. In this arrangement the US government announced that it would cancel US$30 million of debt payments owed by Indonesia in return for increased protection of Sumatra's forests.[17] This exchange is essentially a reframing of the debt-for-nature exchange (see Chapter 2, this volume).

C. Debt-for-Development Exchanges

This section provides a brief overview of debt-for-development exchanges. As this theme is covered at length elsewhere in this volume, this section focuses on the key principles, strengths and weaknesses of exchanges that should be considered for the analysis in this chapter. Both debt and development are highly contentious issues, with histories marked by both successes and terrible failures. Any consideration of debt-for-adaptation exchanges is inevitably tied up with these debates. Despite this, in recent years debt-for-development exchanges have been identified as having a significant capacity for furthering progress towards meeting the Millenniums Development Goals (MDGs).[18]

It is widely acknowledged that there can be a wide range of benefits as a result of debt-for-development exchanges.[19] The International NGO Forum on Indonesian Development (INFID) identified a range of benefits from these exchanges, including the reduction of overall debt levels, the provision of additional sources of funds for development and the stimulation of local economies. Similarly, Jubilee Australia identified benefits for the debtor nation.[20] These include not needing to find new money in the budget and increasing total overseas development assistance (ODA). These perceived strengths are inevitably accompanied by perceived weaknesses.

Ruiz asserts that a number of concerns should be considered in relation to debt-for-development exchanges.[21] For example, debt exchanges may legitimise dubious debt, they may fall short of international commitments to debt cancellation, they can be expensive to administer and they can reinforce conditionality. INFID reinforces some of these claims and recognises that debt-for-development exchanges can have negative effects on local currency and side-step national priorities.[22]

[17] Charlie Parker et al., *The Little Climate Finance Book*.
[18] International NGO Forum on Indonesian Development (INFID), *Debt Swaps for Indonesia: A Proposal for Improving Their Effectiveness* (Jakarta: INFID, 2006).
[19] Ibid.; Jubilee Australia, *A Debt-for-Development Swap with Indonesia* (Sydney: Jubilee Australia, 2007); Marta Ruiz, *Debt Swaps for Development* (Brussels: European Network on Debt and Development, 2007).
[20] Jubilee Australia, *A Debt-for-Development Swap with Indonesia*.
[21] Ruiz, *Debt Swaps for Development*.
[22] INFID, *Debt Swaps for Indonesia*.

A common conclusion of papers on this topic is that within appropriate parameters debt exchanges can play a constructive role in poverty reduction. In response to the various concerns Ruiz outlines, a number of principles should be adhered to in any debt-for-development exchange.[23] These principles underpin the proposals this chapter subsequently outlines. Debt-for-development exchanges should always be voluntary, should be transparent and should not include illegitimate debt. They should not be framed as the key solution to poverty, debt or climate change vulnerability.

III. THREE CONCEPTUALISATIONS

This section will explore three theoretical conceptualisations of how debt-for-adaptation exchanges might be considered. As noted previously this section will utilise the adaptation continuum conceptualisation presented in Figure 18.1. This involves exploring how debt-for-adaptation exchanges could function using both the vulnerability and the impacts focus of adaptation.

A. *Exchanges Targeted at Specific Climate Impacts*

The first proposal utilises the impacts end of the adaptation continuum. Under this scenario a portion of debt that is cancelled could be utilised for a specific adaptation project that addressed a specific climate impact. In this example the process could be visualised as the following:

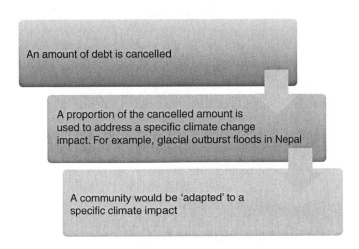

An amount of debt is cancelled

A proportion of the cancelled amount is used to address a specific climate change impact. For example, glacial outburst floods in Nepal

A community would be 'adapted' to a specific climate impact

---

[23] Ruiz, *Debt Swaps for Development*.

This pathway could function in a similar way to Australia's debt-for-health exchange with Indonesia whereby Australia cancelled A$75 million of Indonesia's debt in exchange for a A$37.5 million investment by Indonesia in the Global Fund to Fight AIDS, Tuberculosis and Malaria within Indonesia. In terms of adaptation, this proposal could be linked with the National Adaptation Programs for Action (NAPAs) whereby the least developed countries (LDCs) have identified their adaptation priorities. The sources of funding for the majority of these NAPAs have not been identified.

One key advantage of such an exchange is that it would be clearly associated with adaptation to specific and verifiable climate change impacts. However, this form of exchange would also be limited, as there are very few examples that fit this criterion. Most communities that are being affected by climate change are also suffering from other stressors such as conflict, poverty and governance issues. It is difficult to delineate specific climate impacts. Nonetheless, a range of small-scale opportunities exist in relation to the NAPAs.

B. *Unconditional Debt Reduction*

At the other end of the debt spectrum, this proposal considers how unconditional debt reduction might contribute to adaptation to climate change. The underlying idea of this scenario is that debt cancellation can increase spending on sectors such as social services and infrastructure. The vulnerability framing from the adaptation continuum suggests that reduction in general vulnerability has the potential to enhance a society's capacity to adapt to climate change. This form of debt-for-adaptation exchange could be conceptualised as follows:

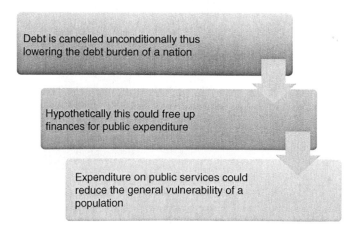

Debt is cancelled unconditionally thus lowering the debt burden of a nation

Hypothetically this could free up finances for public expenditure

Expenditure on public services could reduce the general vulnerability of a population

There are a number of precedents for unconditional debt reduction. For example, some national debts were cancelled under the Highly Indebted Poor Countries (HIPC) Initiative. Whilst there are many critiques of this initiative, there is some evidence that debt cancellation resulted in increased public expenditure on crucial social services. A key benefit of this proposal is that it may be favoured in the eyes of the recipient government. This model respects the sovereignty of recipient governments and provides them the flexibility to allocate freed-up finances in a manner they see fit.

However, there are potential barriers to this model of debt-for-adaptation exchanges. For example, there is no guarantee that the debt cancellation would have the desired impact in relation to adaptation. It would be very difficult to verify the benefits or outcomes in terms of adaptation. In addition, it may not benefit the most vulnerable, it may not reduce vulnerability to climate change and it may not be used in a socially equitable way. The relationship between climate change and adaptation and unconditional debt relief is likely to be contested.

In response to some of the barriers that have been noted, mechanisms could be developed to monitor national investment in general vulnerability reduction, and perhaps even broad adaptation measures. This process would need to be mindful of the blurred line that exists between conditional and unconditional arrangements. This section demonstrates that there is space in international discourses to consider unconditional debt relief in response to the inequity of climate change and inevitable costs of adaptation.

C. General Exchanges That Target Climate Vulnerable Sectors

This final proposal fits somewhere between the first two. In this scenario, debt is cancelled and then a proportion of the cancelled amount is directed towards the strengthening of climate vulnerable sectors. Referring back to the adaptation continuum, activities carried out under this proposal would generally fit within the vulnerability framework. This means that the actions would not have to be specifically correlated to adaptation; rather, they would be aimed at reducing generally vulnerability that stands to be exacerbated by climate change. Examples could include the provision of safe drinking water sources or immunisation against certain diseases that may be exacerbated by climate change scenarios. The ranges of several vector-borne diseases are changing as a result of a change of climate. A key example of such a shift is the movement of the 'mosquito line' up to altitudes where there are large cities, such as Nairobi in Africa. Sectors that may be affected by climate change include water, agriculture, health and forestry. This proposal has a much greater range of expenditure possibilities than the first proposal and a clearer connection to reducing vulnerability to climate change and greater opportunity for accountability than the second.

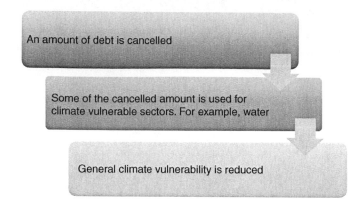

Within the frameworks used in this chapter this is most appropriate in terms of scalability and reproducibility. Some key challenges to this proposal lie in the prioritisation of various sectors for assistance. The following section explores some of the key objections to this model and the concept of debt-for-adaptation exchanges more broadly.

IV. POTENTIAL OBJECTIONS TO CLIMATE CHANGE ADAPTATION EXCHANGES

The consideration of debt-for-adaptation exchanges inevitably results in a discussion of principles. There are many principled and practical objections to the very idea of debt-for-adaptation exchanges. This section explores several of these key objections and discusses potential ways they could be overcome. It does not focus on each of the three conceptualisations that have been presented; rather, it explores overarching critiques. This section is framed mostly from the climate change perspective, as many of the critiques of debt have been covered in other chapters in this book. The principles identified in the following are gleaned from advocacy documents by key NGOs and coalitions.[24] The section provides some examples of potential objections and by no means offers an exhaustive list.

[24] Documents include Julie-Anne Richards, "Fair, Ambitious and Binding: Essentials for a Successful Climate Deal" (2009), Climate Action Network International; Micah Challenge Australia Policy Calls (2010); Make Poverty History Policy Calls (2010); Oxfam Briefing Note (2010), "Climate Finance Post-Copenhagen: The $100bn Questions", Oxfam International.

A. *Key Objections and Principles*

1. Industrialised countries have a historic obligation to provide full, no-strings-attached financial assistance for dealing with climate change impacts in developing countries

This principle is based on the fact that developing countries have contributed very little to the climate change problem and are not responsible for dealing with the impacts. Assistance for dealing with the impacts and future adaptation should be provided in full by those nations that have caused climate change. This has also been framed in terms of climate debt or reparations.

With reasonably flexible conditions on an exchange, finance could be freed up for a recipient country to help it adapt to climate change impacts. The debt-for-adaptation exchanges considered in this chapter could adhere to this principle. An exchange, which is not rebadged ODA, could be a component of meeting the historical obligation for financing whilst also reducing debt burdens.

2. All financing for adaptation to climate change must be additional to existing aid commitments

This is connected to the first objection and it presents a more tangible layer of complexity. Often debt-for-development exchanges are considered within existing aid budgets. For the principle of additionality to be adhered to, any debt-for-development exchange would have to be 'new and additional' to existing aid commitments. Functionally this becomes more complex when we consider the range of definitions of 'new and additional'. For example, a number of NGOs consider 'new and additional' to be finance that is beyond the 0.7% gross national income (GNI) that is argued to be required for the achievement of the MDGs.[25] However, for countries that are not yet meeting 0.7% GNI, this notion is abstract and perhaps unhelpful as anything other than an aspirational principle. An operable understanding of this principle in this context is that 'new and additional' means additional to existing aid commitments.

3. Financing must be predictable and long term

Due to the predicted continuity of climate change impacts, many NGOs and developing nations argue that funding must be predictable and long term.

[25] Micah Challenge Australia Policy Calls 2010; Make Poverty History Policy Calls.

Precedents for debt-for-development exchanges show us that they are generally isolated agreements involved with the short to medium term.

   This hurdle could be overcome through the design of innovative long-term
exchanges. One option would be to redirect all or part of a pre-existing repayment stream from a reduced debt to an agreed-upon development project.
The priorities for adaptation should be regularly reviewed to ensure that the
most urgent adaptation responses are being prioritised. It should be noted that
the conditionality of this proposal may cause objections.

   4. Financing should be delivered primarily through UN mechanisms,
      not bilaterally, in order to prevent the imposition of inappropriate
                conditions motivated by donor country agendas

Developing countries and NGOs have articulated that funding for adaptation
should be delivered through UNFCCC mechanisms. This is in opposition to
other options, such as bilateral aid and multilateral development banks like
the World Bank and Asian Development Bank. There are several reasons for
this preference, with the two foremost being transparency and equity of governance. UNFCCC funds generally offer a transparent process through the
involvement of civil society and a more balanced governance structure with
equal representation from developed and developing country governments.
In addition, the use of UN funds minimises the opportunities for aid to be
used as a tool of foreign policy or to promote nationally based, ideologically
driven agendas.

   Whilst it is difficult to avoid a bilateral component of debt-for-adaptation
exchanges, there are possibilities for adherence to this principle at the expenditure end. For example, in the case of Australia's debt-for-development exchange
with Indonesia, debt is cancelled and Indonesia will subsequently donate
money to the multilateral Global Fund. In this instance the exchange provides an opportunity for Australia to further support a multilateral institution
through its bilateral aid program. In regards to adaptation there are a range of
organisations with multilateral principles similar to those of the Global Fund
for financial contributions, such as the UNFCCC Adaptation Fund.

                           V. CONCLUSIONS

This chapter has conceptually explored potential debt-for-adaptation exchanges
with the aim of identifying emerging opportunities. There are a wide range
of critiques of exchanges that focus on the legitimacy of debt and the justice
implications of climate change. This chapter has drawn attention to some of

these arguments and suggests that they must be substantively debated if such exchanges were ever implemented. Having noted this, this chapter concludes that debt-for-adaptation exchanges should be considered, for the following reasons.

Individuals, communities and organisations have been campaigning for more and better aid for many decades. The majority of wealthy countries that committed themselves to achieving aid levels of 0.7% GNI are still a long way from reaching this target. Inequality between the wealthiest and poorest people on earth has grown significantly since World War II. It will be some time before we see a flow of finances for adaptation to climate change and, indeed, development that meets the calls of campaigners around the world and the cries of the global South. Given this context, there is a compelling argument that every avenue for the transfer of wealth between the wealthiest and poorest people on earth should be considered in order to move us closer to what is needed. Within certain parameters, debt-for-adaptation exchanges could reduce vulnerability to climate change for the poor and enhance adaptive capacity.

The consideration of debt-for-adaptation exchanges rests on philosophical questions concerning the delivery of aid and the treatment of the climate change issue. For example, what is considered legitimate debt? In addition, debt-for-adaptation exchanges pose a number of serious challenges in relation to the strengthening of certain development paradigms. Colonial approaches to development and international banking stand to be reinforced and potentially strengthened. This chapter has posed a number of arguments aimed at overcoming these challenges.

This innovative use of aid money should be considered and operationalised if deemed appropriate by all parties involved. As for all debt-for-development exchanges this should occur within very strict parameters. As noted throughout this chapter, debt-for-adaptation exchanges will inevitably attract strong contestation. It is only within this contested space, where all voices are heard, that we can search for the pathway forward. Debt-for-adaptation exchanges can play a part in leading us towards a more equitable and just global community.

19

Climate Change and Food Security: Building Resilience by Means of Climate Field Schools

Alicia C. Qian and Tanvir A. Uddin

I. INTRODUCTION

Climate change has been described as the greatest challenge that humankind will face in the 21st century. It encompasses both gradually altered weather patterns and extreme climatic events. Irrespective of its root cause, whether anthropogenic or part of ongoing natural processes, climate change has the potential to cause significant social and economic disruption across the globe. Agriculture has been consistently identified as one of the most vulnerable sectors due to its dependence on environmental resources and weather patterns. This in turn poses serious food security concerns for the globe. Key stakeholders in the resulting security dilemma are the farming populations of developing countries whose livelihoods are particularly at risk.

This chapter will explore the potential for climate field schools to address the effect of climate change on food security. First, we highlight how developing countries are acutely vulnerable due to the more pronounced impact climate change has on agricultural production. Second, we propose the use of debt-for-development exchanges to fund climate field schools for farmers as a fruitful adaptation strategy to build resilience and coping capacity.

II. CLIMATE CHANGE AND REDUCED AGRICULTURAL POTENTIAL

The increased intensity and frequency of extreme climatic events has been attributed to climate change. Damages from floods, droughts and windstorms amounted to US$31 billion damage and almost 24,336 deaths in Southeast and South Asia from 1994 to 2003.[1] It is clear that both gradual and acute

---

[1] http://www.emdat.be/old/Documents/Publications/publication_2004_emdat.pdf, accessed August 2, 2010.

environmental strains due to climate change have diminished livelihoods and hampered development in these regions.

Agriculture in particular is highly sensitive to climatic and temperature variation. While additional carbon dioxide gases in the atmosphere will benefit some plants, this will be more than countered by increased global mean temperatures reducing crop yields. For instance, an average increase of 6°C could decrease cereals yields by more than a third.[2] Farmers will need to face challenges, such as increased competition with pests and weeds. As conventional farming is characterised by monocultures, weeds have a competitive advantage in warmer temperatures due to a larger genetic diversity.[3] Further disruptions to the water cycle may occur with the melting of the Himalayan glaciers. This may provide a short-term water supply for irrigation. However, in the long term it may 'disturb monsoon patterns and increase seasonal floods and droughts' in Asia.[4]

Agricultural production is also highly dependent on water and requires regular precipitation. Irregular precipitation will cause major disruptions to both rain-fed and irrigated production by affecting soil moisture retention.[5] Moreover, excessive precipitation could also lead to floods that erode soil and cause extensive damage to crops. Weather variability such as that associated with the El Niño Southern Oscillation (ENSO) has been linked to a shortage of rainfall in regions such as Central America. This intensifies existing agricultural losses caused by hurricanes and floods.[6] In 2005 ENSO caused FJ$11 million damage to Fiji's sugar-cane industry.[7] Combined with irregularities in

[2] Food and Agriculture Organization (FAO) of the United Nations, *Climate Change and Food Security: A Framework Document* (Rome: FAO, 2008), 21, accessed August 2, 2010, ftp://ftp.fao.org/docrep/fao/010/k2595e/k2595e00.pdf.

[3] Lewis H. Ziska, "Climate Change Impacts on Weeds", *Climate Change and Agriculture: Promoting Practical and Profitable Responses*, accessed August 2, 2010, http://www.climate-andfarming.org/pdfs/FactSheets/III.1Weeds.pdf.

[4] Christian Nellemann et al., *The Environmental Food Crisis: The Environment's Role in Averting Future Food Crises*, UNEP Rapid Response Assessment (Norway: United Nations Environment Programme, GRID-Arendal 2009), 6, accessed August 2, 2010, http://www.grida.no/publications/rr/food-crisis/ebook.aspx.

[5] Food and Agriculture Organization (FAO) of the United Nations, "Climate Change, Water and Food Security", Technical Background Document from the Expert Consultation Held on February 26–28 2008, 1, accessed August 2, 2010, http://www.fao.org/nr/water/docs/HLC08-FAOWater-E.pdf.

[6] Edgardo Ayala, "Climate Changes Threatening Food Security", *Inter Press Service News Agency / Global Information Network* (June 15, 2010), accessed August 2, 2010, http://ipsnews.net/news.asp?idnews=51829.

[7] Food and Agriculture Organization (FAO) of the United Nations, *Climate Change and Food Security in Pacific Island Countries* (Rome: FAO, 2008), 7, accessed August 2, 2010, ftp://ftp.fao.org/docrep/fao/012/i1262e/i1262e00.pdf.

the length of growing seasons,[8] stabilising future agricultural potential will be a major challenge.

III. LOCAL RELATIONSHIP BETWEEN CLIMATE CHANGE AND FOOD SECURITY

Food security is driven by a number of complex forces that are both climatic and nonclimatic. Food security encompasses four components: food availability, food accessibility, food utilisation and food system stability.[9] Where one or more components are uncertain, a food system is considered vulnerable. Moreover, food security is influenced largely by environmental factors as well as socioeconomic forces such as trade flows, lack of credit and demographic changes. It has been estimated that 80% of the world's food-insecure people live in rural areas, with half being smallholder farmers.[10] Although decreased food production in itself does not automatically lead to food insecurity, agricultural vulnerability overall does constitute a prominent threat. The relationship is complex. Climate change essentially impacts agricultural production by affecting many biophysical factors. For example, plant growth and water cycles may change, resulting in changes in agricultural output. Thus, climate change can alter local food availability as well as price and food system stability.

Most rural households are not completely self-subsistent but rely on a combination of produced and purchased food. Thus, food security can rarely be achieved in the absence of cash expenditure.[11] Declining yields often reduce income, which influences food accessibility prominently at the local level. Income directly dictates consumption patterns and shapes food utilisation by either expanding or limiting food preferences. Income and warmer temperatures may also increase costs associated with food storage and spoilage. This would consequently affect choices regarding nonperishable foods. There can also be flow-on effects on the nutrition, diseases and health of rural communities. It must be noted, however, that agriculture does not consist only of food crops. Likewise, many communities do not subsist only on local produce. Nonetheless, by virtue of reshaping output and practices, climate change affects agriculture-associated livelihoods and income.

---

[8] Andrew J. Challinor et al., "Crops and Climate Change: Progress, Trends and Challenges in Simulating Impacts and Informing Adaption", *Journal of Experimental Botany* 60(10) (2009): 2775, 2779.

[9] Marc J. Cohen, "Food Security: Vulnerability Despite Abundance", *Coping with Crisis Working Paper Series*, International Peace Academy (2007), 1, accessed August 2, 2010, http://www.fanrpan.org/documents/d00438/Food_security_Cohen_Jul2007.pdf.

[10] Cohen, "Food Security", 2.

[11] UN FAO, *Climate Change and Food Security*, 5.

Climate change also lowers agricultural productivity. Pests and increased irrigation distort farmer input costs, while heat and water stress lowers production. This may affect the temporary availability of food where local markets are affected.[12] In addition, the increased use of biofuels to mitigate emissions also presents ambivalent consequences for agricultural sectors of developing countries. Biofuels have the potential to reduce carbon emissions that contribute to anthropogenic climate change. However, biofuels also compete with food crops for land and other agricultural resources. Furthermore, while biofuels are attractive in that they provide income for farmers, long-term sustainability in global food supplies may be compromised by the disproportionate preference for cash crops over food crops. Under the auspices of climate change, these risks all contribute to the complex and uncertain future of food security.

IV. REGIONAL VULNERABILITIES TO CLIMATE CHANGE

Many developing regions are particularly sensitive to climate change exposure and, by extension, food insecurity. The challenges of poverty and undernourishment will be exacerbated by reductions in agricultural production. Agriculture remains the backbone of many developing economies, and many rural communities are still largely dependent on it for employment. In Asia-Pacific regions, more than 2.2 billion people rely on agriculture for their livelihood.[13] This renders agricultural communities particularly vulnerable to climate change in comparison with their industrialised counterparts.

Some developing countries also suffer disproportionate effects of climate change due to geographic factors. Bangladesh and Tuvalu, with low-lying coastal profiles, are especially vulnerable to coastal regression if sea levels rise. Regions that experience a considerable loss in arable land are also likely to be prone to salt sprays and salinity problems.[14] Furthermore, island countries that rely exclusively on rainwater, such as Vanuatu, could experience severe water shortages.[15] These pre-existing sensitivities will see a more pronounced adverse impact of climate change.

In other countries, traditional crop choices may exacerbate vulnerabilities to varying precipitation levels. The 2005 IFPRI Food Policy Report indicates that food security will become a crucial issue, particularly for East Asia and

[12] Ibid.
[13] Asia Development Bank, "Facts and Figures", accessed August 2, 2010, http://www.adb.org/food-security/facts-figures.asp.
[14] UN FAO, "Climate Change, Water and Food Security", 16.
[15] Ibid., 12

the Pacific.[16] In particular, South Asia has been identified as the most food insecure subregion in the world.[17] This is because these regions rely on heavily irrigated crops such as rice, wheat and maize. They will be comparably more distressed by water scarcity. For developing countries, the lack of financial and technical resources enhances pressures on managing food security and rural livelihoods above and beyond existing development challenges. Furthermore, with disproportionately greater impacts of climate change in the Asia-Pacific region, the effects of climate change could have significant security ramifications for Australia in the future. Hence, Australia must play a leading role in mitigating the consequences of climate change in the region.

A. Related Security Concerns

The impacts of climate change on food security and, by extension, development are cyclical. Food security undermines other aspects of human security. Malnutrition is the main manifestation of poverty. In addition, food security can lead to conflicts over resources. Agricultural losses are often turned into 'contemporary food wars', of which Darfur was an example.[18] Farmers in Indonesia have been in competition for resources to grow subsistence rice for many years. This has resulted in local violence in the past.[19] These related concerns are likely to aggravate existing human security concerns.

With regards to water, Butts argued that, unlike other resources, 'water is an essential resource with no substitutes' and cannot be viably transported in sufficient quantities to support a population.[20] Given population growth, it is predicted that, by 2050, 67% of the world's population may experience water scarcity and one in six people may have insufficient water to meet their requirements for agriculture and domestic use.[21] Given that more than 70%

---

[16] Gerald C. Nelson et al., International Food Policy Research Institute (IFPRI), *Climate Change: Impact on Agriculture and Costs of Adaptation* (Washington, DC: IFPRI, 2009), 5, accessed August 2, 2010, http://www.ifpri.org/sites/default/files/publications/pr21.pdf.

[17] Asia Development Bank and International Food Policy Research Institute, *Building Climate Resilience in the Agricultural Sector of Asia and the Pacific* (Mandaluyong City: Asia Development Bank, 2009), 3, accessed August 2, 2010, http://www.adb.org/Documents/Books/Building-Climate-Resilience-Agriculture-Sector/Building-Climate-Resilience-Agriculture-Sector.pdf.

[18] Cohen, "Food Security", 7

[19] Richel Dursin, "Water Scarcity Dries Up Rice Growers' Livelihoods," *Asia Information Wire / Global Information Network* (July 20, 2006), accessed August 2, 2010, http://ipsnews.net/news.asp?idnews=34035.

[20] Kent Hughes Butts, "The Strategic Importance of Water", *Parameters* 27 (1997): 65, 66, 73

[21] J. S. Wallace, M. C. Acreman and C. A. Sullivan, "The Sharing of Water between Society and Ecosystems: From Conflict to Catchment-Based Co-Management", *Philosophical Transactions: Biological Sciences* 358, no. 1440 (2003): 2011.

of all water consumption is for agriculture, increased competition with industries will lead to water stress and increased prices of cereal crops.[22] Two of the Asian region's largest water sources, the Mekong and Ganges, have historically been sources of tension, which is likely to increase.

As livelihoods experience greater strain, the trend of rural–urban migration in developing countries is likely to be exacerbated. Denser populations concentrated over a smaller area may catalyse further tension between social groups. As well, this phenomenon places burdensome strains on the ability of government and agricultural sectors to provide for all citizens.

B. Escape or Build Resilience?

Security concerns demand urgent action. There is a crucial need to safeguard food security and minimise disruptions in global and local food supplies. The global consequences of unaddressed food insecurity concerns induced by climate change are serious. In 2000 Asia and the Pacific produced 43% of the world's crop production.[23] Disruptions in this region's food supply will also intensify global pressures relating to food security.

At the grassroots level, livelihoods in developing communities are already experiencing increased distress from climate change and food insecurity. This trend is expected to intensify in the future. It has been predicted that 200 million people will be displaced by 2050,[24] creating major tension in destination communities. While migration is one way to cope with the strain imposed by climate change, it is more likely to be a last resort than an early option.[25] Money and lack of existing networks will create impediments for the poor to relocate nationally or migrate transnationally. In the latter case, there is currently no international legal recognition of 'climate change refugees' who flee from the environment as the source of persecution.[26] For the farming population, it is imperative to seek other viable adaptation methods. Climate change is an inescapable global challenge with dire consequences for

---

[22] Timm Sauer et al., "Agriculture and Resource Availability in a Changing World: The Role of Irrigation", *Water Resources Research* 46 W06503 (2010).

[23] Asia Development Bank, "Facts and Figures".

[24] Oli Brown, "Migration and Climate Change", IOM Migration Research Series no. 31 (2007), 11.

[25] Ibid., 23, 36, 38.

[26] Fabrice Renaud et al., United Nations University Institute for Environment and Human Security, "Control, Adapt or Flee: How to Face Environmental Migration?" *Intersections*, no. 5 (2007): 14, accessed August 2, 2010, http://www.each-for.eu/documents/RENAUD%20 2007%20Control,%20Adapt%20or%20Flee%20How%20to%20Face%20Environmental%20 Migration%20UNU-EHS.pdf.

the food insecurity and livelihoods of vulnerable people. We explore one such resilience-focussed approach to aid communities in the next section.

V. FUNDING CLIMATE FIELD SCHOOLS USING DEBT-FOR-DEVELOPMENT EXCHANGES

Climate field schools (CFSs) provide a new means to address some of the major impacts of climate change on agriculture. Typically, CFSs are modelled on the operation of farmer field schools (FFSs). Thus, the first part of our discussion defines and examines the operation of FFSs. Moreover, by observing the experiences of FFSs, many important lessons may be adopted by the CFS program, as both programs are based on the diffusion of information. Although in their infancy, CFSs have much potential to significantly assist rural farmers in dealing with climate change. This is achieved through the diffusion of information and capacity building rather than by delivering a prepackaged program.

A. *Farmers are Noticing Change*

Farmers are already noticing changes in the environment and weather patterns. Taking Selvaraju et al.'s study of drought-prone, north-west Bangladesh as an example, locals have noticed the following: increased frequency and severity of droughts, increased incidences of pests and diseases and unpredictable rainfall patterns.[27] Whilst farmers have a willingness to adapt, old habits and practices are difficult to alter. The costs of adaptation are often seen as being too great. Also, climate change has shown that traditional knowledge and methods are no longer effective. For instance, in Indonesia, farmers are recording that their traditional knowledge of rainfall and weather patterns (*pranata mangsa*) is no longer working. Furthermore, government policy sometimes ignores the importance of sustainable adaptation. In Bangladesh, successive governments have, understandably, been concerned mainly about increasing food stocks to reduce starvation. These short-term measures often do nothing to address the long-term vulnerability of communities and the fragility of the environment. For instance, the excessive use of fertilisers and groundwater reserves has resulted in severe environmental degradation.[28]

---

[27] R. Selvaraju et al., "Livelihood Adaptation to Climatic Variability and Change in Drought-Prone Areas of Bangladesh: Developing Institutions and Options", Implemented under the project *Improved Adaptive Capacity to Climate Change for Sustainable Livelihoods in the Agriculture Sector* – DP9/1-BGD/01/004/01/99 (Rome: Asian Disaster Preparedness Center, Food and Agriculture Organization of the United Nations, 2006).

[28] M. Alauddin, "Environmentalising Economic Development: A South Asian Perspective", *Ecological Economics* 54 (2004): 251, 255.

B. Farmer Field Schools

FFSs are training programs that utilise participatory methods 'to help farmers develop their analytical skills, critical thinking and creativity, and help them learn to make better decisions'.[29] They were pioneered by the UN Food and Agriculture Organization (UN FAO) to diffuse knowledge-intensive concepts and practice. The programs were scaled up in 1989 to disseminate integrated-pest management (IPM) techniques among rice growers, mainly in Indonesia. In 1994 the National IPM Training Project expanded the pilot program into a nationwide FFS effort in Indonesia with the World Bank. By 1999 some 500,000 farmers in 10,000 villages had been trained and 20,000 farmers had attended 'training of trainers' sessions. Subsequently, large FFS pilot programs were set up in other parts of Asia, Africa and Latin America. The key benefit of FFSs was that, through group interaction, participants sharpened their decision-making abilities. Furthermore, they are empowered by learning leadership, communication and management skills.

C. The Field School Process

In Indonesia, a number of participants were placed into groups of 25 to 30 within each village. The farmer groups were trained in informal schools with weekly meetings over a season-long training course. The farmer-trainers received additional training in order to conduct programs. Subsequently the graduates shared their knowledge and experiences informally with neighbours as well as formally through structured programs. The intended outcome as explained by Feder et al. is that farmer-to-farmer diffusion effects bring about cost-effective knowledge diffusion and financial sustainability.[30] Thus, the key advantage of the FFS program over other agricultural extension efforts is that it is financially sustainable and more effective in disseminating knowledge.

D. Climate Field Schools

Like FFSs, CFSs are an agricultural extension program. CFSs train farmers and equip them with knowledge about sustainable agricultural practices. However, the purpose of CFSs is to assist farmers to understand the challenges and become better equipped to combat the threats posed by climate change.

---

[29] Kenmore (1997), cited in Gershon Feder, Rinku Murgai and Jaime B. Quizon, "Sending Farmers Back to School: The Impact of Farmer Field Schools in Indonesia," *Review of Agricultural Economics* 26, no. 1 (2003): 46.

[30] Ibid., 45, 46.

The conceptual framework is based on training farmers with a set of core skills. The farmers' improved knowledge is then reflected in improved outcomes in cultivation procedures, decisions and crop yields. In the presence of climate change, farmers have to mitigate pre-existing agricultural constraints as well as emerging climatic and environmental constraints. CFSs attempt to address these existing problems as well as prepare farmers for future climatic variation.

E. CFS Program Content

In Winarto et al.'s words, the CFS program attempts to 'transform global climate change modelling observations into locally actionable adaptation practices'.[31] To achieve this, one can envision many features of potential CFS programs. Designing successful programs would include:

- an understanding of the impacts of climate change and identifying the specific issues that are relevant to each community;
- practicable adaptation strategies to mitigate the adverse effects of current climatic variability and extreme events through alternative agricultural practices and income sources;
- incorporating traditional knowledge of weather, agriculture and ecosystems and local adaptation strategies;
- building institutional and technical capacity among clients and supporting agencies in government, nongovernment organisations (NGOs) and the corporate sector; and
- raising awareness about climate change and its effects, and flagging longer-term issues related to it and how to best prepare for them.

F. Theoretical Explorations

Despite the lack of empirical studies of FFSs (and almost none of CFSs), the theoretical aspects of the field schools are sound. First, poor knowledge is a major barrier for farmers. Even though farmers notice the effects of climate change, they are not aware of the best practices to address it. There is considerable evidence of the existence of beneficial learning spill-overs in agricultural practice amongst farmers.[32] Farmers often maximise their marginal

---

[31] Y. Winarto et al., "Climate Field Schools in Indonesia: Coping with Climate Change and Beyond", International Society for Agricultural Meteorology, accessed August 2, 2010, http://www.agrometeorology.org/topics/accounts-of-operational-agrometeorology/climate-field-schools-in-indonesia-coping-with-climate-change-and-beyond.

[32] Gershon Feder, "The Relation Between Farm Size and Farm Productivity", *Journal of Development Economics* 18, no. 2–3 (1985): 297.

profitability and reduce their losses by relying on their neighbours. Moreover, experimentation is an integral part of agriculture, and so farmers will adopt new methods by observing the experiences of other farmers.

Furthermore, farming and rural communities have traditionally built up considerable social capital in tackling common challenges. Examples of common challenges include resource scarcity and the adoption of new technologies such as high-yield varieties. Social capital denotes the social bonds and norms that are important for sustainable livelihoods. They are the structure of relations or the 'glue' that support productive activities.[33] Four central aspects of social capital readily apply to environmental challenges. These include relations of trust, reciprocity and exchanges; common rules; norms and sanctions; and connectedness, networks and groups. Intervention programs that focus on these aspects of social capital (such as field schools) are more effective than regulations and economic incentives. The latter are costly to implement and do not necessarily change habits in the long term. Thus, these approaches are far less effective in empowering farmers to adopt sustainable practices.[34]

VI. UTILISING THE EXPERIENCE FROM FFSS

There are diverging views about the effectiveness of, and returns from, FFS programs. For present purposes, a review of the literature can help identify the positive and negative aspects of these programs. FFS studies provide valuable insights for implementing future CFS programs.

Primarily, the FFS approach has been praised as an effective form of human capital investment. It has also been useful in assisting the agricultural extension projects of government and NGOs. Moreover, there is evidence that FFSs result in higher yields for farmers.[35] They can be extremely beneficial for rural communities due to their multidimensional learning outcomes. Most FFS programs (such as UN FAO) incorporate content relating to crop yields, environment, family health, as well as human and social capital. CFSs should minimise this and aim to undertake a holistic approach to climate change and the development challenges faced by farmers at the microlevel.

On the other hand, some authors have identified problems with FFS programs and question the positive outcomes mentioned earlier.[36] However, in practice most of the deficiencies actually relate to program design and

---

[33] Coleman (1988, 1990) cited in Feder et al., "Sending Farmers Back to School".
[34] For a study of successful social capital and environment projects, see J. Pretty and H. Ward, "Social Capital and the Environment", *World Development* 29, no. 2 (2001): 209, 213, table 1.
[35] These studies were cited in Feder et al., "Sending Farmers Back to School", 45.
[36] Ibid., 46–47.

management.[37] These include bureaucratic inefficiency, which reduces program outcomes when there is collaboration with government agricultural departments. Due to poor program design in some instances, the most crucial issues are not adequately addressed and important messages are not effectively communicated to farmers. These are generally the weaknesses that are inherent in 'publicly operated, staff-intensive, information delivery systems'.[38] Another problem that can readily be addressed is the tendency to conduct programs in a 'top-down' manner. Rather than participatory approaches being taken to train farmers, information is conveyed as a technological package.[39] This should be avoided, as it undermines the central tenets of a participatory approach to the field schools.

FFSs have been effective in some cases and less effective in others. Hence, careful planning must be undertaken in the design of CFS programs. Program managers must address both logistical challenges and the content of the information they wish to disseminate. The debt-for-development funds must be managed and administered by an appropriate body that is capable of undertaking this task. Whilst discussion of the management of CFSs is beyond the scope of this chapter, local and grassroots organisations must be consulted.

The nature of climate change and its problems demand emphasis on adaptation (with a particular development focus) in climate change–affected areas. New uses of official development assistance are needed to grapple with the existing and emerging challenges. The new strategies must improve information access, deliver the latest knowledge and assist in identifying alternative, technically viable options for livelihood adaptation. Moreover, these programs must be cognisant of changing socioeconomic/climatic conditions. Rather than delivering a technological 'package', local knowledge and traditional adaptation responses have to be integrated into program content. Furthermore, there must be a significant focus on institutional and individual capacity building to establish more efficient and sustainable adaptation programs. Consequently, affected communities can adopt new practices and adapt existing practices to reduce long-term vulnerability to climate change. CFS programs that address these essential criteria can be recommended as worthy investment projects for debt-for-development exchange.

---

[37] Ibid., 59.
[38] Feder et al. (2001), cited in ibid., 45.
[39] Axxin (1988), cited in ibid., 46.

20

Debt-for-Security Exchanges

Ross P. Buckley

I. INTRODUCTION

The rule of law is essential to good governance and development. In the words of Alexander Downer, Australia's former Minister for Foreign Affairs, 'Sustainable broad-based [economic] growth is impossible in countries which cannot guarantee public safety.... In violent or insecure environments, inevitably the poor pay the highest price.'[1]

The foregoing chapters have illustrated that debt exchanges can be used to address a broad range of development goals. This chapter argues the mechanism has a largely untapped potential – to fund security-enhancing projects. Two examples are explored in this chapter: using debt exchanges to fund peace initiatives in Mindanao and nuclear nonproliferation activities.

II. MINDANAO

Civil conflict has being going on for five centuries in Mindanao in the Philippines, and it is now the second-oldest conflict in the world.[2] This insecurity encourages people to join vigilante groups while discouraging them from investing in their future through agriculture, education, infrastructure and resource protection.[3]

---

[1] AusAID, "Australian Aid: Approaches to Peace, Conflict and Development" (November 2005) 1, accessed August 2, 2010, http://www.ausaid.gov.au/publications/pdf/ausaid_peace.pdf.

[2] Salvatore Schiavo-Campo and Mary Judd, "The Mindanao Conflict in the Philippines: Roots, Costs, and Potential Peace Dividend", Paper No. 24, *The World Bank Social Development Papers Conflict Prevention & Reconstruction* (February 2005): 1.

[3] Alexander Downer, "Australia's Overseas Aid Program, 2005–06" (May 10, 2005), accessed August 2, 2010, http://www.budget.gov.au/2005–06/ministerial/html/ausaid.htm.

Conflict in Mindanao is a complex problem. It is concentrated in rural Muslim-majority communities and originated from the Moro clans' resentment of the increasing number of Christian settlers and Christian central control. The Moro National Liberation Front (MNLF) emerged in the 1960s, and Muslim resistance developed into armed conflict. More recently, the Moro Islamic Liberation Front (MILF) has also emerged. The MNLF is the government's main opponent, and the MILF is a more religiously focussed resistance group. Although religious differences have shaped the conflict, its roots lie in the clans' conflicting interests regarding control over land and the resentment felt by the Moros about their inferior status. The situation is convoluted by the existence of several indigenous clans. They have been dominated and relocated by each of the settling colonisers and are regularly looked down upon by both the Christians and the Moros.[4]

The current situation in Mindanao is much more complicated than can be seen from its history. Among the Christians there is tension between the elite and the majority. Within the Muslim clans there is constant conflict, which often elicits military intervention. This is aggravated by widespread banditry, including violence, extortion and kidnapping for ransom.

Numerous attempts have been made to bring the violence under control. Most recently efforts have involved the creation of the Government–MILF Joint Ceasefire Coordinating Committee on the Cessation of Hostilities (JCCCH), which is charged with monitoring any violation of the ceasefire agreement. In addition, an agreement has been made to establish an international monitoring team to be led by Malaysia for the purpose of strengthening the peace process. In the past a major hurdle to negotiations has been the Moro's desire for a geographical area where they can promote their culture, religion and way of life.[5]

Conflict in Mindanao has killed 120,000 people and displaced a further 2 million since 1970[6] and has severely repressed economic and social development.[7] Armed conflict between the Philippine government and the MILF in 2008 led to a further 750,000 people being displaced and an estimated 400 killed. Life expectancy and socioeconomic indicators in Mindanao lag behind the rest of the Philippines. In addition to being a deterrent to FDI in the Philippines, conflict in Mindanao discourages any worthwhile investment

---

[4] Schiavo-Campo and Judd, "The Mindanao Conflict in the Philippines", 2.
[5] Ibid., 3.
[6] Michael Vatikiotis, "Resolving Internal Conflicts in Southeast Asia: Domestic Challenges and Regional Perspectives", *Contemporary Southeast Asia* 28(1) (2006): 31.
[7] Downer, "Australia's Overseas Aid Program"; Schiavo-Campo and Judd, "The Mindanao Conflict in the Philippines", 2.

by local farmers and reduces the profitability of crops in conflict- afflicted regions.[8] On a social level, extended conflict reduces levels of education and health, increases the level of poverty and causes a collective loss of hope.

In 2005 the World Bank pledged US$50 million to rehabilitate 5,000 villages in conflict-affected areas in Mindanao and in the South.[9] Japan and the United States have also made separate agreements to assist in post-conflict development.[10] In addition to improving the international image of the Philippines, resolving the conflict will facilitate enormous gains in economic and social development for the conflict-affected areas and subsequently allow the poorest Filipinos to improve their quality of life. According to a 2005 UN development report, additional economic opportunities may exist in Mindanao rebel-controlled areas that are believed to be rich in oil, gas, copper and gold.[11]

Security and poverty in Mindanao are complex, and overlapping problems and recent developments have confounded development projects. A comprehensive approach is necessary for peace to be achieved in Mindanao. Peace initiatives must include the unresolved issues from the 1996 Peace Agreement and the concerns of the indigenous people.[12] A noninclusive approach could be counterproductive in the long term by creating new tensions between clans. Post-conflict assistance programs must target Muslim and indigenous communities equally to provide the needed facilities, resources and training.[13] Care must be taken to prevent new economic and social tensions, to restore the trust of the people and to break the cycle of violence.[14]

A. Debt-Exchange Proposal Focussed on the Conflict in Mindanao

In September 1996 the Final Peace Agreement (FPA) was signed by the Government of the Republic of the Philippines (GRP) and the MNLF under the auspices of the Organization of the Islamic Conference under

---

[8] Schiavo-Campo and Judd, "The Mindanao Conflict in the Philippines", 7.

[9] Vatikiotis, "Resolving Internal Conflicts in Southeast Asia".

[10] The Ministry of Foreign Affairs of Japan, "Dispatch of Senior Advisor for Reconstruction and Development of Mindanao to International Monitoring and Support Team in Philippines" (2006), accessed August 2, 2010, http://www.mofa.go.jp/announce/announce/2006/10/1010. html; United States Ministry of Foreign Affairs, "Foreign Operations, Export Financing, and Related Programs (Foreign Operations)" (2007), 19, accessed August 2, 2010, http://www. state.gov/documents/organization/60300.pdf.

[11] Mindanao Economic Development Council, "Mindanao" (2004), accessed August 2, 2010, http://www.medco.gov.ph/medcoweb/mindanao.asp.

[12] Schiavo-Campo and Judd, "The Mindanao Conflict in the Philippines", 9.

[13] Ibid.

[14] Ibid.

the leadership of Indonesia.[15] The FPA seeks to address the political, social, cultural and religious foundations of the conflict in the southern Philippines. The signing of the FPA shows a commitment to peace.[16] While the signing of a peace treaty was heralded as a step forward, the militant arm of the separatist movement, the MILF, continued to operate distinct from the political arm with the objective of forming an Islamic separatist state. It was estimated that in the four years after the peace process the MILF increased its membership from 8,000 to 15,600.[17]

The fragile peace brought by the FPA was disrupted in August 2008. The catalyst for MILF violence was a decision by the Supreme Court of the Philippines which held that the expansion of the autonomous region in Muslim Mindanao was unconstitutional. Autonomy was given to three Muslim provinces in Mindano following a 1989 plebiscite. The autonomous region was expanded in 2001 and again in 2006. Following the 2008 court case, the government cancelled the Memorandum of Agreement on Ancestral Domain.[18] The MILF launched attacks against civilians, which led to fighting with the Philippine government. The conflict continued until the Philippine government and MILF declared a suspension of military activities on July 23 and 24, respectively.[19] Peace talks resumed on December 8, 2009. A commitment to ongoing talks with the new Filipino administration was agreed upon in June 2010.[20]

The recent bout of conflict in Mindano has displaced approximately 750,000 people. In 2009 the region had the highest number of new internally displaced persons worldwide.[21] Amnesty International, which has been in the area since the resumption of the peace process, has asserted that both the Philippine military and the MILF have failed to comply with international humanitarian law, with widespread incidents of human rights violations.[22] As

---

[15] Nieves Confesor, "The Philippines: In Search of a 'Transformed' Society – Building Peaceful Social Relations" (Expert Group Meeting, UN Division of Social Policy and Development, UN HQ, New York, November 21–23, 2005), 6; Mindanao Peaceweavers, "Is the Philippines at War with the US?" (November 30, 2005), accessed August 2, 2010, http://www.mindanao-peaceweavers.org/index.php?option=com_content&task=view&id=214&Itemid=1.

[16] Confesor, "The Philippines".

[17] Senator Gregorio B. Honason, "On Peace and Insurgency: President Estrada and Conflict in Mindanao", *Karainlam* 15(2) (2000): 238.

[18] AusAID, "Philippines", accessed August 2, 2010, http://www.ausaid.gov.au/country/country.cfm?CountryId=31.

[19] Amnesty international, *Philippines: Shattered Lives Beyond the 2008–2009 Mindanao Armed Conflict* (London: Amnesty International, 2010), 2.

[20] Mandel T. Subuter and Edd K. Usan, *Binay to MIL: Resume Peace Talks with GRP* (Manila: Manila Bulletin Publishing Company, August 12, 2010).

[21] Amnesty International, *Philippines*, 2.

[22] Ibid., 4.

a result of the conflict, Mindanao has fallen further behind the rest of the nation in terms of development indicators. The United Nations Development Program found that 7 of the 10 provinces ranked worst on the country's human development ratings are in Mindanao.[23] The US State Department has reported that the worsening economic situation in Mindanao has led to a substantial increase in the trafficking of women and children from the poor farming communities in the area.[24]

Any sustained peace will most likely involve community-based initiatives. Avoiding future outbreaks of violence will depend on a fair social structure that gives all clans an equal opportunity to participate in the governance of the community. Efforts must also be made to overcome mistrust and resentment between clans. It has been suggested that the success of peace initiatives in Mindanao must focus on three goals:

1. The peace process in Mindanao must be community based and reflect the basic values of all Filipino communities.
2. The peace process must create a fair social structure where all individuals are free to engage in peaceful competition for the success of their political programs based on an electoral system.
3. The peace process must seek a peaceful resolution to the armed conflict without blame or surrender, one that restores dignity to all people.[25]

Community-level peace initiatives have been designed by communities to fit with their own image of peace. These have included projects promoting peace advocacy and education, community-based peace building, peace centres and secretariats, mediation initiatives and inter-religious dialogues. An example of a community-level peace initiative is the Mindanao Peace and Development Initiative (MAPD). MAPD is a joint government and community effort to respond to the increased level of violence and tension of the 1990s. MAPD's achievements include affirming the shared desire for peace, placing concerns about religion and community-related issues on the table for discussion and proposing courses of action to address these concerns.

MAPD has also encouraged the formation of other peace initiatives, such as the Mindanao Peaceweavers. The Peaceweavers are a broad-based network whose goal is to engage communities in support of the peace initiative. The Peaceweavers believe, given the extended period of conflict and the damage it has done, that peace can be achieved only by starting at the local level.

[23] Integrated Regional Information Networks, "Philippines: Mindanao Conflict Fuels Trafficking", March 31, 2010, http://www.irinnews.org/report.aspx?ReportId=88631.
[24] United States State Department, "Trafficking in Persons Report 2010", available at http://www.state.gov/g/tip/rls/tiprpt/2010/, p. 270.
[25] Confessor, "The Philippines", 8.

The Mindanao Peaceweavers have investigated the factors that led to the wars in Sulu between the MNLF and the military in February and November 2005. These conflicts alone displaced 70,000 civilians and have caused persisting fear and insecurity among the people. Since then there have been an alarming number of incidents in Sulu implicating Filipino marines. There are accusations of rape, murder and kidnapping and the release from custody of marines suspected of killing innocent civilians without investigation. US soldiers in Mindanao have allegedly taken part in these attacks alongside Filipino marines.[26]

The Peaceweavers have called on the police to assert supremacy over the military, to conduct formal independent investigations into allegations against marines and to take the appropriate action to bring about justice for the victims.[27]

Programs like the MAPD and Peaceweavers that engage communities in initiatives to create a sustainable peaceful environment have a fundamental role to play in keeping the peace. Currently the Peaceweavers are seeking to promote constructive dialogue between stakeholders in the present conflict. Local programs like these may be better placed than international organisations or government organisations to achieve these ends. As stated by Vice President Binay, '[T]he end of armed conflict is key to bringing development and growth to the region'.[28] Renewing such efforts that existed before the breakdown of the FPA in 2008 is essential.

Achieving peace in Mindanao will stop the cycle of violence, mistrust and fear that is preventing social and economic development. Once the violence has ended, new social structures can be established to facilitate continued communication and allow shared or fairly distributed ownership of resources and shared community governance.

III. DEBT FOR NONPROLIFERATION

In 2002 a new legislative initiative was enacted in the United States that illuminated the potential breadth of uses to which debt exchanges might be put, not only for conservation purposes like previous initiatives, but also as a tool to promote national security. The 2002 Russian Federation Debt Reduction for Nonproliferation Act authorised the US President to reduce Soviet-era debt

[26] Mindanao Peaceweavers, "Is the Philippines at War with the US?".
[27] Mindanao Peaceweavers, "A Call for an Impartial Probe on Marines' Involvement in the Killings, Bombings in Sulu" (March 29, 2006), accessed August 2, 2010, http://www.mindanaopeaceweavers.org/index.php?option=com_content&task=view&id=316&Itemid=1.
[28] Subuter and Usan, *Binay to MIL*.

owed to the United States, in exchange for an agreement with Russia that the debt reduced be invested in nonproliferation programs agreed to by the two nations.[29] Enactment of the debt exchange as a tool for nonproliferation drew specifically from the example provided by 'past debt-for-environment exchanges'.[30] Unlike the case of debt-for-nature legislation, there was no reluctance expressed to use external debt for this purpose, and the Act passed both houses of Congress with broad bipartisan support.

At the time of enactment in 2002, there had been a growing concern over the rate of proliferation in the international community. In a G8 meeting that year, it was decided that Russia should be provided with additional nonproliferation assistance. The United States committed to $10 billion, with an additional commitment of $10 billion from other G8 nations over 10 years.[31] The heightened concern about the threat of proliferation of nuclear weapons was seen in the United States in new legislation to apply stricter funding embargoes on Iran.[32] A 2001 report by the Non-Proliferation Project of the Carnegie Endowment for International Peace focussed attention squarely on the situation in Russia, and painted an alarming picture of the risk that undervalued and underpaid Russian nuclear experts may be tempted to sell their knowledge to states supporting terrorism.[33] Congresswoman Tauscher stated that 'the reports findings are terrifying',[34] and a consensus emerged on the need for a response by the United States.

James Fuller, a nuclear scientist in the field of US–Russian nonproliferation and arms control, was a leading advocate in the debate about debt for nonproliferation. He argued that debt-for-national-security exchanges had been utilised previously by the United States. The first example was the cancellation in 1991 of 70% of Poland's debt to the United States, a reduction of $2.5 billion, in an effort to stabilise Poland as a market-oriented democracy. The second example was also from 1991, when Congress agreed to cancel $7 billion of Egypt's debt to the United States in recognition of Egypt's role in

---

[29] Russian Debt for Nonproliferation Act, 22 U.S.C. § 5929, (2002).

[30] 22 U.S.C. 5929 § 1312(a)(9).

[31] Congressional Record – House H6465 (September 23, 2002).

[32] The Iran Nuclear Proliferation Prevention Act of 2002 required the Secretary of State to assess the International Atomic Energy Agency's projects in Iran for their consistency with US nuclear nonproliferation goals in order to continue US funding. See Susan B. Epstein, "Foreign Relations Authorization, FY 2003: An Overview", CRS Report RL 31370 (November 8, 2002), accessed August 2, 2010, http://fpc.state.gov/documents/organization/10086.pdf.

[33] Congresswoman Ellen Tauscher, "Reflections on Legislation: Time to Act – A Review of Legislation to Prevent the Proliferation of Nuclear Weapons", *Seton Hall Legal Journal* 26 (2002): 327.

[34] Ibid.

the Persian Gulf coalition. The third example was Congress' agreement to forgive $700 million debt owed by Jordan in 1994 by way of recognition for its stabilising influence in the Middle East.[35]

More recently, in the aftermath of the Iraq war, Congress agreed to cancel all of Iraq's $3.5 billion debt to the United States, after the United States had persuaded other Paris Club creditor nations to cancel 80% of Iraq's loans from them. This is a quite extraordinary degree of debt relief, given that Iraq is not even poor by global standards (gross national income per capita in Iraq was estimated by the World Bank to be in the range of US$736 to $2,935 per annum)[36] and Iraq has the world's second-largest oil reserves.[37]

These examples illustrate that debt reduction can be a powerful political tool. The Russian Federation Debt Reduction for Nonproliferation Act, however, imposes significant stipulations on how the debt that is reduced must be used. In this respect, it is similar to the stipulations imposed on the Polish debt reduction, where debt was redirected into an established Polish EcoFund. Indeed, Fuller recommended that the legislation require the establishment of a Russian Nonproliferation Fund, on the model of the Polish EcoFund, in order to encourage additional funding from developed nations, foster Russian governance and create a viable long-term financing tool.[38] This requirement of a Nonproliferation Fund was not adopted, reflecting a concern that. the funds not be managed by another administrative body.

Russia is a prime candidate for debt-reduction initiatives. At the time of enactment, Russia's external debt stood at US$147 billion, of which $71 billion was from the Soviet era, and $2.7 billion of this debt was owed to the United States.[39] However, Congress highlighted that the purpose of the legislative initiative was not to provide debt relief, as Russia was meeting its international financial obligations, but to provide new funding to nonproliferation efforts.[40] The Act does not provide for any overt debt forgiveness, as the entirety of the

[35] James Fuller, "Debt for Nonproliferation: The Next Step in Threat Reduction", (January–February 2002), *Arms Control Today*, accessed August 2, 2010, http://www.armscontrol.org/print/975.

[36] World Bank, 2004 World Development Indicators (2004), 14–16.

[37] Ross P. Buckley, "Iraqi Sovereign Debt and Its Curious Global Implications", in *Beyond the Iraq War: The Promises, Perils and Pitfalls of External Interventionism*, eds. Michael Heazle and Iyanatul Islam (London: Edward Elgar, 2006), 141–155.

[38] "Loose Nukes, Biological Terrorism, and Chemical Warfare: Using Russian Debt to Enhance Security, Hearing Before the House Committee on International Relations" (July 25, 2002) (testimony by James Fuller), accessed August 2, 2010, http://www.nti.org/e_research/official_docs/labs/pnnl072502.pdf.

[39] Congressional Record – House H6465 (September 23, 2002); and Fuller, "Debt for Nonproliferation".

[40] Fuller, "Debt for Nonproliferation".

value of the debt reduced must be invested in agreed-upon nonproliferation programs and projects.[41]

The Act was couched in wording that appeals strongly to national security concerns and commences with the statement that 'it is in the vital security interests of the United States to prevent the spread of weapons of mass destruction'. Particular interest lay in ensuring the safety of 'weapons and weapons-usable nuclear material' in Russia, which would involve a cost that might not be able to be borne by Russia alone.[42] While US funding for Russian threat-reduction programs totalled $750 million in 2001,[43] this was recognised as insufficient to tackle the urgent threat.[44]

The Act gives the US President authority to reduce Soviet-era debt following entry into force of a Russian Federation Nonproliferation Investment Agreement between the two nations.[45] Each project and program funded must be agreed upon by the President and is to be subject to monitoring and auditing by the US government. Further stipulations require that the funds not be subject to taxation by the Russian government and that 75% of the funds be spent within Russia.[46] Under the Act, 10% of the funds freed by the reduction may, however, be invested in a Centre for an Independent Press and the Rule of Law, intended to encourage the growth of independent media within Russia. While the President is not required to direct funds for this purpose, it was strongly urged by Congress, due to concerns over the suppression of independent media.[47]

The power of the President to reduce debt for the purposes of nonproliferation is constrained by two legislative stipulations. Firstly, debt can be reduced only to the amount previously appropriated by Congress for debt-reduction purposes.[48] Secondly, there are certain implementation prerequisites. Before any agreement can take place, the President must verify that Russia has made 'material progress in stemming the flow of sensitive goods, technologies, material and knowledge' relating to the production of nuclear weapons.[49]

No debt-reduction agreements have yet been signed with Russia under the Russian Federation Debt Reduction for Nonproliferation Act, because the US government has thus far not been satisfied that material progress has been achieved in reducing the threat of the flow of sensitive goods and information.

[41] 22 U.S.C. 5929 § 1315(a)(1).
[42] 22 U.S.C. 5929 § 1312.
[43] Fuller, "Debt for Nonproliferation".
[44] 22 U.S.C. 5929 § 1312.
[45] 22 U.S.C. 5929 § 1314(a)(1).
[46] 22 U.S.C. 5929 § 1315.
[47] Congressional Record – House H6466 (September 23, 2002).
[48] 22 U.S.C. 5929 § 1312 (a)(2).
[49] 22 U.S.C. 5929 § 17.

A report issued by the United States confirmed that US assistance would not be forthcoming until certain 'implementation issues' – including 'taxation, transparency, access, and, particularly, liability protections' – were resolved by Russia.[50]

In the same report, President Bush also cited the failure of other G8 nations to meet their funding commitments for nonproliferation as another barrier to the willingness of the United States to enter into further funding commitments.[51] The Russian Federation Debt Reduction for Nonproliferation Act has, as one of its express aims, the encouragement of other nations to provide more extensive funding for nonproliferation.[52]

The respective importance attached by the US administration to the implementation efforts by Russia itself and the joint funding actions of its G8 partners is not clear. What is clear, however, is that, unsupported by efforts from the international community and in the absence of other compelling reasons to act unilaterally, the United States has to date been unwilling to work alone to fund further nonproliferation efforts.

Again, it will be interesting to see whether this is an initiative that the Obama administration chooses to reinvigorate. Thus far there have been no steps towards the use of the debt-for-nonproliferation legislation. Certainly, the problem and threat of proliferation remain, and the need for US leadership in this field is as acute as ever, particularly given the recent expiry of the Strategic Arms Reduction Treaty.[53]

IV. CLIMATE CHANGE AND RESOURCES PRESSURES AS A SECURITY THREAT

Another issue of relevance to the use of these techniques to address security concerns is the significant, but perhaps not yet fully understood link to be drawn between the state of the environment and human conflict. Access or lack of access to natural resources and water can trigger conflict. For example,

[50] "Report to the Congress on implementation of Public Law 107–228, Authority for Russian Federation Debt Reduction for Nonproliferation", 108th Congress, 2d Session, House Document 108–171, 2004.

[51] Ibid.

[52] Fuller, "Debt for Nonproliferation".

[53] In April 2009 Presidents Obama and Medev commenced negotiations for a new, legally binding agreement on reducing and limiting strategic and offensive arms to replace the START agreement, which was to expire on December 5, 2009. While no agreement was reached at the expiry date, both nations agreed that the START agreement would remain in force indefinitely whilst negotiations on a successor agreement continued. See President of Russia, "Joint Statement by the United States of America and the Russian Federation in Connection with the Expiration of the Treaty on the Reduction and Limitation of Strategic Offensive Arms" (press release, December 4, 2009), accessed August 2, 2010, http://www.ln.mid.ru/brp_4.nsf/ e78a48070f128a7b43256999005bcbb3/a3706a3fc9bfobf5c32576850026de6c?OpenDocument.

one of the underlying tensions between Israel and Syria is the issue of access to water. In both the Democratic Republic of Congo and Haiti, the United Nations Environment Programme (UNEP) has reported that environmental degradation has been a major cause of political unrest and conflict.[54] It has been estimated that approximately 5 million people were killed in armed conflicts during the 1990s related to the exploitation of natural resources[55] and that one-quarter of the 50 active armed conflicts in 2001 were 'motivated' largely by conflicts over resources.[56] Indeed, the army was called out in Peru in 2009 to support the police in quelling protests by indigenous peoples related to oil, gas and timber resources in the Amazon.[57]

University of Toronto researchers have concluded that, in countries as diverse as Haiti, Pakistan, the Philippines and South Africa, 'severe environmental stress multiplied the pain caused by such problems as ethnic strife and poverty'.[58] In regions experiencing low-level conflict, the risk of escalation to full-scale civil war approximately *doubles* immediately following a year of abnormally low rainfall.[59] In 2004 the United Nations High-Level Panel on Threats, Challenges, and Change concluded:

> Poverty, infectious diseases, environmental degradation and war feed one another in a deadly cycle.... Environmental stress, caused by large populations and shortages of land and other natural resources, can contribute to civil violence.[60]

Environmental degradation also leads to an increasing number of refugees.[61] The United Nations High Commissioner for Refugees, António Guterres,

54 Alister Doyle, "UN Aims to Study Link Between Environment, Wars", *Planet Ark World Environment News*, January 14 2004, accessed August 2, 2010, http://www.planetark.com/dailynewsstory.cfm/newsid/23429/story.htm.
55 Rudy S. Salo, "When the Logs Roll Over: The Need for an International Convention Criminalizing Involvement in the Global Illegal Timber Trade", *International Environmental Law Review* 16 (2003): 142.
56 David R. Francis, "Fueling the Fire: 'Resource Wars' Spurred by Assets of Developing Nations", *Christian Science Monitor*, December 6 2002.
57 BBC News, "Peru Army Call for Amazon Protest", May 17, 2009, accessed August 2, 2010, http://news.bbc.co.uk/2/hi/americas/8054043.stm.
58 Thomas Homer-Dixon, "Terror in the Weather Forecast", *New York Times*, April 24, 2007, accessed August 2, 2010, http://www.nytimes.com/2007/04/24/opinion/24homer-dixon.html?_r=1&th&emc=th& oref=slogin.
59 Professor Charles Vörösmarty, "Drought as a Contributor to Civil War: Results from a Global Spatial Analysis", Speech delivered at a seminar entitled *Climate–Security Connections: An Empirical Approach to Risk Assessment*, Washington, DC (March 6, 2007).
60 "Report of the High-Level Panel on Threats, Challenges, and Change, A More Secure World: Our Shared Responsibility", UN Doc A/59/565 (December 1, 2004), para. 22.
61 United Nations High Commission for Refugees, "2007 Global Trends: Refugees, Asylum-seekers, Returnees, Internally Displaced and Stateless Persons" (2008), accessed August 2, 2010, http://www.unhcr.org/statistics/STATISTICS/4852366f2.pdf.

concluded in 2008 that climate change leads to the dislocation of people 'by provoking conflicts over increasingly scarce resources, such as water' and, due to its impact on the environment, 'was a trigger of extreme poverty and conflict'.[62]

Environmental degradation can be both a cause and a consequence of armed conflict. While more work must be done to accurately determine the nature and extent of the link between environmental degradation, poverty and conflict, the logic of some form of connection appears to be undeniable, as was recognised by the United Nations Security Council in 1992:

> The absence of war and military conflicts amongst States does not in itself ensure international peace and security. The non-military sources of insta-bility in the economic, social, humanitarian and *ecological* fields have become threats to international peace and security. The United Nations membership as a whole needs to give the highest priority to the solution of these matters.[63]

Indeed, because environmental degradation can give rise to social upheaval and conflict, many states now assess environmental concerns, including resource conservation and sustainable development, 'in strategic terms'.[64] In the *Gabcíkovo-Nagymaros Project* case, the International Court of Justice acknowledged that the concerns of Hungary in relation to damage to its envi-ronment constituted an 'essential interest' of that country, within the mean-ing of that expression in the context of the international law of defence of necessity.[65] Moreover, the effects of environmental destruction can, and often do, have transboundary consequences, thus undermining the stability and security of neighbouring countries, regions and even the broader interna-tional community.

---

[62] Julian Borger, "Conflicts Fuelled by Climate Change Causing New Refugee Crisis, Warns UN", *Guardian*, June 17, 2008.

[63] United Nations Security Council, Note by the President of the Security Council, Presidential Statement S/23500 (January 31, 1992), in Catherine Tinker, "'Environmental Security' in The United Nations: Not a Matter for the Security Council", *Tennessee Law Review* 59 (1992): 787 (emphasis added).

[64] Ryan James Parsons, "The Fight to Save the Planet: U.S. Armed Forces, 'Greenkeeping,' and Enforcement of the Law Pertaining to Environmental Protection During Armed Conflict", *Georgetown International Environmental Law Review* 10 (1998): 444; Jutta Brunneé, "Environmental Security in the Twenty-First Century: New Momentum for the Development of International Environmental Law", *Fordham International Law Journal* 18 (1995): 1742. See also Michael K. Murphy, "Note: Achieving Economic Security with Swords as Ploughshares – The Modern Use of Force to Combat Environmental Degradation", *Vanderbilt Journal of International Law* 39 (1999): 1181, 1214, 1219.

[65] *Gabcíkovo-Nagymaros Project (Hungary v. Slovakia)* (Judgment) [1997] ICJ Rep 7, para 53.

In order to consider the linkages between environmental concerns and international human security, in April 2007 the United Nations Security Council held its first-ever debate on the impact of climate change on international peace and security.[66] In the same month, 11 retired US generals and admirals released a detailed report[67] in which they argued that the environmental impacts of climate change constituted a 'threat multiplier' in fragile parts of the world, which would 'exacerbate conditions that lead to failed states – the breeding grounds for extremism and terrorism'.[68] They highlighted the situations in Darfur and Somalia as examples of conflicts stemming from struggles over scarce natural resources.[69] United Nations Secretary-General Ban Ki-moon has said that the effects of climate change were partly to blame for the ongoing conflict in Darfur.[70] Shortly after his inauguration as President in January 2009, Barack Obama spoke of the risk of 'violent conflict' stemming from unchecked global warming.[71]

All of these concerns raise many questions as to how best to address the myriad threats caused by environmental degradation and climate change. The recently concluded Copenhagen Accord in reality offers very little by way of tangible solutions – and is, in any event, not a binding document. It would now be opportune for the United States to revisit its debt-for-nature legislative schemas with a view to assessing their relevance and applicability as one possible way to counter rising climate change and security concerns. Obviously, these techniques are of themselves no panacea; however, there is no sense in ignoring the possibilities these initiatives offer as a part of the broad matrix of actions required to mitigate the threats posed to the maintenance of international peace and security.

[66] See United Nations Security Council, "Security Council Hold First-Ever Debate on Impact of Climate Change on Peace, Security, Hearing Over 50 Speakers", UN Doc SC/9000 (press release, April 17, 2007), accessed August 2, 2010, http://www.un.org/News/Press/docs/2007/sc9000.doc.htm.

[67] CNA Corporation, "National Security and the Threat of Climate Change" (April 2007), accessed August 2, 2010, http://securityandclimate.cna.org/report/National%20Security%20and%20the%20Threat%20of%20Climate%20Change.pdf.

[68] "Warming and Global Security", *New York times*, April 20 2007, accessed August 2, 2010, http://www.nytimes.com/2007/04/20/opinion/20fri2.html.

[69] Ed Pilkington, "UK to Raise Climate Talks as Security Council Issue", *Guardian*, April 16, 2007.

[70] BBC News, "UN, Sudan to Discuss Darfur Plan", accessed August 2, 2010, http://news.bbc.co.uk/2/hi/africa/6760781.stm.

[71] Andrew C. Revkin, "Bush's Environmental Legacy in Play: Obama Reshaping Some Policies and Building on Others: Climate Change", *International Herald Tribune*, February 7–8, 2009. See also Allan Behm, "Climate Change and Security: The Test for Australia and Indonesia – Involvement or Indifference?" APSNet Special Report 09–01S, February 12, 2009, accessed August 2, 2010, http://www.globalcollab.org/Nautilus/australia.

21

Promoting Good Governance through ICT Systems: Improving Transparency and Reducing Corruption

Emmanuel T. Laryea

I. INTRODUCTION

This chapter proposes that investment in information and communication technology (ICT) systems through a debt-for-development exchange can be used to promote good governance, and in turn development, in developing countries. It proceeds on the basis that deficient (or poor or bad) governance in developing countries is a principal cause of their underdeveloped conditions.

Many heavily indebted developing countries are resource rich.[1] The seeming paradox of poverty and debt amidst heavy resource endowments has been the subject of much study and writing.[2] Some have called the situation the 'resource curse', suggesting a correlation between resource endowments and poverty and underdevelopment.[3] Others

---

[1] See, e.g., Joseph Siegle, *Remedying the Natural Resource Curse* (Geneva: UNESCO, 2009), accessed July 31, 2010, http://www.cdi.anu.edu.au/featured_articles/featured-articles_dowloads/ISSJ_705.pdf.

[2] See, e.g., Mohammed Ali Alayli, *Resource Rich Countries and Weak Institutions: The Resource Curse Effect* (Berkeley: University of California, 2005), accessed July 31, 2010, http://are.berkeley.edu/courses/EEP131/fall2006/NotableStudent05/Resource%20CurseM_Alayli.pdf.

[3] Halvor Mehlum, Karl Moene and Ragnar Torvik, "Institutions and Resource Curse", *Economic Journal* 116 (2006): 508; Tim Harford and Michael Klein, "Aid and the Resource Curse: How Can Aid Be Designed to Preserve Institutions?" *Public Policy for the Private Sector* 291 (2005): 1, accessed July 31, 2010, http://www.eldis.org/vfile/upload/1/document/0708/DOC20032.pdf; Richard Auty, *Resource-Based Industrialization: Sowing the Oil in Eight Developing Countries* (New York: Oxford University Press, 1990); Alan Gelb, *Windfall Gains: Blessing or Curse?* (New York: Oxford University Press, 1988); Jeffrey D. Sachs and Andrew M. Warner, "Natural Resource Abundance and Economic Growth", National Bureau of Economic Research Working Paper No. 5398, (Cambridge, MA, 1999). See also Ian Gary and Terry Karl, *Bottom of the Barrel: Africa's Oil Boom and the Poor* (Baltimore: Catholic Relief Services, 2003), 5; Jeffrey Sachs and Andrew Warner, "The Big Push, Natural

disagree,[4] as does this author. Arguably, it is the quality of governance that determines whether the availability of natural resources (and related revenues) will be positive or negative for a nation.[5] Strong political will and institutions underpinning sound governance can ensure that the economies of resource-rich countries are efficiently and effectively managed for the betterment of those countries and their peoples.[6] That is what distinguishes resource-rich developed countries (such as Australia, Canada, Norway and the United States) from the many resource-rich but poor developing countries. The poverty and indebtedness are due to factors other than the presence (or even lack) of natural resources.

Some of the factors that have been proffered to explain the underdevelopment of resource-endowed economies include human geography,[7] culture,[8] colonialism and conspiracy of world powers[9] and deficient governance (or

Resource Booms and Growth", *Journal of Development Economics* 59 (1999): 43–76; X. Sala-i-Martin and A. Subramanian, "Addressing the Natural Resource Curse: An Illustration from Nigeria", IMF Working Paper 03/019 (Washington, DC: International Monetary Fund, 2003); Jeffrey Sachs and Francisco Rodriguez, "Why Do Resource-Abundant Economies Grow More Slowly?" *Journal for Economic Growth* 4 (1999): 277–303; Oxfam, "Lifting the Resource Curse: How Poor People Can and Should Benefit from the Revenues of Extractive Industries", Oxfam Briefing Paper No. 134 (2009), 9. Ravinder Rena, "Dealing with Africa's Resource Curse" (2007), Global Policy Forum online, accessed July 31, 2010, http://www.globalpolicy.org/component/content/article/198/40125.html.

4   See, e.g., Christa Brunnschweiler and Erwin Bulte, "The Resource Curse Revisited and Revised: A Tale of Paradoxes and Red Herrings", *Journal of Environmental Economics and Management* 55 (2008): 248–264; Christa Brunnschweiler, "Cursing the Blessings? Natural Resource Abundance, Institutions, and Economic Growth", *World Development* 36 (2008): 399–419; Erika Weinthal and Pauline Luong, "Combating the Resource Curse: An Alternative Solution to Managing Mineral Wealth", *Perspectives on Politics* 4(1) (2006): 435–53; Anne Boschini, Jan Pettersson and Jesper Roine, "Resource Curse or Not: A Question of Appropriability", *Scandinavian Journal of Economics* 109 (2007): 593–617.

5   Joseph Seigle, "Governance Strategies to Remedy the Natural Resource Curse", *International Social Science Journal* 57 (2009): 45; M. Mehrara, S. Alhosseini and D. Bahramirad, "Resource Curse and Institutional Quality in Oil Countries" (2008), Munich Personal RePEc Archive (MPRA) Paper No. 16456, accessed July 31, 2010, http://mpra.ub.uni-muenchen.de/16456/1/MPRA_paper_16456.pdf; George B. N. Ayittey, *Indigenous African Institutions* (Ardsley-on-Hudson, NY: Transnational Publishers, 1991).

6   Harford and Klein, "Aid and the Resource Curse", 1; Daniel Kaufmann and Aart Kraay, "Growth without Governance", *Economia* 3 (2002): 169–229.

7   See, e.g., David S. Landes, *The Wealth and Poverty of Nations: Why Are Some So Rich and Others So Poor?* (New York: W. W. Norton, 1998).

8   See, e.g., Lawrence E. Harrison and Samuel P. Huntington (eds.), *Culture Matters: How Values Shape Human Progress* (New York: Basic Books, 2000); Lawrence E. Harrison, *Who Prospers: How Cultural Values Shape Economic and Political Success* (New York: Basic Books, 1992). Contrast with Hernando de Soto, *The Mystery of Capitalism: Why Capitalism Triumphs in the West and Fails Everywhere Else* (New York: Random House, 2000), 4.

9   See, e.g., Sambit Bhattacharyya, "Root Causes of African Underdevelopment", *Journal of African Economies* 18(5) (2009): 745–780; Nathan Nunn, "The Long-Term Effects of

poor or bad governance).[10] While there may be some validity in the causative effects of each of the listed factors, this chapter argues that governance deficiencies are the critical cause. It goes on to suggest that the deployment of appropriately targeted ICT systems can enhance governance and improve economic development (and human rights).

The chapter thus proceeds, first, to discuss issues of good governance (Section II). It starts by looking at the concept of good governance, noting that there is no single definition that is universally accepted. It adopts a description that encapsulates a few generally acknowledged elements, namely democracy, rule of law, transparency and accountability, low corruption and effective and efficient economic management. It goes on to specify corruption and economic mismanagement as debilitating manifestations of poor governance often bred by deficiencies in the other elements of good governance. Sections III and IV then discuss, respectively, corruption and economic mismanagement. Section V examines how information technology systems can enhance governance. Section VI outlines conditions necessary for the proposals to work, and Section VII concludes the chapter.

II. GOOD GOVERNANCE

It must be noted at the outset that the concept of 'good governance' (or even 'governance') is difficult to define succinctly.[11] The reasons are that the term 'is heavily value-laden'[12] and can be general in its orientation, admitting of a multiplicity of issues.[13] Not only has the concept evolved over time, it has been

Africa's Slave Trades", *Quarterly Journal of Economics* 123(1) (2008): 139–176; Nathan Nunn, "Historical Legacies: A Model Linking Africa's Past to Its Current Underdevelopment", *Journal of Development Economics* 83(1) (2007): 157–175.

[10] See, e.g., Siegle, "Governance Strategies"; Mehrara, Alhosseini and Bahramirad, "Resource Curse"; Claudio Ciborra and Diego D. Navarra, "Good Governance, Development Theory, and Aid Policy: Risks and Challenges of E-Government in Jordan", *Information Technology for Development* 11(2) (2005): 141; Al-Jurf, "Good Governance and Transparency: Their Impact on Development", *Transnational Law and Contemporary Problems* 9 (1999): 193, 198–199. See also World Bank, *Sub-Saharan Africa: From Crisis to Sustainable Growth* (Washington, DC: World Bank, 1989), 60, where, in explaining Africa's development problems, the Bank stated that 'underlying the litany of Africa's development problems is a crisis of governance'.

[11] See, e.g., Francis Botchway, "Good Governance: The Old, the New, the Principle and the Elements", *Florida Journal of International Law* 13 (2001): 160–161; Thomas G. Weiss, "Governance, Good Governance and Global Governance: Conceptual and Actual Challenges", *Third World Quarterly* 21(5) (2000): 795–814; Gerry Stoker, "Governance as Theory: Five Propositions", *International Social Science Journal* 50 (1998): 17–28.

[12] Botchway, "Good Governance", 162.

[13] Ibid.

discussed in different contexts and given different meanings or emphases in particular contexts.

While discussions of the substance or elements of governance have long been around,[14] the contemporary origin of the term 'good governance' is attributed to the World Bank, in its 1989 World Development Report.[15] The report made extensive reference to the term, and subsequently expounded upon it in 1992, 1994 and 1997.[16] In 1997 the World Bank announced that good governance is a *conditio sine qua non* to development.[17] Even then, the Bank's definition (or description) of the term 'governance' has varied to include 'the exercise of political power to manage a nation's affairs'[18] and the manner of exercising power for economic and social development.[19] The Bank's view of good governance as a major variable of economic development brought focus to this issue.[20]

A number of other development-oriented institutions have also considered governance as an important issue.[21] The International Monetary Fund incorporated governance as a criterion for assistance in 1997.[22] The United Nations Development Programme (UNDP) stated in 1997 that 'it is only with good governance that we can find solutions to poverty, inequity, and insecurity'.[23] The UNDP describes 'good governance' as the processes and structures that guide political and socioeconomic relationships, and lists its ingredients as participation, rule of law, transparency, accountability, responsiveness, consensus orientation, equity, effectiveness and efficiency and strategic vision.[24] Within this is 'political governance', which refers to the process of decision making

---

[14] See ibid., 165.

[15] See Amado Tolentino, "Good Governance Through Popular Participation in Sustainable Development", in Konrad Ginther et al. (eds.), *Sustainable Development and Good Governance* (The Hague: Martinus Nijhoff, 1995), 136; Botchway, "Good Governance", 162.

[16] See World Bank, *Governance and Development* (Washington, DC: World Bank, 1992); World Bank, *Governance: The World Bank's Experiences* (Washington, DC: World Bank, 1994); Botchway, "Good Governance", 162–163.

[17] World Bank, *World Development Report: The State in a Changing World* (Washington, DC World Bank, 1997); Botchway, "Good Governance", 163.

[18] World Bank, *Sub-Saharan Africa*, 60.

[19] World Bank, *Governance: The World Bank's Experiences*, xiv.

[20] Botchway, "Good Governance", 162–163.

[21] Ibid., 163.

[22] See, generally, International Monetary Fund, *Good Governance: The IMF's Role* (Washington, DC: IMF, 1997); International Monetary Fund, *IMF Code of Good Practices on Fiscal Transparency: Declaration Principles* (Washington, DC: IMF, April 16, 1998).

[23] United Nation Development Programme, "Foreword", *Governance for Sustainable Human Development* (UNDP: UNDP Policy Document, January 1997), accessed July 31, 2010, http://mirror.undp.org/magnet/policy/chapter1.htm#b.

[24] Ibid.

to formulate policy; 'administrative governance', which refers to the system of policy implementation; and 'economic governance', which includes decision-making processes that determine and affect a country's economic activities and its relationships with other economies, which have fundamental implications for equity, poverty and quality of life.[25] In 2002 the importance of good governance for development was incorporated in the Monterrey Consensus.[26]

Scholars too have examined the concept of good governance and its impact on development, albeit with different emphasis at various times.[27] For instance, Max Weber outlined the functions of a bureaucracy that would facilitate development, calling for strict observance of rule of law and legal rationality, and advising against the mixing of private interest with the public responsibility of the bureaucrat.[28] The rise of the law and development theory in the 1960s is also notable.[29] So too are more recent works, such as those by Rose-Ackerman,[30] Kaufman[31] and Fitzgerald,[32] among others.

[25] Ibid.

[26] The Monterrey Consensus is a document adopted at the United Nations International Conference on Financing for Development, held in Monterrey, Mexico, March 18–22, 2002. More than 50 Heads of State and 200 Ministers of Finance, Foreign Affairs, Development and Trade together with the Heads of the United Nations, the IMF, the World Bank and the World Trade Organization, prominent business and civil society leaders and other stakeholders participated in the event. See United Nations, "Monterrey Consensus on Financing for Development" (2002), accessed July 31, 2010, http://www.un.org/esa/ffd/monterrey/MonterreyConsensus.pdf; United Nations, "Financing for Development: Building on Monterrey" (2002), accessed July 31, 2010, http://www.un.org/esa/ffd/documents/Building%20on%20Monterrey.pdf.

[27] See, e.g., Tolentino, "Good Governance Through Popular Participation"; Patrick McAuslan, "Good Governance and Aid in Africa", *Journal of African Law* 40 (1996): 168.

[28] See, generally, Wolfgang J. Mommsen, *The Age of Bureaucracy: Perspectives on the Political Sociology of Max Webber* (New York: Harper & Row, 1974); David M. Trubek, "Max Weber on Law and the Rise of Capitalism", *Wisconsin Law Review* 3 (1972): 720–753; Botchway, "Good Governance", 165.

[29] See Thomas M. Franck, "The New Development: Can American Law and Legal Institutions Help Developing Countries?" *Wisconsin Law Review* 3 (1972): 767, 770–778.

[30] Susan Rose-Ackerman, *Corruption and Government: Causes, Consequences, and Reform* (Cambridge: Cambridge University Press, 1999).

[31] Daniel Kaufman, "Myths and Realities of Governance and Corruption", in World Economic Forum (ed.), *Global Competitiveness Report, 2005–2006* (London: Palgrave Macmillan, 2005), 81–98, accessed July 31, 2010, http://papers.ssrn.com/sol3/papers.cfm?abstract_id=829244&rec=1&srcabs=386904. The author defines 'governance as the traditions and institutions by which authority in a country is exercised for [the] common good. This includes: the process by which governments are selected and replaced; the capacity of the government to formulate and implement sound policies effectively; and the respect of citizens for the institutions that govern economic and social interactions among them'.

[32] Fitzgerald et al. describe governance as 'working and listening to citizens in order to manage the public's resources and respond to the needs and expectations of citizens as individuals,

Notwithstanding the difficulty of defining good governance, most in the discipline appear content with a description or a list of elements for the term.[33] Elements, or principles, generally accepted include transparency and accountability, low levels of corruption, efficient and equitable management of resource revenues, democracy and rule of law.[34] Each of these principles is broad and hardly amenable to easy or precise definition. In fact, what each of these elements entails may be not only controversial, but also contradictory. For instance, an equitable allocation of resources may not be efficient in the short term.[35]

Ignoring the problems with precise meanings, if the proposition is accepted that these elements are good for development, then a deficiency in one or more will have an impact on development. It is beyond the scope of this chapter to discuss all of the elements in detail or the possible permutations of deficiencies and their likely effects. Within the limited space available, this chapter selects for further discussion corruption and inefficient management (or mismanagement) of resources, as two major governance deficiencies in developing countries that cause underdevelopment. The other elements will, inevitably, be alluded to in the course of the discussions.

III. GOVERNANCE DEFICIENCIES: CORRUPTION AND ECONOMIC MISMANAGEMENT

This section discusses corruption and economic mismanagement as manifestations of poor (or deficient) governance. It is not uncommon for the two terms to be used interchangeably, as, broadly viewed, corruption may entail mismanagement and vice versa. However, in this chapter, the two terms are given narrow definitions and are discussed separately.

---

interest groups, and society as a whole'. Governance includes active co-operation and engagement in policy processes among all stakeholders, including citizens. See P. Fitzgerald, A. McLennan and B. Munslow, *Managing Sustainable Development in South Africa*, 2d ed. (New York: Oxford University Press, 1997).

[33] Botchway, "Good Governance", 61.

[34] Daniel Kaufmann, A. Kraay and A. Mastruzzi, "Governance Matters, III: Governance Indicators for 1996–2002", Policy Research Working Paper No. 3106 (Washington, DC: World Bank, 2003). See also A. Iimi, "Escaping from the Resource Curse: Evidence from Botswana and the Rest of the World", IMF Staff Papers, Vol. 54, No. 4 (Washington, DC: International Monetary Fund, 2007), 672–673.

[35] An example may be given of a policy to provide electric power to a remote and economically depressed part of a country. It may be equitable for the inhabitants there but economically inefficient, in the short term at least. See Botchway, "Good Governance", 162.

A. *Corruption*

1. Definitional Issues

The term 'corruption' is used in several contexts to describe myriad situations or actions.[36] In this chapter the conventional definitions are considered. With slight differences, the common definitions include 'the abuse of public trust for private gain',[37] 'the illegal use of power for personal gain',[38] the 'misuse of public power for private or political gain' and 'a violation of established rules and ways of doing things with the aim of obtaining private gain or profit'.[39] These definitions may have different emphasis, but most focus on the public aspect. That is, they focus on the misuse of public office for private gain. The discussions in this chapter will, similarly, focus on the public aspect.

Corruption, of course, also exists within the private sector.[40] Zimiring and Johnson[41] cite as an example of abuse of private power an estate agent who sells property to a friend for less than its market price. To give a personal example, while the author was visiting Ghana in 2009, he had to buy an automobile part for the repair of a damaged car. The author requested an invoice. Perhaps thinking the author needed the invoice to account to his superior, the storekeeper asked the amount the author would like written on the invoice. The storekeeper was apparently suggesting over-invoicing without any prompting by the author, in order to defraud any superior to whom he thought the author was to report (irrespective of whether that superior was a private or public entity). The author understands that the practice is very widespread and well understood among Ghanaians. Of course, there is a public (administration) dimension to the pervasiveness of such a practice. First, it thrives because traders operate largely in an

---

[36] See Susan Rose-Akerman, "The Challenge of Poor Governance and Corruption" (2004), Copenhagen Consensus Challenge Paper, 1, accessed July 31, 2010, http://www.copenhagenconsensus.com/files/filer/cc/papers/governance_and_corruption_300404_(0.7mb_version).pdf.

[37] Michael Todaro and Stephen Smith, *Economic Development*, 8th ed. (New York: Addison-Wesley, 2003), 711.

[38] Franklin E. Zimring and David T. Johnson, "On the Comparative Study of Corruption", *British Journal of Criminology* 45(6) (2005): 793.

[39] Augustine Nwabuzor, "Corruption and Development: New Initiatives in Economic Openness and Strengthened Rule of Law", *Journal of Business Ethics* 59 (2005): 121.

[40] See, e.g., Vito Tanzi, "Corruption Around the World: Causes, Consequences, Scope, and Cures", IMF Working Paper (1998), 8, accessed July 31, 2010, http://www.imf.org/external/pubs/ft/wp/wp9863.pdf; and Zimiring and Johnson, "On the Comparative Study of Corruption", 7–8, where the authors cite as an example of abuse of private power an estate agent who sells private property to a friend for less than the market price he could get.

[41] See Zimiring and Johnson, "On the Comparative Study of Corruption", 7–8.

informal environment where they do not account for, or pay tax to, the government based on their turnover. They keep little or no accounting records of any significance. Second, the practice has flourished because of lax laws.

Thus, for the purpose of this chapter, 'corruption' is defined as the misuse or illegal use of power or position, public or private, for personal or political gain.[42] It may be argued that there is no readily discernible private or inappropriate gain accruing to the storekeeper in the present example so the practice is not captured by this definition. However, by willingly offering to collude, the storekeeper may have hoped to gain future business from the customer, which is a benefit. The definition captures most activities usually considered corrupt (and illegal in most countries), such as the payment and receipt of bribes, embezzlement, fraud, misappropriation of public resources for private use, nepotism and cronyism.[43] These form the largest part of corruption and are the most destructive to developing economies.

2. Kinds of Corruption

This subsection outlines four main categories that are common in developing countries, though it should be noted that there are several more varieties in which corruption may manifest.[44] The categories adopted here are bribery in the provision of public goods and services (including investment approvals); bribery in the judicial system; bribery in government procurement; and misappropriation of public resources.

A. BRIBERY IN THE PROVISION OF PUBLIC GOODS AND SERVICES. Bribe extraction by providers of government services is a major problem in developing countries. This can be pervasive, and damaging. Unfortunately, citizens, foreigners, investors and consumers all have to deal with government departments at various times. To take an example, an investor may need from government regulatory bodies a number of approvals, registrations, licences, exemptions and permits to establish and run a business. This often requires a number of steps and dealings with bureaucrats who often have the power (*de*

---

[42] A distinction may be drawn between "co-operative corruption", where the offender aims at creating alliances or social popularity (the type discussed here), and "predatory corruption", where the perpetrator seeks to keep rather than share the gains (the more familiar type). See Zimiring and Johnson, "On the Comparative Study of Corruption", 7–8.

[43] Rose-Akerman, "The Challenge of Poor Governance and Corruption", 1.

[44] Patrick Maegher has proposed a similar categorisation. See Patrick Meagher, "Combating Corruption in Africa: Institutional Challenges and Responses" (Washington, DC: IMF, June 1997), 2–17, accessed July 31, 2010, http://pdf.usaid.gov/pdf_docs/PNACA964.pdf.

jure or *de facto*) to grant, expedite, delay or deny what is being applied for.[45] This creates the potential for the extraction of bribes, and advantage is often taken by public officials of their position. Sometimes progress on the application is intentionally frustrated, so the applicant is compelled to pay bribes in order to expedite the processing. At other times, the capacity of the department concerned may be low and systems outmoded, so that the department is unable to cope with demands for its services. This creates a backlog and prompts applicants who may be in a hurry to pay 'speed money'.

As is noted later with respect to the consequences of corruption, investments, and therefore job creation and economic growth, may suffer as a result. However, as also noted in Section V, the deployment of ICT systems can help reduce the problems faced by recipients of government services and ameliorate the incidence of bribery.

B. BRIBERY IN THE JUDICIAL SYSTEM. The judicial process is subject to three forms of corruption. The first two forms occur in matters between private individuals or firms, on the one hand, and government, on the other. The first is usually present when the judiciary is not independent, and results in illegal rulings in favour of government, though there may not be direct bribes paid.

The second form manifests in situations where private individuals pay bribes to judicial officers (often together with representatives of governments) in order to avoid or minimise sanctions for breaches of the law, including tax evasion, environmental damage, infringements of workers' rights and embezzlement.

The third form is encountered in matters between private individuals or firms, and involves the making of illegal rulings in favour of one party in return for favours from that party, usually monetary payments.

All forms of bribery in a judicial system undermine the rule of law, and diminish the enjoyment and enforcement of rights and respect for and observance of obligations. These undermine trust and confidence in the system, which leads to costly and inefficient methods of doing business (e.g., gravitating towards self-enforcing deals such as spot-market sales, rather than running the risk of needing to go before unreliable courts).[46]

C. BRIBERY IN GOVERNMENT PROCUREMENT. Government contracting is critical in developing countries and is often a fertile ground for corruption. It takes many forms, including collusion and bid rigging, and payoffs to government officials for the award of particular contracts. This may result in the wrong supplier or contractor being awarded contracts, with attendant consequences.

[45] Ibid., 3.
[46] Ibid.

As the kickbacks must be recouped somehow, there will be over-invoicing, resulting in a waste of resources, or skimping on quality or quantity of materials, resulting in shoddy products.

D. MISAPPROPRIATION OF PUBLIC RESOURCES. This type of corruption includes embezzlement of government funds, theft of other public resources and civil service fraud. It is rampant in many developing countries. It results in loss of revenue and assets to the state, and a consequent lack of resources for legitimate government business.

3. 'Petty' and 'Grand' Corruption

A distinction is sometimes drawn between 'petty corruption' and 'grand corruption'.[47] 'Petty corruption' is used in the context of relatively small bribes often collected by public servants. Even then, the pettiness of the corruption refers only to the size of each transaction and not to its total impact on government income or policy or the efficiency of the economy. 'Grand corruption', on the other hand, refers to corruption that takes place on higher levels of government and involves large amounts of money or value to public officials.

Both petty and grand corruption do manifest in the four categories outlined earlier. However, some scholars have suggested that petty corruption should be formalised as acceptable practices within certain societies, while grand corruption is to be combated.[48] In this chapter no such distinction is made, for two reasons. First, the supposed petty corruption can be debilitating to development. Indeed, the suggestions made in this chapter for combating corruption are aimed at eliminating, foremost, the types of corruption that may be described as petty corruption, as the suggestions are aimed at public administrative systems. Second, there are governments that may not engage in grand corruption but nonetheless strive to fight petty corruption, as they consider it detrimental to the development of their country.

4. Causes of Corruption

Various explanations have been given for the prevalence and magnitude of corruption.[49] The reasons can be contentious. It is not feasible to examine

---

[47] See, e.g., Susan Rose-Ackerman, "'Grand' Corruption and the Ethics of Global Business," *Journal of Banking and Finance* 26 (2002): 1889–1918.

[48] Nwabuzor, "Corruption and Development", 122.

[49] Undoubtedly, there is some degree of corruption in every country, but the magnitude, degree, incidence and pervasiveness vary greatly among countries. See, e.g., Sandrine Tolotti et al., "Nations United in Sleaze", *World Press Review* 43 (1996): 18; Frank Anechiarico and James

here the debates regarding the causes of, or conditions conducive to, corruption. This chapter simply notes a few of the discussed causes, particularly the conditions that enable corruption to prevail.

A. POVERTY. Some have suggested that the high incidence of corruption in developing countries is attributable to the presence of large-scale poverty within those countries. The argument is that the existence of poverty and low salaries encourages antisocial and unethical behaviour such as bribe taking.[50] That argument seems to be supported by evidence suggesting a correlation between income levels (per capita) of countries and their incidence of corruption (i.e., their performance on corruption measurement indices). It should be noted, however, that often the perpetrators of corruption are the 'rich' in those poor countries. The elites, who are much better off than most in poverty-ridden jurisdictions, tend to engage in corruption, grand corruption. Their corrupt behaviour may not necessarily be explained by their economic position.

B. LIMITED ECONOMIC FREEDOM. The absence of economic freedom is also said to encourage corruption.[51] Economic freedom is defined as 'the absence of government constraint or coercion on production, distribution and consumption of goods and services that are beyond the extent necessary for citizens to maintain and protect liberty itself'.[52] The absence of economic freedom means the government owns and runs much of the national economy, with attendant inefficiencies. Those in charge wield enormous power over public assets, which they use to profit themselves. Moreover, a lack of economic freedom tends to generate illegal markets, which foster corruption.

Of course, simply because an economic entity is government owned does not necessarily mean those in charge should or would be corrupt. There are state-owned enterprises in the developed world that have operated profitably. For instance, before its partial privatisation by the Australian federal government, Telstra, the nation's biggest telecom entity, operated efficiently and profitably, contributing to the federal government's revenue stream.

B. Jacobs, *The Pursuit of Absolute Integrity: How Corruption Control Makes Government Ineffective* (Chicago: University Of Chicago Press, 1996), 9.
[50] See, e.g., Nwabuzor, "Corruption and Development".
[51] Ana Eiras, "Make the Rule of Law a Necessary Condition for the Millennium Challenge Account" (2003), accessed July 31, 2010, http://www.heritage.org/Research/Reports/2003/03/Make-the-Rule-of-Law-a-Necessary-Condition.
[52] Nwabuzor, "Corruption and Development", 125.

C. ABSENCE OF EFFECTIVE RULE OF LAW. The concept of rule of law lacks a precise definition but is understood to cover ideals that subject the exercise of powers held by leaders to certain constraints provided by a framework of public norms.[53] It encompasses three elements: the supremacy of the law and absence of arbitrariness; equality before the law; and constitutional law as part of the ordinary law of the land.[54] Rule of law ensures that political power is not abused. Without the rule of law, there would be no mechanism to stop private abuse and public mismanagement.[55] In an environment of very weak rule of law, national assets are stolen by elites, often with impunity. People take matters into their own hands, using whatever means they can, including corruption, to advance their self-interest. It also means that corrupt practices, if they constitute crime under the nation's laws (and corruption is illegal in most jurisdictions), go largely unpunished. This then reinforces the practice.

D. DISCRETION AND UNCERTAINTY. Closely aligned with the absence of rule of law is discretion and uncertainty. Where public officials have unduly wide discretion in relation to activities, probably because there are no rules and regulations, or any existing rules are ambiguous, administrators have an opportunity to extract bribes.[56]

E. ABSENCE OF DEMOCRACY. As the saying goes, 'Power corrupts, and absolute power corrupts absolutely'.[57] In autocratic jurisdictions, where the power of the leadership is effectively subject to little or no limitation, abuses are most likely to occur. It is entirely possible for there to be a benevolent dictator who, despite any absolute powers he or she may wield, is incorrupt and governs with the utmost interest of the governed at the fore. However, experience shows that such situations are rare. Dictatorial regimes have tended to be most corrupt. Thus democracy helps to control corruption.

---

[53] J. Waldron, "The Concept and the Rule of Law", New York University School of Law Public Law and Legal Theory Research Paper Series Working Paper No. 08–50 (2008), 5.

[54] A. V. Dicey, *An Introduction to the Study of the Law of the Constitution*, 10th ed. (London: Macmillan, 1959), 193–194. See also I. Saunders and K. Le Roy (eds.), *The Rule of Law* (Sydney: Federation Press, 2003), 5.

[55] Eiras, "Make the Rule of Law a Necessary Condition".

[56] See Tanzi, "Corruption around the World", 10–15.

[57] This quotation is attributed to John Emerich Edward Dalberg Acton (1834–1902), a British historian and moralist, who was otherwise known simply as Lord Acton, in a letter to Bishop Mandell Creighton in 1887. http://www.phrases.org.uk/meanings/288200.html, accessed July 31, 2010.

But what is democracy? Any particular effort to define democracy has attracted criticism.[58] This may be due to its overtly political character. Perhaps the easiest definition is that which takes democracy as a form of governance based on some degree of popular sovereignty and collective decision making.[59] Democracy may be appreciated from procedural, institutional and social viewpoints. Procedurally, democracy encapsulates the legitimacy of the opposition, the protection of freedoms (of expression and association), free and fair elections, universal suffrage and equity.[60] Subjecting to the citizenry the mandate of the political leadership means they have to be wary of corruption, among other things. If they are not, and are considered to be corrupt, they would be voted out of government. Consequently, it is not uncommon to see political opposition in developing countries portraying incumbents as corrupt and promising anticorruption if voted into office.[61] Such campaigns are almost always popular.[62]

F. ABSENCE OF TRANSPARENCY AND ACCOUNTABILITY. Corruption and bribery typically operate, and thrive, in opacity.[63] Transparency in a system that enables the citizenry to know what, why, how and by whom decisions are taken, appointments are made and resources are allocated reduces corruption and engenders trust and confidence in the system.

Accountability, in this context, is an available framework to subject actions and decisions of public officials to oversight, and ensures not only that the formulation of government initiatives is scrutinised but that those implemented meet their planned objectives. It also ensures that government responds to the needs of the citizenry and contributes to the reduction of corruption.

[58] M. Saward, "Democratic Theories and Indices of Democratization", in D. Beetham (ed.), *Defining and Measuring Democracy* (London: Sage, 1994), 6–8.
[59] T. Landman, "Democracy Analysis", in International IDEA, *Ten Years of Supporting Democracy Worldwide* (Stockholm: International IDEA, 2005), 20.
[60] It should be noted that the list is not exhaustive. There is no complete set of democratic procedures, and there is no sufficient set of elements for democracy. See, generally, R. Dahl, *Polyarchy: Participation and Opposition* (New Haven, CT: Yale University Press, 1971).
[61] In Ghana, during the lead up to the 2000 elections, the main opposition party (the New Patriotic Party, NPP) campaigned mainly on the corruption of the incumbent and promised a "zero tolerance of corruption" if voted into power. And it succeeded. For more information, see "The Challenges Facing Anti-Corruption in Ghana", *Ghana Integrity Initiative Quarterly Newsletter GII Alert* 23 (December 2009): 9, accessed July 31, 2010, http://www.tighana.org/newsletters/GII_ALERT_23.pdf.
[62] It must be noted that democracy is not simply about holding elections; it entails far more than that. Organising elections for the sake of it, without freedom and fairness, does not meet the most basic element of democracy and would not produce the positive outcomes of democracy alluded to in this paragraph.
[63] Kaufnam, "Myths and Realities", 83.

5. Consequences of Corruption

The negative impact of corruption on development is well documented. Established evidence from cross-country empirical studies has confirmed the negative impact of corruption on institutions, democracy, investments, growth and productivity, policy processes, property rights and consequently overall development.[64] Some of these consequences are outlined in the following subsections.

A. WASTE OF NATIONAL RESOURCES. Corruption leads to a diversion of economic resources from legitimate uses.[65] It leads to suboptimal resource allocation, as resources that ostensibly are meant to benefit the public are diverted to private benefits, reducing the quality and cost effectiveness of public works.[66] This may result in shoddy, faulty or dangerous pieces of infrastructure (such as roads, hospitals and drains), which not only may deprive the citizenry of the expected benefits, but may cost them more – in repairs or reconstruction, and even lives in cases of unsafe and inferior constructions.[67]

B. EFFECTS ON GOODS AND SERVICES PROVIDED. Corruption can adversely affect the quality of goods and services produced in a given economy. Companies that are burdened with 'under-the-table payments' will try to contain their costs by cutting corners.

Where cost cutting cannot compensate for the bribes paid, they are passed on by way of higher prices, feeding into inflation and reducing the international competitiveness of products from the jurisdiction. The inflationary effects of corruption can be self-perpetuating, as when artificially high contract prices fuel hyperinflation, reduce GNP and per capita income and raise unemployment.[68]

C. DISCOURAGEMENT OF INVESTMENT. A high incidence of corruption increases transaction costs for business, undermines trust and confidence in

---

[64] See Rose-Ackerman, *Corruption and Government.*

[65] See Cynthia Kemper, "Law Aims at More Than Bribes", *Journal of Commerce* (1999): 4.

[66] Neil H. Jacoby et al., *Bribery and Extortion in World Business: A Study of Corporate Political Payments Abroad* (New York: Macmillan, 1977), 142.

[67] See Jeffrey P. Bialos and Gregory Husisian, *The Foreign Corrupt Practices Act: Coping with Corruption in Transnational Economies* (New York: Oceana Publications, 1997), 147.

[68] Konyin Ajayi, "On the Trail of a Spectre-Destabilisation of Developing and Transnational Economies: A Case Study of Corruption in Nigeria", *Dickson Journal of International Law* 15 (1997): 546.

the security of investment and therefore discourages investment from both domestic and foreign sources.[69] It is not uncommon for residents of developing countries with a high incidence of corruption to invest their capital (often obtained through corrupt activities) abroad.

D. SELLING SHORT NATIONAL RESOURCES. In return for private benefits, corrupt public officials may grant to foreign investors contracts that are one sided in favour of the investors, depriving their country of the necessary benefits. Underpinning most foreign investments in resources are contractual arrangements either with a state (the host state or its agency) or a private entity (or entities) in which the resources to be exploited are vested. Ownership of natural resources is determined primarily by domestic law, though international law also plays an important part, particularly in resources that transcend international borders[70] or in areas of undefined boundaries.[71] In most countries, natural resources are vested in the state.[72] Thus, the contractual arrangement, which may range from permit or license for exploration and discovery to substantive contracts for development, production and distribution, is often between the investor and the state (or its agencies).

The primary object of the investor is to procure profits, obtaining the maximum possible risk-adjusted return on its investment over the life of the investment. Normally, the broad primary objective of the host state is the general public interest of economic development, translating into expectations

---

[69] Soma Pillay, "Corruption – the Challenge to Good Governance: A South African Perspective", *International Journal of Public Sector Management* 17(7) (2004): 586–605; Nwabuzor, "Corruption and Development", 129–130.

[70] See Nico Schrijver, *Sovereignty over Natural Resources: Balancing Rights and Duties* (Cambridge: Cambridge University Press, 1997). An example of resources that may transcend international borders is oil reservoirs that extend beneath national borders (see A. Ifesi et al., "International Unitisation of Oil and Gas Fields: The Legal Framework of International Law, National Laws, and Private Contracts", *Oil, Gas & Energy Law* 5(2) (2007); Roger Knight et al., "Deep Water: How West Africa Compares with Gulf of Mexico", *Oil & Gas Journal* (2003): 42; Bruce Kramer and Gary B. Conine, "Joint Development and Operations", in Ernest Smith et al. (eds.), *International Petroleum Transactions* (Denver: Rocky Mountain Mineral Law Foundation, 2000), 640; Rainer Lagoni, "Oil and Gas Deposits Across National Frontiers", *American Journal of International Law* 73 (1979): 215. Another example is transboundary fish stocks that can move across territorial waters in an ocean or fish stocks in a lake that is bordered by two or more states (such as Lake Victoria, which is bordered by three African countries – Kenya, Tanzania and Uganda).

[71] See, e.g., Ifesi et al., "International Unitisation"; David M. Ong, "Joint Development of Common Offshore Oil and Gas Deposits: 'Mere' State Practice or Customary International Law", *American Journal of International Law* 93 (1999): 771.

[72] Kirsten Bindemann, "Production Sharing Agreements: An Economic Analysis", Oxford Institute for Energy Studies (1999), 8, accessed July 31, 2010, http://www.oxfordenergy.org/pdfs/WPM25.pdf.

of maximum revenue from the exploited resources, job creation (direct and indirect), provision of training and skills upgrade, transfer of technology to the host state, increased capital stock and spin-off of new and allied industries. However, history has shown that the interest of most governments of host developing countries is often private benefit, not public interest of economic development. Most resource-rich developing countries are characterised by 'those in political offices working hard to ensure that the rest of the population receives almost no benefit from the resources with which their countries have been abundantly endowed'.[73]

E. MISUSE OF SKILLS AND MANPOWER. Because of corruption, inappropriate use is often made of a nation's scarce skills and manpower. Less qualified or inappropriate people may be appointed to critical positions, leading to bad and ineffective policies.[74] Also, valuable management time and money may be spent on monitoring projects and conducting investigations into cases where corruption or suspicions of it have been alleged.

F. UNDERMINING OF DEVELOPMENT. Corruption's effects of lack of investment, suboptimal allocation of resource, waste of resources and selling short all have a dampening effect on the efforts of any nation to achieve political and economic development.

Corruption can lead to apathy among the citizenry, undermining the desire to work hard, creativity and nation building. As Frisch put it, corruption can kill 'the development spirit – nothing is as destructive to a society as the rush to quick and easy money which makes fools of those who can work honestly and constructively'.[75]

IV. ECONOMIC MISMANAGEMENT

Though closely related to corruption (and, broadly viewed, corruption is a form of mismanagement), 'economic mismanagement' is here distinguished from corruption and its consequences. Mismanagement in this context refers to the inefficient allocation of resources (or misallocation of resources), though not actuated by corruption – that is, the allocation of resources to

---

[73] Emeka Duruigbo, "Permanent Sovereignty and People's Ownership of Natural Resources in International Law," *George Washington International Law Review* 38 (2006): 33, 34.

[74] This is discussed further in Section IV.

[75] D. Frisch, "Effects of Corruption on Development in Corruption", Paper presented at a conference entitled *Democracy and Human Rights in West Africa*, Africa Leadership Forum, Cotonou (1994), 60–61.

suboptimal uses or for suboptimal returns. Simply put, it is the wasting of resources. Governments can be wasteful in the same way private individuals can be wasteful. Mismanagement may stem from incompetence, bad advice, poor judgement, ignorance or, some may argue, social constraints.[76]

Misallocation of resources is quite common in developing countries. There are several examples, from the building of palaces and other edifices, instead of basic public and productive infrastructure (e.g., roads, schools, hospitals, water and sanitation, governance institutions and technology), to opulence, bizarre largesse and the conclusion of investment contracts that are bad for the nation. Examples of suboptimal uses of available resources and bad deals for the state are discussed in the following subsections.

A. *Suboptimal Allocation of Available Resources*

The issue here is the use of funds (often borrowed) on patently unproductive projects.

1. Ghana

Two examples are given here. First, the previous Ghanaian government decided to build, in 2005, a new presidential palace (later named 'Jubilee House' following public criticism)[77] costing hundreds of millions of borrowed dollars (not including the value of land already owned by the government). The structure was built with unprecedented speed in order for the incumbent to move in for a short time (less than three months) before the end of his second term in 2008, after which he became ineligible for a further term. The 'palace' was built while most public infrastructure is in a deplorable state. For instance, there is no ultimate referral hospital in the country. So when politicians are sick, they are flown abroad (mostly to the United Kingdom and South Africa) at a huge cost to the citizenry. Apart from the obvious unfairness of such a practice to ordinary citizens,[78] the practice seems to ignore the

---

[76] Social constraints can broadly be described as prevailing social conditions that inhibit government from implementing economically prudent, but socially tough reforms that may disturb existing cohesion within the country. On mismanagement stemming from social constraints, see Jo Ritzen, William Easterly and Michael Woolcock, "On 'Good' Politicians and 'Bad' Policies: Social Cohesion, Institutions, and Growth" (2000), World Bank Policy Research Working Paper No. 2448, accessed July 31, 2010, http://econ.worldbank.org/external/default/main?pagePK=64165259&piPK=64165421&theSitePK=469372&menuPK=64216926&entityID=000094946_0009200531267.

[77] The name 'Jubilee House' referred to Ghana's 50th anniversary of independence from the British on March 6, 1957, the golden jubilee falling on March 6, 2007.

[78] The politician is transported to a developed country for treatment at the expense of the ordinary citizen, but the ordinary citizen has to make do with what is available locally.

fact that timely diagnosis and treatment can be critical. Precious time may be lost when patients have to be flown for hours to hospitals in foreign countries for treatment. Thus, the political elites are exposed to serious risks by relying on treatment abroad instead of building and equipping at least one ultimate referral hospital in the country for everyone.[79]

The second example is that hundreds of millions of borrowed dollars were lavished on celebrations of Ghana's golden jubilee in 2007. This occurred at the same time that Ghana was issuing sovereign bonds to the tune of US$750 million on the international capital market, in September 2007.[80]

The loans for the presidential palace, for the jubilee celebrations, and from the issued bonds and several more millions obtained from bilateral and other sources, which have been used largely for unproductive ventures, remain to be serviced and repaid. That borrowing for unproductive ventures is a cause of debt and economic crises is well documented.[81]

2. Cote d'ivoire

Félix Houphouët-Boigny, a former (and long-serving) President of Cote d'Ivoire,[82] is known to have built the largest church in the world, the Basilica of Our Lady of Peace of Yamoussoukro, in a part of the country that is woefully lacking in basic infrastructure. Constructed between 1985 and 1989 at a cost of US$300 million, the construction was a huge impost on the country's national debt.

B. *Bad Investment Contracts for the State*

It was noted in Section III.A.5.d that corrupt public officials may grant to foreign investors contracts that are one sided in favour of the investors in return for private benefits. One-sided contracts in favour of investors that deprive a state of adequate benefits may result from factors other than corruption, such as incompetence, neglect of duty on the part of public officials, bad advice,

---

[79] In February 2010, a 56-year-old former Ghanaian Minister of Agriculture passed away soon after arriving in Israel for treatment for an undisclosed ailment. While one cannot say with certainty that delay occasioned by the need to transport the patient abroad contributed to his death, this author wonders whether the risk posed by the time delay is not appreciated by the political elites of the country.

[80] See Joanna Chung, "Ghana Makes International Bond Debut", *Financial Times*, September 28, 2007. Lucy Adoma Yeboah, "Ghana's Eurobond Wins Award," December 31, 2007, http://lucyadoma.blogspot.com/2007/12/ghana-eurobond-wins-award.html.

[81] See Ross Buckley, "A Tale of Two Crises: The Search for the Enduring Reforms of the International Financial System", *UCLA Journal of International Law & Foreign Affairs* 6 (2001): 1, 18–20.

[82] Félix Houphouët-Boigny ruled from August 7, 1960, until his death on December 7, 1993, at the age of 88 years.

poor judgement or ignorance. Two examples are given in the following subsections, though the presence of corruption cannot be ruled out.[83]

1. Liberia

In the midst of high commodity prices and international competition for
resources, Liberia granted to foreign investors lopsided concessions on iron
ore and rubber in 2005.[84] It took an outcry from civil society groups and support from Liberia's donor partners for the government to renegotiate two major
such concessions, yielding several improvements to the fiscal take of the country.[85] In signing the initial contract, the government obviously neglected to
secure for the country reasonable outcomes from the deal.

2. Ethiopia

On May 14, 2009, the Ethiopian government signed a Product Sharing
Agreement (PSA) with the Canadian energy company Epsilon Energy Ltd for
the exploration of petroleum.[86] The agreement covers some 79,345 square kilometres in northwest Ethiopia, nearly 8% of the approximately 1,100,000 square
kilometre total area of the country, and provides for the initial percentage split
of profit oil in the event of discovery at 80% for Epsilon and 20% for Ethiopia.[87]
The contract followed an earlier Study Agreement that Epsilon concluded
with the Ethiopian government in June 2008, which enabled Epsilon to use a
combination of satellite remote sensing, hydrology, gravity and magnetic technologies to identify areas that potentially hold oil reserves. Epsilon identified
the areas of the country's north-west, towards Ethiopia's border with Sudan,
for inclusion in the PSA with the Ethiopian government, for exploration and,
if oil is discovered, production.[88]

[83] Corruption often occurs in secrecy, so the imprudent contracts may well have been actuated
by corruption on the part of the public officials that is not yet public.
[84] See Raja Kaul, Antoine Heuty and Alvin Norman, *Getting a Better Deal from the Extractive
Sector: Concession Negotiation in Liberia, 2006–2008* (New York: Revenue Watch Institute,
2009), accessed July 31, 2010, http://www.revenuewatch.org/news/publications/getting-a-
better-deal.php.
[85] Ibid.
[86] "Epsilon Energy Signs PSA with Ethiopia", *Energy Business Review: Oil & Gas Exploration*
(May 14, 2009), accessed July 31, 2010, http://oilgasexploration.energy-business-review.com/
news/epsilon_energy_signs_psa_with_ethiopia_090514; "Epsilon Energy Signs Production
Sharing Agreement in Ethiopia" (Epsilon news release, May 14, 2009), available on the Epsilon
Web site, accessed July 31, 2010, http://www.epsilonenergyltd.com/pdf_folder/05.14.09%20
Ethiopia.pdf; "Epsilon Signs PSA with Ethiopia", *Petroleum Africa News* (May 15, 2009),
accessed July 31, 2010, http://petroleumafrica.com/read_article.php?NID=7621.
[87] Ibid.
[88] "Epsilon Energy Signs Production Sharing Agreement in Ethiopia"; "Epsilon Energy Signs
PSA with Ethiopia".

As Ethiopia has yet to discover oil in commercial quantity, ceding all of the most prospective areas of the country (neighbouring Sudan has proven oil reserves) in one contract to one company appears to be ill advised. A prudent approach would have been to demarcate the areas for exploration, and possible exploitation, into clear blocks, release them in batches over time and invite competitive bidding from investors. In a climate of international competition for mineral and petroleum resources, the value of blocks is likely to appreciate with successful discoveries in neighbouring blocks.

V. HOW ICT CAN ENHANCE GOVERNANCE

It has thus far been argued that governance deficiencies are the critical cause of underdevelopment and poverty in developing countries. The discussion has focussed on corruption and economic mismanagement as debilitating examples and manifestation of deficient governance. This is generally acknowledged by multilateral international development institutions, aid agencies, international civil society and academics.[89]

Efforts have been made to ameliorate those deficiencies without much success.[90] These efforts have often focussed on traditional themes, such as the promulgation of international conventions against corruption,[91] codes and guides, domestic legislation (to criminalise corruption and, in some jurisdictions, protect whistle blowing) and public sector reform.[92]

---

[89] See, e.g., United Nations, "Monterrey Consensus on Financing for Development", clauses 11–17; and United Nations, "Financing for Development: Building on Monterrey" (2002), accessed July 31, 2010, http://www.un.org/esa/ffd/documents/Building%20on%20 Monterrey.pdf.

[90] See, e.g., Stephen R. Salbu, "Information Technology in the War against International Bribery and Corruption: The Next Frontier of Institutional Reform", *Harvard Journal on Legislation* 38 (2001): 67.

[91] Examples are (1) the United Nations Convention Against Corruption (UNCAC), adopted on October 31, 2003, and entering into force on September 15, 2005, after Ecuador became the 30th country to ratify it; as of June 30, 2010, there were 140 signatories and the Convention had been ratified, accepted, approved or acceded by 137 countries (states parties); (2) the OECD Anti-Bribery Convention (officially the OECD Convention on Combating Bribery of Foreign Public Officials in International Business Transactions), which is aimed at reducing corruption in developing countries by encouraging sanctions against bribery in international business transactions carried out by companies based in the Convention member countries; the convention was signed on December 17, 1997 and came into force on February 15, 1999; as of July 28 2010, 38 countries had ratified the convention; (3) the African Union Convention on Preventing and Combating Corruption, adopted July 11, 2003; (4) the Inter-American Convention Against Corruption (IACAC), adopted by member countries of the Organization of American States on March 29, 1996; it came into force on March 6, 1997.

[92] Kaufman, "Myths and Realities", 90.

This section discusses an additional method: the deployment of ICT, including e-governance, in developing countries to fight corruption, engender transparency and enable the citizenry and civil society to contribute more to public policy formulation and resource allocation. This is not to suggest that ICT has never been considered an instrument for fighting corruption and improving governance. As will be seen, e-governance is now considered a potential tool for fighting corruption. Salbu argued, more than a decade ago, that the global diffusion of information technology via the Internet has the potential to promote transparency and democracy.[93] The discussion here includes not only current e-government applications, but also the deployment of other ICT supporting equipment to enforce or prosecute anticorruption programs, and the need for associated public education. It also discusses how and why the proposal in this chapter would work and suggests funding through a debt-for-development exchange scheme – debt for ICT (Debt4ICT).[94]

A. *Use of ICT Systems to Improve Governance*

This section discusses e-governance (in its most basic description, the use of ICT to deliver government services) and the use of ICT equipment to enhance the enforcement of anticorruption programs.

1. e-Governance

Like many of the terms or concepts already discussed, there is no one universally accepted definition of e-governance (or e-government). Several definitions abound in the literature. Examples include 'the use of ICTs, and particularly the Internet, as a tool to achieve better government',[95] 'the use of information and communication technologies in all facets of the operations of a government organization',[96] 'the use of technology to enhance the access to and delivery of government services to benefit citizens, business partners

[93] See Salbu, "Information Technology", 89–102.
[94] In fact, Debt4ICT has been mooted in the past, but in the broad context of bridging the digital divide. See, e.g., Gerolf Weigel, "SDC Approach and Priorities In Knowledge/ICT for Development", Paper delivered at the ICT Collaboration Meeting with Development Agencies, ITU/HQ, Geneva (January 21–22, 2002), 14, accessed July 31, 2010, http://www.itu.int/ITU-D/resmob/documents/ICT_Collaboration_Jan2002/19-SDC-Suisse.pdf.
[95] OECD, "The e-Government Imperative: Main Findings", OECD *Policy Brief* (2003), 1, accessed 31 July, 2010, http://www.oecd.org/dataoecd/60/60/2502539.pdf.
[96] C. E. Koh, and V. R. Prybutok, "The Three-Ring Model and Development of an Instrument for Measuring Dimensions of e-Government Functions", *Journal of Computer Information Systems* 33(3) (2003): 34–39.

and employees[97] and 'the use of … ICT … to promote more efficient and cost-effective government, more convenient government services, greater public access to information, and more government accountability to citizens'.[98] The focus of the definition may simply be on ICT-enabled government or ICT for governance transformation, in some cases extending to citizen engagement and participation in governance. In this chapter, e-governance is defined as the use of ICT tools to create a transparent interaction between government and citizens (G2C – government to citizens), government and business enterprises (G2B – government to business enterprises) and the relationship between government departments (G2G – interagency relationship) to enhance government service delivery and to achieve better governance.

In recent times e-governance has been identified as a potential tool for improving governance in developing countries, combating corruption, enhancing economic growth and alleviating poverty.[99] In terms of combating corruption, the provision of public goods and services, including approval for investments and licences and the granting of permits for various activities, is a major avenue for predation by bureaucrats. The public often does not know the required processes and requirements, timelines within which processes should be expected to be completed (often there are none) or the chain of responsibility within the relevant department. On the other hand, appropriate records are not maintained by government departments, no audits are carried out and bureaucrats have unnecessarily wide discretion. These combine to provide perfect conditions for bribe extraction, as public officials

---

[97] "At the Dawn of e-Government: The Citizen as Customer" Deloitte Research Paper (2000), 1, accessed August 10, 2010, http://www.egov.vic.gov.au/pdfs/e-government.pdf.

[98] Clay G. Wescott, "e-Government to Combat Corruption in the Asia Pacific Region", Paper presented at the 11th International Anti-Corruption Conference, Seoul, Republic of Korea, May 25–28, 2003, 1, accessed July 31, 2010, http://www.adb.org/Governance/egovernment_corruption.pdf. See also Clay G. Wescott, "E-Government in the Asia-Pacific Region", *Asian Journal of Political Science* 9(2) (2001): 1–24; D. G. Garson, *Public Information Technology and E-Governance* (Sudbury, MA: Jones and Bartlett Publishers, 2006).

[99] See, e.g., Thomas Barnbeck Andersen, "E-Government as an Anti-Corruption Strategy", *Information Economics and Policy* 21 (2009): 201; Vicente Pinilla, Lourdes Torres, and Sonia Royo, "Is E-Government Leading to More Accountable and Transparent Local Governments? An Overall View", *Financial Accountability & Management* 26(1) (2010): 3; UN Public Administration Programme, "United Nations-Government Survey", 2010 (2010), 1, accessed July 31, 2010, http://www2.unpan.org/egovkb/global_reports/10report.htm; and Subhash Bhatnnagar and Christine Apikul, United Nations Development Programme, "Fighting Corruption with e-Government Applications" (2006), APDIP e-Note 8, 1, accessed July 31, 2010, http://www.apdip.net/apdipenote/8.pdf, arguing that '[a] well-planned e-government strategy can make leaps into building a more efficient, accountable and transparent government. If planned with representation from key stakeholders, e-government applications can rebuild citizen trust in government, promote economic growth by improving interface with business, and empower citizens to participate in advancing good governance'.

are able to frustrate users into bribe payment. The system leaves users at the mercy of bureaucrats.

The implementation of ICT systems could eliminate the conditions conducive to bribe extractions. To do so, first, the exact processes and required documents should be published both in print and online. This will give users prior knowledge of the processes to follow. Second, realistic timelines should also be pre-published, so that users know when to expect the processes to be completed and can plan appropriately. Publishing timelines would also put pressure on the relevant public officials of the service provider to act, as reasons would have to be given for not meeting published schedules. It would also provide performance indicators by which assessments and audits could be carried out. Third, the chain of responsibility within the relevant service provider should be outlined. In particular, avenues for enquiry and lodgement of complaints should be clearly outlined, together with a timeline within which a response to complaints can be expected. Fourth, to the extent possible, and this would be the case for most services, the application, monitoring and enquiries should be offered online. Fifth, service providers should be required to maintain appropriate records. This would be easier and cheaper in an online environment, as recording can be automated. Sixth, there should be regular audits, and complaints by dissatisfied users should be investigated swiftly. Possible sanctions, to be set at appropriate levels, for breaches by public officials should be pre-published.

If appropriately implemented, such an e-governance application not only would diminish the opportunities for corruption, but would make public administration more transparent and efficient. It would also make officials within the relevant government departments more accountable and responsible, as well as, potentially, engender patriotism and public support, all of which would enhance governance. There are a few proven cases of e-governance projects in developing countries that have yielded such benefits. Three, one in South Korea and two in India, are briefly discussed here.

A. SEOUL METROPOLITAN GOVERNMENT'S OPEN SYSTEM. In this example, the Seoul Metropolitan Government (SMG) initiated what it described as an anticorruption program, called Online Procedures Enhancement for Civil Applications (OPEN), in January 1999.[100] The aim was to open up to the public governmental procedures and processes for managing civil applications,

---

[100] See Yong Hyo Cho and Byung-Dae Choi, "E-Government to Combat Corruption: The Case of Seoul Metropolitan Government", *International Journal of Public Administration* 27(10) (2005): 719.

so as to remove factors precipitating corruption.[101] Three other principles underpinned the project: (1) to punish corrupt officials with certainty; (2) to enhance transparency in the administrative process; and (3) to secure citizen–government co-operation to drive out corruption.[102]

Civil applications for permits and approvals were analysed by a reviewing team, which identified 26 categories of civil applications that most frequently caused irregularities and inconvenience to citizens. These included building permits and inspection; approval and sanction of entertainment establishments and song bars; and decisions about and change of urban development plans. Those categories were moved online to the OPEN Web portal. The system contained information on application procedures for each of the categories and contact information of departmental persons-in-charge, so that citizens could monitor applications and raise questions in the event any irregularities were detected. Some 5,000 employees in 485 city departments dealing with such applications were trained to operate the system, after which unique user names and passwords were assigned to each individual trainee for accessing the system and making entries.[103] Surveys conducted in the years following the implementation of OPEN reported a sharp drop in the incidence of corruption.[104]

B. THE BHOOMI PROJECT. The Bhoomi Project is an online system developed to computerise records of land rights (including tenancy and cultivation) held by farmers in the state of Karnataka, in India.[105] The computerisation process began in 1991, but not until March 2002 was the task completed in

[101] Ibid., 721.
[102] Ibid., 722. 'This project is widely recognized as an effective example of political and managerial commitment to transparency and for its impact on corruption'. See Bhatnnagar and Apikul, "Fighting Corruption", 2.
[103] See Bhatnnagar and Apikul, "Fighting Corruption", 2.
[104] Bhatnnagar and Apikul found that while a total of 83 corrupt practices by civil servants were reported in 1998, no case was filed from 2000 to 2004. But contrast with "OPEN (Online Procedures Enhancement for Civil Applications) System", accessed July 31, 2010, http://www.stockholmchallenge.org/project/data/openonline-procedures-enhancement-civil-applications-system, which states that the 'number of disciplinary measures taken against government officials involved in bribery scandals or embezzlement between 1997 and 2001 was 95 cases in 1998, 104 in 1999, 78 in 2000, and 45 in 2001, showing a sharp decrease'. Both agree, however, that there was a sharp drop in the incidence of corruption. See also Cho and Choi, "E-Government to Combat Corruption", 728–730, which confirms that the project resulted in a drop in the incidence of corruption.
[105] *Bhoomi* means 'land'; the project was specifically on land records. See Bhatnnagar and Apikul, "Fighting Corruption", 2. See also "Digitisation of Land Records: Bhoomi Project"; for further information on the project, see http://www.it.iitb.ac.in/~prathabk/egovernance/egov_success_stories_bhoomi.html.

all subdistricts.[106] Prior to the Bhoomi Project, an estimated 9,000 village accountants (VAs), each serving three to four villages, maintained the land records in the area. These records were not open to the public. The record holders leveraged their position to extract bribes from farmers who tried to obtain copies of the Record of Rights, Tenancy and Crops (RTC), a record that is mandatory for various purposes, including crop loan applications and concessions linked to the size of the landholding.[107] Requests for copies of the records took months instead of days. Requests for alteration of the records, called 'mutation' (say, upon sale or inheritance of a land parcel), which officially requires a maximum of 30 days, took one to two years to process. Farmers had to pay bribes to obtain copies of their records or procure changes in entries; 'over two-thirds paid more than INR 100 [about US$2] compared with the official service fee of INR 2 [about US$0.043]'.[108] As the records held by VAs were not open to public scrutiny, there was considerable scope for manipulation.[109] Oversight of the VAs and the accuracy of records suffered as the number of records multiplied over generations and accountant supervisors were burdened with numerous other regulatory and development tasks.[110]

The Bhoomi Project computerised some 20 million land records by capturing legacy data records maintained by the VAs, allowed a copy of the RTC to be obtainable by anyone after providing the name of the owner or plot number and paying a fee of INR 15 (about US$0.33) at computerised kiosks in the 180 subdistrict offices. Clients can see the transaction online. Application for change of ownership (mutation) can be filed at the kiosk. The requests are processed on a first-come-first-served basis, and processing takes no more than 30 days, if the request is valid. Following verification, a notice is automatically generated by the computer system to the affected parties and the system updates the particular land record. Operators of the computerised system are made accountable for their decisions and actions through a log-in system. The project involved the organisation of a series of workshops for planning,

[106] Rajeev Chawla and Subhash Bhatnagar, "Online Delivery of Land Titles to Rural Farmers in Karnataka, India" (2004), Paper delivered at _Scaling Up Poverty Reduction: A Global Learning Process and Conference_, Shanghai, May 25–27, 2004, 1, accessed July 31, 2010, http://info. worldbank.org/etools/docs/reducingpoverty/case/96/fullcase/India%20Bhoomi%20Full%20 Case.pdf?q=bhoomi.

[107] Rajeev Chawla, "Bhoomi, Bangalore, Karnataka", accessed July 31, 2010, http//www.apdip. net/resources/case/in03), 1; Rajeev Chawla and Subhash Bhatnagar.

[108] See Andersen, "E-Government as an Anti-Corruption Strategy", 202. 'Bribes typically ranged from about US$2.40, but could exceed $200 if details on the records were to be written in a deliberately ambiguous fashion.' See Chawla and Bhatnagar, "Online Delivery of Land Titles", 1.

[109] Chawla, "Bhoomi, Bangalore, Karnataka", 1.

[110] See Chawla and Bhatnagar, "Online Delivery of Land Titles", 2.

the production of guidelines in the use of the online system and an extensive training program that covered more than 9,000 village officials and revenue inspectors.

An independent evaluation of the project has indicated that bribes have decreased significantly, if not ceased. The official service fee was increased from INR 2 (about US$0.043) to INR 15 (about US$0.33), but is still far less than the average bribes paid (in excess of US$2). Turnaround time from application for a copy of the records to the time of receipt by the applicant was reduced from 3–30 days[111] to 5–30 minutes.[112] The participatory nature of the project is said to have contributed to its success.

Crucially, the project is financially self-sustainable.[113] The state government injected an initial amount of INR 244 million (about US$5.2 million), including INR 13 million (about US$280,000) into the capacity development of public officials.[114] INR 180 million (about US$3.86 million) was recovered within the first three years of the project's becoming fully operational.[115] The higher official service fees (from INR 2 to INR 15), which is still much lower than the average bribes paid by applicants under the manual system, and better revenue recovery by the government have been positive for all (except, of course, the VAs).

C. THE GUJARAT BORDER CHECKPOSTS PROJECT. In the Gujarat Border Checkposts project in India, ICT systems were installed at some 10 remote interstate border checkposts for the inspection of trucks and issuance and collection of fines (for overloads) and taxes.[116] Prior to that, checking and issuance

---

[111] As 'village accountants were not easily accessible, and it took them 3–30 days to provide such records, depending on the record's importance for the farmer – and the bribe paid to the accountant'. See ibid., 1.

[112] Andersen, "E-Government as an Anti-Corruption Strategy", 202.

[113] Rahul De', "Evaluation of E-Governance Systems: Project Assessment vs Development Assessment", in M. A. Wimmer et al. (eds.), *Proceedings of the Electronic Government, Fifth International Conference* (Krakow, 2006), *Lecture Notes in Computer Science*, Vol. 4084, 317, 321; Rahul De' and Chiranjib Sen, "The Complex Nature of e-Government Projects: A Case Study of Bhoomi, an Initiative in Karnataka, India", in Ronald Traumullaer (ed.), *Proceedings of the Electronic Government, Third International Conference*, Zaragoza, Spain, August–September 2004, *Lecture Notes in Computer Science*, Vol. 3183, 556; Chawla, "Bhoomi, Bangalore, Karnataka", 4.

[114] See Chawla, "Bhoomi, Bangalore, Karnataka", 4.

[115] Ibid.

[116] See "Case of Gujarat Interstate Border Checkposts: e-Governance Causes Reduction in Corruption and Increase in Tax Revenues". See also Centre for Electronic Governance Indian Institute of Management, Ahmedabad, "Computerized Interstate Check Posts of Gujarat State, India: A Cost Benefit Evaluation Study" (November 2002), accessed July 31, 2010, http://www1.worldbank.org/publicsector/bnpp/Gujarat.PDF.

of fines were done manually. Officials at the checkposts were known to be corrupt. The new system saw the introduction of smart card driver's licences and the installation of computers and communication networks to collect fines and taxes. In the computerised process, all the checkposts were (and still are) monitored at a central location using video cameras installed at every checkpost cabin. The video camera captures the registration number of all trucks approaching the checkpost and converts it to a digital form accessible from a central database. An electronic weighbridge captures the weight, and the computer automatically issues a demand note for a fine. Drivers can use a stored value card for payment.

The new system produced a threefold increase in tax collection over two years, from US$12 million to US$35 million, paying back the total project cost of US$4 million in just six months.[117] Vehicles are cleared in 2 minutes, instead of the 30 minutes they spent under the manual system. Video monitors reduced the incidence of harassment of truckers by public officials. The large and medium transport owners are happy with the system because they know the exact date and time their drivers passed the checkpost and the exact amount payable (or paid). The pre-paid card means that drivers do not have to carry much money and thus avoid the risks associated with that.

D. OTHERS. Misuraca found some successes in case studies of e-governance projects in Senegal, Ghana and Uganda.[118] A good example is Ghana's GCNet, an automated customs clearance system, which is discussed in greater detail later. Andersen cites examples in Argentina and the Philippines.[119] After a detailed study of 149 countries, he established that e-government reduces corruption.[120] Thus, the potential for ICT applications tools to combat corruption is significant.

2. Equipping Anticorruption Units

In jurisdictions of endemic corruption, e-governance alone is unlikely to be a sufficient corruption-combating and public management tool, particularly

---

[117] Ibid.
[118] See Gainluca Carlo Misuraca, "e-Governance in Africa, from Theory to Action: A Practical-Oriented Research and Case Studies on ICTs for Local Governance" (2007), accessed July 31, 2010, http://delivery.acm.org/10.1145/1150000/1146659/p209-misuraca.pdf?key1=1146659& key2=2870171821&coll=GUIDE&dl=GUIDE&CFID=100459369&CFTOKEN=47872062; Gainluca Carlo Misuraca, *E-Governance in Africa: From Theory to Action – A Handbook on ICTs for Local Governance* (Trenton, NJ: Africa World Press, 2007).
[119] See Andersen, "E-Government as an Anti-Corruption Strategy", 202.
[120] Ibid.

where corruption goes unpunished. Thus, in addition to implementing e-governance systems (in government departments), equipping (or establishing and equipping, where none already exists) a strong anticorruption investigative unit with appropriate legal powers, skills and gadgets should be considered. It is important that there is an oversight unit to investigate, proactively and reactively, and prosecute infractions.

Provision of the necessary ICT logistics, such as covert operational and surveillance systems, including hidden recording devices that can be used to collect evidence, should be considered. In the Gujarat Border Checkposts project discussed earlier, installed overt video equipment stemmed the corrupt practices of public officials. However, there may be areas where anticorruption agencies would have to be proactive, particularly in areas where comprehensive ICT systems are yet to be deployed. Officers equipped with covert gadgets could pretend to be ordinary citizens seeking services to ascertain operational levels, attitudes and incidents of corruption. Offenders should then be prosecuted under law in open courts observing all due processes.

Of course, there is a big danger that such a unit and/or the equipment provided would be abused in various ways. First, the unit's work and evidence may be used selectively, such as to target and prosecute political opponents. Second, the judiciary may be corrupt and side with the government even if the evidence is scant. Third, operatives of the unit may use the equipment inappropriately (some may consider it a source of power), such as to invade people's privacy, and harass and blackmail ordinary citizens. Fourth, operatives lacking integrity may use their position to frame citizens, such as to settle personal scores. Thus, careful consideration must be given to the recruitment of personnel and deployment of ICT equipment for such operations. Strict criteria, including a high level of integrity, must be formulated and satisfied by appointed officers of the unit. The track record of government must be carefully analysed by any donors contemplating assisting such governments before this kind of assistance is given. Appropriate laws must be enacted and checks put in place to forestall possible misuses.

B. Public Education

In addition to the training of public officials who would operate the implemented ICT systems to deliver services, there would be a need for a high level of public education about the anticorruption initiative, which would have to be funded. The education would need to explain to the citizenry the reasons for, and mechanisms of, the anticorruption campaign, as it is particularly important that the public is carried along. Citizenship rights, entitlements and responsibilities would have to be ensured. This would energise civil society to support government action.[121]

Functional ICT literacy or capability may also need to be provided to certain categories of persons within the country. Intended users of the system would have to be able access it. For many in developing countries, both young and old, basic ICT skills needed to access G2C services online may be absent. That would pose challenges, for which consideration would have to be given. It may be that this would be done through schools. Most homes are likely to have young people in schools. Equipping them with functional ICT skills means they would be able to assist their older relations who may need such skills.[122]

C. Funding Through Debt4ICT Schemes

Obviously, implementing e-governance, deploying the ICT equipment for enforcement purposes as discussed and educating the public would all involve costs – initial capital and training costs, and ongoing maintenance and development costs. Most developing countries cannot afford to pay these costs. This is acknowledged by the international community, as a result of which some aid has been, and continues to be, provided. For instance, the World Bank recently approved more than US$44 million in funding for Ghana's e-governance project.[123] 'The World Bank has already given eastern and southern African countries about USD424 million to expand e-governance systems in the region'.[124] Kenya, Nigeria, Rwanda, Burundi and Madagascar are all implementing World Bank–funded e-governance projects.[125] In December 2009, the World Bank approved US$2.3 million zero-interest credit for the Commonwealth of St. Vincent and the Grenadines to implement an Organization of Eastern Caribbean States (OECS) regional e-government integration program. The integrated e-government program is expected to reduce the cost of doing business and improve the efficiency, quality and transparency of public services.[126]

[121] See, e.g., Michela Wrong, *It's Our Turn to Eat* (London: Fourth Estate, 2009).
[122] Training school-age persons would have the additional benefit of developing ICT skills for the future.
[123] See "World Bank Moves to Improve E-Governance in Africa" (news item by Affiliated Network for Social Accountability, ANSA-Africa, July 8, 2010), accessed July 31, 2010, http://www.ansa-africa. net/index.php/views/news_view/world_bank_moves_to_improve_e_governance_in_africa/.
[124] Ibid.
[125] Ibid.
[126] See World Bank, "St. Vincent and the Grenadines: WB Approves US$2.3 Million for OECS Regional E-Government Integration Program" (press release 2010/192/LAC, December

Funding through Debt4ICT schemes would complement current programs. Most of the ongoing programs are aimed at broad public infrastructure to support ICT implementation. Debt4ICT programs can aim at specific, microlevel projects, such as land registries (like the Bhoomi Project), law enforcement projects (such as the Gujarat Border Checkpost project), permits and licence application and issuance (such as the Seoul metropolitan government's OPEN System), and customs and excise clearances and revenue collection (such as Ghana's GCNet, discussed later). The debt-for-development mechanism (in this case Debt4ICT) is particularly suitable for such projects, for the following reasons.

1. Suitability of Debt4ICT Mechanisms

In a debt-for-development exchange, an agreed-upon external debt of a country is bought by a donor or investor at a discount and cancelled, provided that the government of the debtor country undertakes to allocate the savings to an identified project.[127] In a debt-for-equity exchange, the external debt may be sold by an investor to the debtor government in return for a discounted amount of local currency, which must then be invested as capital into a local business.[128] The mechanisms may be used for multilateral, bilateral or commercial debt. They may be used by governments, multilateral institutions, nongovernmental organisations (NGO) or investors. The application is divided into 'participation by creditor governments and multilateral institutions' and 'participation by investors'.

A. PARTICIPATION BY CREDITOR GOVERNMENTS AND MULTILATERAL INSTITUTIONS. Debt to creditor governments or multilateral institutions may be cancelled in exchange for the debtor country investing in an e-governance project in a designated government department or agency for service delivery, transparency, information flow and combat of corruption. The implementation can be done incrementally, starting with one or a few departments at modest costs. Key performance indicators should be outlined at the beginning, against which the project's effectiveness can then be assessed, giving guidance for possible expansion to other departments.

16, 2009), accessed July 31, 2010, http://web.worldbank.org/WBSITE/EXTERNAL/COUNTRIES/LACEXT/OECSEXTN/0,,contentMDK:22420632~menuPK:339300~pagePK:2865066~piPK:2865079~theSitePK:339287,00.html.
[127] See Ross Buckley, "Debt-for-Development Exchanges: The Origins of a Financial Technique" *Law and Development Review* 2(1) (2009): 26.
[128] Ibid.

As fees are usually charged for government services, but often the revenues leak into the private pockets of public officials (and rarely paid into government coffers), the ICT implementation may bring revenue gains to government. This was the case in the Bhoomi and Gujarat examples. The government may also make savings in administrative expenses.[129] Not only may these gains make the project financially self-sustainable, they may yield surplus funds for other projects and development programs. Donors would find such outcomes appealing.

Citizens of developed creditor (donor) countries are likely to support an initiative directed at combating corruption in developing countries. There are many in developed countries who genuinely support aid for developing countries but who are equally concerned about the rampant corruption and its debilitating effects on the development efforts. They will welcome a project to combat corruption in the aid recipient countries, as a possible means of removing significant barriers to development in many of these countries.

Deployment of ICT systems in government departments would yield efficiency gains for the citizens, government and investors (domestic and foreign). The gains would include time and cost savings for all, as well as capacity building in ICT skills that would result in further benefits. It could accelerate the adoption of ICT by the private sector, yielding a 'multiplier effect'. In fact, the World Bank has called on governments in developing countries to adopt e-governance in order to drive the adoption of ICT in their economies.[130]

The deployment of ICT systems would also enhance government information capture and storage for uses such as analysis and planning. Donor countries, institutions, civil society groups and researchers have often been frustrated by the lack of data from developing countries. They would find useful relevant information gleaned from installed ICT systems.

Further, the increased government revenues, efficiency gains, potentially better resource management and related benefits of decreased corruption that may result from the ICT deployments are likely to enhance development over time, lift the country out of the poverty trap and make it less dependent on aid. It would enhance the efficacy of future grants.

B. PARTICIPATION BY INVESTORS. Deployment of ICT systems for government service delivery can be commercially based, and therefore amenable to

[129] For instance, an e-government project in Uganda, the District Administrative Network Program, yielded concrete savings in administrative expenses. See Misuraca, "e-Governance in Africa", 217.
[130] See Indrajit Basu, "Adopt E-Governance to Drive ICT Penetration, Says World Bank" (July 17, 2009), accessed July 31, 2010, http://www.digitalcommunitiesblogs.com/international_beat/2009/07/adopt-egovernance-to-drive-ict.php.

private sector investment, particularly in a public–private partnership (PPP). We have already seen in the Bhoomi and Gujarat Checkpost projects the quick recovery of initial capital investments and the profit potentials afforded by the projects. Another example is the Ghana Community Network Services Ltd (GCNet), incorporated in October 2000 under a PPP to establish and operate a single window customs electronic clearance system in Ghana.[131] The initial funding for the project (US$5.3 million) was raised in the form of shareholdings as follows: Ghana government (represented by Ghana Customs Excise and Preventive Service), 20%; SGS (Société Générale de Surveillance, SA), 60%; Ghana Shippers Council, 10%; Ecobank, 5%; and Ghana Commercial Bank, 5%.[132] The GCNet overhauled the cargo clearance process at Ghana's ports, reviewing and streamlining the procedures (including training some 1,500 people) and providing an interface with all stakeholders.[133] Total investment exceeded the initial capital, as the system was rolled out and expanded (US$7 million had been spent by 2004),[134] but it is, obviously, predominantly funded and owned by the private sector.

Not only has the implementation of the GCNet led to a drop in corruption by customs officials[135] and a substantial increase in government revenue collection at the ports,[136] it has also been paying good dividends to all shareholders, both private and government.[137] While implementation of the project started

[131] See Luc De Wulf and José B. Sokol (eds.), *Customs Modernization Initiatives: Case Studies* (Washington, DC: World Bank, 2004), 19–32; "The Ghana TradeNet and Customs Management System (GCNet)," accessed July 31, 2010, http://www.intracen.org/serviceexport/pdf/Ghana-2007/06Nov07/GCNet_061107.pdf.

[132] De Wulf and Sokol, *Customs Modernization Initiatives*, 22. See also "Ghana TradeNet and Customs Management System (GCNet)", ibid; and SGS's Web site, "Ghana Community Network (GCNet)", accessed July 31, 2010, http://www.singlewindow.sgs.com/ghana_community_network_gcnet_singlewindow.

[133] Such as Ghana customs, Ghana ports authority, customs brokers, freight forwarders, commercial banks, insurance companies, freight terminals, airport freight handling operators, Ministry of Trade, Ministry of Finance and Economic Planning, Revenue Agencies Governing Board, the Central Bank (Bank of Ghana), Statistical Service Bureaux, Narcotics Control Board, Driver and Vehicle Licensing Authority, Shippers' Council, Free Zone Board, Standards Board, Environmental Protection Agency and the Minerals Commission. See SGS Web site and "The Ghana TradeNet and Customs Management System (GCNet)".

[134] See De Wulf and Sokol, *Customs Modernization Initiatives*, 22.

[135] Ibid., 29: 'The losers [from the implementation of GCNet] are those CEPS personnel who had previously benefited from substantial facilitation payments that traders had offered to accelerate cargo clearance, to close their eyes when cargo left port premises without a declaration, or to accept declarations that included underinvoicing and erroneous product classifications so as to lower the amount of duties due'.

[136] See ibid., 28–29; Vitus A. Azeem, "Ghana", in Dieter Zinnbauer, Rebecca Dobson and Krina Despota (eds.), *Global Corruption Report, 2009: Corruption and the Private Sector* (Cambridge: Cambridge University Press, 2009): 180–184, 183.

[137] See "The Ghana TradeNet and Customs Management System (GCNet)," 15.

at the major ports in Accra and Tarkoradi, the private partners, particularly
SGS, have been keen to roll out the system to cover all border posts between
Ghana and its neighbouring countries due to its success.

Such a project may be used for a debt-for-equity scheme. An investor may sell
an external debt to the debtor government in return for a discounted amount
of local currency to be invested in an ICT project that is commercially viable.
Private sector, commercially operated e-governance systems would be particularly useful in developing countries. This is because users of the public sector
delivery methods are often highly inefficient in most developing countries.
Many e-government initiatives have failed in developing countries, in part
because of that.[138] Private sector–operated systems are likely to be more efficient and sustainable. Users may have to pay more, above current official rates,
but that may still be less than the bribes they pay to public officials to obtain
those services, as seen in the Bhoomi example. Moreover, the efficiency, time
savings and reliability that may come with the private sector delivery may be
worth the extra costs. Of course, an appropriate regulatory framework would
have to be put in place to avoid gouging by private monopolies.

Two potential objections to the proposal spring to mind. First, its adoption
may be inflationary, which may be economically destabilising.[139] However, efficiency and productivity gains that may result from the e-government application may offset, or reduce, the impact of the capital injection. Moreover, any
sizeable inflationary problems may be solved by a gradual implementation of
the project, to avoid sudden monetary injection into the system. Second, ICT
equipment needed to establish the project may have to be imported. Local currency to be paid to the investor may therefore be inadequate for the project. One
way of overcoming such a problem is to design the project within a framework
of joint venture, partnering with parties that can afford the equipment. The
local currency payment from the debt–equity project may be used primarily for
labour and other inputs whose costs are payable in local currency. Thus, while
there are potential pitfalls, they can be addressed with appropriate design.

2. Compatibility with Other Initiatives

The deployment of ICT systems to combat corruption in developing countries
will complement other initiatives with similar aims. These include the work
of Transparency International (TI) and the Extractive Industry Transparency
Initiative (EITI). TI is an international NGO that has been at the forefront

---

[138] See Danish Dada, "The Failure of E-Government in Developing Countries: A Literature
Review", *Electronic Journal on Information Systems in Developing Countries* 26(7) (2006): 1.
[139] Buckley, "Debt-for-Development Exchanges", 29–31.

of fighting corruption internationally and raising public awareness of the problem.[140] Originally founded in Germany in May 1993 as a not-for-profit organisation, it is now organised as a group of some 100 national chapters across the globe, with an international secretariat in Berlin. It has published an annual Corruption Perceptions Index (CPI) since 1995. It also publishes an annual Global Corruption Report, a Global Corruption Barometer and a Bribe Payers Index.[141] TI's work and publications are now widely regarded.

The EITI is an international initiative that aims to strengthen governance by improving transparency and accountability in the extractives sectors of resource-rich developing countries in order to foster economic growth and development and to reduce poverty. It is a coalition of governments, compa-nies, civil society groups, investors and international organisations. Though it was launched in London in 2003, its validation methodology was not agreed upon until September 2008, and its current governance structure formalised in February 2009. The initiative has received, and continues to receive, the endorsement and support of most of the world's biggest oil, gas and mining companies. It has received the support of international institutions—financial, economic and political. Resource-rich countries, the target of the initiative, are joining. As of July 31, 2010, there were three compliant countries, 27 candi-date countries, most of them African, and five more that have signalled their intention to join.[142]

The efforts of these entities are increasingly compelling governments in developing countries to take steps to tackle corruption. In particular, TI's work was instrumental in the formulation of the international conventions previously mentioned, and EITI is making resource-rich developing countries more transparent. The infusion of ICT systems from debt-for-development exchange schemes would further those steps.

VI. CONDITIONS FOR EFFECTIVENESS

As already noted, there have been tremendous efforts in the past two decades or more to combat corruption in developing countries. Most have been ineffective.[143] In many countries there has not been any noticeable reduction in the incidence of corruption for a considerable period. A logical question thus arises as to why the suggestions in this chapter would be effective. The

[140] See Hongying Wang and James N. Rosenau, "Transparency International and Corruption as an Issue of Global Governance", *Global Governance* 7 (2001): 25.
[141] For more information on TI, see http://www.transparency.org/.
[142] For more information on the EITI, see the EITI Web site at http://eitransparency.org/eiti.
[143] Salbu, "Information Technology".

suggestions would be effective if certain conditions prevail. These are the presence of democracy, rule of law and the political will to combat corruption, improve governance and enhance the management of national assets.

A. Democracy

It was noted earlier that the absence of democracy is a cause of, or contributes to, the prevalence of corruption in countries.[144] This suggests that the presence of democracy itself could prevent corruption. However, we also know that there are countries with a high incidence of corruption that are seemingly democratic.[145] So democracy does not necessarily prevent corruption. But democracy is essential for the diffusion of ICT systems in government departments to combat corruption, for the following two reasons.

First, democracy would give citizens a voice to probe and challenge public officials and government departments. It would allow them to pursue infractions of their rights. In an oppressive regime, the citizenry would not be as able or willing to challenge government departments, as they might risk being seen as antigovernment and be persecuted as such.

Second, where elements of the government are corrupt, they may be inclined to resist the anticorruption initiative.[146] However, in a democracy, civil society and opposition parties could make an issue of the government's resistance to the initiative. The citizenry could put pressure on government. Opposition parties might promise to adopt the initiative for the benefit of the nation (even if their real motivation was, perhaps, political opportunism). This could lead to two possible outcomes. Either the government would back down (and adopt the initiative) or there would be a regime change that ushered in a new government that was receptive to the initiative.[147] Either way, the outcome would be positive.

B. Rule of Law

Like the absence of democracy, the absence of an effective rule of law was identified as a cause of, or contributor to, corruption in developing countries.[148]

[144] See Section III.A.4.e.
[145] A few examples are India, Indonesia, Ghana, Nigeria and Kenya.
[146] Thanks to Julia Roy, of the Faculty of Law at the University of New South Wales, for raising this issue.
[147] This is not to suggest that an issue on an anticorruption initiative would solely determine the outcome of an election. However, in developing countries, corruption and anticorruption are often major issues for the electorates.
[148] See Section III.A.4.c.

The presence of an effective rule of law is necessary, for a few reasons. First, it ensures that citizens have enforceable rights against government, among other things, including for breaches that corruption exacts on them. Second, anticorruption initiatives such as those suggested in this chapter can be used corruptly. They can be used for political witch-hunting – for example, prosecuting political opponents to nullify their political ambitions. An effective rule of law is, therefore, necessary to guard against such possibilities and to protect people.

C. Political Will

As noted with respect to democracy, funding ICT systems to combat corruption in developing countries may be workable even if a government may not be particularly keen on it, as long as a robust democracy exists. However, it would be far easier and better if there were genuine political will to combat corruption from all sides, both government and opposition. In such an environment, there would be more effort, co-operation and support for the initiative. The good news is that there are countries out there where government and opposition seem united against corruption.[149] Those countries would benefit from Debt4ICT schemes aimed at helping them implement anticorruption initiatives like those discussed in this chapter.

VII. CONCLUSION

This chapter has argued that governance deficiencies are the major cause of underdevelopment in resource-rich but poor developing countries. It has identified corruption and mismanagement as critical elements. The chapter has analysed how the deployment of appropriately targeted ICT systems can enhance governance and improve economic development, and has examined some success stories that may serve as guides. Necessary conditions for the effectiveness of the proposal discussed in this chapter have been identified as democracy, rule of law and political will. This means the proposal may not be viable in some developing countries, particularly countries under dictatorships. Donor countries and institutions may have to be selective in implementing the proposals. However, there are plenty of potential candidates for such schemes.

---

[149] Thanks to Professor Ross Buckley, of the Faculty of Law at the University of New South Wales, for pointing this out to me.

22

Using Debt Exchanges to Enhance Public Accountability to Citizens

Bill Walker

I. BACKGROUND: ASSESSING DEBT RELIEF AND ADDRESSING CAUSES OF DEBT CRISES

Debt relief has proved to be a highly efficient form of aid and has helped foster social development and economic growth in low-income countries. Thus recent debt-relief initiatives are to be welcomed, while recognising they are no panacea and have some caveats attached.[1]

Under certain circumstances, there may be certain negative implications of these initiatives for future aid allocations to highly indebted poor countries (HIPCs) or non-HIPCs. The degree to which these countries are affected depends critically on two factors: (1) the degree to which debt relief is additional to traditional official development assistance (ODA) flows and (2) the degree to which aid donors reallocate existing aid allocations because they are providing debt relief. The higher the degree of additionality, the higher are the costs to creditors. The higher the reallocation of the HIPCs' traditional aid, the lower are the benefits to the HIPCs.[2]

In general these implications seem unlikely to apply to debt exchanges, as long as they remain at their current modest levels. Even if exchanges were to expand 10-fold – a much larger expansion in their use than seems likely in the near future – their impact in increasing additionality to traditional ODA and in reallocating traditional ODA is likely to remain modest, and thus be free of the negative implications that Gunter flags.[3]

---

[1] S. J. Staats, "Debt Relief No Panacea, Birdsall Tells Senate Foreign Relations Committee" (2008), accessed April 28, 2008, http://blogs.cgdev.org/globaldevelopment/2008/04/debt_relief_no_panacea_birdsal.php.
[2] B. G. Gunter et al., "Robbing Peter to Pay Paul? Understanding Who Pays for Debt Relief", *World Development* 36(1) (2008): 1–16.
[3] Ibid.

Although debt cancellation has now reduced significant portions of the debt burden of the poorest and most indebted countries, much of the impact of the HIPC Initiative has been to remove debt that had simply become unpayable. Cancellation has not addressed and cannot by itself address the root causes of the debt crisis. A major reason for incorporating conditionality into various debt-relief initiatives was to address these root causes.

The HIPC Initiative employed conditionalities requiring improved *macroeconomic* governance by government as the major prerequisite of debt relief, along with the formulation of poverty reduction strategies (PRSs). However, these conditionalities, being macroeconomic, paid little attention to central principles of improved governance (such as public transparency and democratic voice and accountability) or to deficits at more localised levels of governance. Over the past few decades local-level governance has become much more important because of the shift towards decentralisation of government – administratively, fiscally and democratically – in many developing countries. One important goal of decentralisation was to ensure that vital public services were closer and more responsive to ordinary citizens.

Alongside macroeconomic conditionalities, 'country ownership' has been a central principle of the HIPC Initiative. PRSs were the major vehicle through which such ownership was to be realised. However, country ownership has, at best, translated into truncated forms of ownership by *governments*, with parliaments and other state institutions often being quite marginal. *Democratic or citizen* ownership has been largely overlooked in discussions of 'country ownership'. Because of this, genuinely democratic oversight of the governance of debt continues to be minimal. This is a major lacuna in the design of contemporary debt-relief schemes. It is surprising that many leading donors strongly espouse 'democracy', 'democratisation' and 'accountability' in other important contexts, but see these principles at best as having only limited or narrow relevance to the governance of debt.

Poor governance is one of the leading causes of debt crises, particularly the failure to make responsible decisions accountably and transparently.[4] When considering the sustainability of overall levels of public debt, responsible governance requires wise decision making about incurring specific debts and the uses to which funds acquired through loans are put. It also requires responsible budgetary allocation and effective management of these funds to reduce

---

[4] Various debt campaigns have, of course, focussed on aspects of governance, primarily at the national level. There have been calls to improve debt governance at various levels include debt audits, a fair and transparent arbitration process for debt and debt tribunals.

poverty and to benefit ordinary citizens. Too often, various aspects of such governance have been and are weak, especially avenues for public scrutiny of governance. Weak governance continues to undermine the resolution of the HIPC crisis and to spawn major new debt crises. If we fail to learn from and address the root causes of each crisis, it is far more likely that debt crises will continue to recur.

II. INADEQUACY OF ODA, DEBT RELIEF AND DOMESTIC FUNDING FOR HUMAN DEVELOPMENT

The debt crisis in HIPCs and other developing countries has undermined financial follow-through on a series of high-minded and well-intentioned declarations from UN summits, particularly during the 1990s. These summits culminated with the Millennium Declaration of 2000, which included the Millennium Development Goals (MDGs). Many of the summit agreements reached and goals thus set – on sustainable development, reforms to gender relations, social development and other issues central to human development – have remained largely unfulfilled, particularly in South Asia and sub-Saharan Africa. Even the modest MDG to halve world poverty over 25 years[5] – for which resources were clearly available but political will was lacking – appears unlikely to be reached at country level, especially in many indebted countries. MDG targets critical to human development such as those for health and education are unlikely to be achieved in many of these countries. ODA has been too inadequate, too poorly directed sectorally, too weakly focussed on poverty and too inconsistent to fill massive persistent fiscal gaps. ODA for essential services in many HIPCs and other indebted countries remains seriously deficient.

Meanwhile, despite the pledges of many governments to increase spending on human development, the domestic budgetary priority given to the basics of human development – health, education, water and sanitation – has often been weak.[6] This weak commitment has been further undermined by poor governance. Two aspects of this are of major concern. First, very high rates of leakage of government expenditure on human development continue to be commonplace in many countries, which undermines basic service provision.

---

[5] The baseline for this MDG goal was backdated to 1990s, thus allowing 25 years for its realisation.

[6] Public Expenditure Tracking Surveys, which are one tool used to track sectoral public expenditure, typically show that in many developing countries with weak governance more than 50% of key line items in a sectoral budget (e.g., essential drugs for health and textbooks for schools) often 'go missing'.

Second, governance measures applied to the same sectors continue to overlook fundamental issues of inequity and inequality.[7]

On the other hand, the evidence – particularly from East Asia and Latin America, but also from other countries with political will and fiscal space to fund basic services – has been that the public provision of essential health care and other inexpensive social services has cut mortality rapidly even in tough economic circumstances, and that political democracy has contributed to the provision and utilisation of such social services in a wider range of ways than is sometimes recognised.[8]

It is clear that traditional ODA and existing levels of debt relief have been insufficient to address such fundamental issues. However, poor governance at all levels, from the global to the local, has undermined the effectiveness of ODA and been a major cause of unpayable debt.

In summary, then, ODA that is poorly directed, inadequate and of insufficient quality and the ongoing impact and legacy of debt crises combined with poor governance continue to undermine human development.

III. IMPROVING BASIC SERVICE DELIVERY, GOVERNANCE AND HUMAN DEVELOPMENT

Decentralising government, and especially its services, has been one major response over the past three decades to improving governance, furthering human development and devolving political power. However, its results have often been disappointing. The trend towards decentralising government services to local levels has been beset by many problems. Inadequate funding and weak devolution of power have been particularly debilitating factors. The low priority accorded to local-level basic services from ODA and domestic funding sources, the latter often severely underbudgeted over decades in order to service excessive debt levels, has exacerbated these problems. More recently, however, HIPC Initiative debt relief has provided modest budget increases to services such as health and education, and has opened the way for policies of universal provision of public services such as primary education and primary health care. While such policies thus sought to increase the reach of services (e.g., by removing public health fees or introducing universal

---

7 UNESCO, *Overcoming Inequality: Why Governance Matters Paris* (Geneva: UNESCO, 2009).
8 J. W. McGuire, *Wealth, Health, and Democracy in East Asia and Latin America* (New York: Cambridge University Press, 2010); S. K. Mehrotra and E. Delamonica, *Eliminating Human Poverty: Macroeconomic and Social Policies for Equitable Growth* (London: Zed Books, 2007).

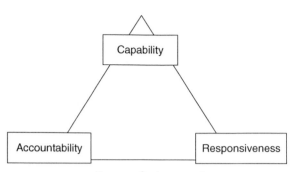

FIGURE 22.1. Synergy for improved governance.

primary education), public services themselves have deteriorated as a result of their wider availability and increased uptake. Some services have been simply swamped. In many HIPCs and other indebted developing countries, these services are now so overrun or understaffed that quality is often poor. Thus, modest levels of debt relief have trickled down as more widely spread access to public services, but have often been undermined by poor quality of service delivery, often accompanied by a lack of key supplies like basic drugs for health centres or textbooks for schools. Many of the fundamental problems in public services continue to be problems of poor governance, especially weak accountability and poor transparency. At the local level – where service delivery matters – the problems remain messy and intractable, and unlikely to be solved by line and planning ministries, which are too removed from these realities. One possible solution involves a demand-led approach. This could employ demand for service reform, while supplementing service funding in ways that increase governments' responsiveness to citizen service users. Performance could be improved by co-ordinating successive improvements in their accountability and responsiveness to citizen users, while steadily building service capability.

This would imply appropriately funding the capability, responsiveness and accountability of three fundamental aspects of local governance of services, such as health, education and water. There is considerable potential for synergy, both between sectors and within key areas of governance (Figure 22.1)

In essence, debt relief could be used to help create virtuous circles of successively improved governance and funding of services, by successively improving their responsiveness and capability. This would have the additional benefit of improving the effectiveness of ODA, which may encourage donors over time to increase their levels of funding.

Of the three, considerable effort and funding have been directed towards building state capability in service provision. The results, however, have mostly been disappointing, particularly because they have been very poorly linked with demands for accountability and responsiveness to citizens at the grass roots. These two central issues of governance have not received the attention – and funding – that they warrant, nor have they been adequately linked to efforts to increase government capability. Thus, the state still remains weakly accountable and at times largely unaccountable to the people at the grass roots for governance, including the governance of debt, which was supposed to benefit the people.

However, what is the current climate for improving governance, to what extent does the political will exist and where do major gaps lie? As Sirleaf has commented:

> A growing group of sub-Saharan countries are embracing democracy and good governance, instilling stronger macroeconomic management, and benefiting from significant debt relief. These countries are beginning to show results with faster economic growth, the beginnings of poverty reduction, and improvements in social indicators. At the same time, some of the most protracted conflicts around the continent have come to an end, including in Angola, the DRC, and Sierra Leone.[9]

Meanwhile, creating accountable and effective states has come to occupy the heart of the development agenda, with accountability, transparency and participation espoused as desirable, indeed essential, for such states.[10] In the words of Hawes, 'Without transparency, citizen participation is less well informed and less effective. Without accountability, those in positions of power can safely ignore the will of the people'.[11]

There has been a tendency to focus upon electoral accountability. But although it is important, it has been relied on far too much. It is but one dimension of accountability, weakened by its periodic nature. In practice, its promise has far exceeded what it has delivered.

However, despite the central importance of governance for development, progress towards better governance is slow and very uneven. Many serious governance challenges remain. While some countries have made progress in governance and anticorruption efforts over the past decade, others have failed to improve, exhibiting little progress. Others have regressed in

[9] E. J. Sirleaf and S. Radelet, "The Good News Out of Africa: Democracy, Stability, and the Renewal of Growth and Development", in *CGD Essay* (Washington, DC: Center for Global Development, 2008).

[10] M. Robinson, *Budgeting for the Poor* (Bassingstoke, NY: Palgrave Macmillan, 2008).

[11] G. Hawes, "Making Governments More Accountable: The Impact of Civil Society Budget Analysis and Monitoring – International Budget Project" (2008), accessed September 7, 2010, http://www.internationalbudget.org/resources/briefs/brief2eng.htm.

some key dimensions.[12] Progress in improving weak transparency and poor accountability in relation to public spending, which were key causes of the debt crisis, is especially poor. Eighty percent of the world's governments fail to provide adequate information to the public so that the public can hold them accountable for managing their money, and the overall state of government budget transparency has been found to be deplorable.[13] These glaring weaknesses continue to undermine the effectiveness of both ODA and debt relief in reducing poverty and are likely to be a major reason for the failure to achieve key MDGs relating to health and education in sub-Saharan Africa and India.[14]

While trends towards improved governance should be encouraged, major weaknesses, particularly in accountability and transparency, remain. While these are of concern to donors, their efforts have met with limited success. Meanwhile, the fundamental role of citizens of affected countries, who are the parties most affected by poor governance, in extracting accountability between elections has been very narrowly and weakly addressed.

Collier argues that accountability is one of two public goods (along with security) essential to development and points to its crucial importance in 58 countries, which include almost all HIPCs.[15] Accountability by countries is important not just for debt, but for all finances for whose stewardship a government is responsible. Electoral responsibility, once seen largely as the panacea for holding democratic governments accountable, is now increasingly being questioned. Because it failed so comprehensively in so many 'democratically governed' countries during the debt crisis of the 1980s and 1990s, it cannot be relied on as a mechanism for improving the governance of debt. Unless countries can control their leaders' greed for wealth and power, they cannot generate other public goods and services, such as schools, health services, roads and courts, all of which are essential for human development. This is especially true of HIPCs, which are characterised by high levels of poverty and where such essential services routinely fail the poor.[16] Indeed, the provision of the most important public services such as health is often heavily skewed towards

[12] D. A. Kaufmann et al., "Governance Matters, VIII: Aggregate and Individual Governance Indicators, 1996–2008", Policy Research Working Paper, World Bank (2009).
[13] Open Budget Initiative Web site, accessed September 7, 2010, http://openbudgetindex.org/; "Open Budgets. Transform Lives: The Open Budget Survey, International Budget Partnership", accessed September 7, 2010, http://openbudgetindex.org/files/FinalFullReportEnglish.pdf.
[14] D. Kaufmann, "To Meet the Millennium Development Goals, Think Governance" (2010), accessed September 6, 2010, http://www.ansa-africa.net/index.php/views/news_view/to_meet_the_millennium_development_goals_think_governance/.
[15] P. Collier, *Wars, Guns, and Votes: Democracy in Dangerous Places* (New York: Harper, 2009).
[16] S. Devarajan and R. Reinikka, *Making Services Work for Poor People* (Washington, DC: World Bank and Oxford University Press, 2003).

the rich, instead of towards the poor, who most need them.[17] Lastly, these problems have been exacerbated over some decades by a long-term undermining of services by International Monetary Fund (IMF) policies, such as IMF-imposed wage ceilings in both health and education, which constrain governments' ability to hire enough trained professionals and to increase investment in social sectors.[18]

Debt exchanges have a valuable but underrecognised role, particularly in the fairly large but unfilled role debt relief can play between periodic, occasional, larger-scale debt cancellation (as in the HIPC Initiative) and the various short- to medium-term measures HIPCs use to manage debt in between larger-scale cancellations. Further, to the extent that the underlying causes of each debt crisis are addressed, the need for periodic large-scale cancellation should decrease.

The particular niche of debt exchanges is in bilateral debt. Thus it is not being suggested that they are a panacea for debt crises, but they can contribute towards a set of overall solutions. Only certain countries with bilateral debt would be likely candidates for this type of proposed debt exchange. These countries would most likely:

1. be HIPCs, or other heavily indebted developing countries excluded from the HIPC Initiative;
2. be able to service their debt; and
3. have governments interested in improving governance, particularly though greater participatory governance, such as through decentralisation.

For such countries, could debt exchanges function in such a way as to address this deficit in democratic accountability for, and transparency regarding, debt and for the failure of services? Are debt exchanges to improve governance feasible? And if so what aspect(s) of governance?

Largely missing from the governance of sovereign debt are the impoverished citizens who are supposed to benefit from it – the same citizens whom basic services largely fail. Accountability to citizens has two aspects: answerability and enforceability. In other words, those who provide services (e.g., health workers and teachers) and governments responsible for their provision must be answerable for adequate levels of service provision, and users must be able

[17] A. S. Yazbeck *Attacking Inequality in the Health Sector: A Synthesis of Evidence and Tools* (Washington, DC: World Bank, 2000), 1.
[18] A. A. Marphati, "The Adverse Effects of International Monetary Fund Programs on the Health and Education Workforce", *International Journal of Health Services* 40(1) (2010): 165–178.

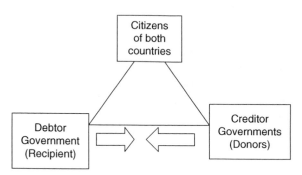

FIGURE 22.2. Citizens' role in the governance of debt.

to enforce reasonable provision levels to which they are entitled. Currently, accountability for public services largely fails these citizens because neither service providers nor governments are answerable, and citizens cannot require the accountable provision of services.

Later, we point to practical solutions to this dilemma. But here we note several issues that point towards solutions. First, the central issue here is the failure in democratic accountability to provide services to citizens, which is a core failure of governance.[19] Second, impoverished citizens, including children, are on average sicker and less educated than those who are better off, and as a result they suffer from a lack of human development and its wide-ranging, lifelong consequences. Third, because these citizens depend on having adequate public health, education and other services, they have reason – motivation – to address the deficit in democratic accountability. They simply cannot afford alternatives such as competent private services, and such alternatives are often not accessible to them anyway. What they lack is the opportunity to seek needed reforms. Figure 22.2 indicates the role that citizens of both creditor and debtor countries should have as those to whom the governments of these countries should be democratically accountable.

Having touched on why citizens of HIPCs would welcome the new type of debt exchanges being proposed, we now ask what could make such exchanges attractive to governments:

1. Improving governance continues to be a major part of many bilateral and multilateral donors' agendas. It remains influential in determining the amount of aid HIPCs receive.
2. Countries are increasingly ranked according to their governance performance, and such rankings continue to proliferate.

[19]   Collier, *Wars, Guns, and Votes.*

3. Increasingly there is evidence that governments can increase their legitimacy with their populations by increasing the capability, accountability and responsiveness of service delivery.
4. In such contexts, debt exchanges can provide stable and predictable – though probably modest – income flows.

IV. MOVING TOWARDS SOLUTIONS THAT ADDRESS SYSTEMIC CAUSES

Important causes of the ongoing debt crisis in many countries remain unaddressed. Many of the central issues are political: powerlessness, voicelessness, lack of accountability by governments towards citizens and missing or limited transparency in making loans and managing debt.

Weak accountability is an endemic cause of the debt crisis. It pervades failures in the debt system, both on the creditor and the debtor sides. On the debtor side, many breakdowns in accountability for loans and managing debt by governments to citizens have been criminal. Reliance on governments being internally accountable often does not work. So how might this gap be bridged by alternatives, such as those that allow citizens to hold their governments accountable?

Given debt's immiserating impacts on ordinary citizens and the denial of basic human rights to food, water, health and education during debt crises, how can debt cancellation and relief be *empowering* for them? Debt exchanges have the potential to be win–win – to fund innovative ideas for development financing while providing debt relief – but also win–win–wins, doing both these things while also increasing the accountability of governments to their citizens and thus empowering them with a voice about development financing while also addressing a key root cause of the debt crisis.

Potential ways for debt exchanges to be *empowering* could include:

1. Ensuring debt-relief benefits to those who need them most (ordinary citizens) by channelling them equitably, and by as direct means as possible, into basic local services, economic empowerment and environmental sustainability, tailored to context: *social, economic and environmental empowerment*. Debt exchanges, for example, could address the increasing impact of climate change on local communities and assist them in implementing adaptation strategies.
2. Rectifying systemic failures and gaps in accountability. *Political empowerment* is important for addressing poverty as characterised by powerlessness and voicelessness.

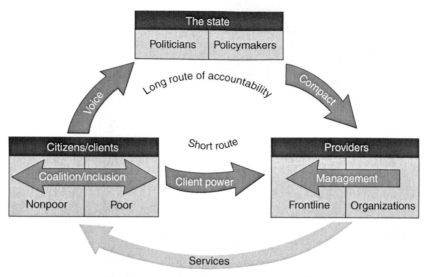

The long and short routes to accountability.

3. Making governments responsive to empowered citizens and able to serve them: *governments empowered to serve, acting responsively and responsibly.*

For this to happen, accountability must be within the reach of ordinary citizens. But national governments are often remote from citizens, making lines of accountability long and thus greatly weakening their impact.[20]

So there is clearly a need to shorten the lines of accountability, particularly in contexts of decentralisation, so that citizens are able to much more directly influence the accountability of, and thus sanction, frontline service providers such as teachers and nurses. Further, three fundamental barriers to participation by citizens in exacting accountability must be addressed:[21]

1. The lack of citizen capacity is a barrier because meaningful participation in governance processes requires skills and knowledge that impoverished people typically do not possess.

---

[20] Devarajan and Reinikka, *Making Services Work for Poor People.*
[21] S. R. Osmani, "Participatory Governance: An Overview of Issues and Evidence", in *Participatory Governance and the Millennium Development Goals (MDGs)*, Publication based on the Expert Group Meeting on Engaged Governance: Citizen Participation in the Implementation of the Developmental Goals Including the Millennium Development Goals (MDGs), New York, November 1–2, 2006, New York (New York: United Nations, 2008), 28–29.

2. Incentives can be lacking because of opportunity, psychological and other costs of participation in public affairs. Citizens need to see that gains in participation outweigh its costs.

3. Power in its various forms is possibly the most serious barrier of all. Systematic asymmetries of power are inherent in unequal societies and between citizens and power holders, including service providers. While power can be used to deny accountability, it is also necessary to facilitate more equitable relationships.

Various promising and established social accountability approaches exist to bridge these gaps. Some have been proved to have major effects both in improving governance and in reducing poverty.[22] Other approaches, such as public expenditure tracking surveys, have been used to considerably increase transparency about government expenditures.[23] One participatory approach to accountability specifically designed to address each of these three barriers is Citizen Voice and Action (CV&A).

V. IMPROVING ACCOUNTABILITY, BEGINNING LOCALLY: THE CASE OF CITIZEN VOICE AND ACTION

CV&A is a hybrid, community-based social accountability tool, combining elements of three other social accountability tools: social auditing, community scorecards and citizen report cards.

First used as a community scorecard process by CARE Malawi, this approach was further developed by the World Bank in the Gambia and by World Vision in more than 10 countries, many of which are HIPCs. Its goal is to enable and empower communities to influence the quality, efficiency and accountability of their local health, education and other local public services. A simple diagram showing how CV&A works to improve bottom-up accountability is given in Appendix 1.

Under CV&A, communities meet with staff members, administrators, local representatives and politicians in their local health clinic or school. They assess

---

[22] G. Baiocchi et al., "Evaluating Empowerment: Participatory Budgeting in Brazilian Municipalities", in *Empowerment in Practice: From Analysis to Implementation* (Washington, DC: World Bank, 2006), 95–128; M. Bjorkman and J. Svensson, "Power to the People: Evidence from a Randomized Field Experiment on Community-Based Monitoring in Uganda", *Quarterly Journal of Economics* 124(2) (2009): 735–769.

[23] Z. Ojoo, *Open Budgets Transform Lives: The Open Budget Survey*, International Budget Partnership (Washington, DC: International Budget Partnership, 2008); R. Reinikka and J. Svensson, "Local Capture: Evidence from a Central Government Transfer Program in Uganda", *Quarterly Journal of Economics* 119(2) (2004): 679–705.

the standards of these services, comparing what is present in the facility (e.g., number of staff members, drug supplies, equipment) against standard national entitlements promised by the government. Indicators of performance in areas of concern are agreed and voted upon, and problems are diagnosed. Together the community then decides what actions it wishes to take to improve services. Typically, responsibilities for such actions are spread among staff members, community members, politicians and other officials. An action plan provides clarity about reforms agreed upon and allows monitoring of progress in these reforms.

As both education and health care are underfunded, there is considerable scope for increasing funding to meet basic standards, while using civic monitoring to improve local accountability. At one primary school in Uganda, through CV&A parents learnt that whilst their school's teacher–student ratio was one teacher to every 186 students, the government's standard was one teacher per 55 students. Within months of initiation of the community process, and as a direct result of CV&A processes, the school gained two additional teachers.

This pattern is common in almost all sub-Saharan Africa countries where access to free primary schooling has been universalised – sometimes as a result of HIPC debt relief. However, rapid expansion in enrolments has degraded quality and has not been matched by adequate funding.[24]

Similarly, in the health sector in Uganda very large funding gaps in health care exist. For example, essential medicine requirements for the provision of minimum health care standards have been estimated to be US$8 per capita (including antiretroviral treatment, vaccines and artemisinin-based combination therapy (ACT) compared with current government funding levels in FY 2006–2007 of US$1.70 per capita.

CV&A also includes subcounty and subdistrict dialogues, which allow citizens to engage in dialogue with officials to encourage public accountability and transparency at the respective government levels, where key government decisions affecting local services are made or from which actions for reform can be taken.

CV&A and other similar approaches are showing that it is possible to lift levels of accountability for public services and that considerable scepticism about the capability and will of citizens to reform public services is not warranted. These approaches are showing how governance can be reformed through local-level democratisation. They also show it is possible to repair fragile or broken

---

[24] K. Lewin and K. Akyeampong, "Education in Sub-Saharan Africa: Researching Access, Transitions and Equity', *Comparative Education* 45 (2009): 143–150.

relationships between citizens and the state through constructive dialogue between service providers, government officials and citizens, beginning locally.

A growing number of other social accountability approaches are being used to increase accountability of local and national governments. Among these are approaches that enhance accountability for financing, whether from domestic budgets or aid grants, including debt funding. These can increase levels of civic confidence and trust in government capability to deliver basic services.

Participatory budgeting is another such social accountability approach. This began in Brazil but has now spread to dozens of developing countries. It gives citizens a far more direct voice in how government budgets are spent than elections do and has been shown to yield impressive development outcomes.[25]

Social accountability approaches such as CV&A are paralleled by other promising approaches that encourage public accountability and responsibility for reforms in areas other than public health and education services at the local level. These include approaches that focus on local economic development (PACA) and natural resource management (such as the Farmer Managed Natural Regeneration discussed in Chapter 15). These approaches show that local demand-side, power-back-to-the-people initiatives can improve governance when government becomes a public servant.

There are likely to be a variety of funding mechanisms appropriate for debt exchanges. It is important, however, that these increase rather than undermine accountability. To show that debt-for-governance exchanges are possible, the following presents one promising avenue for funding them that is based on established practice and draws on recent research findings.

VI. SECTOR-BASED SUPPORT: A POSSIBLE DEBT-EXCHANGE FUNDING MECHANISM

Despite considerable controversy and widespread scepticism, budget support has evolved into a reasonably well established aid instrument in some developing countries. It arguably has positive impacts, including improved donor co-ordination and alignment to country strategies and systems. Further, emerging experience and evaluations confirm that budget support can be effective in strengthening the quality of policy dialogue, transparency and accountability in budget management and enhancing donor co-ordination. In summary it can have positive outcomes regarding governance.[26]

[25] Baiocchi et al., "Evaluating Empowerment".
[26] S. Leiderer, "Budget Support as an Aid Instrument: Neither Pandemonium nor Panacea", Briefing Paper, Deutsches Institut für Entwicklungspolitik/German Development Institute, Bonn, 2010.

Sector-based support (SBS) is one major modality of budget support for ODA that is widely used, for example, by donors in Africa, alongside general budget support (GBS). It is characterised by the fact that ODA is channelled via the recipient government's treasury and uses government budget execution systems. Other inputs accompanying the flow of funds relate to that sector.[27]

Because it allows funding to be sectorally focussed, SBS could assist debt exchanges to have sufficient focus in order to encourage better accountability. Like all types of budget support, SBS has shortcomings. However, many of these are symptomatic of the disconnect between government and ordinary citizens, which social accountability approaches such as CV&A help to address.

A major study reviewing SBS in 10 sectors in six African countries (all of which are HIPCs) was recently completed by the Overseas Development Institute. This found that overall 'SBS is a potentially important and effective modality for supporting improved service delivery in developing countries'.[28] This research suggests that favourable consideration should be given to SBS as a possible mechanism for governance debt exchanges. SBS and social accountability could be mutually beneficial, in the interests of improved local governance.

Policy dialogue in budget support is typically led by line ministry policy and planning departments, but frontline providers and citizens are excluded. CV&A, with its proven approach to local-level dialogue, involving bureaucrats, service providers and citizens, could provide an important way to democratise policy dialogue in the interests of service reform, beginning locally.

How might debt relief through SBS or other modalities work when combined with demand-led governance? Figure 22.3 sketches how debt relief could foster mutually beneficial empowering and accountable relationships between government and impoverished citizens, with support from local and international civil society.

SBS has been successfully used for debt relief in Uganda, and this experience indicates it could potentially be also used for debt exchanges. One key question to be addressed is how to ensure that all debt exchanges are additional to ODA and domestic funding.

In summary, a new type of debt exchange is needed: what I tentatively call debt for local governance (DfLG).

[27] T. Williamson and C. Dom, *Making Sector Budget Support Work for Service Delivery: An Overview* (London: Overseas Development Institute, 2010).
[28] Ibid.

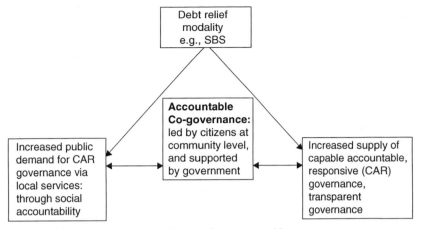

FIGURE 22.3. Debt exchanges for accountable co-governance.

A. *What Would DfLG Entail?*

Centrally, DfLG would be built on partnerships of mutual accountability between local governments and citizens, facilitated by community service organisations, preferably enabled or at least encouraged by national governments and donor creditors. Despite being closer to citizens than are other government levels, local governments are often greatly underresourced. Thus their capacity to be responsive to clearly identified local reforms that are needed is greatly undermined. When such reforms are also based on well-articulated democratic demand by affected citizens (e.g., through social accountability), their legitimacy is further increased. Providing predictable flows of funding to enhance local government capacity, responsiveness and accountability is likely to yield dividends of improved governance over time.

This chapter has made some specific suggestions about the form that debt-for-governance exchanges might take, but there are no doubt many others. One recommendation is that other strategic options in exchanges to improve governance be considered and those showing the most promise be adequately researched. For example, another tactic to build the virtuous cycle of improved capability, accountability and responsiveness in local governance could be to gradually introduce beneficial taxation reforms, such as those involving decentralisation of tax collection. By providing a transitional fiscal strategy, this can aid the longer-term sustainability of democratic governance reforms introduced through debt-for-governance exchanges.

VII. DEBT EXCHANGES FOR LOCAL GOVERNMENT IN ACTION

Creditor country C agrees to forgo specified bilateral debt obligations X of debtor country D in exchange for a promise that D will use the funds to allow citizens to monitor service delivery via an appropriate social accountability approach (such as CV&A), while apportioning part of the funding to improve local essential service delivery, including in response to citizen-generated proposals for reforms.

One possible funding modality for this is SBS, if this is being used in the country. Instead of repaying or servicing its debt, D would then contribute X towards SBS to be used as described.

A second possible mechanism for funding could be participatory budgeting, which is increasingly being used across the world. The debt exchange would provide a top-up of funding for essential services of say 20%, the allocation of which for reform of local services would be decided democratically by citizens through social accountability processes.

C will be concerned whether D will use the funds this way, or whether D will reduce other social/local development spending in lieu of debt-exchange funding. So monitoring after the exchange is important. DfLG envisages that citizens would have a significant role in this.

Also, if C writes off the debt, it has no recourse if D does not keep its side of the bargain, as it is unlikely D will agree to reinstate the obligation. So a better option may be for C to offer merely to forgo debt servicing each year on certain conditions – for example, as long as the budget support or program expenditures are clearly additional as required. Evidence of progressively improved service delivery may also be part of any bilateral arrangement. This year-by-year approach is likely to be important to provide assurance of accountability. Accountability, as well as being related to the appropriate allocation of funds, may also be tied to specified outcomes of their application.

How would progressive improvements in service delivery be judged? CV&A could provide one possible answer, by allowing citizens to periodically vote on (and thus rate) the adequacy of reforms in public service delivery. Proven means such as citizen scorecards or report cards would allow citizens both to deliberate and to vote on progress being made. Such processes could allow ordinary citizens to periodically exercise some degree of democratic sanction over the continuation of the exchange, which could itself also have intrinsic benefits. The arrangements regarding any mix of straight debt relief in the exchange can be tailored according to the relationship between debtor and creditor government, and the incentives deemed to be appropriate. The overriding principle should be that the goal is to improve governance and accountability rather than to undermine it.

VIII. CONCLUSION

Addressing governance issues, including those fundamental to debt crises, constitutes a much larger and longer-term project than can be addressed in this chapter. It requires addressing issues beyond accountability and transparency, and would need to consider these systemically, from local and national up to global levels. However, the deficit in both debtor and creditor governments' democratic accountability to their citizens is a critical factor for human development, which needs considerably more attention than it has received to date. This chapter outlines one modest proposal with practical steps that could be adopted to help address one of the central factors giving rise to debt crises. Debt-for-local-governance exchanges have potential benefits for ordinary citizens and for debtor and creditor governments. Where the political will exists, this type of exchange could be applicable to a significant group of indebted developing countries, many of them HIPCs.

APPENDIX I: KEY ELEMENTS IN CITIZEN VOICE AND ACTION APPLIED TO LOCAL SERVICE DELIVERY

Citizen Voice and Action is a local-level advocacy approach that uses citizen education, service auditing and monitoring and dialogue between communities and government in order to improve public services like health and education that have an impact on the daily lives of ordinary people. Since 2005 hundreds of local government services in a growing number of countries on all continents have been transformed by the hard work of communities implementing CV&A.

CV&A works by educating and mobilising citizens, equipping them with skills and tools to monitor government services and facilitating a process to improve those services. CV&A includes one preparatory phase shown in Appendix 1 ("Organisation and Staff Preparation") and three implementation phases ("Enabling Citizen Engagement," "Engagement via Community Gathering" and "Improving Services and Influencing Policy").

PHASE ONE: ORGANISATION AND STAFF PREPARATION

Before beginning CV&A, implementing NGO staff and partners need to make some basic preparations, such as the following:

- getting a grasp of the situation within each country in relation to citizen and governance issues;

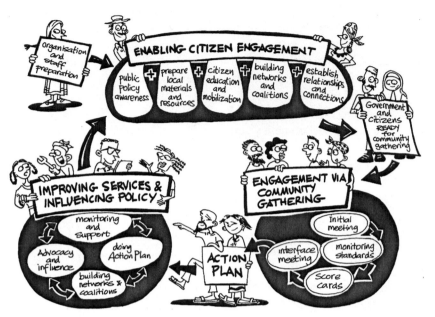

APPENDIX 1. Key Elements in Citizen Voice and Action Applied to Local Service Delivery.

- training staff, partners and stakeholders to facilitate CV&A within communities, recognising the broader issues that relate to citizenship and governance within their country;
- ensuring that CV&A complements National Office Strategy;
- contextualising the CV&A materials. We encourage adapting CV&A in order to respond to the civil society spaces that exist and use context analysis tools to better understand the power structures in society.

As a result of this phase, the NGO implementing CV&A should have the staff capacity and organisational structure and strategy necessary to implement CV&A successfully.

PHASE TWO: ENABLING CITIZEN ENGAGEMENT

This phase builds the capacity of citizens to address issues of governance and provides the foundation for subsequent phases. We know that for citizens to engage governments effectively, they need support and awareness. So this stage involves a series of processes that raise awareness of the meaning of citizenship, accountability, good governance and human rights. An important aspect is that citizens learn about how abstract human rights translate into concrete commitments by their government under national law. For example, the "Right to Health" (Article 25 of the Universal Declaration of Human Rights) in a particular country might pertain to a child's right to receive vaccinations at the local clinic or the community's right to have two midwives present at the local clinic, as stated under national law. Citizens also learn about government budgets associated with various inputs to public services.

CV&A thus lays the groundwork for staff members to mobilise communities toward ensuring that these rights to deliver public services, policies and budgets are respected. As a result of this phase, communities should be ready to work with governments in a constructive and productive manner.

PHASE THREE: ENGAGEMENT VIA COMMUNITY GATHERING

This phase entails a series of linked participatory processes that focus on assessing the quality of public services (like health care and education) and identifying ways to improve their delivery.

Community members who use the service, service providers (such as clinic and school staff members) and local government officials are all invited to participate. The process is collaborative, not confrontational. Simply put, nobody wants an underperforming school or clinic in their community, and local authorities are often eager to work with citizens to improve these essential facilities.

PHASE FOUR: IMPROVING SERVICES AND INFLUENCING POLICY

In this fourth phase, communities begin to implement the action plan that they created as a result of the Community Gathering process. Citizens and other stakeholders act together to influence policy at both local and higher levels. In effect, communities organise what amounts to a local-level campaign, with objectives, targets, tactics and activities designed to influence the individuals who have the power to change the situations they face at the local level.

Often communities will work with other communities to identify patterns of government failure across large geographic areas. In response, communities come together in coalitions in order to influence progressively higher levels of government in order to solve the problems they face.

As a result of their advocacy, communities tend to see marked improvements in the services that they depend upon on a daily basis. Once communities see the success they can achieve, they will usually begin the monitoring process again, focusing on increasingly complex and challenging issues. Thus, CV&A is designed to function cyclically and sustain a new working relationship between communities and governments over the long term.

Conclusion

Ross P. Buckley

Debt-for-development exchanges have much to offer developing countries and donor countries that wish to promote debt cancellation and/or aid budgets.

I. PRINCIPAL ADVANTAGES OF DEBT-FOR-DEVELOPMENT EXCHANGES

This financial technique has at least five benefits:

1. Debt-for-development exchanges provide funding for much needed development projects.

2. Debt-for-development exchanges promote debt reduction. Debt reduction is critical for many developing countries. In 2005, the G8 nations resolved that the International Monetary Fund (IMF), the concessional lending arm of the World Bank, and the African Development Bank should cancel all of their debts to poor countries that comply with the requirements of the World Bank's debt-relief program, the Highly Indebted Poor Countries (HIPC) Initiative. This became known as the MDRI, the Multilateral Debt Reduction Initiative. This total cancellation of debt will certainly assist those nations that receive it, but only 24 nations currently qualify for such total debt cancellation, and only a further 17 can potentially become eligible in the future.[1]

Yet many nations not poor enough to qualify for such relief labour under stultifying debt overhangs. For instance, in 2007 Indonesia's total external debt stood at US$137.4 billion, which was 31.7% of GDP and represented 104.5% of total exports.[2] In 2008 the Philippines' total external debt was US$53.5 billion,

---

[1] International Monetary Fund, "A Factsheet: Multilateral Debt Relief Initiative" (January 2009), accessed August 2, 2010, www.imf.org/external/np/exr/facts/mdri.htm.
[2] See International Monetary Fund, "Country Report No. 08/299" (September 2008), accessed August 2, 2010, www.imf.org/external/pubs/ft/scr/2008/cr08299.pdf.

which represented 33.4% of GDP.[3] Debt-for-development exchanges offer debt relief to debt-constrained nations such as these and many others that are not eligible for relief under HIPC initiatives.

3. Debt-for-development exchanges give donor countries considerable control over how the debtor country will spend the funds that otherwise would have been applied to debt servicing. Well-structured exchanges can also promote transparency and accountability in how the savings generated by debt relief are applied. Greater control, transparency and accountability can encourage donor nations to cancel more debt than they otherwise would.

4. Debt-for-development exchanges camouflage debt relief for donor countries. Debt relief is often a politically sensitive topic in donor countries. For instance, the announcement by the Australian government of the Debt2Health exchange with Indonesia was greeted without adverse comment in the Australian media. Yet if the Australian government had announced the straight cancellation of A$75 million of debt owed by Indonesia, one would anticipate adverse comment in the media, particularly from the radio 'shock-jocks', arguing that here is another A$75 million that Indonesia can now use to buy arms to use, one day, against Australia (as utterly unlikely as such a development is in geo-strategic terms). The delivery of the debt relief as part of a debt-for-health exchange camouflaged it and insured it against such a reception. Exchanges make debt relief more politically palatable for donor country governments.

5. Debt-for-development exchanges allow creditors to advance ends that serve the creditor as well as the debtor. In our increasingly interconnected, globalised world, donor countries have a strong interest in projects in developing countries that will directly benefit the donor country. Examples include projects to reduce greenhouse gas emissions, to fund nuclear nonproliferation efforts and to mitigate the risks of outbreaks of swine flu and avian influenza.

II. TWO POSSIBLE DISADVANTAGES OF DEBT-FOR-DEVELOPMENT EXCHANGES

Debt-for-development exchanges have two potential downsides. It is arguable that exchanges entail a loss of sovereignty for the debtor nation if the debt relief was going to be granted anyway, as the exchange simply gives to the donor country a degree of control over how the saved funds will be expended that

---

3 "Philippines Quarterly Economic Update – January 2009", Report for the World Bank, accessed August 2, 2010, http://siteresources.worldbank.org/INTPHILIPPINES/Resources/PhilippinesQuarterlyEconomicUpdateWorldBankJanuary2009asofJan23.pdf.

it would not otherwise have had. This is exemplified by France's consistent misuse of the technique by imposing exchanges on debt that France was obligated to cancel as part of the HIPC or Paris Club initiatives (considered in Chapter 7).

However, generally this objection overlooks the fact that bilateral debt relief outside the HIPC or MDRI frameworks is uncommon, and debt-for-development exchanges encourage many more instances of debt relief than they provide control over the proceeds of cancellations that would have occurred anyway. France's misuse of the technique is very much the exception rather than the rule.

It is also arguable that exchanges may be used to get rid of illegitimate or odious debt. Illegitimate debt is debt lent for irresponsible purposes, typically to promote industries in the creditor, not the debtor, nation. The best example of debt being treated as illegitimate is to be found in the decision in 2006 by Norway to cancel US$80 million of its loans to a number of developing countries, which had been extended to fund the purchase of vessels built in Norway. The debt was cancelled in recognition that the loans were made by Norway to promote employment in its ship-building industry, not responsibly to aid the debtor nations' development.[4]

Odious debt is much a narrower concept than illegitimacy. The idea is that sovereign debt is odious if (1) it is incurred for a purpose that does not benefit the people of the debtor nation, and (2) it is incurred without the consent of the people. The reasoning is that '[t]his debt is not an obligation for the nation; it is a regime's debt, a personal debt of the power that has incurred it, and consequently it falls with the fall of this power.'[5] The concept is that it is appropriate for a people to have to repay loans incurred by a dictator without their consent if the loans were used to build hospitals or public infrastructure but not if the funds were used for purposes that don't benefit the people.[6]

[4] Marta Ruiz, "Debt Swaps for Development: Creative Solution or Smoke Screen?" (European Network on Debt and Development, October 2007), 9, accessed August 2, 2010, http://www. eurodad.org/uploadedFiles/Whats_New/Reports/Debt_swaps_ENG(2).pdf; "Norway Makes Ground-Breaking Decision to Cancel Illegitimate Debt" (European Network on Debt and Development, October 3, 2006), accessed August 2, 2010, www.eurodad.org/whatsnew/articles. aspx?id=302 (includes text of official Norwegian government press release, in English).
[5] M. Kremer and S. Jayachandran, "IMF Seminar: Odious Debt" (2002), 3–4, accessed August 2, 2010, www.imf.org/external/np/res/seminars/2002/poverty/mksj.pdf.
[6] R. Rajam "Odious or Just Malodorous?" *Finance and Development* 54 (2004): 54–5; P. Adams, "Iraq's Odious Debts" (Cato Institute Policy Analysis No. 526 2004), 2; M. Kremer and S. Jayachandran, "IMF Seminar: Odious Debt", 3–4.

If a donor government is selecting debt for use in an exchange, it may be likely to offer first for exchange debt that may be illegitimate or odious. This is natural – most governments will take an opportunity to bury past actions that smell less than sweet. As discussed in Chapter 10, this causes civil society networks such as the international Jubilee network to seek audits for all debt offered for use in exchanges to ensure that illegitimate or odious debt is not used in exchanges.[7] Clearly it is preferable for illegitimate or odious debt to be cancelled outright because of its compromised status. However, as is explored in Chapter 11, as debt cancellation on these grounds is exceedingly unlikely (Norway being the only instance to date), the issue for international civil society is whether, given the crushing debt overhang in many poor nations, it is better simply to support all exchanges that result in the reduction of debt and the application of funds to worthwhile developmental programs, without insisting on the somewhat idealistic requirement that debt used in these exchanges be audited to ensure that it is free of any taints whatsoever.

Some commentators have criticised these exchanges on the grounds that they make no substantial difference to the level of a nation's indebtedness or that the development projects typically funded are small.[8] These are fatuous criticisms in my view. Indonesia is better off directing A$37.5 million into the fight against tuberculosis than having to service and repay A$75million in loans to Australia. Australia is better off with a healthier neighbouring country, both due to the risk of transmission of tuberculosis to Australians and, far more important, because of the greater social stability likely in a healthier nation with more to spend on social programs and poverty relief. Of course, these are very small steps. In national terms they are tiny amounts. Debt exchanges are invariably about small steps, but given the magnitude of the challenges facing humanity small steps are better than no steps at all. The need to make big steps doesn't in any way invalidate the contribution of small ones.

Apart from the issues of debtor nation sovereignty and potential illegitimacy of debt used in exchanges, there seem to be few other grounds upon which objection to these exchanges is possible. Certainly the major criticism levelled at debt–equity schemes, that they are highly inflationary, doesn't apply to debt-for-development schemes, as they have, perhaps sadly, never been operated at a scale sufficient to have an impact on a nation's money supply.

[7] See, e.g., Jubilee Australia, "Inquiry into Australia's Relations with Indonesia", Submission No. 37, October 31, 2002, accessed September 6, 2010, http://web.archive.org/web/20060920113352/ www.aph.gov.au/house/committee/jfadt/indonesia/subs/subindo37.pdf.

[8] See, e.g., Danny Cassimon and Jos Vaessen, "Theory, Practice and Potential of Debt-for-Development Swaps in Asian and the Pacific", *Economic Systems* 31 (2007): 12.

III. A NEW PARADIGM FOR DEVELOPMENT

The current conventional development paradigm is a failure. One way to assess its effectiveness is to answer the question 'How many nations that were developing in 1950 are now developed?'

The definition of a developed country is not settled. The IMF has identified 34 'advanced economies',[9] and with the recent invitations to join extended to Israel, Estonia and Slovenia, membership in the Organisation for Economic Development and Co-operation (OECD) will also shortly increase to 34 nations. However, there are significant differences between the two groupings.[10] For instance, Chile and Mexico are OECD members but are not considered advanced economies by the IMF.

So there are a range of credible answers to the question of which countries have developed in the past 60 years, but most answers would probably include Hong Kong, Israel, Singapore, South Korea and Taiwan (treating Hong Kong and Taiwan as separate countries for these purposes). If one treats the Yangtse Delta region of China, centred on Shanghai, as a separate economic entity, it may also qualify for developed status, and one could perhaps add to the list Malaysia, Turkey and some of the Emirates. But that is about it – only perhaps 5 to 7 of the 130 underdeveloped nations have graduated to developed status in the past 60 years.

Of these nations that have undoubtedly developed in this period, governments have enjoyed a much larger role in Singapore, South Korea and Taiwan than the development policies advocated by the World Bank, IMF and US Treasury Department, the Washington Consensus policies, would permit. Governments in those countries have directed much economic activity.

Equally, most of the development success stories in this period are to be found in East Asia, and of these, only one, that of the island state of Hong Kong, has largely followed Washington Consensus policies.

It is a time for a new development paradigm, one that actually works. New paradigms require new thinking, new ways of perceiving issues. The chapters in Part IV of this volume have identified some thinking that has to change:

'Local trees are no good, they are worthless scrubby bushes that get in the way of ploughing the fields. What this country needs is good, tall straight foreign trees raised in nurseries and planted into this barren land'.

'The mangroves are gone now, we cannot afford to replant and restore them'.

---

[9] International Monetary Fund, *World Economic Outlook* (New York: IMF, 2009).
[10] Ibid.

'This country cannot afford even the most basic social welfare protection schemes. These may be a good idea in rich countries, but cannot work here'.

'We cannot afford to spend money now adapting to climate change or teaching our farmers how to adapt, we are poor and should leave this until it is a pressing problem'.

'Giving poor people a voice isn't going to make a difference to anything. Government departments are never going to really be accountable to poor people'.

All these sentiments seem superficially sensible, yet Chapters 15 through 19 and 22 offer multiple examples of how wrong this thinking is.

This type of thinking must be replaced by a mindset of capability and capacity – a mindset that poor countries have the ability and capacity to help themselves. Perhaps nowhere is this perspective needed more than in countering the common belief that '[t]his country is poor. It cannot rely upon its own savings, but needs to borrow capital from abroad to prosper'.[11] This entirely neglects the fact that less affluent local people do have savings but that these are typically inefficiently intermediated to other borrowers. It neglects the fact that the elites, who are in all developing countries, have massive savings that they typically invest offshore. And it neglects the lessons of history – that foreign capital will be denominated in foreign currency and carry floating interest rates, so that both the exchange and interest rate risks of the loans will fall upon those least able to bear and hedge against them, the debtor nation.

Most developing countries do not have freely convertible currencies, and as capital is typically raised in foreign currencies, debt service must be funded from export revenues.[12] The reliance upon foreign capital thus intensifies the pressure to move away from subsistence agriculture towards growing cash crops for export. This neglects the extreme historical volatility of agricultural commodity prices. Planting coffee, tea or cocoa looked mighty attractive when prices were at historical highs. However, when prices fall by three-quarters, 'old-fashioned' crops that fed the village, irrespective of the prices the exchanges in Chicago put on commodities, look awfully attractive to people who cannot eat their coffee beans.

Poor nations typically have more domestic resources than they utilise and typically do not need foreign capital nearly as much as the foreign commercial

---

[11] Explored in Chapter 14.
[12] Ross P. Buckley and Peter Dirou, "How to Strengthen the International Financial System by Improving Sovereign Balance Sheet Structures", *Annals of Economics and Finance* 2 (2006): 257–69.

banks, or their handmaiden, the IMF, will tell them they do. Furthermore, this foreign capital will come with profoundly destabilising side-effects, such as exchange rate and interest rate risk, and its proclivity to flee when times turn hard, which foreign advisors will tend to ignore. Developing countries often have considerable, grossly underutilised financial resources and, as is explored in Chapter 14, debt-for-development exchanges could be used to fund mechanisms to utilise these financial resources in productive ways.

The greatest contribution that debt-for-development exchanges could make would be to support this much needed shift towards a new development paradigm, a mindset of capability and capacity. This is a lofty, and important, goal. The good news, however, is that until exchanges start to empower this paradigm shift, every well-structured debt-for-development exchange results in the cancellation of some debt owed by a poor country and the liberation of some funds for a worthwhile development project. Each exchange thus makes the world a little better place, which is no bad thing while we await the fundamental changes needed to lift billions of people from poverty and hardship.

Index